COUNSEL AND COMMAND IN EARLY MODERN ENGLISH THOUGHT

While it has often been recognised that counsel formed an essential part of political discourse in early modern England, the precise role that it occupied in the development of political thinking has remained obscure. This comprehensive and rigorous study of early modern English political counsel establishes the importance of the relationship between political counsel and the discourse of sovereignty. Tracing the changes and evolution of writings on political counsel during the 'monarchy of counsel', from the end of the Wars of the Roses to the end of the English Civil War, Joanne Paul examines English thought in its domestic and transnational context, providing an original account of the relationship between counsel and emerging conceptions of sovereignty. Formed at the conjunction of the history of political thought and English political history, this book grounds textual analysis within the context of court politics, intellectual and patronage networks and diplomacy.

JOANNE PAUL is Senior Lecturer in Early Modern History at the University of Sussex where her research currently focuses on Thomas More's *Utopia*, as well as the Dudley family during the reign of the Tudors. Winner of the 2014 Sir John Neale Prize for Tudor History, she is a Fellow of the Royal Historical Society. She is the author of *Thomas More* (2016), and numerous articles in journals such as *Renaissance Quarterly, Renaissance Studies* and *Hobbes Studies*.

IDEAS IN CONTEXT

Edited by David Armitage, Richard Bourke, Jennifer Pitts and John Robertson

The books in this series will discuss the emergence of intellectual traditions and of related new disciplines. The procedures, aims and vocabularies that were generated will be set in the context of the alternatives available within the contemporary frameworks of ideas and institutions. Through detailed studies of the evolution of such traditions, and their modification by different audiences, it is hoped that a new picture will form of the development of ideas in their concrete contexts. By this means, artificial distinctions between the history of philosophy, of the various sciences, of society and politics, and of literature may be seen to dissolve.

The series is published with the support of the Exxon Foundation.

A list of books in the series can be found at the end of the volume.

COUNSEL AND COMMAND IN EARLY MODERN ENGLISH THOUGHT

JOANNE PAUL

University of Sussex

CAMBRIDGE
UNIVERSITY PRESS

University Printing House, Cambridge CB2 8BS, United Kingdom

One Liberty Plaza, 20th Floor, New York, NY 10006, USA

477 Williamstown Road, Port Melbourne, VIC 3207, Australia

314-321, 3rd Floor, Plot 3, Splendor Forum, Jasola District Centre, New Delhi - 110025, India

103 Penang Road, #05-06/07, Visioncrest Commercial, Singapore 238467

Cambridge University Press is part of the University of Cambridge.

It furthers the University's mission by disseminating knowledge in the pursuit of education, learning and research at the highest international levels of excellence.

www.cambridge.org
Information on this title: www.cambridge.org/9781108748254
DOI: 10.1017/9781108780407

First published 2020
First paperback edition 2022

A catalogue record for this publication is available from the British Library

Library of Congress Cataloging in Publication data
NAMES: Paul, Joanne, author.
TITLE: Counsel and command in early modern English thought / Joanne Paul.
DESCRIPTION: Cambridge, United Kingdom ; New York, NY : Cambridge University Press, 2020. | Series: Ideas in context | Includes bibliographical references.
IDENTIFIERS: LCCN 2019031565 (print) | LCCN 2019031566 (ebook) | ISBN 9781108490177 (hardback) | ISBN 9781108780407 (epub)
SUBJECTS: LCSH: Political consultants – Great Britain – History. | Prerogative, Royal – Great Britain – History. | Legitimacy of governments – Great Britain – History. | Great Britain – History – Tudors, 1485–1603. | Great Britain – History – Stuarts, 1603–1714. | Great Britain – Politics and government – 1485–1603. | Great Britain – Politics and government – 1603–1714.
CLASSIFICATION: LCC DA300 .P34 2020 (print) | LCC DA300 (ebook) | DDC 320.01/1–dc23
LC record available at https://lccn.loc.gov/2019031565
LC ebook record available at https://lccn.loc.gov/2019031566

ISBN 978-1-108-49017-7 Hardback
ISBN 978-1-108-74825-4 Paperback

Contents

Acknowledgements

As this project emerged out of my PhD, and has been at least ten years in the making, there is a long list of people to whom I owe a debt of gratitude. In order to avoid, however, producing an acknowledgement section as long as the book itself, I will try to confine my thanks here to those who had a direct role in this iteration, which is markedly different to the content of my PhD work.

I must begin my thanks here as I did in my PhD, with Quentin Skinner, who did not cease his support and mentorship when my PhD ended but has continued to champion my work in the intervening years. Likewise, thanks are owed to James Tully, who continues to inspire, unswervingly challenging me to retain a sense of contemporary relevance to my historical work through his example. Comparable inspiration and support have been drawn from other stellar academics, historians and writers I am blessed to call friends, exemplars and mentors, including, but not limited to, David Armitage, Teresa Bejan, Adrian Blau, Richard Bourke, Matthew Champion, David Colclough, Jeffrey Collins, Hannah Dawson, Lindsey Fitzharris, Catherine Fletcher, Andrew Hadfield, Eva Johanna Holmberg, Courtney Herber, Susan James, Kristine Johanson, Carole Levin, Sarah Lewis, Shiru Lim, Vanessa Lim, Suzannah Lipscomb, Kate Maltby, Helen Matheson-Pollock, Kurosh Meshkat, Edmund Neill, Julia Nicholls, Estelle Paranque, Rebecca Rideal, Kirsty Rolfe, Lorenzo Sabbadini, Sophie Smith and Sarah Wilford. I am also extremely grateful to my PhD examiners, Stephen Alford and Angus Gowland, not least for letting me pass, but also for spending so much time in my viva on the topic of revisions and publication, essential to the production of this book.

This group of expert counsellors (if I may) played no small part in helping me secure my position at the University of Sussex, where I've had the benefit of working with yet more generous people, who have supported my work in a plethora of ways. I must begin with Iain McDaniel, who has been an unfailing friend and support in every aspect of my academic life since my application to Sussex and my comrade in intellectual history since arriving there. Thanks as well to the rest of my amazing colleagues, and especially to Hester Barron, Liz James, Laura Kounine, Claire Langhamer, Melissa Milewski and Lucy Robinson, who have all been there in moments when I needed someone to pick me up, brush me off and send me back out into the fight.

Pep talks, coaching and general propping-up were also frequently provided by my dear friends, caring family and, at times, my cat, who deserves a mention in these acknowledgements for putting up with my weird work habits as much as anyone else. I am grateful to rely for such patience, alongside a great deal of encouragement and support, on the wonderful James Darrall, who likewise has to live with me and has been putting up with this book since the beginning, when I followed through on the threat to bring it with me on our first holiday together.

Liz Friend-Smith at Cambridge University Press has been working with me on this book for longer than it's healthy to remember, for which I am very appreciative. I am grateful as well to the anonymous readers, especially to the very helpful reader who graciously agreed to go through the manuscript (at one point well over 150,000 words long) twice. I owe a great debt to several institutions, most especially Queen Mary, University of London, who supported my doctoral research in every way conceivable, and University of Sussex, who have supported me in turning it into a book. Thanks are also due to the British Library, National Archives, Institute for Historical Research and Senate House, London for having everything I could possibly need to produce what you read here, including deeply warming cups of tea.

My final thanks are to those who took time out of their overloaded schedules in recent years to read selections of what follows and provided feedback: Adrian Blau, Virginia Cox, Andrew Hadfield, Vanessa Lim, David Mitchell, Arthur Walzer and Samuel Garett Zeitlin, as well as the members of the Early Career Writing Group at Sussex History. Academia is (and needs to be) a collaborative exercise, and these readers, alongside all the wonderful people who have supported me in a myriad of other ways, embody this spirit through their exemplary generosity. Thank you.

Introduction

> *To a perfect common wealth these two things be required, the pen and the swoorde, that is, councell and good letters in deliberating of affaires, and the sworde in the execution of the same.*[1]

There was a deep-seated tension present in early modern English political thought: the 'paradox of counsel'.[2] On the one hand, it was a long-standing requirement that monarchs receive counsel in order to legitimise their rule. On the other, this condition had the potential to undermine their authority if the monarch was required to act on the counsel given. In other words, if counsel is obligatory, it impinges upon sovereignty. If it is not, it then becomes irrelevant and futile. The working out of this essential problem defines much of the political thinking produced during the English 'monarchy of counsel', roughly from the end of the Wars of the Roses to the end of the English Civil War.[3] It is the purpose of this book to document attempts to grapple with this fundamental problem: the necessarily challenging relationship between counsel and command.

In working out this problem, political thinkers shifted the grounds of discussion from counsel to command and generated the modern political discourse that we associate with English thought from the mid-seventeenth century onwards. Due to developments in the discourse of counsel through traditional humanist, Machiavellian and reason of state iterations, as well as circumstantial factors, such as the age, gender and personalities of succeeding monarchs, the debate over counsel and command came to a head in the context of the English Civil War. There were two available options. First that counsel was obligatory, and especially ought to directly

[1] Claude Paradin, *The Heroicall Deuises* (London, 1591), 231.

[2] Judith Ferster, *Fictions of Advice: The Literature and Politics of Counsel in Late Medieval England* (Philadelphia: University of Pennsylvania Press, 1996), 39–40.

[3] J. G. A. Pocock, 'A Discourse of Sovereignty: Observations on the Work in Progress', in *Political Discourse in Early Modern Britain*, ed. Nicholas Phillipson and Quentin Skinner (Cambridge: Cambridge University Press, 1993), 395–6.

guide the monarch in cases of emergency or incapacity (which could include 'seducement' by privately interested counsellors), in which case the best, most transparent and state-interested source of such counsel was parliament. In such a view, parliament becomes essentially sovereign: counsel mutates into command. Or, second, counsel was not obligatory, and must be shown to be absolutely subject to the monarch. This reduces counsel to its most basic and ineffectual functions. In either of these cases, counsel disappears into command, either becoming it or being subjugated to it, and sovereignty emerges as the primary concept of political thinking.

It is probably because of this conceptual disappearing act that counsel, as a political idea, has received less attention in the scholarship than sovereignty, though the significance of the counsellor in Renaissance thought has long been acknowledged. Arthur Ferguson's *The Articulate Citizen and the English Renaissance* attempts to document the way in which 'citizens of Tudor England' connected their communication of grievances to the defense of the 'commonwealth of the realm'.[4] J. G. A. Pocock's formative *Machiavellian Moment* also recognises the way in which English humanism 'developed its civic awareness by projecting the image of the humanist as counselor to his prince', noting the way in which this image was in tension with the ruler's imperium.[5] These analyses were given a greater sense of background and significance in Quentin Skinner's *Foundations of Modern Political Thought*, in which he connects this figure of the 'citizen-counselor' to the study of rhetoric and the re-emergence of republican thought.[6]

This has developed, more recently, into a republican account of the role of counsel, at odds with the absolutist account of sovereignty associated with Hobbes. As Eric Nelson puts it, 'The Renaissance occupies a paradoxical place in the history of political thought. It is famous for having nurtured two diametrically opposed, although similarly extreme theoretical positions: republicanism and absolutism.'[7] Such tension erupts in the English Civil War, an event which is seen to toll the death knell for the discourse of counsel.[8]

[4] Arthur B. Ferguson, *The Articulate Citizen and the English Renaissance* (Durham, NC: Duke University Press, 1965).

[5] J. G. A. Pocock, *The Machiavellian Moment: Florentine Political Thought and the Atlantic Republican Tradition* (New Haven: Princeton University Press, 2009), 338–40.

[6] Quentin Skinner, *The Foundations of Modern Political Thought: Volume I: The Renaissance* (Cambridge: Cambridge University Press, 1978), 113–38, 219–42.

[7] Eric Nelson, 'The Problem of the Prince', in *The Cambridge Companion to Renaissance Philosophy*, ed. James Hankins (Cambridge: Cambridge University Press, 2007), 319.

[8] Pocock, 'Discourse of Sovereignty', 395; John Guy, 'The Rhetoric of Counsel in Early Modern England', in *Tudor Political Culture*, ed. Dale Hoak (Cambridge: Cambridge University Press, 1995), 292–310.

While previous studies have acknowledged the conflict between counsel and command, they have not highlighted the way in which seventeenth-century arguments about sovereignty were rooted in longstanding claims about counsel. In political history, as John Watts has suggested, 'much more attention has been given to the growth of central government, the functioning of clientage networks, the changing structures of political society and the securing of compliance' than to counsel.[9] This has been countered by the generation of what John Guy has called the 'new political history' of Tudor England. This 'new political history' attempts to draw connections between the work of historians such as A. F. Pollard and John Neal on the governmental, bureaucratic and administrative aspects of Tudor politics, and that of historians such as Quentin Skinner, who study political ideas.[10] This changed focus, in the words of Stephen Alford,

> emphasises the importance of studying the interaction between people, institutions, and ideas; of combining archival research with a sensitivity to literary and iconographical sources; of recognizing political language, and in particular the vocabulary of counsel; of understanding the impact of classical writing on sixteenth-century notions of duty and service, and the effect this eventually had on concepts of the state; and on the wider reach of the polity.[11]

A number of studies in recent decades, emerging out of such an approach, have taken the discourse of counsel as central. John Guy was the first to attempt a categorisation of two 'vocabularies' of the 'rhetoric of counsel': 'feudal-baronial' and 'humanist-classical'.[12] Both A. N. McLaren and Jacqueline Rose have suggested additions to Guy's vocabularies, highlighting 'godly' or 'religious' counsel.[13] The edited volume produced by Rose, *The Politics of Counsel in England and Scotland*, traces the role of counsel from the late thirteenth to early seventeenth centuries in England and Scotland, and pushes scholarship forward, especially on the role of medieval political thought and practice, Elizabeth's relationship with counsel and

[9] John Watts, 'Counsel and the King's Council in England, c.1340-c.1540', in *The Politics of Counsel in England and Scotland, 1286–1707*, ed. Jacqueline Rose (Oxford: Oxford University Press, 2017), 63.

[10] John Guy, *Tudor Monarchy* (London: Hodder Education Publishers, 1997), 1–8; Stephen Alford, 'Politics and Political History in the Tudor Century', *The Historical Journal* 42, no. 2 (1999): 535–48.

[11] Alford, 'Politics and Political History', 535.

[12] Guy, 'The Rhetoric of Counsel', 292–310. I will not be writing according to these two 'languages', though my analysis falls primarily into Guy's 'humanist-classical' vocabulary.

[13] A. N. McLaren, 'Delineating the Elizabethan Body Politic: Knox, Aylmer and the Definition of Counsel 1558-88', *History of Political Thought* 17, no. 2 (1996): 225; Jacqueline Rose, 'Kingship and Counsel in Early Modern England', *The Historical Journal* 54, no. 1 (2011): 47–71.

the continuing importance of counsel to seventeenth-century English thought.[14]

Despite such interest, there remains no comprehensive full-length study of early modern political counsel in England, which traces the working out of the paradox of counsel in the period Pocock identifies. This book attempts to provide such an account, by outlining the wider intellectual context in which these debates took place. In so doing, this study makes three contributions to the study of counsel in particular and early modern English intellectual history in general. First, as has been stated above, it provides an account of the move from the monarchy of counsel to modern notions of sovereignty, making the argument that the paradoxes inherent in the discourse of counsel prompt this transition. Second, it contributes to an understanding of the boundaries of this change, in particular the division between public and private that is essential to modern ideas of politics. Not only does this relate to the rejection of private counsellors in favour of public conciliar institutions, based on notions of the corruption of private interest, but also growing ideas regarding political amoralism, especially in the reason of state tradition. As the understanding of the figure of the counsellor and his essential skills develops, so does the generation of a set of ideas about what constitutes political knowledge and, indeed, 'the political'. Thus, third, this study contributes a new perspective on the development of modern 'political science', by tracing the moves from moral philosophising to historical knowledge to the observation of contemporary affairs in the writings about the counsellor.

[14] Jacqueline Rose, ed., *The Politics of Counsel in England and Scotland, 1286–1707*, Proceedings of the British Academy (Oxford: Oxford University Press, 2016). Several books have been written on the role of counsel in medieval literature – both political and personal; see Rosemarie Deist, *Gender and Power: Counsellors and Their Masters in Antiquity and Medieval Courtly Romance* (Heidelberg: Winter, 2003); Ferster, *Fictions of Advice*. The relationship between counsel and the monarch in the Elizabethan context has also been the subject of a number of treatments, see A. N. McLaren, *Political Culture in the Reign of Elizabeth I: Queen and Commonwealth 1558–1585* (Cambridge: Cambridge University Press, 2004); Natalie Mears, 'Counsel, Public Debate, and Queenship: John Stubbs's "The Discoverie of a Gaping Gulf", 1579', *The Historical Journal* 44, no. 3 (2001): 629–50; Susan Doran, 'Elizabeth I and Counsel', in *The Politics of Counsel in England and Scotland, 1286–1707*, ed. Jacqueline Rose (Oxford: Oxford University Press, 2017), 151–61; Mary Thomas Crane, '"Video et Taceo": Elizabeth I and the Rhetoric of Counsel', *Studies in English Literature, 1500–1900* 28, no. 1 (1988): 1–15; Dale Hoak, 'A Tudor Deborah?: The Coronation of Elizabeth I, Parliament, and the Problem of Female Rule', in *John Foxe and His World*, ed. Christopher Highley and John N. King (Aldershot: Ashgate, 2002), 73–89. Finally, the role of counsel in the breakdown of the relationship between monarch and parliament has also been touched on; for instance, David Colclough highlighted the role of the discourse of counsel in the development of parliamentary arguments regarding free speech in England, and particularly associating it with the concept of *parrhesia*; David Colclough, *Freedom of Speech in Early Stuart England* (Cambridge: Cambridge University Press, 2005).

This study is formed at the intersection of the history of political thought and political history, and takes as fundamental, as others such as Greg Walker have done, that texts regarding counsel and the counsellor were inherently political.[15] In the words of David Colclough, 'political discourse is not a prelude to or commentary on political action: it is political action'.[16] Along with Peter Lake, there is an attempt in this book to expand the category of 'political thought' to include 'attempts to "think about politics"', which includes much of the work on political counsel.[17] An intellectual or political history that concerns itself exclusively with ideas such as sovereignty or institutional bodies such as parliament misses this extra-institutional, extra-state form of political intervention, perhaps to the detriment of the perceived legitimacy of such modes of action. It is hoped that this historical study prompts new ways of considering our own political circumstances and ideas, reflecting on the role of political discourse and means of communicating public opinion.

—

The scope of this book is the 'monarchy of counsel', from the turn of the sixteenth century to the middle of the seventeenth. There is, however, a relevant longer perspective to consider. The tension between counsel and command in Western political thought goes back as far as its earliest writings. Malcolm Schofield has drawn attention to the ways in which the *Iliad* is shot through with references to the importance of *euboulia* – usually translated as 'good counsel' – and the way in which it forms a necessary balance with military power.[18] Polydamas and Hector are born on the same night, but whereas Hector was superior 'with the spear', Polydamas is 'far superior in words'.[19] This is a divine balance set between martial and advisory ability, for 'God gives one man feats of war, but in the heart of another farseeing Zeus places a good understanding, and

[15] Greg Walker, *Writing Under Tyranny: English Literature and the Henrician Reformation* (Oxford: Oxford University Press, 2007), 143.

[16] Colclough, *Freedom of Speech*, 124–5.

[17] Peter Lake, *Bad Queen Bess?: Libels, Secret Histories, and the Politics of Publicity in the Reign of Queen Elizabeth I* (Oxford, New York: Oxford University Press, 2016), 5.

[18] Malcolm Schofield, *Saving the City: Philosopher-Kings and Other Classical Paradigms* (London: Routledge, 1999), 11; Paul Woodruff, 'Euboulia as the Skill Protagoras Taught', in *Protagoras of Abdera: The Man, His Measure*, ed. J.M. van Ophuijsen, M van Raalte and P. Stork (Leiden: Brill, 2013), 182–8; Jeannine Quillet, 'Community, Counsel and Representation', in *The Cambridge History of Medieval Political Thought c.350–c.1450*, ed. J. H. Burns (Cambridge: Cambridge University Press, 1988), 545.

[19] Homer, *Iliad*, 18.251–2, quoted in Schofield, *Saving the City*, 15; see also the discussion of Nestor as counsellor-figure in Hanna M. Roisman, 'Nestor the Good Counsellor', *The Classical Quarterly* 55, no. 1 (2005): 17–38.

from him many men get advantage and he saves many'.[20] This balance between sword and word provides the foundation for the mutually supportive relationship between counsel and command.

But they are also in conflict. In the medieval period, Marsilius of Padua builds on a theological distinction between *praeceptum* and *concilium* to mark out a clear distinction between religious and temporal authority.[21] Priests, Marsilius sets out, are forbidden from involvement in civil activities.[22] Their only role is (quoting from II Timothy 4.2) 'exhortation, submission, censure and reproof' for '[the priest] can never engage in compulsion'.[23] Marsilius reinforces this lesson with reference to II Corinthians 8:8–10: 'I do not speak like a commander [*non quasi imperans dico*] ... but I give counsel [*consilium*] in this matter'.[24] This sort of 'authority' is specifically not coercive but 'instructional or managerial', comparable to the role of the physician, who, despite being learned for the purpose of preserving health nevertheless 'cannot compel anyone to observe a suitable diet, nor avoid a harmful one, by imposing some punishment on the persons or property of patients', a comparison drawn from Aristotle.[25] Counsel cannot involve punishment, or else it mutates into law, and thus command.[26] Even when it is recommended that a monarch take counsel of priests or experts, he is emphatically not subject to them, and this does not constitute any diminution of his use of the sword of sovereignty.[27] To say, that 'the temporal sword must be drawn "by the will

20 Homer, *Iliad*, 13.730–4, quoted in Schofield, *Saving the City*, 16.

21 See Quillet, 'Community, Counsel and Representation', 546.

22 Marsilius of Padua, *Defensor Minor and De Translatione Imperii*, ed. Cary J. Nederman (Cambridge: Cambridge University Press, 1993), 6.

23 Marsilius of Padua, *Defensor Minor*, 6.

24 Marsilius of Padua, *Defensor Minor*, 9.

25 Marsilius of Padua, *Defensor Minor*, 10, 51; Aristotle, *Politics*, trans. H. Rackham (Cambridge, MA: Harvard University Press, 1944), 6.13.1145a6-9.

26 On counsellors themselves, Marsilius associates them with prudence, and sees their role as guiding a ruler on 'what is expedient for the polity'; Marsilius of Padua, *The Defender of Peace: The Defensor Pacis*, ed. Alan Gewirth (New York: Columbia University Press, 1967), 77. Nevertheless, on the question of the relative importance of the moral quality of each, Marsilius is clear: the moral character of the ruler is of prime importance, that of counsellors secondary. Drawing once again on Aristotle, he also notes the value of a multitude of voices gathered in a council, for 'each one listening to the others, their minds are reciprocally stimulated to the consideration of truth at which not one of them would arrive if he existed apart or separately from the others', Marsilius of Padua, *Defensor Pacis*, 42. As Cary J. Nederman, *Community and Consent: The Secular Political Theory of Marsiglio of Padua's Defensor Pacis* (London: Rowman & Littlefield, 1995), 111 points out, for Marsilius, an elected monarchy would also solve the problem of evil counsellors.

27 Marsilius of Padua, *Defensor Pacis*, 400. Notably, the prince's authority is limited by the law and legislator, see Serena Ferente, 'Popolo and Law: Late Medieval Sovereignty in Marsilius and the Jurists', in *Popular Sovereignty in Historical Perspective*, ed. Richard Bourke and Quentin Skinner (Cambridge: Cambridge University Press, 2016), 112–13. It is this authority, and not counsel, which ensures that the prince does not enslave his subjects.

of the priest and at the command of the emperor"' means that it ought to be drawn by the counsel of the priest, which is distinct from 'command or coercive authority'.[28] If this were confused, for instance in the case of excommunication, 'on the one hand, all the civil kings of the leading men and people would be useless; on the other hand, priests could make individuals and communities subject to them temporally and civilly.'[29] As he sets out in *Defensor Pacis*, the polity would be threatened by a 'multiplicity of governments'.[30] The separation of counsel and command is thus essential to an early understanding of sovereignty.

Marsilius' view of this necessary distinction is in contrast to many of the authors in the medieval *speculum principis* genre, who set out a powerful, even governing, role for counsel. John of Salisbury's *Policraticus* sets out clearly the importance of counsel 'from men of letters' to the king, especially if he is illiterate.[31] For John of Salisbury, the king occupies the place of the head, and 'is regulated solely by the judgement of his own mind'.[32] That being said, counsel and admonishment are essential to a prince who has gone astray, and should be embraced before any consideration of resistance.[33] Others, such as Christine de Pisan, go further, suggesting that 'the good prince shall be governed by the wise', just as 'the ancients governed themselves by philosophy'.[34] Pisan advances a vision of wise counsel as the true authority governing a successful (virtuous) state, placing the counsellor at the head of the political community. That is not to say that it is not a help if the king is also wise and learned, but it is more important to place one's hope for the good of the realm in the counsellors of a prince, rather than the prince's own wisdom.[35] Perhaps no other text was clearer or more influential on this point than the pseudo-Aristotelian *Secretum secretorum*.[36] Underscoring the idea that many minds produce more prudent governance, the figure of Aristotle reminds Alexander that 'prudent counsayll make thy chefe pryncesse' for he 'arte but one

28 Marsilius of Padua, *Defensor Pacis*, 401. 29 Marsilius of Padua, *Defensor Minor*, 33.

30 Marsilius of Padua, *Defensor Pacis*, 163. Nederman, *Community and Consent*, 128 here draws a comparison with Hobbes.

31 John of Salisbury, *Policraticus: Of the Frivolities of Courtiers and the Footprints of Philosophers*, ed. Cary J. Nederman (Cambridge: Cambridge University Press, 1990), xv, 44.

32 John of Salisbury, *Policraticus*, 69. 33 John of Salisbury, *Policraticus*, 70.

34 Christine de Pisan, *The Book of the Body Politic*, ed. Kate Langdon Forhan (Cambridge: Cambridge University Press, 1994), 43.

35 For Pisan, such advisers are not equated with the nobles, who 'responsible for guarding the republic' and who ought to 'love the wise and to govern by their advice', rather than being such wise advisers themselves; Pisan, *The Book of the Body Politic*, 58, 59.

36 See Steven J. Williams, *The Secret of Secrets: The Scholarly Career of a Pseudo-Aristotelian Text in the Latin Middle Ages* (Ann Arbor: University of Michigan Press, 2003), 24–5.

man'.[37] Notably, the insistence on good counsel to augment the limitations of the singular ruler means that counsel is given a place of near equality with the authority of the king.[38] As Judith Ferster makes clear, the *Secretum* is based on the fundamental assumption that, in order to cultivate virtue, the king must be ruled and – no matter how frustrating – must accept that rule: 'Alexander conquered the world because he was conquered by Aristotle.'[39] Good counsel is not only necessary to good command, but must have the force of command if the end is good rulership. To interpret good counsel as anything other than a dictate for virtuous action is to risk giving into vice. After all, the Lydgate translation, produced in 1511 for the young Henry VIII, takes as its title the paradoxical 'pun': *The Gouernaunce of Kynges and Prynces*.[40]

In England, this discourse became especially important with the overthrow of Richard II in 1399, which prompted reflection on the proper role of counsel. Critics of Richard were clear that his perceived failure to take counsel from the correct sources ought not to be repeated by his successor, Henry IV.[41] John Gower's *Confessio Amantis*, originally written in the 1380s and dedicated to Richard II, but revised and re-dedicated to Henry IV upon Richard's overthrow, reiterates the centrality of counsel to good governance.[42] Works such as Gower's, the anonymous *Mum and the Sothsegger* and Thomas Hoccleve's *Regement of Princes* all seek to more fully define the counsellor-figure, moving from an otherworldly distant philosopher, to a man of the court. Importantly, this counsellor constrains the monarch; as Hoccleve writes, 'Counceil may wele be likenede to a bridelle, Which that an hors kepethe up from fallyng.'[43] These debates and tensions take centre-stage in the Tudor and early Stuart period as we shall see.

[37] John Lydgate, *Gouernaunce of Kynges and Prynces* (London, 1511), sig. B, ii^{v}; F, iv^{r}.

[38] Ferster, *Fictions of Advice*, 48–9.

[39] Ferster, *Fictions of Advice*, 44, 45, 49.

[40] See DeWitt T. Starnes, 'Introduction', in *The Gouernaunce of Kynges and Prynces, the Pynson Edition of 1511; a Translation in Verse* (Gainesville: Scholars' Facsimiles & Reprints, 1957), xii.

[41] Ferguson, *Articulate Citizen*, 69; See Janet Coleman, 'A Culture of Political Counsel: The Case of Fourteenth-Century England's "Virtuous" Monarchy vs Royal Absolutism and Seventeenth-Century Reinterpretations', in *Monarchism and Absolutism in Early Modern Europe*, ed. Cesare Cuttica and Glenn Burgess (London: Routledge, 2012), 19–29. As Ferster, *Fictions of Advice*, 2–3 points out, the medieval period saw weaknesses in kingship that led to the power of the council, and thus would have prompted reflections on the relationships between kings and councillors.

[42] John Gower, *The Complete Works of John Gower*, ed. G. C. Macaulay, vol. 1 (Oxford: Clarendon Press, 1901), VII.4150–56; See Ferster, *Fictions of Advice*, 108–36.

[43] Thomas Hoccleve, *Thomas Hoccleve: The Regiment of Princes*, ed. C. Blyth (Kalamazoo: Medieval Institute Publications, 1999), ln. 4929–30; quoted in Lester Kruger Born, 'The Perfect Prince: A Study in Thirteenth- and Fourteenth-Century Ideals', *Speculum* 3, no. 4 (1928): 501.

This book also suggests that the 'discourse of counsel' diminishes significantly in importance past the middle of the seventeenth century. Rose has made persuasive arguments for the extension of the study of counsel beyond the usual cut off of the English Civil War or Wars of the Three Kingdoms,[44] though others such as Linda Levy Peck have suggested this moment 'put an end to the political culture of court and counsel'.[45] Certainly counsel remained a part of political discourse up until the Act of Union (if not beyond), but in a much more limited – and as Rose herself notes – 'liminal' fashion. Counsel was an outdated vocabulary which sat uneasily with new political languages and realities. As she suggests, 'parliamentary authority was also the source of the decline of both councils and counsel' and counsel did not fit well with the 'driving force of interest': 'Interest might lobby; it did not have to (pretend to) counsel.'[46] In other words, the continued use of vocabularies of counsel in the decades following 1651 were vestiges of what had come before, a period in which counsel was a central and dynamic element of political thinking.

One of the more tentative theories of this book is that there is something unique about the English articulation of the discourse of counsel: that the English were more concerned about the problems and paradoxes of counsel than their continental counterparts. Consistently in the analysis of what follows we see that when non-English texts – classical or continental – are translated into English, greater emphasis is put on counsel and the counsellor. This attention to counsel is most likely due to the coming together of a combination of factors, including the role of counsel in justifying the overthrow of Richard II, the impression that England was, as John Fortescue famously put it, a 'dominium politicum et regale', the role of parliament in the Royal Supremacy, the succession of 'weak' monarchs (detailed in Chapter 5) and the fact that, according to the Royal Supremacy, the head (or governor) of the Church of England was a member of the laity, thus requiring counsel from the more godly. The comparative work required, however, to isolate the distinctive variables in the English case is not possible within the scope of this book.

44 Jacqueline Rose, 'Sir Edward Hyde and the Problem of Counsel in Mid-Seventeenth-Century Royalist Thought', in *The Politics of Counsel in England and Scotland, 1286–1707*, ed. Jacqueline Rose (Oxford: Oxford University Press, 2017), 249–69; Jacqueline Rose, 'Councils, Counsel and the Seventeenth-Century Composite State', in *The Politics of Counsel in England and Scotland, 1286–1707*, ed. Jacqueline Rose (Oxford: Oxford University Press, 2017), 271–94.

45 Linda Levy Peck, 'Kingship, Counsel and Law in Early Stuart Britain', in *The Varieties of British Political Thought, 1500–1800*, ed. Gordon J. Schochet, J. G. A. Pocock and Lois Schwoerer (Cambridge: Cambridge University Press, 1994), 115.

46 Rose, 'Councils, Counsel and the Seventeenth-Century Composite State', 293.

This study is limited to English texts – both texts published in England and texts written in or translated into the English language – and I am attentive to the particular choices made by English translators of classical or continental texts. It is also impossible to consider English thought in this period as being formed in isolation from continental ideas. For this reason, many of the chapters of this book deal exclusively or almost exclusively with texts written and published outside of England by non-English authors (such as those of Erasmus, Castiglione, Machiavelli, Botero, Bodin and others), some of which were only later translated into English.

—

The counsellor is central to Renaissance humanists in England as in Europe, as the figure who mitigates the tyranny of hereditary monarchy and introduces republican themes of active citizenship into non-republican political contexts. This view is outlined in Chapter 1, by considering the work of three leading humanists who dealt with issues of counsel-giving: Erasmus, Thomas More and Baldassare Castiglione. In particular, these writers dealt with the issue of the efficacy of counsel, the 'problem of counsel', often thinking through it in terms provided by Seneca's letters. Regardless of their views on this question, it was clear for each of these writers that counsel should have profound influence over the ruler, one that often placed the humanist counsellor in a position of authority over his prince.

In the context of Henry VIII's Break with Rome and his perceived unwillingness to listen to the 'right' counsel, English humanist writers interrogated even more deeply the questions raised by Erasmus, More and Castiglione. Chapter 2 examines, in particular, the work of Thomas Starkey and Thomas Elyot, and the way in which they focus especially on the theme of 'right-timing' in counsel. Both suggest that their predecessors had got it wrong; timeliness does not mean waiting for the ideal moment, but seizing any available moment, even if this means speaking one's censorious counsel publicly. Both Starkey and Elyot also go further in enforcing the leadership of the counsellor over the prince; commonwealth, prince and counsellor are all unfree if good counsel does not rule.

This 'orthodox humanist' model of counsel – in which the counsellor leads or guides the prince to virtue – is challenged by the rise of a reversed vision of the relationship between counsellor and ruler, set out in the work of Machiavelli and explored through the course of Part II. In *The Prince* Machiavelli presents an inversion of the model treated in Part I by placing the counsellor very clearly under the control of the monarch.

As set out in Chapter 3, the monarch's prudence guides his counsellors, not the other way around, thanks in large part to Machiavelli's more pessimistic account of counsellors' self-interest. Counsellors, in this tradition, are required to guide the prince in navigating the demands of *kairos* (the opportune moment) and *paradiastole* (rhetorical description) using and dismissing virtue as circumstances dictate. Scholars have often overlooked the importance of *kairos* to Machiavelli's and Machiavellian thought, but it becomes clear that it forms the foundation of the moral flexibility for which Machiavelli becomes famous.

Essential, as well, to the Machiavellian tradition is the redefinition of prudence, explored in Chapter 4, in the works of writers such as Innocent Gentillet and Justus Lipsius. Rather than being a virtue, prudence becomes the means by which opportunities and the necessity of deception are known. Even those writing against Machiavellianism accept some of its basic tenets, including this redefined notion of prudence, which becomes associated with the political, as opposed to private, sphere. In the work of the essayists, such as Michel de Montaigne and William Cornwallis, this division between public and private is rearticulated according to the individuals involved; private individuals must obey the principles of traditional morality, but those in the public sphere must occasionally deviate from these norms, even at the peril of their souls. This is written into an understanding of counsel, situated within this morally flexible public political arena.

These fundamental conceptual shifts coincide with other changes in the political discourse brought about by the political realities of 'weakened' monarchs (a minor, Edward VI, and two women, Mary I and Elizabeth I). Chapter 5 notes the implications of Machiavellianism in a changed political context, in which the monarch is not considered strong or prudent enough to be a powerful guiding force to self-interested counsellors. According to the humanist model, such monarchical insufficiencies necessitate the rule of wise counsellors. Contrastingly, the Machiavellian approach to counsel raises concerns regarding the ways in which self-interested counsellors may seek to control these monarchs for their own ends. This tension is often resolved by the requirement that counsel comes not from private counsellors, but more trustworthy sources, such as histories (the 'counsel of the dead') or, increasingly, from parliament.

Part III treats the language of reason of state and its implications for early Stuart politics. Chapter 6 introduces this vocabulary, largely through the work of Giovanni Botero and those who follow him. Reason of state sets out the bounds of what might be considered necessary to secure the well-being of the state. Fundamental to the reason of state tradition is the language of 'interest' which allows for the expression of a clear dichotomy between the private interests of the counsellor and the interests of the state, now fully articulated. This leads many writers, such as Fray Juan de Santa Maria and Philippe de Béthune, to articulate an even clearer boundary between counsel and command. Distrustful of rhetoric and even history, writers in this tradition mark 'observation' of contemporary affairs as the essential content of counsel, gleaned primarily from travel writings. From an educated moral guide to the prince, seen in Part I, the counsellor becomes a straightforward transmitter of factual information.

If the tension between counsel and command is rooted in the assertion that obligatory (including rhetorically influential) counsel becomes command (i.e. infringes upon sovereignty), then the seventeenth century presents three potential answers to that problem. The first, the Stuart royalist account, is to continue, nevertheless, to try to subdue counsel. It neglects to take into account the necessary 'paradox of counsel' at its heart, and therefore fails. The second is to accept this transformation of counsel into command, and to fit it into other justifications of the legitimate sources of sovereignty. This parliamentarian account is far more successful than the royalist and accepts that counsel and therefore command are placed in the institution of parliament, resolving a century-old debate by accepting what had been seen as an unacceptable outcome: counsel becoming command. Finally, and this is the Hobbesian move, one could reject that counsel should be 'influential' in the way previously conceived, instead firmly subjugating it to sovereignty. This Hobbesian sovereignty revives a firm distinction between counsel and command by refuting the importance of many of the concepts central to the discourse, especially the role of prudence and rhetoric, thereby going far beyond the royalist attempt to simply reassert counsel's inferiority. Thus, the two most successful answers to the paradox of counsel simply accept the consequences of the problem, either allowing counsel to become command or to become essentially trivial.

Understanding sovereignty's roots in the 'monarchy of counsel' raises questions about the continued relevance of counsel to political thought and action (and indeed the blurred line between them), and possibilities for political theorising which moves beyond sovereignty. At the very least, it presents a picture of early modern political thought that allows us to see past modern preoccupations with a politics defined by sovereignty.

PART I

CHAPTER 1

The Humanist Counsellor

Humanism had taken root in England by the middle of the fifteenth century and was beginning to compete for a place in its universities by the turn of the sixteenth, often thanks to a productive scholarly exchange between England and Italy.[1] The character of the Italian and Northern European Renaissances brought the emerging conciliar figure to the fore, presenting him consciously as a way of mitigating the threats of personal monarchical sovereignty by connecting him with neo-republican ideas.[2] In a monarchical context, the republican orator-citizen became the counsellor, who still had a role in freeing the commonwealth through his speech; where there was no opportunity to establish a republic, this active citizen became the counsellor.[3] The counsellor was the manifestation of republican ideals: not just the *vita activa* (or active life) but also introducing limits on the tyranny of the monarch. This, inevitably and intentionally, created a conflict between counsel and command, especially given the

1 See Markku Peltonen, *Classical Humanism and Republicanism in English Political Thought, 1570–1640* (Cambridge: Cambridge University Press, 2004), 2–3, 7–8; Roberto Weiss, *Humanism in England During the Fifteenth Century* (Oxford: Basil Blackwell, 1957). It has been suggested that humanism did not establish itself in the schools under the latter half of the sixteenth century; see Jo Ann Hoeppner Moran, *The Growth of English Schooling, 1340–1548: Learning, Literacy, and Laicization in Pre-Reformation York Diocese* (Princeton: Princeton University Press, 2014), 216–19; E. R. Kintgen, *Reading in Tudor England* (Pittsburgh: University of Pittsburgh Press, 1996), 20.

2 Cary J. Nederman, 'Rhetoric, Reason, and Republic: Republicanisms – Ancient, Medieval, and Modern', in *Renaissance Civic Humanism: Reappraisals and Reflections*, ed. James Hankins (Cambridge: Cambridge University Press, 2000), 252–3; See Cary J. Nederman, 'Nature, Sin and the Origins of Society: The Ciceronian Tradition in Medieval Political Thought', *Journal of the History of Ideas* 49, no. 1 (1988): 7–9; James M. Blythe, '"Civic Humanism" and Medieval Political Thought', in *Renaissance Civic Humanism: Reappraisals and Reflections*, ed. James Hankins (Cambridge: Cambridge University Press, 2000), 65.

3 Skinner, *Foundations*, 116–17; see also Walker, *Writing Under Tyranny*, 143: 'The relationship between prince and counsellor was, then, the lynchpin of the humanist conception of the state'. Of course, as Anthony Grafton, 'Humanism and Political Theory', in *The Cambridge History of Political Thought 1450–1700*, ed. J. H. Burns (Cambridge: Cambridge University Press, 1991), 17 points out, a dedication to civic service did not always go alongside a commitment to republican ideals. See also Nelson, 'The Problem of the Prince', 319.

power of the rhetorical tools for giving counsel espoused by these humanist writers.

It was consistent with both humanism and the growth of political bureaucracy that humanistically educated 'new men' took roles as counsellors in the courts of both early Tudor kings.[4] Such men had the skills to manage quotidian political business as well as acting as mediators – and occasional buffers – between the king and his subjects. Early Tudor kingship was 'intensely personal', with private relationships defining structures of power.[5] This generated a role for the counsellor as close personal companion to the king, at times even '*alter rex*'.[6]

Such a blurring between counsel and command was consistent with the writings on the topic produced by leading humanists of the time, including Erasmus, More and Castiglione. Each accepted that good counsel should, to varying degrees, rule the prince. At the heart of their writings remains, however, a question about the efficacy of counsel in a hereditary monarchy. Often overlooked in this debate is importance of Seneca, who provides the basis for the discussion of the effectiveness of counsel in all three writers' works, contrasting principles learned through instruction from precepts gathered through counsel. Erasmus presents a pessimistic view on the question of the value of counsel if the prince has not been well educated, which is why he turns to the figure of the tutor, rather than the counsellor, in shaping the virtue of the prince in his *Institutio*. His suggestion is taken up by More, who presents the contrary view in his *Utopia*, maintaining that regardless of the virtue of the prince's education, the learned man still has a duty to try to counsel the prince when the right moment comes. Castiglione attempts a resolution of the question, by combining both instructor and counsellor in the same figure, his ideal courtier, who speaks rhetorically sweetened truth to the prince in the right moment to guide him to virtue. Castiglione also goes furthest in explicitly asserting the power of the counsellor over the prince as a means to restore republican liberty in a monarchical context, though it is clear for all three writers that virtuous counsel ought to rule.

i Erasmus and the 'seeds of morality'

At first glance Erasmus may seem an unlikely starting point for a study of the English discourse of counsel. For one, he never seems wholly convinced

[4] See Steven Gunn, *Henry VII's New Men and the Making of Tudor England* (Oxford: Oxford University Press, 2016), 109, 113.

[5] Gunn, *Henry VII's New Men*, 39.

[6] Gunn, *Henry VII's New Men*, 320.

of the efficacy of counsel and, second, he was not English. Few of his texts were translated into English in the period in question, and those that were did not deal explicitly with the role of the counsellor. Nevertheless, as 'arguably the most widely read author in early sixteenth-century Europe', with connections to England, it is essential to use his ideas as a starting point.[7] Furthermore, as we shall see, his friend and colleague Thomas More, perhaps the best-known English writer on counsel in the period, was responding directly to some of Erasmus' comments on counsel, particularly his dismissal of the utility of political advice. This dismissal was based on a debate contained within two of Seneca's letters, which Erasmus himself translated. Without understanding the connection to Seneca, both More's and Erasmus' comments about the efficacy of counsel are difficult to grasp.

Any republicanism in Erasmus is tempered by his attachment to monarchy as the system defended by most philosophers and analogous to the rule of God.[8] He does, however, also suggest that the best monarchical government would be an elected one. There were two major issues with personal hereditary monarchy for Erasmus. The first was the limitations of a singular ruler, a theme in the literature on counsel since Aristotle, and which often drew on his image of collective prudence in the *Politics*: 'For it is possible that the many, though not individually good men, yet when they come together may be better, not individually but collectively . . . the multitude becomes a single man with many feet and many hands and many senses, so also it becomes one personality as regards the moral and intellectual faculties.'[9] Erasmus also relies heavily on Plutarch for this view. In the essay 'That a Philosopher Ought to Converse Especially with Men in Power', Plutarch notes that those who study philosophy have an inclination to 'converse with the prominent and powerful', just as a well-trained physician will want to 'cure the eye which sees for many'.[10] Erasmus likewise writes to the English king, Henry VIII, in a preface to his translation of Plutarch's *How to Tell a Flatterer from a Friend*, easily one of the

[7] Gregory D. Dodds, *Exploiting Erasmus: The Erasmian Legacy and Religious Change in Early Modern England* (Toronto: University of Toronto Press, 2009), xi.

[8] Erika Rummel, *Desiderius Erasmus* (London: Continuum, 2004), 56.

[9] Aristotle, *Politics*, 1281a43–b9. For more on what Aristotle calls the 'doctrine of the wisdom of the multitude' see Jeremy Waldron, 'The Wisdom of the Multitude: Some Reflections on Book 3, Chapter 11 of Aristotle's Politics', *Political Theory* 23, no. 4 (1995): 563–84. For the medieval roots of Erasmus' text see Richard F. Hardin, 'The Literary Conventions of Erasmus' Education of a Christian Prince: Advice and Aphorism', *Renaissance Quarterly* 35, no. 2 (1982): 154–5.

[10] Plutarch, 'That a Philosopher Ought to Converse Especially with Men in Power', *Moralia*, trans. Frank Cole Babbitt (Cambridge, MA: Harvard University Press, 1927), vol. 1, 1.

most influential classical writings on the theme of counsel in the period, 'One who all by himself looks out for the good of thousands of other men must have extremely clear vision. Therefore it is proper for a ruler to be provided with many eyes, that is, with many prudent and loyal friends.'[11] Erasmus also repeats the metaphor of the fountain or ever-flowing cup from Plutarch. Those who, in Plutarch's words, 'constantly corrupt rulers or kings or tyrants' have the effect of 'putting deadly poison, not into a single cup, but into the public fountain which, as they see, everyone uses'.[12] In such a vision, the prince becomes no more than an instrument through which others' influence flows to the commonwealth.

Second, and relatedly, an unelected monarch is an unknown in regard to his or her ability to rule in line with reason. Erasmus repeats the idea, from the psuedo-Aristotelian *Secretum secretorum* and other medieval texts, that the prince 'will not be able to be a king unless reason is king over you'.[13] It would be best if philosophers could rule directly, as in Plato's republic, but this is often unrealistic.[14] Personal hereditary monarchy is not the best option, but it can be rendered more in line with humanist ideals by means of those who surround and assist the monarch, mitigating his limitations and weaknesses.

This means that the ruler ought to be ruled by others, such as his 'friends', who offer him counsel. In the *Panegyricus*, written in 1503 for Archduke Philip of Austria, Erasmus suggests that 'a state is more fortunate, and probably safer, whose prince is wicked, than one in which the prince's friends are wicked, because, one bad person can be corrected by several good ones, whereas many bad ones cannot by any means be triumphed over by one person, however good'.[15] The ideal scenario, of course, is a good prince who only admits good counsel, but

11 Erasmus, *Erasmus and His Age: Selected Letters of Desiderius Erasmus*, ed. Hans J. Hillerbrand (New York: Harper and Row Ltd, 1970), 64. Erasmus' translation of Plutarch's text, alongside Isocrates' *To Nicocles*, were published with the 1516 edition of *The Education of the Christian Prince*. For the influence of Isocrates on *The Education of the Christian Prince* see Hardin, 'Literary Conventions', 155–6.

12 Erasmus, *The Education of a Christian Prince*, trans. Lisa Jardine (Cambridge: Cambridge University Press, 1997), 2, 11 from Plutarch, 'Philosopher Ought to Converse', 3.

13 Erasmus, *Education*, 52; see Lydgate, *Gouernaunce of Kynges and Prynces*, sig. B, iiv; F, ivr; Starnes, 'Introduction', xii.

14 In the *Republic*, wisdom (not *phronesis*) and command are combined in the philosopher-kings, who conceivably have no need for external counsel (or even, indeed, practical wisdom); see Plato, *The Republic*, ed. Paul Shorey (Cambridge, MA: Harvard University Press, 1969), 428b.

15 Erasmus, *Panegyric*, in *Education*, 131. Erasmus attributes the maxim that it is better to have a bad prince than bad friends of the prince to Marius Maximus via Lampridius. It is the same conclusion that John Gower had come to in *Confessio Amantis*; Gower, *The Complete Works*, VII.4157ff; see Ferster, *Fictions of Advice*, 127.

being realistic, counsellors are more influential than the monarch: if they are good, good will follow; if they are bad, no matter the goodness of the prince, they will prevail. Erasmus articulates a similar maxim in a text composed in 1516 for Philip's son, the future Emperor Charles V, *Institutio principis Christiani*. He repeats the suggestion that it is better to have a bad ruler than that those around the prince are malicious, 'In some ways it is a more acceptable situation for the state when the prince himself is bad than when his friends are: somehow or other we put up with a single tyrant . . . to satisfy a whole entourage of tyrants is a very heavy burden.'[16] He does not repeat, however, the corrective influence of good 'friends' in the *Institutio*, which is generally more pessimistic about the positive power of counsel than the *Panegyricus*.

In the *Institutio*, the redemptive republican power is placed in the tutor rather than the counsellor: 'Where there is no power to select the prince, the man who is to educate the future prince must be selected with comparable care.'[17] Developing the Plutarchan images of the all-seeing eye and the ever-flowing fountain, Erasmus suggests that 'a country owes everything to a good prince; but it owes the prince himself to the one whose right counsel [*recta ratio*] has made him what he is'.[18] Reason, which is instituted by the tutor, actually rules the prince. In the *Institutio*, it is not *counsel* but *instruction* which overrules command.[19]

The different approaches between these two texts appear to result from Erasmus' engagement with Seneca's letters shortly before publishing his *Institutio*. Erasmus produced a translation of the letters in 1515, *Lucubrationes omnes*, having begun work on the translation while in England in 1513. It was on sale in London by early 1516 and More reported positively on its reception.[20] In the letter 'On the Value of Advice' (Letter 94), published in Erasmus' collection as '*Vtrum pars philosophiae sup[er] fluat disputatio & solutio, & de annotatione contra malum popularis opinionis*', Seneca makes a distinction between the *decreta* and *praecepta* of

16 Erasmus, *Education*, 71. 17 Erasmus, *Education*, 6.

18 Erasmus, *Education*, 6. The translation of *recta ratio* as 'right counsel' has led to some confusion here.

19 It is this emphasis on education over counsel which prompts Hardin to suggest that 'In the *Education*, as in the later *Apophthegmata*, the object is less to counsel princes than to show them how to be their own counselors'; 'Literary Conventions', 161. Alistair Fox, 'English Humanism and the Body Politic', in *Reassessing the Henrician Age: Humanism, Politics and Reform, 1500–1550*, ed. Alistair Fox and John Guy (Oxford: B. Blackwell, 1986), 51 draws a distinction with More on this point.

20 Robert B. Hardy, 'A Study of Erasmus's Editions of the Works of Lucius Annaeus Seneca' (Honours Dissertation, Oberlin College, 1986), 4, 11.

philosophy.[21] Seneca suggests that, although precepts – related to particulars and advice-giving – 'do not remove error, nor do they rout [*expugnant*] our false opinions on the subject of Good and Evil' they are still useful.[22] Advice 'engages the attention and rouses us'; it is, he says, 'a sort of exhortation'.[23] It serves to 'stir' the 'seed of everything that is honourable [*honestum*]', which is naturally within the soul, 'as a spark that is fanned by a gentle breeze develops its natural fire'.[24] Importantly, precepts are not the same as commands, for they do not coerce but 'plead' [*exorant*].[25] They are considered side by side, however, by Seneca, who suggests that as 'one is helped by commands [*imperio*]' so 'one is helped also by advice [*admonitione*]'.[26]

Notably, Seneca gives the corresponding case in the next letter, 'On the Usefulness of Basic Principles' or '*Non esse petendum quod impetrate uolueris. De differentia inter decreta & praecepta* . . . ', where he establishes that *praecepta* alone are not enough either, for precepts can only take hold 'when the will is receptive; and sometimes they are applied in vain, when wrong opinions obsess the soul'.[27] As a counterweight to what he said in his previous letter, Seneca writes that the 'upset condition of morals' of his time requires 'something stronger' than just advice; 'in order to root out a deep-seated belief in wrong ideas, conduct must be regulated by doctrines [*decretis*]', but to it must be added 'precepts, consolation and encouragement', for without them they will not prevail.[28]

Erasmus emphasises the importance of early instruction, without which later counsel will not be of any use, drawing directly on the vocabulary from Seneca's letters, and particularly siding with Letter 95. The 'seeds of morality', he suggests, must be sown early, so 'they may gradually germinate and mature and, once they are set, may be rooted in him throughout his whole life'.[29] It is 'fruitless', Erasmus maintains, 'to give advice on the principles of government

[21] Lucius Annaeus Seneca, *Lucubrationes omnes*, ed. Desiderius Erasmus (Basel, 1515), 313–20. See I. G. Kidd, 'Moral Actions and Rules in Stoic Ethics', in *The Stoics*, ed. John M. Rist (Berkeley: University of California Press, 1978), 252–4 for the difference between *decreta* – 'definite and fixed' 'rules of practice' – and *praecepta* – which are harder to define, but involve more specificity and flexibility. See also John Schafer, *Ars Didactica: Seneca's 94th and 95th Letters* (Göttingen: Vandenhoeck & Ruprecht, 2009), 10–11.

[22] Lucius Annaeus Seneca, *Moral Letters to Lucilius (Epistulae Morales Ad Lucilium)*, ed. Richard Mott Gummere 3 vols (Cambridge, MA: Harvard University Press, 1917–1925), 94.21.

[23] Seneca, *Letters*, 94.25. [24] Seneca, *Letters*, 94.29. [25] Seneca, *Letters*, 94.37.

[26] Seneca, *Letters*, 94.44.

[27] Seneca, *Lucubrationes omnes*, 320–6; Seneca, *Letters*, 95.4; Seneca, *Letters*, 95.4; see Andreas Heil and Gregor Damschen, *Brill's Companion to Seneca: Philosopher and Dramatist* (Leiden: Brill, 2013), 714.

[28] Seneca, *Letters*, 95.35. In particular here he draws attention to the importance of recognising *paradiastole*.

[29] Erasmus, *Education*, 5.

without previously setting a prince's mind free from those popular opinions which are at once most widely held and are yet most fallacious'.[30] Counsel later in life is useless without instruction as a child. Erasmus seeks the person who can 'eradicate from his pupil's mind whatever shameful and vulgar ideas may somehow have taken root, and to implant those that are healthy and worthy of the Christian prince'.[31]

Erasmus' rejection of counsel is linked to a general pessimism about the quality of men who generally make up a prince's court, the entourage of tyrants he references in the *Institutio*; it is they who plant false opinions in the prince, which only instruction can uproot. The 'plague of flattery' is rife in the courts of Europe, caused by the self-interest of counsellors who have 'rival interests among themselves'.[32] Drawing directly on Plutarch's 'How to Tell a Flatterer from a Friend', Erasmus writes that 'the most pernicious flatterers of all are those who operate with apparent frankness but in some remarkable way contrive to urge you on while seeming to restrain you and to praise you while seeming to criticise'.[33] It is thus probably better, Erasmus maintains, once again drawing on Plutarch, to learn from books and not from counsellors, to 'learn from these what his friends have not dared to bring to his attention'.[34] As he writes, 'Nobody speaks the truth more honestly or more advantageously or more candidly than do books'.[35] Nevertheless, the prince must attempt to encourage his friends to do the same: to give 'frank advice' and to 'advise him opportunely, advantageously, and amicably', and the prince must forgive those who speak 'clumsily' so that 'no precedent may deter those who would advise him properly from doing their duty'.[36] All of this is dependent, however, on the prince's early instruction. If he was educated in right principles, then bad counsel will do him little ill; if he is not, then no amount of good counsel can save him.

Whether tutor or counsellor, however, Erasmus is clear that the humanist-orator figure must be more powerful than the prince for two main reasons. This first is that the prince needs to follow and act upon good advice or be classed a tyrant. Erasmus in the *Institutio* gives two – related – definitions of tyranny. He writes that the prince should strike a balance – an 'equability of

[30] Erasmus, *Education*, 11. [31] Erasmus, *Education*, 54, 73. [32] Erasmus, *Education*, 56, 57.

[33] Erasmus, *Education*, 57; see Plutarch, 'adulator', 5.

[34] Erasmus, *Education*, 60; see Plutarch, *Moralia*, trans. H. N. Fowler (Cambridge, MA: Harvard University Press, 1936), 3, 52: 'Demetrius of Phalerum recommended to Ptolemy the king to buy and read the books dealing with the office of king and ruler. "For," as he said, "those things which the kings' friends are not bold enough to recommend to them are written in the books."'

[35] Erasmus, *Education*, 64–5. [36] Erasmus, *Education*, 64–5.

temperament' – between tyranny and pliability, neither being obstinate and refusing advice (tyranny), nor 'so pliant as to allow himself to be led this way and that by the opinion of anyone and everyone'.[37] Elsewhere, Erasmus defines tyranny as self-interest.[38] These two definitions – refusing counsel and self-interested rule – do not have to be opposed. If the tutor/counsellor represents the good of the commonwealth, then to refuse such advice in favour of one's own judgement is indeed tyranny.[39] As such, the king is *required* to take such advice, or is a tyrant.

Secondly, the influence of the tutors/counsellors stems from their rhetorical power. Erasmus is happy to use – and advise others to use – rhetorical tools in their counselling. In the prefatory letter of the *Panegyric*, to Nicholas Ruistre, Erasmus professes a distaste for 'all this kind of writing' (panegyrics), because of his preference for 'frank speaking'; however, setting an 'example' before princes in the form of a panegyric can encourage them towards virtue and away from vice.[40] The portrait Erasmus paints of Philip is not accurate, but rather an ideal-type for him to strive for. In *Praise of Folly*, published in 1511, Erasmus' Folly suggests that there are two kinds of flattery. One is 'wholly noxious'.[41] The other 'stems from a sort of ingenuous goodness of heart and is far nearer being a virtue than the critical asperity which is its opposite'.[42] In addition to various other benefits, including 'cheer[ing] the sick' and 'attract[ing] children to pursue the study of letters', this sort of flattery 'offers advice and counsel to princes in the form of praise which doesn't give offense'.[43] Even flattery, of a certain kind, can be used for good ends, in 'leading' the prince to virtue. In the *Institutio*, Erasmus notes that the tutor should use 'an agreeable style of speech', where the matter is harsh.[44] He repeats the same intention in a contemporary letter to the

37 Erasmus, *Education*, 4.

38 Erasmus, *Education*, 25–8, 53; see also Erasmus, *Praise of Folly*, ed. A. H. T. Levi, trans. Betty Radice (London: Penguin UK, 1993), 104–5.

39 Erasmus goes on to include listening to good counsel as one of the criteria that differentiates a good king from a tyrant, *Education*, 28. See Kinch Hoekstra, 'Athenian Democracy and Popular Tyranny', in *Popular Sovereignty in Historical Perspective*, ed. Quentin Skinner and Richard Bourke (Cambridge: Cambridge University Press, 2016), 48–9 on the Aristotelian definition of the tyrant as one who rules 'unaccountably' in his personal interest.

40 Erasmus, *Panegyric*, in *Education*, 112; see David Rundle, '"Not so Much Praise as Precept": Erasmus, Panegyric, and the Renaissance Art of Teaching Princes', in *Pedagogy and Power: Rhetorics of Classical Learning*, ed. Yun Lee Too and Niall Livingstone (Cambridge: Cambridge University Press, 1998), 148–69.

41 Erasmus, *Praise of Folly*, 70. For the puzzles inherent in the text see Anthony Grafton, 'Prelude', in *The Praise of Folly* (Princeton: Princeton University Press, 2015), vii–xxii and Hoyt Hopewell Hudson, 'The Folly of Erasmus', in *The Praise of Folly* (Princeton: Princeton University Press, 2015), xxv–lv.

42 Erasmus, *Praise of Folly*, 70.

43 Erasmus, *Praise of Folly*, 70.

44 Erasmus, *Education*, 13.

humanist Jean Desmarez, adding that he follows the examples of classical authors – such as Isocrates – in 'exhort[ing] rulers to honourable actions under the cover of compliment'.[45] Erasmus does not mind that these are strong and rather deceptive terms. Exhortation is not compulsion, but it is still a sort of control – 'How much easier it is to lead [*dicitur*] a generous spirit than to compel [*trahitur*] it'.[46] Leading a prince through rhetoric is entirely acceptable, even to be encouraged, and perhaps necessary.

This is sometimes more easily done, he suggests, with humour than with harsh rebukes: 'Plato approves of having several rounds at a drinking bout for the reason that some defects can be routed under the cheerful influence of wine which could not be corrected by a stern rebuke. And Horace is of the opinion that humorous advice is no less profitable than serious.'[47] Humour could be a legitimate means for imparting counsel, as long as it remained unspecific and 'did not lapse into raging passion'.[48] As he writes to his friend Thomas More: 'If someone criticizes men's lives without censuring anyone at all by name – now, is such a person really carping, or is he not rather teaching and admonishing?'[49] Honey can be applied to medicine to make it more appealing, and fools and jesters can 'reveal and correct slight faults' without offense.[50] Even Christ employs such methods in the Gospels, and St Augustine, Erasmus suggests, encourages the same.[51] This kind of humour acts as a corrective to vice and the true antidote to the folly of the world.[52]

The 'folly' of the world brings us back to Erasmus' discussion of false opinion and to his discussion of the 'stage-play'. Everything in life has two completely opposed faces: 'All human affairs are like the figures of Silenus described by Alcibiades and have two completely opposite faces, so that what is death at first sight, as they say, is life if you look within, and vice versa, life is death . . . in fact you'll find everything suddenly reversed if you

[45] Erasmus, *Panegyric*, in *Education*, 114–15.

[46] Erasmus, *Panegyric*, in *Education*, 115; on the power of rhetoric to 'move', see Quentin Skinner, *Reason and Rhetoric in the Philosophy of Hobbes* (Cambridge: Cambridge University Press, 1996), 90.

[47] Erasmus, *Erasmus and his Age*, 85.

[48] Erasmus, *Erasmus and his Age*, 85, 59. He repeats the same in his *Praise of Folly*, 57 where he also notes that 'the words which would cost a wise man his life are surprisingly enjoyable when uttered by a clown', before beginning a litany of social, political and religious criticisms through the mouth of Folly herself.

[49] Erasmus, *Erasmus and his Age*, 59.

[50] Erasmus, *Erasmus and his Age*, 85.

[51] Erasmus, *Erasmus and his Age*, 85.

[52] See Claudia Zatta, 'Democritus and Folly: The Two Wise Fools', *Bibliothèque d'Humanisme et Renaissance* 63, no.3 (2001): 533–49; Quentin Skinner, *Visions of Politics: Volume 3* (Cambridge: Cambridge University Press, 2002), 145, 152–8, 168–70; Travis Curtright, 'Thomas More on Humor', *Logos: A Journal of Catholic Thought and Culture* 17, no.1 (2014): 13–35.

open the Silenus.'[53] But it is important to keep the illusion alive, a lesson Erasmus expresses through the use of a stage-play metaphor: 'To destroy the illusion is to ruin the whole play, for it's really the illusion and make-up which hold the audience's eye.'[54] To maintain the play is prudence (which Folly associates with herself), to disrupt it is the sign of wisdom, which Folly seems to suggest is always mistimed: 'A man's conduct is misplaced if he doesn't adapt himself to things as they are, has no eye for the main chance, won't even remember that convivial maxim "drink or depart", and asks for the play to stop being a play.'[55] It is the sign of prudence, not wisdom, to 'wear your illusions with a good grace'.[56]

Here the concept in question is most certainly *decorum*, which had been associated with the idea of the stage-play in Cicero's works.[57] Folly suggests that the wise man is not attentive to *decorum*, and thus disrupts the play.[58] It is unclear here if Erasmus agrees with Folly or not. Certainly, at least, he idealises a figure who can see through the stage-play.[59] As he writes in the *Institutio*, a '"philosopher" does not mean someone who is clever at dialectics or science but someone who rejects illusory appearance and undauntedly seeks out and follows what is good'.[60] But whether his ideal figure would openly overthrow the stage-play or participate in it (knowing it is false) is left open.[61]

It is perhaps intentional that a few pages later Erasmus has Folly appear to contradict this conclusion, now in the language of *kairos*: the opportune moment or 'occasion'.[62] Cicero had also treated *kairos*, under the heading of 'seemliness', and he gives *kairos* a virtuous function; it does not carry any

53 Erasmus, *Praise of Folly*, 43.

54 Erasmus, *Praise of Folly*, 43. For the influence of Lucian on *Praise of Folly* see Hudson 'The Folly of Erasmus', xxxiii–xxxiv.

55 Erasmus, *Praise of Folly*, 45. 56 Erasmus, *Praise of Folly*, 45.

57 See Quentin Skinner, 'Thomas More's Utopia and the Virtue of True Nobility', in *Visions of Politics: Volume 2: Renaissance Virtues* (Cambridge: Cambridge University Press, 2002), 220. Erasmus produced an edition of *De officiis* in 1501, see Hardy, 'A Study', 5.

58 Erasmus, *Praise of Folly*, 40.

59 Dominic Baker-Smith, *More's* Utopia (Toronto: University of Toronto Press, 2000), 44 points out how the 'main targets of humanist satire' were where 'a public sign becomes a totem or substitute for the real thing'.

60 Erasmus, *Education*, 15.

61 Fox, 'English Humanism and the Body Politic', 150 maintains that Erasmus and More disagreed over the stage-play metaphor: 'Whereas for Erasmus the play-acting was part of the corruption to be remedied, for More it constituted the most effective way of ensuring that what could not be made perfectly good was made as little bad as possible.' On both counts it seems more nuance is necessary, and perhaps both agree that the ideal is to recognise and reject the stage-play internally, while participating in it externally.

62 See Joanne Paul, 'The Use of Kairos in Renaissance Political Philosophy', *Renaissance Quarterly* 67, no.1 (2014): 43–78. As Glyn P. Norton, 'Improvisation, Time, and Opportunity in the Rhetorical Tradition', in *The Oxford Handbook of Critical Improvisation Studies*, ed. George E. Lewis and Benjamin Piekut (Oxford: Oxford University Press, 2016), 270 makes clear 'In the plural (*kairoi*),

of the potential amoralism of its Greek roots.[63] To misjudge the time, for Cicero, does not just run counter to one's aims but is also dishonourable. As Cicero states, 'it is dishonourable and a great failing to introduce into a serious matter something worthy of a dinner party, or some frivolous conversation', and the reverse is true as well.[64] Erasmus, like Cicero, seems to reject the sophistic understanding of *kairos*, which allowed for moral flexibility, by satirising it in *Praise of Folly*. Contradicting what she had said of the wise man whose truth interrupts the play, Folly goes on to state that it is only fools 'who speak frankly and tell the truth', whereas a wise man 'has two tongues, as Euripides also says, one to speak the truth with, the other for saying what he thinks fits the occasion'.[65] No longer the incompetent ill-timed philosophical blunderer, such a one 'makes a habit of changing black into white and blowing hot and cold in the same breath' as needed.[66] A wise man might have missed *decorum*, but he seizes occasion for his own ends, using its ability to, as Erasmus had put it, 'turn what is

the word refers to moments of crisis, critical times calling for decision and making their discontinuity with the past'. Holbein contributes an illustration of *kairos* in Erasmus' *Praise of Folly*, despite the fact that the temporal figure in discussion is *fortuna*, not *kairos*. Holbein also designed the printer's mark for Andreas Crantander – an image of *kairos*-and *kairos* graces the frontispieces of the *Lucubrationes omnes*.

63 See Mario Untersteiner, *The Sophists*, trans. Kathleen Freeman (New York: Blackwell, 1954), 119–20; Michael Carter, 'Stasis and Kairos: Principles of Social Construction in Classical Rhetoric', *Rhetoric Review* 7, no. 1 (1988): 101; Phillip Sipiora, 'The Ancient Concept of Kairos', in *Rhetoric and Kairos: and Praxis*, ed. Phillip Sipiora and James S Baumlin (New York: State University of New York Press, 2002), 4; Sharon A. Beehler, '"Confederate Season": Shakespeare and the Elizabethan Understanding of *Kairos*' in *Shakespeare Matters: History, Teaching, Performance*, ed. Lloyd Davis (Newark; London: University of Delaware Press; Associated University Press, 2003), 79.

64 Marcus Tullius Cicero, *Cicero: On Duties*, ed. M. T. Griffin, trans. E. M. Atkins (Cambridge: Cambridge University Press, 1991), 56. Cicero explicitly defines *occasio* in *De Inventione*: 'An occasion is a portion of time having in it a suitable opportunity for doing or avoiding to do some particular thing. Wherefore there is this difference between it and time. For, as to genus, indeed, they are both understood to be identical; but in time some space is expressed in some manner or other, which is regarded with reference to years, or to a year, or to some portion of a year; but in an occasion, besides the space of time implied in the word, there is indicated an especial opportunity of doing something. As therefore the two are identical in genus, it is some portion and species, as it were, in which the one differs, as we have said, from the other.' Cicero goes on to define three 'classes' of *occasio*: 'public, common, and singular'. In the first is included those occasions 'which the whole city avails itself of for some particular cause: as games, a day of festival, or war'. Common occasions are those which 'happens to all men at nearly the same time; as the harvest, the vintage, summer, or winter'. And a singular occasion is that which 'on account of some special cause, happens at times to some private individuals' and he gives as examples 'a wedding, a sacrifice, a funeral, a feast, sleep'; Marcus Tullius Cicero, 'On Invention', *The Orations of Marcus Tullius Cicero*, trans. Charles Duke Yonge, vol. 4 (London: H.G. Bohn, 1853), 1.27.

65 Erasmus, *Praise of Folly*, 56.

66 Erasmus, *Praise of Folly*, 56. Exchanging 'blacke for white' is also associated with flattery in Baldesarre Castiglione, *The Book of the Courtier*, ed. Virginia Cox, trans. Thomas Hoby, (London: J. M. Dent & Sons Ltd/Everyman's Library, 1994), 81; see also Trajano Boccalini, *The New-Found Politicke*, trans. John Florio (London, 1626), 1, 2 (treated in Chapter 6).

honourable into dishonour' to flatter rather than counsel.[67] Thus, kings have 'no one to tell them the truth' and are 'obliged to have flatterers for friends'.[68] Kings prefer what is pleasant, and 'in order to keep their minds untouched by care they give audience only to men who know how to say what is pleasant to hear'.[69] For this reason pleasantness – here associated with 'folly' – must be mixed with truth, as the fool had done, and 'in season'.[70] Just as the flatterer, then, uses occasion to advance self-interested advice, the good counsellor uses it, alongside rhetoric, to advance truth. *Praise of Folly* itself becomes precisely such a text, as the *Panegyricus* had been: 'advice' which is 'cloaked' in order to make it more agreeable.[71]

It is worth noting that the context of the Reformation changes Erasmus' approach somewhat, introducing more caution in regard to frank counsel. Erasmus writes to Luther in 1519 that 'it is more advisable to scream out against those who abuse papal authority than against popes themselves', and 'the same approach I think should be used with regard to kings'.[72] This is not just a worry about revolt, but a strategy for counselling advisedly, as he makes clear to Lorenzo Campeggio a year later, expanding on the advice he gave Luther:

> [Luther] should spare the dignity of rulers, for if they are inopportunely insulted or admonished they do not improve, but rather become embittered and sometimes stir up dangerous storms. As a result, the critic loses his authority and sometimes his life, and the advice its effect. While it is never lawful to oppose the truth, still it is sometimes expedient to conceal it at the right time.[73]

In these few lines Erasmus expresses succinctly the humanist 'problem of counsel' and its connection to right timing. As Erasmus makes clear, if the counsellor mistimes his advice, he risks two possible consequences: (1) making the situation he sought to rectify worse (or at the least not making any change) and (2) a loss of position and perhaps even life. Erasmus' solution is to 'conceal' the truth 'at the right time'. In other words, in certain moments speaking truth frankly will probably only make the situation worse, and so the

67 Erasmus uses similar language in treating *kairos* in his adage *Nosce Tempus*, harkening back to sophistic connotations: 'Such is the force of *Opportunitas*, of Timeliness, that it can turn what is honourable into dishonour, loss into gain, happiness into misery . . . in short, change the nature of everything'; Erasmus, *The Adages of Erasmus*, ed. William Watson Barker (Toronto: University of Toronto Press, 2001), 106.

68 Erasmus, *Praise of Folly*, 56.

69 Erasmus, *Praise of Folly*, 105.

70 Erasmus, *Praise of Folly*, 115.

71 See Hudson, 'The Folly of Erasmus', xlvi.

72 Erasmus, *Erasmus and His Age*, 141.

73 Erasmus, *Erasmus and His Age*, 160.

opportune moment for such frank speech must be chosen carefully. Doing this correctly could solve the problem of counsel. Still better, however, if the prince is well educated by a tutor from the start, avoiding such problems altogether.

ii More and 'uprooting' Vice

The best-known text in the early modern period on the problem of counsel is undoubtedly More's *Utopia*.[74] In this text, More addresses many of the themes touched on by Erasmus, including the Senecan debate on the efficacy of counsel and the stage-play metaphor.[75] He also goes further in connecting these questions to ones about an 'indirect approach' to counsel and the issue of public versus private advice, a topic which preoccupies him intensely, especially after 1517.

Book I of *Utopia*, published in 1516, contains the so-called 'dialogue of counsel', in which the character of Raphael Hythloday debates the value of entering the service (or servitude) of a king with the character of Thomas More (hereafter 'Morus').[76] As has been well established, in Book I, Hythloday advances Platonic arguments for the contemplative life, against Morus' Ciceronianism.[77] Morus argues that Hythloday owes a duty to the commonwealth.[78] A counsellor such as he could be greatly beneficial to the commonwealth by 'mak[ing] [*persuareris*] [the prince] follow . . . straightforward [*recta*] and honorable [*honesta*] courses.'[79] He reinforces this argument with the now-familiar fountain metaphor: 'From the monarch, as from a never-failing spring, flows a stream of all that is good or evil over the whole nation'.[80] Morus' image of the counsellor, drawn from Plutarch as well as Cicero, leads his prince by his persuasive speech to reason and virtue for the benefit of all.[81]

Hythloday objects to Morus, first, that he does not wish to abandon his freedom and, second, that it would not do any good if he did. Echoing

[74] J. H. Hexter, 'Thomas More and the Problem of Counsel', in *Quincentennial Essays on St. Thomas More: Selected Papers from the Thomas More College Conference* (Boone: Albion, 1978), 55–66.

[75] John Michael Parrish has suggested that Seneca's *De Otio* inspired much of the debate in Book I, as well as possibly providing More's original title for *Utopia* – *Nusquama* – but it does not touch on the debate in Letters 94 and 95; John Michael Parrish, 'A New Source for More's "Utopia"', *The Historical Journal* 40, no. 2 (1997): 493–98.

[76] Hexter, 'Thomas More and the Problem of Counsel', 55–66.

[77] Skinner, 'Thomas More's *Utopia*', 213–44.

[78] See Thomas More, *The Yale Edition of the Complete Works of St. Thomas More: Utopia*, ed. Edward Surtz and J. H. Hexter, vol. 4 (New Haven: Yale University Press, 1965), 87; Skinner, 'Thomas More's *Utopia*', 220–2.

[79] More, *Utopia*, 57. [80] More, *Utopia*, 57. [81] See Baker-Smith, *More's* Utopia, 132–3.

Erasmus' pessimism, Hythloday maintains that both kings and courtiers are too self-interested to heed or allow his advice; he would end up speaking counsel too far from the interests of monarchs or would be forced to join in the chorus of sycophancy and corruption.[82] As he concludes to Morus, 'if I tried to obtrude [*ingerere*] these and like ideas on men strongly inclined to the opposite way of thinking, to what deaf ears should I tell the tale!'.[83]

Morus is forced to agree with Hythloday's pessimism regarding the results of his counsel. The issue is with how he delivers his advice, for 'such ideas should [not] be thrust [*ingerere*] on people, or such advice given, as you are positive will never be listened to.'[84] Instead of this 'academic philosophy', which thinks that 'everything is suitable for every place',[85] an adviser must adopt a 'more civil philosophy [*philosophia ciuilior*]',[86] 'which knows its stage, adapts itself to the play in hand, and performs its role neatly and appropriately [*cum decoro*]'.[87] More's Morus, as Erasmus' Folly had done, rejects the stark universalist counsel of the philosopher, advising Hythloday to adopt a counsel which participates in, rather than overthrows, the conventions of the 'play' in which he finds himself: 'Otherwise we have the situation in which a comedy of Plautus is being performed and the household slaves are making trivial jokes at one another and then you come on the stage in a philosopher's attire and recite the passage from the *Octavia* with Nero.'[88]

This involves adopting an 'indirect approach [*obliquo ducto*]'.[89] Erasmus had also touched on this strategy, in a letter to Martin Dorp in 1515, where he suggests that that the praise contained in the *Panegyricus* is nothing more than a 'cloak' for addressing 'indirectly' the same theme that he had in his *Education of a Prince*, namely 'advice as to the type of training a prince should receive'.[90] The idea of using 'indirect' speech in counselling tyrants comes from a source common to Erasmus and More, and indeed all Renaissance humanists: Quintilian. In his *Institutio Oratorio*, Quintilian allows 'ambiguity of expression' in counselling tyrants, as long as one only seeks to avoid 'danger' and not 'giving offense'.[91] Morus agrees with

[82] For the connection between Hythloday and Erasmus see Giulia Sissa, '*Familiaris Reprehensio Quasi Errantis*. Raphael Hythloday, between Plato and Epicurus', *Moreana* 49 (Number 187–188), no. 1–2 (2012): 121–50.

[83] More, *Utopia*, 97. This passage is marked '*Prouerbium*' in the margin.

[84] More, *Utopia*, 99.

[85] Hythloday later demonstrates he's missed this point, wondering 'what did my speech contain that would not be appropriate or obligatory everywhere?', More, *Utopia*, 101.

[86] My translation.

[87] More, *Utopia*, 99.

[88] More, *Utopia*, 99.

[89] More, *Utopia*, 101.

[90] Erasmus, *Erasmus and His Age*, 85.

[91] Quintilian, *Institutio Oratoria*, 9.2.67, quoted in Frederick Ahl, 'The Art of Safe Criticism in Greece and Rome', *The American Journal of Philology* 105, no. 2 (1984): 193.

Erasmus and Quintilian that it is still possible to speak 'openly' when one is speaking 'indirectly'.

The 'indirect approach' is demonstrated in an unfinished work produced by More contemporaneously with *Utopia*, his *History of King Richard the Third.* The character of John Morton, later Bishop of Ely and More's patron, uses such an approach to heal the divisions in the kingdom caused by the usurpation by Richard III. In the final passage of the English version of the text, Morton uses an oratorical strategy outlined by Quintilian in the same book of the *Oratio* cited above:

> The facts themselves must be allowed to excite the suspicions of the judge, and we must clear away all other points, leaving nothing save what will suggest the truth. In doing this we shall find emotional appeals, hesitation and words broken by silences most effective. For thus the judge will be led to seek out the secret which he would not perhaps believe if he heard it openly stated, and to believe in that which he thinks he has found out for himself.[92]

In speaking with Buckingham, Morton begins to indicate some displeasure with Richard and then breaks off 'saying that he had alredy medled to muche with the world, and would fro that day medle with his boke and his beedes and no farther'.[93] This has the intended effect, and Buckingham 'longed ... sore to here what he would haue sayd ... and exhorted him so familiarly' to tell him.[94] Buckingham begs to 'vse [Morton's] faithful secret aduise and counsayle', rather than Morton having to risk life and limb to deliver it to him.[95] Morton uses a tale, reportedly from Aesop, in order to justify his feigned reluctance to comply. Morton communicates to Buckingham, by way of this pleasant fable, that he is reluctant to share even harmless advice, in case it is perceived differently by those in power, and Buckingham laughs, pledging to Morton his protection and confidence. Still Morton holds out, and Buckingham 'longed ... yet moch more to wit what it was' until at last Morton admits that he wishes the governance of the realm had been given to Buckingham, instead of Richard.[96] Morton is able to deliver his advice by feigning reluctance to do so.

92 Quintilian, *Institutio Oratoria*, 9.4, 72–3, quoted in Ahl, 'The Art of Safe Criticism', 194–5.

93 Thomas More, *The Yale Edition of the Complete Works of St. Thomas More: History of King Richard III*, ed. Richard S. Sylvester, vol. 2 (New Haven: Yale University Press, 1963), 92.

94 More, *Richard the Third*, 92.

95 More, *Richard the Third*, 92.

96 More, *Richard the Third*, 93.

The *History* also recalls the Senecan debate on the efficacy of counsel. Morton does not seek to 'pluck out' pride, but to 'prick' it, which allows him to keep his interlocutor 'close w^{t}in his bondes, that he rather semed to folow hym then to lead him'.[97] He applies the same technique to Richard as well: '[Morton's] wisedom abused [Richard's] pride to [Morton's] own deliueraunce & [Richard's] destruction'.[98] Pride cannot be moved, but it can be used.

In *Utopia*, Morus likewise rejects the notion that one must 'uproot' vice: 'If you cannot pluck up wrongheaded opinion by the root, if you cannot cure according to your heart's desire vices of long standing, yet you must not on that account desert the commonwealth.'[99] Hythloday must do his best with the situation: 'What you cannot turn to good you must make as little bad as you can.'[100] Hythloday, echoing Erasmus and Seneca's Letter 95, objects to Morus that if kings are not already philosophers, then his advice will be rejected, 'because they have been from their youth saturated and infected with wrong ideas [*perverto opinio*] . . . If I proposed beneficial measures [*decreta sana*] to some king and tried to uproot from his soul the seeds of evil and corruption, do you not suppose that I should forthwith be banished or treated with ridicule?'[101] Hythloday and More are speaking at cross-purposes, each arguing from the perspective of a different Senecan letter. Hythloday is committed to speaking about *decreta* and abandoning counsel if the king has not been educated properly from his youth (Letter 95). Morus maintains that even if this is the case, advice can do its work (Letter 94). It should be no surprise to find Seneca's letters appearing in *Utopia*; not only had More probably read a draft of the *Institutio*, but Erasmus had begun the production of his translation while in England, perhaps even while staying with More, and it was on the market in London while More was finishing *Utopia* in 1516.[102]

In fact, the entire description of Utopia can be read as a meditation on these themes, which Hythloday points to by suggesting that if he were to tell kings and their counsellors 'the kind of things which Plato creates in his republic or which the Utopians actually put in practice in theirs' he would be unwelcome.[103] The Utopians are the perfect example of the sort of training

97 More, *Richard the Third*, 92–3. 98 More, *Richard the Third*, 90.

99 More, *Utopia*, 99. George of Trebizond had made a similar point in the fifteenth century in regard to the appetite for private property, holding that it ought not to be 'pulled out by the roots . . . You demand the impossible; even if it were possible, it would not be expedient. These things must be tempered by reason, not entirely prohibited'; quoted in Chloë Houston, *The Renaissance Utopia: Dialogue, Travel and the Ideal Society* (Burlington: Routledge, 2014), 27.

100 More, *Utopia*, 101. 101 More, *Utopia*, 87. Emphasis added. 102 Hardy, 'A Study', 4, 12.

103 More, *Utopia*, 101.

and education that Hythloday wishes for, and without which he cannot see his counsel being useful. Utopians are 'trained' in every way so that wrong opinions are corrected.[104] *Opinio* is emphasised throughout *Utopia* as shaping the values of both Europeans and Utopians.[105] In Europe there is a 'false idea of pleasure' (*falsa voluptatis opinio*) and a 'meaningless nobility' (*vana nobilitas*), which is created by those who have a *nobilitatis opinio*.[106] Because Utopians are committed to real and decent – or 'natural' – pleasures, they see through this façade of imagined pleasure generated by 'perverse habit'.[107] The greatest example of this is in the Utopians' treatment of precious metals and gems – as it is marked in the margins: 'Human Imagination [*Opinio*] Gives Value to Gems or Takes It Away'.[108] The Utopians' practice of publicly devaluing gold, silver and jewels means public opinion does not place unnatural or artificial value in them.

One of the most important agents of such public opinion is the priest. Priests are in charge of the 'influence of honor' and 'take the greatest pains from the very first to instil into children's minds, while still tender and pliable, good opinions [*opinio*] which are also useful for the preservation of the commonwealth'.[109] These opinions, Hythloday reports, again in a Senecan vein, once 'firmly implanted in children . . . accompany them all through their adult lives and are of great help in watching over the condition of the commonwealth', which cannot decay, except 'from wrong attitudes [*ex perversis opinionibus*]'.[110] Notably, in Utopia there is a clear divide between counsel and command when it comes to the role of priests, like that in Marsilius of Padua (see Introduction). It is the priests' 'function to give advice and admonition' but 'to check and punish offenders [*coercere*] belongs to the governor and the other civil officials'.[111] Priests have the all-important job of reforming *opinio*, but no punitive power. Their role is, as Hythloday is at pains to stress, essential, and since this work correcting opinions is not done in Europe, his counsel is useless.

Amongst Hythloday's well-trained Utopians, counsel can do its work; Utopia's entire political structure is based on the importance of counsel.[112]

[104] More, *Utopia*, 35; 'They have very few laws because very few are needed for persons so educated [*instituere*]', More, *Utopia*, 195.

[105] Richard A. McCabe, '"*Ut Publica Est Opinio*": An Utopian Irony', *Neophilologus; Groningen, Netherlands* 72, no. 4 (1988): 633–9 traces the uses of *opinio* in *Utopia*.

[106] More, *Utopia*, 169; see Joanne Paul, *Thomas More* (Cambridge: Polity, 2016).

[107] More, *Utopia*, 173. [108] More, *Utopia*, 169. [109] More, *Utopia*, 229.

[110] More, *Utopia*, 229. My translation. [111] More, *Utopia*, 229.

[112] John Guy, 'The Henrician Age', in *The Varieties of British Political Thought, 1500–1800*, ed. Gordon J. Schochet, J. G. A. Pocock and Lois Schwoerer (Cambridge: Cambridge University Press, 1994), 21 suggests the opposite, that 'the Utopian institutions which Hythlodaeus meticulously describes in

In each of Utopia's fifty-four cities, households elect syphogrants, who elect tranibors. These counsel the *princeps* (at least once a day), who is elected by the syphogrants. Over the entire island rules a General Council, comprised of 'three old and experienced citizens' from each city.[113] As Erik de Bom has suggested, the political system of Utopia is designed to limit the power of a prince, who cannot be guaranteed to have moral virtue.[114] In this way, Book I and Book II both comment on how counsel can be used to guide a prince to virtue, though this does not solve the problem of its efficacy in perverse Europe.

Along with counsel, deliberation is also key to Utopia's political system, though it is strictly regulated. Decisions are not made on the day when they are debated, so people will not vote obstinately and self-servingly, according to the opinion voiced during the debate, but rather upon reflection on the good on the commonwealth as a whole.[115] And discussion of matters of public interest are not permitted outside of these (plentiful) public fora: 'to take counsel on matters of public interest outside the senate or the popular assembly is considered a capital offense'.[116] The reason for this harsh measure is that the Utopians fear the 'tyrannical oppression of the people'.[117] As everything is oriented in Utopia towards the common rather than the private interest, removing such discussions from a public to a private context is treated with the severest penalty.[118]

Thus it is the '*publica ... opinio*' or 'estimation of the common people' which the Utopian customs overthrow, causing Morus to doubt whether such things could be seen in the commonwealths of Europe.[119] On this Hythloday would agree, as in Europe 'Pride is too deeply fixed in men to be easily plucked out'.[120] As Morus concludes, this is not foreseeable in Europe, but his earlier statements imply he does not think that this

Book II allot only the most superficial role to "good counsel"'. This appears to overlook the frequency of consultation between tranibors and *princeps*, as well as the way in which a single conciliar institution (such as the Utopian General Council) still embodies the principles of counsel through deliberation. That being said, it is true that in Utopia it is *institutio* rather than *concilio* which maintains order and virtue by removing false opinion.

113 See the figure explaining this system in Paul, *Thomas More*, 43. The conciliar structure of Utopia's political system reflects More's belief in the superiority of the General Council as the representative body of the Church; see Paul, *Thomas More*, 83–115.

114 Erik De Bom, 'Realism vs Utopianism', in *Utopia 1516–2016: More's Eccentric Essay and Its Activist Aftermath*, ed. Han van Ruler and Giulia Sissa (Amsterdam: Amsterdam University Press, 2017), 109–42.

115 More, *Utopia*, 125. 116 More, *Utopia*, 125. 117 More, *Utopia*, 125.

118 See Paul, *Thomas More*; Baker-Smith, *More's* Utopia, 156. 119 More, *Utopia*, 247.

120 More, *Utopia*, 245.

means that counsel cannot have a positive effect. The counsellor can still work to reform the commonwealth, even if long-standing vices are not 'plucked out'.

This counsel must be communicated, however, via the proper (private) channels, as More, like Erasmus, is keen to point out, especially after the rise of Lutheranism from late 1517. As he writes in his *Confutation of Tyndale's Answer*, a decade and a half after *Utopia* and in the midst of the debates over the Reformation, even when it is merited, it is 'a lewde thinge to suffre any prynce, estate, or gouernour, to be brought in sclaunder amonge the comen people'.[121] This can only lead disobedience and sedition. Even if a prince is so blinded by 'priuate affection towarde theyr owne fantasies' that they cannot see their faults, then it is their 'confessours and counsaylours' who are to take the role of correcting the prince, as well as 'euery man that of good mynde [who] wolde in good maner declare his owne good aduyce toward his prynce and his countrey'.[122] This, however, must be done 'to [the prince's] owne person or suche other of his counsayle' but not 'in vnthrifty company' or in 'sclaunderous bylles' that are 'blow[n] abroad'.[123]

For this reason, though perhaps with a touch of irony, More writes in his *Apology* a few years later, if he disagreed with laws already made, 'in place and tyme conuenyent I wolde gyue myne aduyce and counsayle to the chaunge' but would not 'put out bookes in wrytynge abrode amonge the people agaynste them'.[124] Even if the laws contravened God's law, then publishing such objections to them would not do those who lacked spiritual understanding any good, whereas the 'secrete aduyse and counsayle maye bycome euery man'.[125] By 1532, More is content that even his own books be put to the flames, rather than anyone take harm from them.[126] A counsellor has to judge the 'time and place' very carefully in giving his advice, or risk doing more harm than good.

More directly addresses the theme of right-timing in regard to speech in his *Four Last Things*, written in 1522 but never published. He suggests that speech must wait for the right moment in order to reform listeners. There is 'as scripture saith, time to speke & time to kepe thy tong'.[127] When the

[121] Thomas More, *The Yale Edition of the Complete Works of St. Thomas More: The Confutation of Tyndale's Answer*, ed. Louis A. Schuster, Richard C. Marius and James P. Lusardi, vol. 8 (New Haven: Yale University Press, 1973), 590.

[122] More, *Confutation of Tyndale's Answer*, 591. [123] More, *Confutation of Tyndale's Answer*, 591.

[124] Thomas More, *The Yale Edition of the Complete Works of St. Thomas More: The Apology*, ed. J. B. Trapp, vol. 9 (New Haven: Yale University Press, 1979), 96.

[125] More, *Apology*, 96–7. [126] More, *Confutation of Tyndale's Answer*, 179.

[127] Thomas More, *The Yale Edition of the Complete Works of St. Thomas More: English Poems, Life of Pico, the Last Things*, ed. Anthony G. Edwards, Katherine Gardiner Rogers and Clarence H. Miller,

'comunicacion is nought and vngoldy, it is better to holde thy tong & thinke on some better thing the while' than to listen to or support what is being said: Hythloday's position.[128] However, More goes on to say, it is even better 'properly to speake, & with som good grace and pleasant fashion, to break into some better matter'.[129] This approach 'shalt not onely profite thy selfe', which would have been accomplished through silence, 'but also amende the whole audience, which is a thynge farre better and of muche more merite'.[130] In other words, if one is self-interested, then silence is the best course. However, if one wants to benefit others, then it is better to use 'good grace and pleasant fashion' (rhetoric) to steer the topic of conversation away from ungodly topics. If it is the case that one can really 'find no proper meane to breake the tale' and one cannot just 'commaunde silence' amongst the other speakers, then silence is better than to 'blunt forth rudely, and yrryte them to anger', which will only provoke more discussion of the topic you wished to avoid.[131] Until the right moment comes about, which will truly mitigate vice, silence is the best course. When that right moment does come, however, counsel is the duty of the public-oriented citizen.

iii Castiglione and the 'veile of ignorance'

The widely read *Il libro del Cortegiano*, written between 1513 and 1527 by the Italian humanist Baldassare Castiglione, published in Italian in 1528 and in English in 1561, is at its heart a text about effective counsel.[132] Castiglione engages with many of the same themes as Erasmus and More, most effectively resolving the Senecan debate, and also going furthest in explicitly outlining the governing power of the counsellor over his prince.

It is in the final book of the dialogue, through Ottaviano Fregoso, that Castiglione makes clear that the ideal courtier, who the interlocutors have been constructing, has higher ends, related to giving counsel:

vol. 1 (New Haven: Yale University Press, 1997), 136. This a reference to Ecclesiastes 3.7, which in the Greek uses the term *kairos*. More translates the poem describing *kairos* in his *Latin Poems*: 'On the God Opportunity From the Greek'.

128 More, *The Last Things*, 136. 129 More, *The Last Things*, 136.

130 More, *The Last Things*, 136–7. 131 More, *The Last Things*, 137.

132 For Castiglione's connections to Renaissance humanism see Virginia Cox, 'Introduction', in *The Book of the Courtier* (London: J. M. Dent & Sons Ltd/Everyman's Library, 1994), xxii–xxvi; Albury, *Castiglione's Allegory*, 3–4; For his knowledge of humanist texts see Guido Rebecchini, 'The Book Collection and Other Possessions of Baldassarre Castiglione', *Journal of the Warburg and Courtauld Institutes* 61 (1998): 17–52.

> the ende therfore of a perfect Courtier . . . is to purchase him, by the meane of the qualities whiche these Lordes have given him, in such wise the good will and favour of the Prince he is in service withall, that he may breake his minde to him, and alwaies enfourme him francklye of the trueth of everie matter meete for him to understande without feare or perill to displease him.[133]

The courtier ought to have the ability to stand up to the prince when he has a mind to do anything 'unseemlie' and to set him 'in the way of vertue'.[134] The courtier is to bring the prince to virtue through 'traininge [*indurre*]' or 'helping'.[135] The qualities given to the courtier by the participants in the dialogue will allow him to 'drive into his Princes heade' the importance of the virtues, and the disaster that shall befall him if he chooses to engage in vice.[136] Acknowledging that it can be dangerous for subjects to know better than those who rule over them, Ottoviano nevertheless maintains that kings need to learn from others how best to govern.[137]

Like Folly and Morus, Castiglione's lead speaker Ottaviano rejects the unadorned counsel of the 'grave Philosopher' who would show a prince 'plainlie and without enie circomstance [*apertamente e senza arte alcuna*] the horrible face of true vertue and teache them good maners and what the lief [sic] of a good Prince ought to be, I ame assured they wolde abhorr him at first sight, as a most venimous serpent or elles they wolde make him a laughinge stock, as a most vile matter.'[138] To 'bende [*indurgli*]' the prince to virtue, the courtier must use all of the skills available to him to 'purchase him the good will and allure unto him the minde of his Prince, that he maye make him a free and safe passage to comune with him in every matter without troubling him'.[139] As for Erasmus, this can be accomplished by

[133] Castiglione, *Courtier*, 295. The fourth book was added when Castiglione revised *The Courtier* 1518–21 and 1524–27, possibly as a way of gaining employment, see Cox, 'Introduction', xx–xxi; Lawrence V. Ryan, 'Book Four of Castiglione's *Courtier*: Climax or Afterthought?', *Studies in the Renaissance* 19 (1972): 156–79.

[134] Castiglione, *Courtier*, 295. W. R. Albury, *Castiglione's Allegory: Veiled Policy in the Book of the Courtier (1528)* (Burlington: Ashgate, 2014) makes the argument that the ultimate purpose of the text is to make a more specific argument about the education of Francesco Maria della Rovere.

[135] Castiglione, *Courtier*, 296. [136] Castiglione, *Courtier*, 295. Original is just 'show his prince'.

[137] In the original, Castiglione refers here only to examples from the past, but Hoby adds 'the exhortations and lessons of such as they deemed meete to correct those faults', which could have a different meaning. Castiglione, *Courtier*, 298.

[138] Castiglione, *Courtier*, 298–9.

[139] Castiglione, *Courtier*, 299. See Alfredo Bonadeo, 'The Function and Purpose of the Courtier in "The Book of the Courtier" by Castiglione', *Philological Quarterly* 50, no. 1 (1971): 36–46 for how the 'qualities and skills imparted to the Courtier . . . create the conditions through which he can captivate the admiration and esteem of the public and win the favor and confidence of the prince' (37).

sweetening the harshness of the truth and virtue, and 'in this wise maye he leade him throughe the roughe way of vertue (as it were) deckynge yt about with boowes to shadowe yt and strawinge it over wyth sightlye flouers, to ease the greefe of the peinfull journey in hym that is but of a weake force'.[140]

Ottaviano is not ashamed of using such forceful language to describe the relationship between the courtier and the prince, for the former ought to be 'beguiling [the prince] with a holsome craft [*ingannandolo con inganno salutifero*]', as physicians do when they sweeten a cup of medicine in order to make children drink from it.[141] It is not compulsion, but it is 'emotional manipulation' through language.[142] The veil of pleasure, when used for good ends, is different than those who use the same 'honest and pleasant maners and their good qualities a cloke for an ill end'.[143] Castiglione, too, employs the fountain metaphor from Plutarch to note the importance of the prince as a conduit for good or evil, and to mark out the one who poisons it as the most pernicious figure in the realm.[144] Paraphrasing Isocrates' opening in his Letter to Nicocles, another oft-cited and influential classical work on counselling-giving, Castiglione makes clear that the courtier-counsellor as described ought to be seen by the prince as giving him 'not the thinges whiche foolish persons give, whiche is, golde, or silver, plate, garmentes, and such matters . . . but that vertue, which perhappes among all the matters that belong unto man, is the cheefest and rarest, that is to say, the maner and way to rule and to reigne in the right kinde'.[145]

Like Erasmus, Castiglione's Ottaviano maintains that the work of a counsellor is to determine the difference between truth and illusion and dispel the 'veile of ignorance' which causes errors and vice in men.[146] Thus virtue comes through right-thinking (the rule of reason) and vice through ignorance (the rule of the appetites).[147] This is not to say, however, that it is possible to 'roote out [*estirpar*]' affections.[148] Instead, and here Castiglione goes further than Erasmus and is more explicit than More, vices can be used

[140] Castiglione, *Courtier*, 299. For Castiglione's knowledge of Erasmus, see Rebecchini, 'The Book Collection and Other Possessions of Baldassarre Castiglione', 20. My thanks to Virginia Cox for her assistance in this and other matters in this chapter.

[141] Castiglione, *Courtier*, 300. For this history of this idea see Albury, *Castiglione's Allegory*, 132–6.

[142] Albury, *Castiglione's Allegory*, 142. For more on how Castiglione's ideal courtier uses deceit on his prince, see Daniel Javitch, 'Il Cortegiano and the Constraints of Despotism', in *Castiglione: The Ideal and the Real in Renaissance Culture*, ed. Robert W. Hanning and David Rosand (New Haven: Yale University Press, 1983), 24–7.

[143] Castiglione, *Courtier*, 300. [144] Castiglione, *Courtier*, 300.

[145] Castiglione, *Courtier*, 308. Isocrates, *The Orations of Isocrates Volume 1*, trans. J. H. Freese (London: George Bell & Sons, 1894), 2.1. Machiavelli also uses this passage, see Chapter 3.

[146] Castiglione, *Courtier*, 303. [147] Castiglione, *Courtier*, 305–6. [148] Castiglione, *Courtier*, 307.

as an aid to virtue, causing the person in question to pursue it: 'anger, that helpeth manliness: hatred against the wicked, helpeth justice'.[149]

But what about the question posed by Seneca, and addressed by both Erasmus and More: can anyone, even the perfect courtier, successfully impart these virtues to the prince if bad habits and opinion have taken root? Ottaviano uses similar language as Seneca to maintain that although nature gives man the 'seed' of virtue, it requires a *maestro*[150] to 'stirr up and quicken in us these morall vertues' as well as 'weedinge' out the 'briers and darnell of appetites'.[151] Without *disciplina*, the 'roote' of these virtues can be lost forever.[152] Thus Castiglione appears to side with Erasmus that instruction is essential to the virtue of the prince, though he gives this job to the courtier, counselling an adult lord. He solves the Senecan dilemma by giving both the power of instruction and counsel to a counsellor-figure, his 'courtier'. As such, Ottaviano is happy to rename the courtier the *institutor* ('Instructor') of the prince, though he defends the name of *perfetto cortegiano*, as Aristotle and Plato were such courtiers in the past.[153] Aristotle, for Ottaviano, represents the model courtier, someone who mingled 'bare truth' with 'courtliness' in instructing Alexander the Great, as did Plato with Dion.[154] As W. R. Albury has argued, Ottaviano himself also becomes a model courtier in *The Courtier*: jesting and directly admonishing when the circumstances call for each.[155]

Castiglione also touches on the importance of timely speech, which Count Lodovico da Canossa suggests 'raise[s] the affections'.[156] The orator, for Lodovico, ought to vary with the time, not being always grave, but also engaging in jests and 'mery conceits'.[157] In fact, even things that are fundamentally good or pleasant can be destroyed if the timing is wrong: 'many things that of them selves be worthie praise, oftentimes in practisyng theym out of season seeme moste foolish'.[158] It is the character of Federico Fregoso, the brother of Ottaviano, who is most dedicated to this idea, repeating it often in the course of the dialogue, directly quoting from the classical texts on the subject of *kairos*.[159] It is also Federico who advocates

149 Castiglione, *Courtier*, 307–8. 150 Hoby gives 'teacher', Castiglione, *Courtier*, 303.

151 Castiglione, *Courtier*, 303. Recall Seneca, *Letters*, 94.29: advice 'stir[s] . . . the seed of everything that is honourable'.

152 Hoby gives 'teaching', but again the meaning is ambiguous, Castiglione, *Courtier*, 303.

153 Castiglione, *Courtier*, 336–7. 154 Castiglione, *Courtier*, 338.

155 Albury, *Castiglione's Allegory*, 122–3. Although as Albury, 125 points out, at no point does Ottaviano suggest that the prince ought to be embarrassed in the way that he embarrasses Gaspare.

156 Castiglione, *Courtier*, 65. 157 Castiglione, *Courtier*, 65.

158 Said by the figure of Guiliano de' Medici, Castiglione, *Courtier*, 86.

159 Castiglione, *Courtier*, 106–8, 117, 121–2.

for a more flexible approach to flattery,[160] and the use of jests, with a mind to *decorum*.[161]

Castiglione, like Erasmus and More, sets out the liberating power of counsel in a monarchical context. Echoing Erasmus, Ottaviano maintains that a monarchical regime is best, because it is closest to nature. Pietro Bembo, another discussant, objects, arguing that it is unconducive to natural liberty, by which man ought to be able to rule himself.[162] Under the rule of the king man is in 'strict bondage. But in Commune weales well in order this libertie is well kept [*strettissima servitú. Ma nelle republiche bene instituite si serva pur questa libertà*]'.[163] Ottaviano maintains that it is the courtier-counsellor who can maintain such liberty under the rule of a king. If it is the case that liberty is not license, but 'to lyve accordynge to good lawes', and obedience natural, Ottaviano reasons, then natural liberty can indeed be maintained in a monarchy, but only if the king is good and wise.[164] This is best achieved 'yf he be helped forwarde with the instructions, bringing up, and art [*educazione ed arte*] of the Courtier'.[165] Such a prince, ruled by reason, will be like a carpenter's square, making the rest of the people good through his example.[166] Liberty, in the truest sense, is only achieved if the king is ruled by good counsel.

This is best accomplished, Ottaviano maintains, in a mixed monarchy, with institutional councils. A good king ought to 'pike out a certein number of Gentilmen emonge his subjectes, of the noblest and wisest, wyth whom he shoulde debate all matters, and give them authority and free leave to uttre their minde franklye unto him without respect'.[167] This 'Counsell of the nobilitie' should be joined to a 'counsell of the commons', and thus the state will 'have the fourme and maner of the three good governmentes, which is, a kingdome, men of the best sorte, and the people'.[168] In this way, Ottaviano is happy to concede that the prince so counselled becomes a 'good Governour [*governatore*]' rather than a good

[160] Castiglione, *Courtier*, 120.

[161] Castiglione, *Courtier*, 150. The importance of *decorum* is repeated by Bernardo Bibbiena, Castiglione, *Courtier*, 159. For more on Federico's arguments, and their connections to Ottaviano's in Book 4, see Cox, 'Introduction', xviii-xix. For the political weight of the jokes in Castiglione, see JoAnn Cavallo, 'Joking Matters: Politics and Dissimulation in Castiglione's Book of the Courtier', *Renaissance Quarterly* 53, no. 2 (2000): 402–24.

[162] Bembo and Fregoso represent the 'respectable' (i.e. oligarchic) face of republicanism (Venice and Genoa), whereas popular Florentine republicanism is represented by the absent and exiled Giuliano de' Medici; with thanks to Virginia Cox for this addition.

[163] Castiglione, *Courtier*, 309.

[164] Castiglione, *Courtier*, 311.

[165] Castiglione, *Courtier*, 312.

[166] Castiglione, *Courtier*, 313.

[167] Castiglione, *Courtier*, 320.

[168] Castiglione, *Courtier*, 321.

prince, for everything actually belongs to the people, and not to the prince.[169]

Castiglione addresses head-on the issue that sits at the heart of the humanist construction of the counsellor: surely such a figure becomes greater than the king himself? This objection is raised to Ottaviano, who begins first by conceding that the courtier is not *wholly* responsible for the goodness of the prince, for nature has its role too. Returning to the Senecan debate, he notes that if the prince is not inclined by nature towards goodness, the courtier's efforts will be in vain.[170] The prince's mind is like soil, in which, if barren, no amount of careful tilling will produce fruit. Thus, the counsellor is not quite all powerful; he cannot make a truly bad prince good. Second, the prince is also responsible for practising virtue, which serves to cultivate it; the courtier cannot do this for him. But even if the prince is so 'wise and good of himselfe' that he does not need counsel, then the courtier can still be on hand if he has need and shield him against corruption by understanding the truth of matters, like a physician.

In the end, however, Ottaviano agrees that he has produced a rare and impressive figure, who stands to compete with the prince for pre-eminence.[171] This lesson is drawn out by the Duchess, who tells Ottaviano that 'it may be said, that you are not onlie the perfect Courtier whom we seke for, and able to instruct your prince well, but also (if fortune be so favourable on your side) ye maye be the good Prince your self, whiche shoule not be withoute great profit to your Countrey'.[172] Through the construction of the perfect courtier, the prince is reduced to governor, and the counsellor – as *institutor* – raised to the level of the prince.

Through an examination of these three leading writers, a humanist model of counsel clearly emerges in which the prince is ruled by good counsel in order to preserve republican notions of liberty and political involvement in a monarchical context. Central to this discussion is a Senecan debate, drawn from Letters 94 and 95, over the efficacy of counsel in the case where poor

169 Castiglione, *Courtier*, 329–30.

170 Castiglione, *Courtier*, 334. Bonadeo, 'The Function and Purpose of the Courtier', 42–3 suggests that the courtier's skills 'establish a strong ascendancy over the lord' and 'It is indeed the prince who has to make himself worthy of being served by the Courtier'; Albury, *Castiglione's Allegory*, 158, 230 takes the argument further, suggesting that should the prince be truly wicked, it is up to the courtier to overthrow the prince.

171 Castiglione, *Courtier*, 335–6.

172 Castiglione, *Courtier*, 332. As Cox points out in the footnote to her edition, Ottaviano became Doge of Genoa in 1513.

education has allowed perverse opinions to root in the prince's mind. Erasmus and More seem to present contrary sides of this debate in the *Institutio* and *Utopia* respectively, and Castiglione attempts a resolution by placing both instruction and counsel in his ideal counsellor. It is Castiglione who most explicitly engages with the dangerous question of the power given to the counsellor to 'rule' the prince, even using rhetoric and deception to 'lead' him to virtue, implying that in such a model the counsellor does indeed hold authority over the prince. All three writers are also attentive to the debate over right timing in giving counsel, and both Erasmus and More, especially after the Reformation, are keen to stress that silence is best until the right moment appears, at which point frank counsel can do its job of reforming the listener and thus the commonwealth. It is in the context of Henry VIII's Break with Rome that this question of right-timed counsel mitigating tyranny becomes central to the discourse of counsel, empowering the counsellor even further to control his prince.

CHAPTER 2

The Right-Timing of Counsel

The first generation of humanists examined here, Erasmus, More and Castiglione, all dealt with the issue of right-timing and appealed to the vocabulary of *kairos* to do so. These writers, as Plato and Cicero had been, were keen to remove any sense of sophistic moral flexibility from *kairos*.[1] Erasmus and More, especially after the beginning of what would become known as the Reformation, were also clear that silence was the best course until the opportune moment, when frank speech could correct vices. Before that, 'raylynge and iestynge vppon any maner of estate' could only produce harm, thanks to the ignorance and naivety of the masses.[2] Erasmus is especially clear on the right moment as a solution to the much-pondered 'problem of counsel'.

The events of the Henrician Reformation served to put pressure on the problem of counsel and especially on its proposed timely solution.[3] A second generation of English humanists took up the question, thinking more deeply about what the opportune moment was and how it related to the question of frank counsel. Thomas Starkey makes this issue central to his *Dialogue Between Pole and Lupset*, criticising More's approach, though he never resolves the problem fully. It is Thomas Elyot, in his works published in 1531 and 1533, who writes at length on the issue of right-timing and counsel, coming, like Starkey, to a critique of the 'silence until *kairos*' strategy espoused by Erasmus and More.

These writers are also directly concerned with the relationship between counsel and command. In the context of the late 1520s and 1530s, theirs is a concern that counsel does not have enough authority over command, and that it will need to be supported or bolstered in some fashion to have its proper influence. For Starkey, this means an institutional solution,

[1] Melissa Lane, *Method and Politics in Plato's Statesman* (Cambridge: Cambridge University Press, 1998), 3–4; for Cicero on *kairos* see Chapter 1.

[2] More, *Confutation of Tyndale's Answer*, 592. [3] See Walker, *Writing Under Tyranny*.

a formal council to rule the king with good advice. Elyot does not go so far, but he does appear to reject More's insistence that counsel be given in private, noting that when the demands of the time call for it, public 'raylynge and iestynge' might be the only means available to speak truth to power. For Starkey and Elyot, it must be the case that prudent counsel rules the prince; the alternative is unbridled tyranny, a familiar concept in the context of the Break with Rome.

i Starkey and Tarrying Time

The most contentious text of this period to tackle the problem of counsel and to pit counsel against command was, perhaps for that reason, never put into print: Thomas Starkey's *A Dialogue Between Pole and Lupset*, written between 1529 and 1532, with some few revisions following until about 1535.[4] Perhaps because it was not printed, few have studied the *Dialogue* in depth. The exception is T. F. Mayer, who has highlighted Starkey's conciliarism,[5] networks[6] and wider intellectual context.[7] Mayer establishes the likelihood of Starkey having read *Utopia*,[8] but there exists no reading of the *Dialogue* as a direct reply to it, despite the explicit references in the text, shown below. In addition, the language of time and occasion that runs throughout the text has been entirely overlooked, though these are fundamental to an understanding of the text and Starkey's place in the discourse of counsel tradition.

Starkey was a Henrician humanist, intimately acquainted with the tenets of civic humanism, thanks to an education at Oxford and time spent in France and Italy.[9] The *Dialogue* was originally intended to be given to Reginald Pole, one of its interlocutors, as a way of persuading him to take on a more public role, as we shall see. However, by the 1530s, Starkey had abandoned this idea, and turned his attention instead to joining Henry VIII's court himself, presenting the *Dialogue* as a statement of his education and experience.[10] Pole's departure from

[4] Thomas F. Mayer, 'Introduction', in *A Dialogue Between Pole and Lupset* (London: Royal Historical Society, 1989), x–xii; Thomas F. Mayer, 'Faction and Ideology: Thomas Starkey's Dialogue', *The Historical Journal* 28, no. 1 (1985): 1–12.

[5] Thomas F. Mayer, 'Thomas Starkey, an Unknown Conciliarist at the Court of Henry VIII', *Journal of the History of Ideas* 49, no.2 (1988): 207–27.

[6] Mayer, 'Faction and Ideology', 1–25.

[7] Thomas F. Mayer, *Thomas Starkey and the Commonwealth: Humanist Politics and Religion in the Reign of Henry VIII* (Cambridge: Cambridge University Press, 2002).

[8] Mayer, *Thomas Starkey*, 35–6.

[9] Mayer, 'Introduction', vii–viii.

[10] Mayer, *Thomas Starkey*, 2.

England in 1532, however, ruined this plan as well, as Pole, and by extension Starkey, came under suspicion from the Crown.[11]

Like *Utopia*'s opening in More's embassy to Flanders, Starkey's *Dialogue* is set in real-world circumstances. Starkey was sent to Paris with Reginald Pole and Thomas Lupset in October 1529 in order to solicit favourable opinions regarding Henry VIII's annulment.[12] This trip was probably the origin-point for Starkey's reflections. Unlike *Utopia*, however, the conversation remains grounded in the real-world – and specifically English – context, despite the fiction of the discussion itself. This specificity is part of the argument that Starkey makes against More's text.

The dialogue opens with Lupset's appeal to Pole, in similar words to those used by the character of Peter Gillis in *Utopia*:

> I have much and many times marvelled . . . why you, Master Pole, after so many years spent in quiet studies of letters and learning, and after such experience of the manners of man, taken in diverse parts beyond the sea, have no before this settled yourself and applied your mind to the handling of the matters of the common weal here in our own nation.[13]

He moves quickly from benefit to friends to the benefit of the whole commonweal, noting in a Ciceronian vein that 'to this all men are born and of nature brought forth: to commune such gifts as be to them given, each one to the profit of the other, in perfit civility, and not to live to their own pleasure and profit, without regard of the weal of their country'.[14] Much of the opening debate of *Utopia* is thus resolved, and quickly, as Pole agrees that it 'cannot be denied but that it is a goodly thing to meddle with the matters of the common weal', though he objects that before so doing, he ought to first 'learn to rule myself', and then attempt to rule others.[15] The contemplative life is better, he maintains, for 'the perfection of man resteth in the mind and in the chief and purest part thereof' so that 'prudence and policy were not to be compared with high philosophy'.[16] This separation of the lives is rejected by Lupset, however, who maintains that a *vita mixta* is not only best, but indeed required to achieve the ends of both lives:

[11] Mayer, 'Introduction', viii. [12] Mayer, *Thomas Starkey*, 89–90.

[13] Thomas Starkey, *A Dialogue Between Pole and Lupset*, ed. Thomas F. Mayer (London: Royal Historical Society, 1989), 21. See More, *Utopia*, 55. The reference to 'here in our own nation' was added to the MS, see Starkey, *Dialogue*, 1. For Starkey's awareness of More and other contemporary and classical works see Mayer, *Thomas Starkey*, 20–36.

[14] Starkey, *Dialogue*, 22. [15] Starkey, *Dialogue*, 23. [16] Starkey, *Dialogue*, 23.

> albeit that high philosophy and contemplation of nature be of itself a greater perfection of man's mind, as it which is the end of the active life, to the which all men's deeds should ever be referred, yet the meddling with the causes of the common weal is more necessary and ever rather and first to be chosen, as the principal mean whereby we may attain to the other. For hither tendeth all prudence and policy: to bring the whole country to quietness and civility, that every man, and so the whole, may at the last attain to such perfection.[17]

Starkey's Lupset holds that knowledge and virtue are worthless if they are not combined with 'use and exercise', and this pertains especially to 'the chief virtue whereunto tend all the other' which is 'the communing of high wisdom to the use of other'.[18] In sum: 'To this every honest man meddling in the common weal ought to look chiefly unto; this is the mark that every man, prudent and politic, ought to shoot at: first to make himself perfit, with all virtues garnishing his mind, and then to commune the same perfection to other. For little availeth virtue that is not published abroad to the perfit of other.'[19] The active and contemplative lives must go together to the end of protecting and reforming the commonwealth, a conclusion not that distinct from points gleaned from previous humanist writers, including Thomas More.

Pole concedes Lupset's point, but raises another: accepting that 'every man ought to study to help his country', the issue remains of 'time and place'.[20] Like Hythloday, Pole objects that the 'labour' of 'wise men' will be 'spent in vain' in 'time of tyranny' or in a place where rulers 'are bent only to their private weal'. In such circumstances 'What think you . . . the counsel of a wise man should avail? Without doubt it should be laughed at, and nothing at all it should be regarded, no more than a tale told among deaf men.'[21] Pole gives examples of Plato, Cicero and Seneca, whose rulers did not benefit from their counsel, and cites the same tale as Hythloday of those who, being dry, go out into the rain to warn others, getting themselves wet in the process.[22] Those who 'without regard of time or place' give their counsel obtain nothing but to become corrupt themselves.[23] In Starkey's Pole, therefore, we see the objections raised by Hythloday, echoing Erasmus and Seneca, placed explicitly in the context of a concern for *decorum* and *kairos*. Starkey is unambiguous in his critique of this objection. Lupset replies that those who think about 'time and

[17] Starkey, *Dialogue*, 26. [18] Starkey, *Dialogue*, 26. [19] Starkey, *Dialogue*, 24.
[20] Starkey, *Dialogue*, 36. [21] Starkey, *Dialogue*, 36.
[22] Starkey, *Dialogue*, 37; only in this case the tale is misattributed to Plutarch, rather than Plato.
[23] Starkey, *Dialogue*, 37.

place' in this way go too far to the extreme: 'too narrowly and so curiously they ponder the time and the place, that in all their lives they nother find time nor place'; they look for 'Plato's common weal' and 'in such expectation they spend their life'.[24] Lupset thus roundly answers Hythloday's objection that only in Utopia should he give his advice; while waiting for this perfect context he will let the commonwealth fall to pieces around him.

Even if one was to pay attention to 'time and place', he goes on, one would find 'occasion' in the rule of Henry VIII, who does listen to good advice; he rules in line with justice and equity 'after he is thereof informed and surely instruct by his wise counsellors and politic men'.[25] Of course, this is a classic panegyric approach like that used by Erasmus, though it is worth noting what power Henry's counsellors are meant to have over him; he rules only *after* he is informed and instructed by his counsellors. Lupset is also making a broader point, however: all the Hythlodaean objections about circumstances miss the crucial point by focusing on the wrong element of *kairos*, which is not delaying until the perfect moment, but seizing an available opportunity with the aim of doing one's 'office and duty'.[26] This is the major critique that Starkey raises of More's *Utopia* and is a significant theme running throughout his text.

There may be reason for 'abstaining from the entreaty of matters of the common weal' in respect of time, but the greater consideration should be in 'taking the time when it is, and taking occasion when it offereth itself . . . Let not occasion slip; suffer not your time vainly to pass, which without recovery fleeth away; for, as they say, occasion and time will never be restored again'.[27] With this in mind, and so that he 'may be in the matter more ripe whensoever occasion shall require', Pole decides to 'devise [that is, imagine, conjecture] touching the order of our country and common weal', with Lupset's added plea that they do so not 'without respect both of time and place', like those (e.g. More's Hythloday) who follow the example of Plato, but instead speak specifically and directly to the issues touching their commonwealth at that time.[28] Pole agrees, and they retire to dinner, to begin their discussion, as is proper, in the morning.

[24] Starkey, *Dialogue*, 38. [25] Starkey, *Dialogue*, 38. [26] Starkey, *Dialogue*, 39.

[27] Starkey, *Dialogue*, 38–9.

[28] Starkey, *Dialogue*, 39–40. A reference perhaps to Aristotle's connection between circumstance and counsel, see Aristotle, *Nicomachean Ethics*, trans. H. Rackham (Cambridge, MA: Harvard University Press, 1926), 1104a; Tarik Wareh, *The Theory and Practice of Life: Isocrates and the Philosophers*, Hellenic Studies Series 54 (Washington, DC: Center for Hellenic Studies, 2013), 4.

In so doing, they return to the conversation they had begun the day before, seeking to discover the ills of the commonwealth, which are unsurprisingly founded in issues surrounding counsel. On the first day of the dialogue, Lupset had maintained that the problems of the world come not from 'the society and company of man', but rather from those qualified to keep 'good order and civility' who run from the task.[29] Once again utilising language from the Senecan texts, Lupset holds that it is the job of such men to cultivate the seeds of virtue which are 'rooted and planted' in the hearts of men.[30] Notably, at this point, speaking abstractly, Lupset no longer tries to convince Pole to take on a role as counsellor to a prince, but uses language from republican texts on the topic to try to convince him to – in a sense – counsel the people.[31] It is they who have the seeds of virtue implanted in them that need cultivating, and rather than his influence flowing via the prince as a fountain, it is directly 'communed' to the people.

On the second day, when they consider specifically the 'time and place' of monarchical England, however, the king is once again brought into the equation. The most pressing problem facing England is a familiar one: the system of hereditary monarchy does nothing to ensure against a prince driven by his affections instead of reason. Because of this, the people are ignorant of virtue and therefore miserable, which by 'diligent instruction and wise counsel' should be rectified, if only there was someone to provide it.[32] Adopting Lupset's Senecan metaphor of the seeds of virtue, Pole remarks that if man would 'hear counsel of wise and prudent men' the 'seeds of nature planted in his mind' would not be choked, which causes him to be 'led by ignorance and folly'.[33] As 'the end of all politic rule is to induce the multitude to virtuous living', and as this is done by counsel, it is crucial that counsel be suffused throughout the political system.[34]

This requires, first, that wise men offer their counsel and, second, that it is then spread to the rest of the commonwealth. Even if the first problem is rectified (men like Pole contributing their learning and expertise to the commonwealth), the second would persist, for, Pole argues, 'this is sure, and a Gospel word: that country cannot be long well governed nor maintained with good policy where all is ruled by the will of one not chosen by election, but cometh to it by natural succession', as he is unlikely to have the 'virtue and wisdom' required for such a post.[35] Whereas

[29] Starkey, *Dialogue*, 28. [30] Starkey, *Dialogue*, 31–2.

[31] See Blythe, 'Civic Humanism', 59–66; Daniel Lee, *Popular Sovereignty in Early Modern Constitutional Thought* (Oxford: Oxford University Press, 2016), 79–120.

[32] Starkey, *Dialogue*, 44. [33] Starkey, *Dialogue*, 44. [34] Starkey, *Dialogue*, 61.

[35] Starkey, *Dialogue*, 99.

Erasmus had here inserted the tutor to the prince, More the counsellor and Castiglione his courtier, Starkey institutes a governing council. As bad princes are likely to result from hereditary monarchy, 'I think it nothing expedient to commit to them any such authority and princely power, which is to singular virtue and most perfit wisdom only due and convenient.'[36] Such 'high authority' ought to be given instead to 'the common counsel of the ream [sic] and parliament', for 'What is more contrary to reason than all the whole people to be ruled by him which commonly lack all reason?'.[37] The king ought to be ruled by reason, and so he will be, insofar as he is ruled by counsel – in a council – which is given the high 'princely' power.

The system that Starkey develops from this conclusion is inspired by medieval conciliarism, to which he had been exposed in France and Italy.[38] The control of the tyranny of the king by means of councils paralleled the mitigation of papal tyranny through the General Council. If the pope did not seek the advice of the General Council, he took on 'a certayn clokyd tyranny under the pretext of relygyon'.[39] In the vision presented by Pole in the *Dialogue*, the king likewise would be ruled by a council: fourteen men chosen by the parliament.[40] The council's membership would be predetermined to include four high-ranking nobles, two bishops, four judges and four wise citizens of London. This council would carry the 'authority of the whole parliament' when it was not in session and 'represent the whole body of the people', seeing 'unto the liberty of the whole body of the ream [sic]' and resisting 'all tyranny'.[41] Thus although the council would be chosen by the parliament, it also carried its delegated authority when parliament was not in session, and would have the power to call it in turn.

Starkey makes clear that this council sits at the top of the institutional hierarchy (though its power comes from parliament) and carries the power to 'pass all acts of leagues, confederation, peace and war'.[42] By these means, 'The power of the prince would, after such fashion, be restrained and brought to order', and all other faults and disorders of the commonwealth would be healed.[43] Under this council of fourteen would sit the Privy

36 Starkey, *Dialogue*, 100. 37 Starkey, *Dialogue*, 100, 104.

38 Mayer, 'Thomas Starkey', 207–27; Mayer, *Thomas Starkey*, 79–89.

39 From the MS of Starkey's *Dialogue*, f. 118r-v, quoted in Mayer 'Thomas Starkey', 214.

40 As imprudent as Starkey's recommendation that Henry's authority ought to be limited by a council might have been, it did reflect the spirit of the age. Under the first two Tudor monarchs coun*sel* was increasingly institutionalised into coun*cils*, though politics remained deeply personal; Gunn, *Henry VII's New Men*, 39.

41 Starkey, *Dialogue*, 155–6, 165–6. 42 Starkey, *Dialogue*, 156. 43 Starkey, *Dialogue*, 168.

Council, appointed not by the king, but by them.[44] Under both of these, at last, would sit the king, who is not to do anything 'pertaining to the state of his ream [sic] without the authority of his proper [i.e. Privy] counsel'.[45] As Guy points out, this imposes 'severe restraints of "counsel" on the king's exercise of *imperium*', and even goes so far as to wrest *imperium* out of the hands of the king, and place it directly into a separate conciliar institution.[46] Importantly it does so using as justification the humanist discourse of counsel developed by Erasmus and More.

Starkey's dialogue ends on a pessimistic note, perhaps inspired by his disappointment with Pole's refusal to take the role set out for him in the *Dialogue*. The character of Pole returns to the issue of right-timing, insisting that he ought to 'tarry his time' and wait for 'the prince to call me to this purpose', which Lupset objects is what leads to the 'destruction of all'.[47] He once again asserts that Pole ought not to 'let this occasion slip'.[48] Pole does not have the perfect opportunity to offer his advice, but Lupset insists he ought to make do with the opportunity he does have, or else the commonwealth will suffer. The issue remains unresolved, with Pole promising to discourse about this 'tarrying of time' at some point in the future. The advice of the *Dialogue* is not communicated, because the advice-giver is silent, waiting for the ideal moment.

ii Elyot and Prudent Counsel

No English humanist writes more on the themes of right-timing and counsel than Thomas Elyot. In his works published between 1531 and 1533, Elyot reflects deeply on the role of the counsellor, and the questions raised by his predecessors and contemporaries.[49] Elyot is generally more conservative in his writings than Starkey, especially in the earliest text of this three-year period, *The Boke Named the Governour*. He does, however, in the context of fears of tyranny under Henry VIII, come to articulate the

44 See Guy, 'The Henrician Age', 20.

45 Starkey, *Dialogue*, 156. The Privy Counsel also has a predetermined membership of 'two bishops, four lords, and four of the best learned and politic men' (156).

46 Guy, 'The Henrician Age', 20. 47 Starkey, *Dialogue*, 191. 48 Starkey, *Dialogue*, 190–1.

49 See Robert Sullivan and Arthur E. Walzer, eds., *Thomas Elyot: Critical Editions of Four Works on Counsel* (Leiden ; Boston: Brill, 2018), 'Introduction', 'chapter 2'; F. W. Conrad, 'The Problem of Counsel Reconsidered: The Case of Sir Thomas Elyot', in *Political Thought and the Tudor Commonwealth: Deep Structure, Discourse and Disguise*, ed. Paul Fideler and Thomas Mayer (London: Routledge, 2003), 77–110; F. W. Conrad, 'A Preservative Against Tyranny: Sir Thomas Elyot and the Rhetoric of Counsel', in *Reformation, Humanism, and 'Revolution': Papers Presented at the Folger Institute Seminar 'Political Thought in the Henrician Age, 1500–1550'*, ed. Gordon J. Schochet (Washington, D.C.: The Folger Institute, 1990), 191–206.

need for wise counsellors to rule their prince. He also addresses head-on the issues raised by his predecessors' texts, including the problem of counsel, the definition of *kairos* and the tension between counsel and command.

Elyot joined the humanist circle around Thomas More, though he later disassociated himself from the former Lord Chancellor after his execution in 1535.[50] He entered the service of Henry VIII in 1523, as senior clerk of the king's council. He, however, lost his position in the wake of Cardinal Wolsey's fall in 1529, and so was forced to work his way back into the king's favour. Like others before and after him, Elyot applied his humanist training to write a book which would serve to announce his skills for royal service.[51] The result was *The Boke Named the Governour*, published in 1531.[52]

Purporting to 'treateth of the education of them that hereafter may be deemed worthy to be governors of the public weal', *The Governour* has rightly been compared to both *The Education of a Christian Prince* and *The Courtier* in setting out the skills and training necessary for a good courtier.[53] It should be clear from the title that the text explicitly assumes the conclusion of *The Courtier*: that the good courtier also has an essential political role. The title refers not only to the way in which the well-educated courtier can govern the people through example, persuasion and delegated sovereignty, but also to the way in which he, too, must be governed 'inwardly' in order to accomplish this 'outward' governance.

Whereas More's *Utopia* dismantled social hierarchies, Elyot suggests that hierarchies and inequalities lead to the stability of the realm. In the opening paragraphs of the text he seeks to redefine the relationship

50 Biographical details from Stanford E. Lehmberg, 'Elyot, Sir Thomas (c. 1490–1546), Humanist and Diplomat', *Oxford Dictionary of National Biography*, 2008, https://doi.org/10.1093/ref:odnb/8782; see also Sullivan and Walzer, eds, *Thomas Elyot*, 'Chapter 2'.

51 See Arthur Walzer, 'Rhetoric of Counsel in Thomas Elyot's *Pasquil the Playne*', *Rhetorica: A Journal of the History of Rhetoric* 30, no. 1 (2012): 2. For instance he mentions that if children are raised in the humanistic curriculum that he describes, and then sent to study the law at the age of about 21 – which may parallel his own upbringing – then 'undoubtedly they should become men of so excellent wisdom that throughout all the world should be found in no common weal more noble counsellors', Thomas Elyot, *The Book Named The Governor*, ed. S. E. Lehmberg (New York: Dent, 1962), 52.

52 Walker, *Writing Under Tyranny*, 149–50, 170–7 and Sullivan and Walzer, eds, *Thomas Elyot*, 15–17 draw attention to the contextual considerations which may have impacted this text, namely Henry's Great Matter.

53 Elyot, *The Governor*, xiii; Stanford E. Lehmberg, *Sir Thomas Elyot, Tudor Humanist* (Austin: University of Texas Press, 1960), 74–5; Walker, *Writing Under Tyranny*, 145; Sullivan and Walzer, eds., *Thomas Elyot*, 26. Earlier studies, such as Pearl Hogrefe, *The Life and Times of Sir Thomas Elyot, Englishman* (Ames: Iowa State University Press, 1967), 118 dismiss the comparison with Castiglione, downplaying the political import of his courtier. As we have seen, however, this stems from a misreading of Castiglione's text. Sullivan and Walzer, eds., *Thomas Elyot*, 17 notes that Elyot also models his text after Quintilian's *Institutio*.

between the English 'common weal' and Latin *respublica*, suggesting that use of the former as a translation for the latter is a mistake. Instead, 'public weal' should be used, as it removes any assumption that 'everything should be to all men in common, without discrepance of any estate or condition'.[54] 'Common weal' would be better suited to the Latin '*Res plebia*' than '*Res publica*'.[55] Elyot has no interest in the contribution of the *vox populi*, and is fundamentally elitist in his understanding of who should hold the reins of government.

Elyot, however, runs up against the same problem of monarchy expressed by his predecessors: though the rule of one might be more natural, 'one mortal man cannot have knowledge of all things done in a realm or large dominion, and at one time discuss all controversies, reform all transgressions, and exploit all consultations'.[56] For this reason, it is necessary 'that under the capital governor be sundry mean authorities' so that the king 'shall govern with the better advice, and consequently with a more perfect governance'.[57] Advice is only one part of the governor's role, however, and Elyot is clear that they are governors in a fuller sense as well; having authority committed to them, they 'may be called inferior governors' or 'magistrates' and by their office have 'a representation of governance'.[58] Thus although Elyot professes a preference for monarchy, it is one with a significant delegation of sovereignty, and the education of his governors runs very closely parallel to the education that Erasmus prescribes for the prince, with the same means and ends in mind.[59] These governors must maintain both 'an interior or inward governance, and an exterior or outward governance'.[60] The first pertains to the rule of reason over the passions and affects, the second refers to his governance over the realm, which can only be successful insofar as the first is maintained.

54 Elyot, *The Governor*, 1, 5. Notably, Elyot is not consistent in this, and uses 'common weal' throughout the text. We should recognise in this distinction, however, an early attempt to differentiate between republicanism and democracy; see Sullivan and Walzer, eds., *Thomas Elyot*, 15.

55 Elyot, *The Governor*, 2.

56 Elyot, *The Governor*, 13.

57 Elyot, *The Governor*, 13. As Walker, *Writing Under Tyranny*, 145–8 shows, this lesson is repeated throughout the text.

58 Elyot, *The Governor*, 13. Elyot here appears to be speaking of the sort of delegation of sovereignty associated with magistrates, see Lee, *Popular Sovereignty*, 20.

59 Elyot praises the *Institutio* and recommends it to his reader, as 'there was never book written in Latin that in so little a portion contained of sentence, eloquence, and virtuous exhortation, a more compendious abundance' (40). I thus agree with Walker, *Writing Under Tyranny*, 150 that 'The model of kingship advanced in *The Governor* is in fact far from absolutist in its implications, and far from uncritically supportive of the Royal Supremacy.' Elyot lays out principles and examples which 'reduce the powers of the prince dramatically'. He does, however, support the Royal Supremacy by 1538, in the dedication to his *Dictionary*. My thanks to Arthur Walzer for this point.

60 Elyot, *The Governor*, 183.

They also have the greatest understanding and experience, especially of civil matters, and so like Castiglione Elyot might run into the problem – though he doesn't treat it here – of inferiors more qualified to rule than their superior.[61]

For Elyot, people are fundamentally different in regard to their ability, and especially that most important gift: understanding.[62] The more able one is in this, the more one should be advanced 'in degree or place'.[63] This is not just because of the fundamental justice of meritocracy for Elyot, but for the benefit of the realm, for by placing them on high 'by the beams of their excellent wit, showed through the glass of authority, other of inferior understanding may be directed to the way of virtue and commodious living'.[64] In fact, these 'governors' seek not their own gain, but only the 'preservation of other their inferiors'.[65] Such reasoning also underpins Elyot's clear preference for a monarchical regime and unequivocal rejection of the rule of the multitude, 'which might well be called a monster with many heads'.[66]

What *The Governor* particularly offers is a deep reflection on the importance of prudence to political counsel, and its connections to right-timing and free speech. The relationship between prudence and counsel-giving goes back to the earliest appearances of the concept in Greek writing, to the extent that *euboulia* – 'good counsel' – can also be translated as 'prudence'.[67] It is Aristotle who most clearly, and most influentially, draws a connection between these ideas. Responding to Plato's emphasis on *sophia*, Aristotle shifts attention to *phronesis*: 'to have deliberated well is the characteristic of prudent men [*phronimos*]; Deliberative Excellence [*euboulia*] must be correctness of deliberation with regard to what is expedient as a means to the end, a true conception of which constitutes Prudence [*phronesis*]'.[68] Prudence is Aristotle's 'central virtue' without which the other virtues cannot be possessed.[69] Without virtue prudence

[61] Elyot does maintain that such counsellors will be from the 'Worshipful class', though exceptions may be granted if they are especially qualified.

[62] That being said, like More, Elyot seems to believe in a sort of fundamental equality, as he later goes on to recommend to his governor that he remember 'that thou art verily a man compact of soul and body, and in that all other men be equal unto thee . . . that every man taketh with thee equal benefit of the spirit of life, nor thou hast any more of the dew of heaven, or the brightness of the sun, than any other person' and that death will come to take any worldly authorities away from him just as swiftly as they were given to him (*Governor*, 165).

[63] Elyot, *The Governor*, 4. [64] Elyot, *The Governor*, 4. [65] Elyot, *The Governor*, 5.

[66] Elyot, *The Governor*, 6. See Lehmberg, *Sir Thomas Elyot*, 42–5.

[67] Woodruff, 'Euboulia', 185; see also Roisman, 'Nestor', 30, 38.

[68] Aristotle, *Nicomachean Ethics*, 1142b4; Matthew Giancarlo, '"Al Nys but Conseil": The Medieval Idea of Counsel and the Poetry of Geoffrey Chaucer' (PhD, Yale University, 1997), 29–30.

[69] Aristide Tessitore, *Reading Aristotle's Ethics: Virtue, Rhetoric, and Political Philosophy* (New York: SUNY Press, 1996), 43. Aristotle, *Nicomachean Ethics*, 6.13.

is 'cleverness' and can be quite dangerous.[70] For this reason, prudence is 'virtue in action' – the expression of universal ideals through *praxis*, which is why it provides the means, and virtue the ends. This relationship between prudence and counsel is repeated by medieval Aristotelians, such as Thomas Aquinas: 'it belongs to prudence to be of good counsel', and again: 'Prudence is of good counsel about matters regarding a man's life in its entirety, and its last end.'[71] It is connected to counsel in a double bond, for not only is it the source of good counsel, but it also allows us to recognise and take good counsel: 'it is by prudence that we take counsel rightly'.[72] If we lack prudence in ourselves, we can still get by if we 'follow the counsels of good men', though this is less morally good than if it had come from ourselves.[73]

Elyot provides an almost identical case in *The Governor*. He names prudence as the most essential virtue, 'whereby all other virtues shall enter' and by which the 'mean' and 'maturity' of things shall be known.[74] It is after matters have been 'invented, conjected, perceived, and by long time and often considered' and 'the mind disposeth herself to execution or actual operation' that prudence comes forward and 'teacheth, warneth, exhorteth, ordereth, and profiteth, like to a wise captain that setteth his host in array'.[75] This understanding of prudence is part of the 'inward' governance but also has parallels for external counsel and governance.

This is clearest in the final chapters of *The Governor*, in which Elyot treats the associated ideas of counsel and consultation. Just as prudence comes forward after the matter has been thoroughly weighed, so too after the 'griefs and diseases' of the public weal are 'investigate, examined, and tried' then 'cometh the time and opportunity of consultation' which is 'most necessary for the healing of the said griefs or reparation of decays'.[76] Counsel is the moment at which inner knowledge becomes the knowledge which can advance the good of the realm, and for this reason is the crux of Elyot's argument.[77] Elyot carefully defines 'consultation' as 'the general denomination of the act wherein men do devise together and reason what

70 Tessitore, *Reading Aristotle's Ethics*, 45.

71 Thomas Aquinas, *Summa Theologiae*, trans. W. D. Hughes, vol. 23 (Cambridge: Cambridge University Press, 2006), 53. See J. C. Doig, *Aquinas's Philosophical Commentary on the Ethics: A Historical Perspective* (Dordrecht; Boston: Springer, 2001), 258; Giancarlo, 'The Medieval Idea of Counsel', 114–15; Quillet, 'Community, Counsel and Representation', 545–6.

72 Aquinas, *Summa Theologica*, Vol. 23, 53.

73 Aquinas, *Summa Theologica*, Vol. 23, 53, 55–7.

74 Elyot, *The Governor*, 79–81.

75 Elyot, *The Governor*, 225–6.

76 Elyot, *The Governor*, 236.

77 As Elyot declares at the outset of the penultimate chapter: 'The end of all doctrine and study is good counsel' (238).

is to be done'.[78] Counsel is 'the sentence or advice particularly given by every man for that purpose assembled'.[79] Such consultation – in line with Aristotle's definition of deliberation – has to do with the time 'future or to come'.[80] Elyot sets out that counsel ought to aim at 'three things principally: that it be rightwise, that it be good, and that it be with honesty'.[81] The first, he says, comes of reason, the second virtue, and the third a combination of the first two.[82] With this in place, counsel is 'a perfect captain, a trusty companion, a plain and unfeigned friend'.[83] Consultation is the connecting element between the 'inward' and 'outward' forms of governance, the latter of which he says 'may be called politic'.[84] Developing the work of classical and medieval writers, such as Aquinas, who had noted connections between inward deliberation and outward counsel, Elyot writes that 'consultation ... is the last part of moral sapience, and the beginning of sapience politic'.[85] Elyot here builds into his definition of counsel (or rather consultation) a fundamental separation between moral knowledge and political knowledge. The counsellor is a mediating figure not only between ruler and subjects, but between moral and political philosophy. By ruling himself according to the dictates of the former, the counsellor/governor can ensure good rule by means of the latter.

iii Elyot and Freeing Speech

Elyot's *Governor* sets the humanist model of counsel out clearly, highlighting the key components and concepts as derived from classical and medieval precedents. It is, however, a very neat presentation of this model, without delving into many of the issues associated with the problem of counsel, especially regarding the relative dominion of counsel and command, raised by Castiglione, and the issue of right-timing, raised by Starkey. This is largely to do with its purpose, which was to secure Elyot a position at court, and context, which was only at the cusp of the seismic debates over Henry VIII's Break with Rome. Following the publication of *The Governor*, Elyot served as ambassador to Spain for four short months, sent to try to bring Charles V (the erstwhile recipient of Erasmus' *Institutio*) around on the issue of the annulment of his aunt's marriage to Henry VIII. Elyot was replaced by Thomas Cranmer, and when he eventually returned to England, was out of money and favour. He was

78 Elyot, *The Governor*, 236–7. 79 Elyot, *The Governor*, 237. 80 Elyot, *The Governor*, 237.
81 Elyot, *The Governor*, 237. 82 Elyot, *The Governor*, 237. 83 Elyot, *The Governor*, 237.
84 Elyot, *The Governor*, 238. 85 Elyot, *The Governor*, 241.

opposed to Henry's marriage to Anne Boleyn, which took place in January 1533, and must have been unnerved by Thomas More's resignation from the position of Lord Chancellor, which had preceded the marriage in May 1532. As Walker establishes, Elyot seems to have had a private meeting with Henry in June 1532 in which he expressed his views on the annulment of Henry's first marriage.[86]

Despite being at a distance of only two years, the 1533 texts evidence a dramatically different tone and perspective on counsel, reflecting much more intensely on the problems within the discourse. These are *Pasquil the Playne*,[87] *Of the Knowledge which Maketh a Wise Man*[88] and *The Doctrinall of Princis*.[89] Whereas *The Governor* was straightforward in its advice-giving, these texts adopt a more indirect approach to political commentary. Both *Pasquil* and *Of the Knowledge* are dialogues. *Pasquil* in particular acts upon Isocrates' (as well as Erasmus') suggestion that advice is more easily given by a 'fable or a fantasie' than by 'preceptes', and sets out a 'mery treatise/ wherin plaines [of speaking] and flateri do come in trial'.[90] *The Doctrinall* is a translation of Isocrates' 'Letter to Nicocles', one of the most important Renaissance sources for the discourse of counsel.[91]

Isocrates was a proponent of the importance of *kairos*, especially to advice-giving, and Elyot's translation amplifies this theme even further.[92] Two translations of the relevant passage, a modern rendering of the

86 Walker, *Writing Under Tyranny*, 123–5; see Sullivan and Walzer, *Thomas Elyot*, 20–4.

87 There are two 1533 editions of *Pasquil*, both produced by Thomas Berthelet, the king's printer. One acknowledges Elyot's authorship in the address to the reader, the other does not (and they differ in pagination). I have used the former, which was actually the second of the two to be produced, with Elyot's revisions. As Walker, *Writing Under Tyranny*, 194–5, 201–2 shows, the second version was significantly toned down (and lacked many of the direct allusions to Thomas Cranmer). For Berthelet's role in Elyot's publications, see Pearl Hogrefe, 'Sir Thomas Elyot's Intention in the Opening Chapters of the "Governour"', *Studies in Philology* 60, no. 2 (1963): 133–4. See also Sullivan and Walzer, eds., *Thomas Elyot*, 169, 171–3.

88 The original reads *Of the Knowledeg which Maketh a Wise Man*. I will refer to the text as *Of the Knowledge*, however, in what follows.

89 'Doctrinall' here means 'a book of instruction' (for princes). As Sullivan and Walzer, eds., *Thomas Elyot*, 94 point out, *The Doctrinall* was probably the first printed book to have been translated directly from Greek into English. For the differences between and dating of the two editions (c. 1533 and c. 1539) see Sullivan and Walzer, eds., *Thomas Elyot*, 116–18, 124–33.

90 Thomas Elyot, *The Doctrinall of Princes* (London, 1534), 15^{v}; Thomas Elyot, *Pasquil the Playne* (London, 1533), verso of front page. Elyot's text is prefaced with the same sort of merry tone as *Utopia*. He notes in the address to the reader that his three figures 'communed to gether, as it foloweth/ but where, I had forgoten to aske' (*Pasquil*, 2^{r}).

91 Sullivan and Walzer, eds., *Thomas Elyot*, 94–5.

92 See Ekaterina V. Haskins, *Logos and Power in Isocrates and Aristotle* (Columbia: University of South Carolina Press, 2004), 72–3. See Sullivan and Walzer, eds., *Thomas Elyot*, 107–11 on Elyot as translator of Greek.

original Greek and Elyot's translation, are compared below to show Elyot's emphasis:

> avoid what is in controversy and test men's value in the light of what is generally agreed upon, if possible taking careful note of them when they present their views on particular situations; or, if that is not possible, when they discuss general questions. And when they are altogether lacking in what they ought to know, reject them, (for it is clear that if one is of no use in himself, neither can he make another man wise).[93]

> specially they that be counsailours ought to haue consideration of the occasion, time and oportunitee, if thei can not bringe that to passe, than to reiecte and put awaie as well them whiche speke in all matters generally, as also those that perceiue nothyng that is expedient or necessarie, for it is aparant, and certaine, that he whiche can not be to him selfe profitable, he shall in other mens businesse do nothynge wisely.[94]

Whereas Isocrates had counselled turning to those who can advise on general matters if those who cannot speak to *kairos* are not found, Elyot argues for rejecting such generalising men along with those who have no useful knowledge. Elyot's translation makes clear that the special knowledge pertaining to the counsellor is *kairos*, a suggestion he had also made in *The Governor*, likewise drawing on Isocrates. In demonstrating how counsel appears through the 'parts' of prudence, in *The Governor*, Elyot set out that it is especially present in the element of 'election', which is 'best described by opportunity, which is a principle part of counsel'.[95] This contains a consideration of the various circumstances of the consultation: 'The importance of the thing consulted. The faculty and power of him that consulteth. The time when. The form how . . . ' and so on.[96] Such a statement draws not only on the reading of Isocrates above, but also from Aristotle, who had noted that the circumstantial nature of *phronesis* requires an understanding of *kairos*: 'the agents themselves have to consider what is suited to the circumstances on each occasion [*kairos*], just as is the case with the art of medicine or of navigation'.[97] For Isocrates, Aristotle's contemporary and Elyot's key source in this text, knowledge does not just pertain to particulars, it is the response to infinitely particular circumstances

[93] ἀμφισβητουμένων ἐπὶ τοῦ συνομολογουμένου λαμβάνειν αὐτῶν τὸν ἔλεγχον, καὶ μάλιστα μὲν ἐπὶ τῶν καιρῶν θεωρεῖν συμβουλεύοντας, εἰ δὲ μή, καὶ καθ' ὅλων τῶν πραγμάτων λέγοντας. καὶ τοὺς μὲν μηδὲν γιγνώσκοντας τῶν δεόντων ἀποδοκίμαζε (δῆλον γὰρ ὡς ὁ μηδὲν ὢν αὐτὸς χρήσιμος οὐδ' ἂν ἄλλον φρόνιμον ποιήσειεν), Isocrates, *Orations*, 252.

[94] Elyot, *Doctrinall*, 17^{v}–18^{r}. [95] Elyot, *The Governor*, 85. [96] Elyot, *The Governor*, 85.

[97] Aristotle, *Nicomachean Ethics*, 1104a. See also Aristotle, *Politics*, 6.13.1145a6–9; Tessitore, *Reading Aristotle's Ethics*, 49; Richard Sorabji, 'Aristotle on the Role of Intellect in Virtue', *Proceedings of the Aristotelian Society* 74, no. 1 (1974): 107–29; Wareh, *The Theory and Practice of Life*, 4.

itself.[98] *Kairos*, in fact, defines the boundaries of deliberation, for once the opportune moment is passed, there is no need to deliberate any further.

The Doctrinall, however, does not solve Starkey's problem of how to define the right moment that demands the giving of advice, simply that it is essential to the role of the counsellor. This question is addressed in the other two of the 1533 texts, both which also draw their inspiration from classical sources. *Pasquil* can be most directly connected to Plutarch's 'How to Tell a Flatterer from a Friend', which centres on the issues of *parrhesia* and *kairos*. Plutarch's work had also been an important source for *The Governor*, founding Elyot's call for the allowance of frank speech: 'Oh what damage have ensued to princes and their realms where liberty of speech hath been restrained!'[99] However, such 'liberty of speech is now usurped by flatterers' and so one needs to know how to tell 'admonition from flattery'; to do so one only need look at Plutarch's work.[100]

In 'How to Tell a Flatterer', Plutarch concludes that a friend uses the opportune moment to speak frankly; in the words of the 1603 English translation, 'opportunitie a wise and skilfull friend will not omit, but make especial good use of', for such moments 'open the doore and make way for us to enter, and give us leave to speak frankly'.[101] Plutarch defines the right moment as when 'the time serveth best to represse excessive pleasure, to restraine unbridled choler, to refraine intollerable pride and insolencie, to stay insatiable avarice, or to stand against any foolish habitude and inconsiderate motion'.[102] *Kairos* exists in the opportunity to encourage virtuous action and bridle vice. For Plutarch this 'define[s] . . . the opportunity of free speech'.[103] As *Pasquil* and *Of the Knowledge* show, however, this does not actually tell the reader how to identify such a moment to speak frankly.

The concepts in Plutarch's tract are personified in *Pasquil*. Plain speaking is represented by Pasquil, an embodiment of the Pasquino statue in Rome, upon which residents could post complaints and satires.[104] Through this practice, Elyot notes, Pasquil has become 'rude and

98 Haskins, *Logos and Power*, 72.

99 Elyot, *The Governor*, 108–10.

100 Elyot, *The Governor*, 151.

101 Plutarch, The Philosophie, Commonlie Called, the Morals, trans. Philemon Holland (London, 1603), 110–11; see Richard Broxton Onians, *The Origins of European Thought: About the Body, the Mind, the Soul, the World, Time, and Fate* (Cambridge: Cambridge University Press, 2011), 348 for the relationship between *opportunitas* and *porta*. I have used the 1603 edition here as the most contemporary English rendering of the text to show parallels with Elyot's 1533 vocabulary.

102 Plutarch, *The Morals*, 110.

103 Plutarch, *The Morals*, 110.

104 For Elyot's awareness of the Pasquino statue and verses in December 1532 see Walker, *Writing Under Tyranny*, 182–3. As Walker points out, if this is indeed when Elyot became inspired to write *Pasquil*, then he wrote the first edition of text quickly and in tense circumstances, which may explain why it is more vehement than other texts, and why he seems to endorse Pasquil's bluntness.

homely'.[105] Pasquil debates with two characterizations of flattery, noted to be 'cosens' as there is 'small diuersite betwene [their] condicions':[106] Gnatho, who 'alway affirmed, what so euer was spoke[n] of his maister', and Harpocrates, who favours silence.[107] Elyot tells his reader to 'consider diligently the state and condition of the parson that speketh' in determining for themselves who they believe to be correct.[108] He ends his address to the reader with the plea that 'if it seme to you, that Pasquill sayeth true' then 'in declaringe howe moche ye do fauoure truthe, defende hym ageyngst venemous tunges and ouerthwart wittis', for these 'doeth much more myschieffe, than Pasquillus babillinge', a plea that Pasquil repeats in the final line.[109] Elyot thus accepts from the outset the Janus-faced nature of *parrhesia*, yet concludes that the opponents of truth-speaking are far more dangerous than those who – in an effort to speak truth – offend or prattle, as Pasquil does.

Pasquil's discussion with each counsellor centres on the interpretation of a quote from Aeschylus' *Libation Bearers*. The quotation, as Gnatho gives it, is 'holding thy tonge wher it behoueth the. And spekyng in tyme that whiche is conuenient'.[110] In Aeschylus' original, the character of Orestes addresses the chorus, instructing them: σιγᾶν θ' ὅπου δεῖ καὶ λέγειν τὰ καίρια – 'be silent when there is need and speak only what the occasion demands'.[111] It is worth noting that Elyot adds a second temporal reference 'spekyng *in time*' which has no precedent in the original, further emphasising the way in which *kairos* speaks to a particular moment, not just a specific context.

The dialogue becomes a debate about how best to interpret this line, and – in essence – how best to determine what *kairos* means in regard to giving counsel.[112] Gnatho gives his reading first. He interprets the statement as meaning that 'it behoueth a man to holde his tunge, whan he aforeseeth by any experience, that the thinge, whiche he wolde purpose or speke of to his superior, shall neyther be pleasantly herde nor thankefully

105 Elyot, *Pasquil*, 2r.

106 Elyot, *Pasquil*, 11v–12r. In this edition it reads 'cosen germanes remoued', in the other 1533 edition it reads 'right cosens' (12r).

107 Elyot, *Pasquil*, 2r. Walker, *Writing Under Tyranny*, 184–5 gives several possible contemporary identifications for Gnatho, and one for Harpocrates: Thomas Cramner.

108 Elyot, *Pasquil*, 2r–v. 109 Elyot, *Pasquil*, 2v, 30v. 110 Elyot, *Pasquil*, 5r.

111 Aeschylus, *Aeschylus, with an English Translation*, trans. Herbert Weir Smyth, vol. 2: Libation Bearers, 2 vols (Cambridge, MA: Harvard University Press, 1926), 540. Note that the form here is *kairios*, a variant of *kairos*.

112 As Walzer, 'Rhetoric of Counsel', 8 puts it: 'The theme of *Pasquil the Playne* is the timing of appropriate counsel.'

taken'.[113] He suggests that, when it comes to words, 'oportunitie & tyme alwaye do depende on the affection and appetite of hym that hereth them'.[114] Of course, anyone well read in their Plutarch, as Elyot was, would know that this was an interpretation of *kairos* completely at odds with the one that a good counsellor was meant to adopt. The good counsellor ought to use *kairos* to restrain affections, not to play to them.

In response, Elyot has Pasquil reiterate much of Plutarch's doctrine of *kairos* explored above. Notably, he begins by giving a series of examples in precept form.[115] For instance, 'When men be set at a good soupper, and be busily occupyed in eatynge and drinkinge, though thou be depely sene in philosophie, holde thy tonge and dispute not of temperaunce'.[116] This is juxtaposed with a more formal council setting: 'Whan thou arte sittynge in counsaile aboute maters of weighty importaunce: talke not than of passe tyme or daliaunce, but omittinge affection or dreede, speke than to the pourpose'.[117] If one takes account of the proper occasion, Pasquil tells Gnatho, then the counsel will be even more effective. For example, 'Whan thy frendes be set downe to souper, before the cuppes betwise fylled: reherce the peryll and also dishonesti that hapneth by glotony'.[118] When it comes to councils, the right time comes 'after thou haste either herde one raisonne bifore the, or at the leest weye, in the balaunce of thyne owne raison ponderid the questio[n]'.[119] It is then that one should 'spare not to shew thine aduise, & to speke truely'.[120] Pasquil then proceeds to give Gnatho his definition of the concept of *kairos*:

> Oportunite consisteth in place or tyme, where and whan the sayd affections or passion of wrath be mitigate and out of extremitie. And wordes be called conueniente, whiche haue respecte to the nature and state of the person, vnto whom they be spoken, and also to the detrimente, whiche mought ensue by the vice or lacke that thou hast espied, & it ought not to be as thou hast supposed. For oportunite & tyme for a counsayllour to speke, do not depend of the affection and appetite of hym that is counsayled: mary than counsaylle were but a vayne worde, and euery man wolde do as hym lyste.[121]

113 Elyot, *Pasquil*, fos. 5^{v}–6^{r}. 114 Elyot, *Pasquil*, fo. 6^{r}.

115 These are set with pilcrows, like those that are used in Elyot's *Doctrinall*. A similar use for pilcrows is highlighted in Thomas Tusser, *Five Hundred Points of Good Husbandry* (London, 1580), A1^{v}. My thanks to Claire M. L. Bourne for this information.

116 Elyot, *Pasquil*, fo. 7^{r}.

117 Elyot, *Pasquil*, fo. 7^{r}. This echoes Plutarch's comments that 'we must take heed how we speake broad at a table where friends be met together to drinke wine liberally and to make good cheere: for he that amid pleasant discourses and mery talke mooveth a speech that causeth bending and knitting of browes', Plutarch, *The Morals*, 108.

118 Elyot, *Pasquil*, fo. 7^{r}. 119 Elyot, *Pasquil*, fo. 7^{r}. 120 Elyot, *Pasquil*, fos. 7^{r}; 8^{r}.

121 Elyot, *Pasquil*, fos. 8^{v}-9^{r}.

The affections should *not* be entered into a consideration of opportunity except in terms of their being 'out of extremitie'. Gnatho is thus correct that Pasquil ought to consider 'what, and to whome, and where thou spekist', but he considers the wrong factors in relation to these, and with the wrong ends in mind.[122] Gnatho seeks promotion, Pasquil truth. That is part of what makes Gnatho such a dangerous flatter: he seems to be speaking sense, but in fact is self-serving.

In one thing Gnatho is correct: Pasquil does indeed 'rayle', but this is to do with the state of the world, which has meant that extreme truth-telling of Pasquil's sort is necessary. As Pasquil states at the end of the dialogue, he would 'speake neuer a worde, but sit as styll as a stone' if those 'that be called, wolde alwaye playe the partis of good Counsaylours'.[123] But the world is turned upside-down, so that 'stones do grutche' and 'counsailours be spechelesse'.[124] This idea that the world 'is rou[n]d, and therfore it is euer tournynge' so that 'nowe the wronge side vpwarde, an other tyme the ryghte' runs throughout the text, directly connected to the faulty counsel of Pasquil's interlocutors.[125] Pasquil opens by declaring 'It is a wonder to see the world: Now a daies, the more straunge the better lyked, therfore vnnethe [scarcely] a manne maye knowe an honest man from a false harlotte', upon which enters Gnatho.[126] When Harpocrates arrives, he declares that he will give his master counsel after they both have eaten, prompting Pasquil to declare 'Lo is it not as I sayde, a wonder to se this worlde?', as in 'olde tyme' men used to attend to such important matters in the morning, before dining, recalling Pasquil's juxtaposition of the right timing of eating and counselling.[127] Now 'after noone is tourned to fore noone, vertue into vice, vice into vertue, deuotio[n] into hypocrisie, and in some places men saye/ fayth is torned to herisye'.[128] In

122 Elyot, *Pasquil*, 4r. Elyot translates *decorum* in his *Dictionary* of 1538 as 'a semelynesse, or that which becommeth the person, hauynge respecte to his nature, degree, study, offyce, or professyon, be it in doinge or speakynge, a grace. sometyme it sygnifyeth honestie'; Thomas Elyot, *The Dictionary* (London, 1538), sig. XXX^{v}. Notably this definition has no temporal dimension. Elyot did not blur *kairos* and *decorum*, but rather saw them as mutually supportive for efficacious speech.

123 Elyot, *Pasquil*, 29^{r-v}. 124 Elyot, *Pasquil*, 29^{v}.

125 Elyot, *Pasquil*, 15^{r-v}. See Edwin Howard, 'Sir Thomas Elyot on the Turning of the Earth', *Philological Quarterly* 21 (1942): 441–3; James Redmond, 'A Critical Edition of Sir Thomas Elyot's "Pasquil the Playne"' (PhD, Purdue University, 1971), 165–6.

126 Elyot, *Pasquil*, 3^{r}. 'Harlotte' here means 'a false or evil man, not a loose woman', Redmond, 'A Critical Edition', 154.

127 As Redmond, 'A Critical Edition', 163 points out, this was also in line with expectations of the time; the 1528 Eltham reform paper requires that counsellors 'apply themselves diligently, meeting at ten o'clock in the morning at the latest, and again at two in the afternoon'.

128 Elyot, *Pasquil*, 13^{r}. This 'turning virtue into vice' speaks to the tradition of *paradiastole*. Notably, Elyot may have been the first English writer to attempt to define *paradiastole* in his *Dictionary* of 1538 (sig. Q, iv^{r}): '*Paradiastole*, a dilatinge of a mater by an interpretation'. Elyot's comment on

other words, the timing of affairs has turned virtues into vices. In such a world, Pasquil's bluntness, usually inappropriate, is the only option.[129] As he says, he might otherwise give his counsel in private, but since he is not invited into the chambers of the mighty to correct their vices, he must publish it publicly, so that shame might be a motivating factor for change to a vice-ridden leader.

Gnatho's suggestion, then, that Pasquil's counsel is not listened to because it is too harsh misses the point: Pasquil's counsel is harsh because he was not listened to.[130] In articulating this position, *Pasquil* wades into the Senecan debate, agreeing that once bad counsel – 'false opinions and vicious affectis' – has been 'rootid' in the heart, like 'poyson', then it 'perchaunce be impossible with speche to remoue those opinions, and cure those affectis', unless the evil counsellors who put them there in the first place 'would confesse [their] owne errours'.[131] Pasquil's bluntness is a last resort, caused by the evil counsellors – the Gnathos and Harpocrates – of the world. In some ways this is a position much like Hythloday's – a truth-speaker excluded because of already-existing bad counsel – but Pasquil is no Hythloday, and is desperate, not reluctant, to give his advice. He is not awaiting a utopian scenario, but rather has been shut out. This was Elyot's own position in 1533, supplanted by Gnathos and Harpocrates and forced to articulate his counsel publicly. The ideal opportunity was not possible, so instead it becomes a question of when the urgency of the situation demands the cessation of silence.

A similar question is explored in *Of the Knowledge*, which involves a debate between characters similar to those in first part of *Pasquil*. Plato is the plain-speaker; he has spoken his truth to the Emperor Dionysius, and been punished – enslaved – for it; a reference to a passage from Diogenes Laertius' life of Plato:

> But when Plato held forth on tyranny and maintained that the interest of the ruler alone was not the best end, unless he were also pre-eminent in virtue, he offended Dionysius, who in his anger exclaimed, 'You talk like an old dotard.' 'And you like a tyrant,' rejoined Plato. At this the tyrant grew furious and at first was bent on putting him to death; then, when he had

heresy here is one of two thinly veiled critiques of the Reformation in *Pasquil*. Earlier, Pasquil seems to suggest that had 'Popes, emperours/ kinges/ and cardinalles' listened to his advice, it might have been prevented (9^v–10^r).

129 This is consistent with Isocrates' use of *parrhesia* as well, as Colclough, *Freedom of Speech*, 25 puts it 'The kind of frankness undertaken by both Isocrates and Demosthenes is represented by them as necessary only because the people are under the sway of flatterers'.

130 I thus disagree with the conclusions drawn by Walzer, 'Rhetoric of Counsel', 1–21 and Sullivan and Walzer, eds., *Thomas Elyot*, 'Chapter 5'.

131 Elyot, *Pasquil*, 26^v.

> been dissuaded from this by Dion and Aristomenes, he did not indeed go so far but handed him over to Pollis the Lacedaemonian, who had just then arrived on an embassy, with orders to sell him into slavery.[132]

Notably, in Elyot's version, Plato responds that Dionysius' words 'sauored of Tyranny', which the character of Plato later claims demonstrates his temperance and reserve in counselling the king, as it was not a straightforward accusation of tyranny against the king himself.[133] This rejoinder is, according to Elyot, 'that whiche is best worthy to be called wysedome'.[134] Plato's interlocutor is Aristippus, a hedonist in Laertius' text, who makes Plato's later lessons about the rule of reason stand out all the more clearly.[135] Crucially as well, Aristippus is described as having been much favoured by Dionysius because 'He was capable of adapting himself to place, time and person, and of playing his part appropriately under whatever circumstances.'[136] Like Gnatho, this flattering opportunist makes an ideal foil for the *parrhesiastes*.[137]

Plato appears in the text in slaves' garb, having been sold and almost killed (twice) for the retort he gives to Dionysius. Upon Aristippus' surprise to find Plato in such a situation, for Dionysius had so depended on him and favoured him, Plato tells his story. Dionysius had suddenly become 'wonderful stourdie' – violent and cruel – not allowing other opinions but his own.[138] Plato takes the 'good oportunitie' of Dionysius' request for praise to 'warn hym of his blyndnes and foly'.[139] In other words, like Erasmus and More, the panegyric becomes a means by which to offer counsel, and in Elyot's words, it is specifically an 'oportunitie', like those Pasquil had spoken of. Plato tells Aristippus, who has accused him of speaking too rashly, that he did not immediately speak on Dionysius' tyranny, but instead, 'abydynge oportunitie to speake' on this topic, discussed various others with him first.[140] When the invitation came to speak on the nature of the king, Plato 'reioyced, wenyng to haue founde the oportunitie to speake that I so longe loked for', and he proceeded to give

132 Diogenes Laertius, *Lives of Eminent Philosophers*, trans. R.D. Hicks (Cambridge, MA: Harvard University Press, 1972), 3.18–19. As Arthur E. Walzer, 'The Rhetoric of Counsel and Thomas Elyot's Of the Knowledge Which Maketh a Wise Man', *Philosophy and Rhetoric* 45, no. 1 (2012): 25 points out, this was a popular story in Renaissance England, appearing, for instance, in More's *Utopia* in the debate between Morus and Hythloday; see also Sullivan and Walzer, eds., *Thomas Elyot*, 210.

133 Thomas Elyot, *Of the Knowledeg Whiche Maketh a Wise Man* (London, 1533), 101r–102v.

134 Elyot, *Of the Knowledeg*, sig. A, 6v.

135 Walzer, 'The Rhetoric of Counsel', 27–8.

136 Laertius, *Lives of Eminent Philosophers*, 2.8.66. Notably, this is not a case in which the original in Greek is *kairos*, neither is the Greek *prepon* (Latin *decorum*) used here. See Sullivan and Walzer, eds., *Thomas Elyot*, 30–1, 213.

137 See also Walker, *Writing Under Tyranny*, 198.

138 Elyot, *Of the Knowledeg*, 2v.

139 Elyot, *Of the Knowledeg*, 3r.

140 Elyot, *Of the Knowledeg*, 94v.

counsel designed to restrain the undue affections of the prince.[141] To have waited longer, until Dionysius' passions had waned, would have done little good and much damage, Plato maintains.

Plato and Pasquil thus both articulate Plutarchan arguments in regard to the identification of the right moment against flattering opportunists who would use *kairos* as a way of advancing themselves, fanning rather than putting out the flames of their princes' affections. They do not, however, solve the issue raised by Starkey's Pole and Lupset: even accepting that frank speech must be spoken to counter-act tyranny, when does this take precedence over the ordinary dictates of discretionary silence? What indeed does determine when to speak and when to stay silent?

For this, returning to *Pasquil the Playne*, the title character turns to his second discussant, Harpocrates. Challenging Harpocrates' dedication to silence, Pasquil asks him 'If I perceyued one at thy backe with a swerde drawne, redy to strike the, woldest thou that I shulde holde my peace, or else tell the?'[142] Harpocrates responds that 'Naye, sylence were than oute of season' ('season' being another translation for *kairos*).[143] Pasquil responds that Harpocrates 'wyll season silence' and jokes that 'Marye I wene my lorde shulde haue a better cooke of you thanne a counsayllour.'[144] He asks Harpocrates 'howe thou doest season thy sylence[?]'[145] Harpocrates responds that he does so 'with sugar, for I vse lyttell salte', and Pasquil retorts that this 'maketh your counsayl more swete than sauery'.[146] Harpocrates choice of 'season' makes his advice pleasant but not wholesome.

Having dismissed an undue commitment to silence as flattery, the two characters come to a more pressing issue: what defines the urgency which would necessitate plain speaking? Their debate hinges on the meaning of the word 'imminent', which Pasquil notes is 'a worde taken out of latine,

141 Elyot, *Of the Knowledeg*, 95ʳ. Plato and Aristippus also discuss the issue of right-timing in regard to Plato's rejoinder, which Aristippus suggests should have awaited 'more oportunitie' once Dionysius' 'fume had been passed' (102ᵛ). Plato rejects this suggestion, however, suggesting that such a delay would have in fact lost the opportunity, for Dionysius would have quickly forgotten the exchange, and his words would have had no effect.

142 Elyot, *Pasquil*, fo. 13ᵛ.

143 Elyot, *Pasquil*, fo. 13ᵛ. For the translation of *kairos* as 'season', see James S. Baumlin, 'Ciceronian Decorum and the Temporalities of Renaissance Rhetoric', in *Rhetoric and Kairos: Essays in History, Theory and Praxis*, ed. Phillip Sipiora and James S. Baumlin (New York: State University of New York Press, 2002), 141–4. 'To season' in English has its root in the temporal meaning of 'season', originally referring to allowing fruits, etc to 'season' – i.e. 'to render (fruit) palatable by the influence of the seasons' – before picking them. Thus 'right time' is etymologically linked to this sense of seasoning, and Elyot's pun has even greater meaning.

144 Elyot, *Pasquil*, fos. 13ᵛ–14ʳ. 145 Elyot, *Pasquil*, fo. 15ᵛ. 146 Elyot, *Pasquil*, fos. 15ᵛ–16ʳ.

and not co[m]menly vsed'.[147] Harpocrates defines 'imminent' as 'whan it appereth to be in the instante to be done or to happen: and after some mens exposition, as hit thretned to come'.[148] Pasquil insists, however, that Harpocrates has misunderstood this word, for 'the instant whan it appereth/ that your frend shall be slayne/ and the instante whan he is in sleinge' are in fact not the same, but 'diuerse'.[149] To speak in Harpocrates' 'imminent' moment is to be too late, for then 'it is in the instance of doinge or happening'.[150] Speech is 'in good season' when the danger is imminent in Pasquil's understanding of the term.[151] In other words, the opportune moment for speech is not when the danger is about to occur, but when it is apparent that it will happen (or is likely to happen). Such 'imminent' moments are consistent with the examples that Pasquil had given to Gnatho as well, as in these cases the danger (e.g. gluttony) was apparent, but not yet executed. Pasquil and Harpocrates agree that before this moment speech is dangerous to the speaker, and after it, dangerous to the hearer.[152] This exact moment must be hit, then, to benefit both counsellor and counselled. The problem of counsel comes down to a problem of understanding *kairos*.

This danger which a counsellor ought to prevent is not just physical, as in Harpocrates' example of the sword drawn at his master's back, but like Erasmus, Castiglione, More and Starkey, Elyot addresses the issue of moral danger. As Pasquil puts it, 'a knocke on the heed/ though it be to the scull/ is not so daungerous to be healed as an yuell affection thraste in to thy maisters braynes by false opinion'.[153] Elyot's Pasquil also takes a position on the recurring question of whether it is too late when such affections are 'rooted' in the mind of the hearer by false opinion. Harpocrates challenges Pasquil that 'It semeth that silence shulde nothing profite nor speche

[147] Elyot, *Pasquil*, 19^{r-v}. 'Imminent, Adj.', in *OED Online* (Oxford University Press), accessed 16 January 2019, www.oed.com/view/Entry/91904 records the first use in 1528, though as Redmond, 'A Critical Edition', 168 points out, this refers to manuscript records not printed until the nineteenth century. The first appearance of the word in print may have been Elyot's translation of Plutarch, *Plutarch's Education, or Bringing up of Children*, published between 1530 and 1533 or Elyot's *Governour*, where it appears five times (10^{v}, 61^{v}, 69^{v}, 117^{r}, 207^{r}). Elyot defines *imminens* in his *Dictionary* as 'that whiche is at hande' (LL, iii^{v}).

[148] Elyot, *Pasquil*, 19^{v}.

[149] Elyot, *Pasquil*, 19^{v}. In the 1534 edition which accompanies Elyot's *A Swete and Devoute Sermon*, which contains translations of St Cyprian and Pico della Mirandola, Elyot prefaces this statement with 'ye must remembre that', giving it more rhetorical force. This edition of *Pasquil* has been overlooked by other scholars, but its importance to its dedicatee, Susan Kingston, is highlighted by the context established by Walker, *Writing Under Tyranny*, 227–9. This 1534 edition is an entirely new printing but is not included in the 1539 edition of the same text.

[150] Elyot, *Pasquil*, 19^{v}. [151] Elyot, *Pasquil*, 20^{r}. [152] Elyot, *Pasquil*, 20^{r}.

[153] Elyot, *Pasquil*, 24^{v}.

shulde any thinge auaille/ if the opinions and affectes be so impressed/ that they can not be remoued.'[154] Pasquil, however, maintains that even rooted vices can be 'some what remoued' by 'good perswasio[n], allowing in the possibility of grace'.[155] Thus, 'speche is not onely profitable but also of necessite . . . in healing the diseases/ both of the soule & also the bodie'.[156] Pasquil sides with Seneca's Letter 94, that advice – rhetorically given – can mitigate the effects of vice, if not uproot them.

In line with other humanist texts, which draw on Cicero's *De Officiis*, Pasquil and Harpocrates establish that such a warning is the 'dutie' of a 'good seruaunt' to perform.[157] Such a one should even be willing to sacrifice his life in order to prevent 'perpetuall infamie, the subuercion of the common weale, or vniuersall destruction of all the hoole countrey'.[158] Pasquil calls this lesson the 'point' to which all his 'longe babblynge' has been drawing.[159] As in the *Governour* and *Doctrinall*, then, counsel is the final and most important end of discourse, because it holds saving power in regards to the commonwealth.

Elyot's Plato would agree; what he issued to Dionysius was a warning that has the power to liberate, and he was required to do so based on his position: in order to live up to Dionysius' expectation of Plato's 'wisedome and knowledge'.[160] Because this is what prompted Dionysius' summons, Plato reasons to Aristippus, Plato was required to fulfil this expectation and both act and speak accordingly. Aristippus is forced to agree: Plato ought to 'tell [Dionysius] truthe/ & accordinge to [Plato's] profession': 'that no man is happy, except he be wise and also good'.[161] Such wisdom must not only be held, but acted upon, for 'operation of that whiche is in knowledge called wysedome/ expressynge the wysedome, maketh the vser or exerciser therof to be iustly named a wyse man'.[162] The wisdom which makes a man wise, the two discussants come to in the course of the dialogue, is self-knowledge, which gives knowledge – in turn- of others: 'the knowlege of hym selfe: wherby also he knoweth other', which is to know things 'intelligible' rather than 'sensible', and thus resides in the soul.[163] Plato draws the image of the soul as ruler over the passions, with understanding 'for a chiefe counsayllour'.[164] If the imagination does not consult 'king

[154] Elyot, *Pasquil*, 26ᵛ. [155] Elyot, *Pasquil*, 27ᵛ. [156] Elyot, *Pasquil*, 28ʳ.
[157] Elyot, *Pasquil*, 23ʳ, 23ᵛ. [158] Elyot, *Pasquil*, 24ᵛ.
[159] Elyot, *Pasquil*, 24ʳ. This discussion of the duty of the counsellor, which involves self-sacrifice, further discredits the arguments of Gnatho, whose entire approach to giving advice was self-advancement.
[160] Elyot, *Of the Knowledeg*, 6ʳ.
[161] Elyot, *Of the Knowledeg*, 14ᵛ-15ʳ. Profession here meaning a declaration of faith or opinion.
[162] Elyot, *Of the Knowledeg*, 91ʳ. [163] Elyot, *Of the Knowledeg*, 27ʳ.
[164] Elyot, *Of the Knowledeg*, 51ʳ.

cou[n]saylle of vnderstandyng' it can be moved and persuaded to think that vices be 'good pleasant & profitable'.[165] Without such counsel, the soul becomes 'ministre vnto the sences/ which before were her slaues' and 'holly at their co[m]mandment'.[166] The internal persuasion of the soul is echoed by the same externally, for 'vicious co[m]munication, yl counsayle, and flatery' lead to 'the venemous humour of ylle opinion, wherof commeth vice'.[167] For Elyot's Plato, the rule of understanding's counsel guards against the enslavement of the soul. This model of internal counsel mitigating enslavement parallels the external model that Plato also iterates (in which he takes the role of 'king cou[n]saylle of vnderstandyng') over Dionysius' soul.

As this is the knowledge required to make a man wise, Plato concludes, he was required to bring it into operation before Dionysius in order to fulfil the expectation of his wisdom. He was not, as Aristippus had held, acting rashly. The knowledge which makes him wise, when exercised, is 'in knowledge of hym selfe and other', and particularly the knowledge that the soul ought to rule the appetites; the same knowledge that Plutarch says ought to be communicated in timely counsel.[168] Plato therefore tells Dionysius that the ideal king is one 'in whom the soule had intiere & ful auctorite ouer the sensis & alway kept the affectis in due rule & obedie[n] ce, folowyng only the counsayle of Vndersta[n]ding'.[169] Such a one can rule his people as he rules himself, both by example and by governance.

Importantly, with Understanding as an internal counsellor, such a king can never be deceived by external evil counsel: 'flatterers and glosers, by whome princis be deoured alyue/ and their soules vtterly consumed with moste mortall pestilence, wherwith their cou[n]tries and people be also in perile to be loste & destroyed'.[170] Plato ends on the image of the tyrant, who loses Understanding as a counsellor, and is thus ruled by the appetites and falls easily into the 'snares' of such flatterers, ignoring the words of those who would seek to correct him.[171] One who does not follow the counsel of understanding is enslaved, king or no.

Counsel is thus not a constraining of the king's liberty, but an expansion upon it. John of Salisbury had made a similar point in his *Policraticus*. Since virtue is what leads to freedom and vice to servitude, to censure vice cannot be seen as enslavement. Free speech is essential to this process, as

165 Elyot, *Of the Knowledeg*, 52ʳ. 166 Elyot, *Of the Knowledeg*, 52ʳ.
167 Elyot, *Of the Knowledeg*, 71ʳ. 168 Elyot, *Of the Knowledeg*, 91ᵛ.
169 Elyot, *Of the Knowledeg*, 95ᵛ. Notably, Plato also includes that such a person ought to be 'by the free consent of the people/ chosen or receyued to be a principal ruler and gouernour' (95ᵛ–96ʳ).
170 Elyot, *Of the Knowledeg*, 96ᵛ. 171 Elyot, *Of the Knowledeg*, 97ᵛ.

long as it is done without rashness. A wise man will listen to what is said to him, and 'does not oppose himself to the works of liberty, as long as damage to virtue does not occur'.[172] For this reason, 'it is permitted to censure that which is to be equitably corrected', even if this includes taunts (a departure from Plutarch).[173] He concludes: 'Therefore, man is to be free and it is always permitted to a free man to speak to persons about restraining their vices.'[174] Elyot might agree that it is always 'permitted', but *kairos* dictates when it would actually have positive effect.

Speaking this wisdom according to *kairos* solves a number of the issues with the discourse of counsel: it demonstrates how counsel can be efficacious and it sets out how it can 'rule' a prince without taking away from his liberty. It does not, however, solve the problem of the danger to the speaker; after all, as Aristippus is all too keen to point out, Plato ended up enslaved himself for his freeing speech. Aristippus, like Hythloday and Gnatho, protests that Plato endangered himself in speaking to Dionysius in the way he did, 'without hope of benefite'.[175] Plato maintains, however, that Dionysius 'had no power to indamage my soule, by whose operation I was called a wyse man', whereas if he had chosen not to speak out of fear of bodily harm, he would have 'proued my selfe to haue ben a foole and no wyse ma[n]'.[176] The knowledge which makes Plato a wise man – rule of the passions – requires as well that Plato not act out of fear or hope of promotion. Plato 'declared that my mynde was not subiecte to corporall passions, and consequently not to sensuall affections' in speaking the truth to Dionysius.[177] In fact, Dionysius, 'by takyng libertie from me, and makyng me a slaue, he more declared mi wordis to be true'.[178] Plato is untouched by his physical enslavement because his soul remains free through his choice to speak truth to power. Dionysius, on the other hand, by Plato's words and examples, is shown starkly in his enslavement. Plato concludes that he was indeed never lost, as he 'was neuer transformed or out of that astate, where in a wise man ought alway to be', whereas Dionysius 'hath bothe lost him selfe' by refusing Plato's knowledge, and has lost Plato 'which by [his] counsaile shuldist haue ben to hym so royall a tresure'.[179] Dionysius (and his realm) had the power to be freed by Plato's

172 John of Salisbury, *Policraticus*, 177.

173 John of Salisbury, *Policraticus*, 180. As Jonathan M. Newman, 'Satire of Counsel, Counsel of Satire: Representing Advisory Relations in Later Medieval Literature' (PhD Thesis, University of Toronto, 2009) demonstrates, satire, irony and 'taunts' were often used in Late Medieval counsel literature.

174 John of Salisbury, *Policraticus*, 180.

175 Elyot, *Of the Knowledeg*, 105r.

176 Elyot, *Of the Knowledeg*, 105v.

177 Elyot, *Of the Knowledeg*, 106r.

178 Elyot, *Of the Knowledeg*, 106v.

179 Elyot, *Of the Knowledeg*, 107r.

speech, but regardless of that outcome, Plato himself showed himself to be free in articulating it, even though it resulted in his enslavement.

Elyot goes one step further. Not only is Plato free in his slavery whereas Dionysius is enslaved in his tyranny, but Plato is in fact superior to Dionysius, and indeed all expert counsellors are superior to those they counsel, no matter their station. As he tells Aristippus: 'he that lacketh, in that whiche he doeth lacke/ he is inferior to him of whom he desireth it/ wherfore in as moche as kynge Dionyse to haue benefit of me, became my herer/ he was inferior vnto me.'[180] The person with the greater reason, Plato maintains, is deserving of the greater respect, regardless 'of the astate of the persone that hereth'.[181] This is a variation on the meritocratic tones of *The Governor*, though with a more explicitly radical edge. The dominance of counsel over the prince had likewise been implied in *The Doctrinall*, the title of which speaks to the instruction of the prince. The contents of Isocrates' letter are given as a series of short precepts, identified with pilcrows, giving it a more didactic tone. The prince, or at one point, 'governour',[182] is to take heed of the precepts contained in the 'little booke', which 'prescribe[s] rules' for him.[183] In *Of the Knowledge*, Elyot explicitly places the counsellor above the counselled – even a king – and states outright that the king must listen to (and act upon) the advice of a wise counsellor or be enslaved. Freedom can be found by the rule of good counsel, which Plato demonstrates through his well-timed act of *parrhesia*. Thus, Elyot answers both problems of counsel: wise counsel should indeed rule the king, and the counsellor ought to have no fear of consequences in the performance of his duty.

These first two chapters have outlined a humanist model of counsel, in which pseudo-republican principles – liberty, active citizenship – can be preserved in the context of a monarchy if the prince is ruled by good counsel. This solution quickly raises its own problems, however, most notably the 'problem of counsel': how to ensure that such good counsel is listened to when princes and their courtiers are not necessarily good. To think through the problem of counsel, each of these writers appealed to vocabulary drawn from classical writers, most obviously Cicero, but also clearly Seneca, who thought deeply about the issue of 'uprooting' vice through counsel. Central also to these discussions was the question of 'right-timing' and whether the

[180] Elyot, *Of the Knowledeg*, 102^{v}–103^{r}. [181] Elyot, *Of the Knowledeg*, 103^{r}.
[182] Elyot, *Doctrinall*, 5^{r}; '*monarkhia*' in the original.
[183] Elyot, *Doctrinall*, 2^{r}, 5^{r}. This is a faithful rendering of '*nomotheteo*' in the original.

need to seize the 'opportune moment' results in a mandate to wait for the ideal moment or to speak at the earliest opportunity.

Regardless of the nuances of the debate, there is no question amongst these writers that counsel ought to have authority over the prince, albeit to different degrees and through different means: rhetorical, institutional or otherwise. The realities of the early Tudor polity were, of course, unideal in this case; especially in the second half of his reign, Henry VIII showed a decided disinclination to being ruled by his counsellors. These issues were aggravated by the events of the Henrician Reformation, when many observers worried that Henry VIII listened to no advice, or the wrong advice, in choosing to break with the Catholic Church. This, for instance, is the claim made by the leaders of the Pilgrimage of Grace in 1536, notably a year after the execution of one of the king's former advisers and writer on the problem of counsel, Thomas More, for his failure to align himself with the king's will.[184] Henry VIII, however, was an adult male monarch, and therefore, theoretically at least, capable of ruling without the guidance of counsel, even if the humanists might suggest it bordered on tyranny to do so. By the accession of his young son, however, a new, inverted, model of the relationship between prince and counsellors had been proposed, which generated new problems for the discourse of counsel to come to terms with.

[184] R. W. Hoyle, *The Pilgrimage of Grace and the Politics of the 1530s* (Oxford: Oxford University Press, 2001), 59–62.

PART II

CHAPTER 3

Machiavellian Counsel

The introduction of Machiavellian political thought into the context of an England weakened by perceived monarchical instability – the reign of a minor and two women – opens a new chapter in the history of the English discourse of counsel. Niccolò Machiavelli's works, as well as their interpretation, offer a challenge to what we may now think of as the traditional or orthodox humanist theory of counsel by questioning its fundamental assumptions, most notably the role of counsel as bridling the prince's vices and passions by guiding him to virtuous action. In this new tradition, prudence – still the special skill of the political counsellor – acts to mitigate and navigate the outside forces of fortune and circumstance, rather than functioning to combat the internal motives of the prince, with the aim of achieving what is in the best interests of the ruler. The vocabulary of *kairos* re-emerges here, with a renewed sophistic bent, becoming the variable on which a move towards dissimulation, deception and *paradiastole* rests.

Machiavelli, in *The Prince*, offers a reversal of the traditional humanist model of counsel; the prince's prudence is what determines the quality of the counsel he receives. Answering the recurring question of whether it is better to have a good prince and bad counsellors, or a bad prince and good counsellors, Machiavellians give the contrary answer to the humanists we explored in Chapters 1 and 2: better that the prince be good (in the sense of capable) than his counsellors, as the prince rules his counsellors, not the other way around. To this, Machiavelli adds a strain of cynicism, suggesting that counsellors are unlikely to be good in any case. Counsellors, given Machiavelli's pessimistic account of self-interest in *The Prince*, are not likely to demonstrate the civic spirit that the humanists took to be foundational to their image of the counsellor. Thus, they need to be held in suspicion, and cannot be given any real power. The prince in the Machiavellian tradition clearly commands counsel; counsellors do not command him, or – as we shall see in Chapter 5 – her.

i Machiavelli's *Prince*

Machiavelli consciously places his most famous work, *The Prince*, within the genre of advice-to-princes literature.[1] Machiavelli's text was directly a piece of counsel, to Lorenzo de Medici, designed to demonstrate his abilities as a counsellor.[2] Though it has been widely acknowledged that Machiavelli was acting in this capacity, and that *The Prince* is consciously a part of the advice to princes tradition, little work has been done to analyse Machiavelli's particular approach to counsel, especially his reversal of the traditional humanist model of counsel.[3]

Machiavelli's first engagement with the classical discourse of counsel comes in the opening lines of the dedicatory epistle of *The Prince*, in which he borrows directly from one of the foundational texts in the classical advice-to-princes literature: Isocrates' *To Nicocles*, the same work that Elyot translates and publishes in England in the 1530s.[4] Just as Isocrates had begun his address by acknowledging that most courtiers 'make it a habit, Nicocles, to bring to you who are rulers of kingdoms articles of dress or bronze or of wrought gold',[5] Machiavelli tells his addressee, Lorenzo de' Medici, that 'Those who wish to be viewed with favour by a ruler usually approach him with ... horses, weapons, a cloth of gold, precious stones and similar ornaments'.[6] Isocrates had argued that his gift was the 'finest and the most serviceable present and the most suitable for

[1] The suggestion that we have to read *The Prince* in the context of Renaissance advice-books for princes has been well established; Skinner, *The Foundations of Modern Political Thought*, 128–38. As Maurizio Viroli, 'Machiavelli and the Republican Idea of Politics', in *Machiavelli and Republicanism*, ed. Gisela Bock, Maurizio Viroli and Quentin Skinner (Cambridge: Cambridge University Press, 1991), 149 suggests, what makes Machiavelli radical is not his amoral advice, as this was in line with other Florentine counsel, but that he generalises it by expressing it through the medium of this genre.

[2] It is also, as described by Virginia Cox, 'Machiavelli and the *Rhetorica ad Herennium*: Deliberative Rhetoric in *The Prince*', *The Sixteenth Century Journal* 28.4 (1997): 1109–41, 'a textbook piece of deliberative rhetoric'.

[3] See Quentin Skinner, *Machiavelli: A Very Short Introduction* (Oxford: New York: Oxford University Press, 2000).

[4] Isocrates's works (including the *Ad Nicoclem*, *Panegyricus*, *Panathenaicus* and *Against the Sophists*) were published in Venice and Milan in 1493 and 1513 respectively; Jonathan Stanley Gnoza, 'Isocrates in Italy: The Reception of Isocrates Among the Romans and the Renaissance Humanists'. PhD Thesis, Yale University, 2012.

[5] Isocrates, *Orations*, 2.1.

[6] 3. 'They, that desire to ingratiate themselves with a Prince, commonly use to offer ... Horses and Armes, cloth of gold, pretious stones, and such like ornaments', Niccolò Machiavelli, *Nicholas Machiavel's Prince*, trans. Edward Dacres (London, 1640), sig. A, 5r. Read in consultation with the English manuscript copies published by Alessandra Petrina, *Machiavelli in the British Isles: Two Early Modern Translations of The Prince* (Ashgate Publishing, Ltd., 2009): the Fowler (F) translation of the 1580s and the Queen's College (QC) translation of an undefined date.

me to give and for you to receive'[7] and Machiavelli, likewise, had 'not found among my belongings anything that I hold more dear or valuable' than his gift: *The Prince*.[8] Machiavelli borrows from a text that stresses strongly the need for political counsel to princes, which sets the tone of *The Prince*, locating it within the advice-to-princes genre and figuring Machiavelli as the reimagined political counsellor.[9]

Machiavelli's treatment of the ends to which counsel should be directed is contained largely within the crucial opening passages of Chapter XV. It is here that Machiavelli states most clearly his critique of the classical and humanist advice-to-princes genre.[10] Machiavelli's reference to, and refutation of, these other political writers is direct; he declares that many have written on 'in what ways a ruler should act with regard to his subjects and allies'[11] but what he has 'to say differs from the precepts offered by others'.[12] This is based on his desire 'to write what will be useful [*utile*] to anyone who understands'[13] for which he has thought it 'better to concentrate on what really happens rather than on theories or speculations'.[14] This is probably a comment on Isocrates' distinction between *paraineseis* – advice regarding how one should live – and the advice given by counsellors, which is contingent and specific to circumstances.[15]

[7] Isocrates, *Orations*, 2.2.

[8] Niccolò Machiavelli, *The Prince*, ed. Quentin Skinner and Russell Price (Cambridge; New York: Cambridge University Press, 2000), 3. 'found nothing in my whole Inventory, that I thinke better of, or more esteem', Machiavelli, *Machiavel's Prince*, sig. A, 5^r^. See Albert Russell Ascoli, in *Machiavelli and the Discourse of Literature*, ed. Victoria Ann Kahn and Albert Russell Ascoli (Ithaca: Cornell University Press, 1993), 219–57.

[9] This argument stands in contrast to those, such as Eugene Garver, *Machiavelli and the History of Prudence* (Madison: University of Wisconsin Press, 1987), who claim that Machiavelli 'endows the prince with powers that will make his own position as advisor superfluous' (60) and that he 'reject[s] the value of such a role [as advisor] in the discussion of counsel and advice that appears in chapters 22–23' (63). Although he places the counsellor under the prudential rule of the prince, he still has a role.

[10] Skinner and Prince, 'Introduction', xv–xvii gives this refutation in detail, and Peter Stacey, *Roman Monarchy and the Renaissance Prince* (Cambridge: Cambridge University Press, 2007) focuses on how this attack is concentrated specifically on the work of Seneca in *De clementia*. These chapters are, as Skinner and Prince, 'Introduction', xv put it, 'the most sensational and "Machiavellian" sections of the book'.

[11] Machiavelli, *The Prince*, 54. Notably, in the 1640 edition, this reads as 'what the conditions of a Prince ought to be, and his termes of government over his subjects, and towards his friends', Machiavelli, *Machiavel's Prince*, 117. The modern edition is closer to the original '*i modi e governi di un principe con i sudditi e con gli amici*', Niccolò Machiavelli, *Il Principe*, ed. L. Arthur Burd (Oxford: Clarendon Press, 1891), 282.

[12] Machiavelli, *The Prince*, 54. 'an opinion different from others', Machiavelli, *Machiavel's Prince*, 117.

[13] 'to write for the advantage of him that understands mee', Machiavelli, *Machiavel's Prince*, 117. F: 'to wryte proffitable instructions'; QC: 'to wright matters profitable'.

[14] Machiavelli, *The Prince*, 54. 'fitter to follow the effectual truth of the matter, than the imagination thereof', Machiavelli, *Machiavel's Prince*, 117.

[15] See Sullivan and Walzer, eds., *Thomas Elyot*, 95–101.

The connection between Machiavelli's intent to write for advantage, or *utile*, and his determination that the proper method is thus to study 'what really happens' is a close one, as 'how men live is so different from how they should live that a ruler who does not do what is generally done,[16] but persists in doing what ought to be done, will undermine his power rather than maintain it',[17] and 'If a ruler who wants to act honourably is surrounded by many unscrupulous men his downfall is inevitable.'[18] It is necessary, Machiavelli tells his reader, for the prince to be able to treat honesty as a tool, to 'act immorally when this becomes necessary',[19] or as the 1640 edition puts it, to 'make use of that honestie, and to lay it aside againe, as need [*necessità*][20] shall require'.[21] In other words, Machiavelli entirely modifies the traditional humanist approach to counsel, which is to focus on what *ought* to be done, not what *can* be done.[22]

[16] F: 'for that which becummeth him to do'.

[17] Machiavelli, *The Prince*, 54. 'there is such a distance between how men doe live, and how men ought to live; that hee who leaves that which is done, learnes sooner his ruine, than his preservation', Machiavelli, *Machiavel's Prince*, 118. The passage in QC is more strongly orientated to counsellors, for it reads 'that leauinge what is dunn by menn, and lookinge at theyr duties: they rather instructe them to thaire ruen then to thaire safety'.

[18] Machiavelli, *The Prince*, 54. 'that man who will professe honesty in all his actions, must needs goe to ruine, among so many that are dishonest', Machiavelli, *Machiavel's Prince*, 118. Here F replaces his original use of 'gud' with 'honest' and adds '& vnhonest' after 'euill', drawing more attention to the connection with *honestum*.

[19] Machiavelli, *The Prince*, 55. [20] F: 'necessestie and extremetie of the tyme'.

[21] Machiavelli, *Machiavel's Prince*, 118.

[22] For instance the 1529 *Reloj de príncipes* by Antonio de Guevara, published in English in 1557: 'my purpose is not to tell princes in this booke, what they be, but to warne theim, what they ought to be: not to tel them what they doe, but to aduise them, what they ought to doe'; Antonio de Guevara, *The Diall of Princes*. (London, 1557), aii^{v}; see Keith David Howard, *The Reception of Machiavelli in Early Modern Spain* (Woodbridge: Boydell & Brewer, 2014), 42–4; J. A. Fernández-Santamaria, *The State, War and Peace: Spanish Political Thought in the Renaissance 1516–1559* (Cambridge: Cambridge University Press, 1977), 260–71. The same sentiment is expressed in other mid-century texts, including George Cavendish, *The Negotiations of Thomas Woolsey* (London, 1641), 85: 'every Counsell to a King ought to have respect to Conscience, before the rigour of the Law: *Laus est facere quod decet, non quod licet*', a quotation from pseudo-Senecan *Octavia*, in which Seneca attempts to counsel the tyrannous Nero; Lucius Annaeus Seneca, *L. Annaei Senecae Tragoediae: incertorum auctorum Hercules (Oetaeus), Octavia*, ed. Otto Zwierlein (Oxford: Clarendon Press, 1985), ln. 454. This is same passage referenced by Morus in *Utopia* when he describes the importance of *decorum* in counsel; More, *Utopia*, 99. William Roper's biography of More likewise includes More's advice to Cromwell: 'if you follow my poore aduise, you shall in your Counsell-giuing, euer tell [the king] what he ought to do, but neuer what he is able to do. So shall you shew your selfe a true and faythfull seruant, & a right worthy Cou[n]sellour'; William Roper, *The Mirrour of Vertue in Worldly Greatness; or, The Life of Sir Thomas More, Knight* (London: De la More Press, 1902), 92. This contrast is made clear by a manuscript written around the same time as Cavendish and Roper's biographies and inspired by Machiavelli's *Prince*, which echoes but reverses de Guevara's sentiment: 'our purpose at present is not to show what a prince is permitted to do and what he is not permitted to do, but only to show by what ways and means a prince can maintain or lose his state'; From Peter S. Donaldson, ed., *A Machiavellian Treatise* (Cambridge: Cambridge University Press, 2009), 138.

Machiavelli presents two intertwined critiques of the princely virtues at the outset of Chapter XV.[23] The first is familiar: one cannot expect a single, fallible man to be well-learned and adhere strictly to all the virtues. Although 'everyone will acknowledge that it would be most praiseworthy for a ruler to have all the above-mentioned qualities that are held to be good',[24] such as liberality, piety and so on, 'it is not possible to have all of them' and furthermore, 'circumstances do not permit living a completely virtuous life'.[25] As we have already seen, writers from the medieval period onward had accepted this premise, providing it as the foundation for the necessity of political counsel. Machiavelli, however, takes it in a different direction. He has a very different solution to the problem of the prince. His answer, representing his second critique, is more revolutionary. Even if the prince *could* adopt all the virtues, Machiavelli writes, there is a further skill needed, for 'doing some things that seem virtuous may result in one's ruin, whereas doing other things that seem vicious may strengthen one's position and cause one to flourish'.[26] On occasion a prince must embrace an action which appears as vice in order to pursue his advantage.[27] Thus, the virtues are all but meaningless beyond their appearance to those upon whose esteem the prince's power is based. The prince must be willing to employ the virtues *as necessity dictates*, and in that way, rethink how he conceptualises the virtues as virtues.

As such, Machiavelli has two pieces of advice for the prince. First, he must have prudence: 'one must be sufficiently prudent [*prudente*][28] to know how to avoid becoming notorious for those virtues that would destroy one's power and seek to avoid those vices that are not politically dangerous'.[29] Machiavelli's definition of prudence comes in Chapter XXI, shortly on the heels of his discussion of the other cardinal and princely virtues, and pertains directly to this skill of seeing through the appearance

23 For the princely virtues see Skinner and Price, 'Introduction', xvi.

24 Machiavelli, *The Prince*, 55. 'every one will confesse, it were exceedingly praiseworthy for a Prince to be adorned with all the above nam'd qualities that are good', Machiavelli, *Machiavel's Prince*, 119.

25 Machiavelli, *The Prince*, 55. 'this is not possible, nor doe humane conditions admit such perfection in vertues', Machiavelli, *Machiavel's Prince*, 119–20.

26 Machiavelli, *The Prince*, 55. 'some things we shall find which have the colour and face of Vertue [*virtù*], and following them, will lead thee to thy destruction; whereas some others, that shall as much seeme vice, if we take the course they lead us, shall discover unto us the way to our safety and well-being', Machiavelli, *Machiavel's Prince*, 120.

27 See Cox, 'Deliberative Rhetoric in *The Prince*', 1112, 1116.

28 F: 'so much fursight wisdome and discretioun'. QC: 'bee soe wise'.

29 Machiavelli, *The Prince*, 55. 'it is necessary for him to be so discreet, that he know how to avoid the infamie of those vices, which would thrust him out of his State', Machiavelli, *Machiavel's Prince*, 120.

of vice and virtue to what will be most advantageous.[30] As he writes, 'prudence [*prudenza*] consists in knowing how to assess the dangers, and to choose the least bad course of action as being the right one to follow'.[31] Prudence had been defined in the past in similar terms – an ability to judge good and bad – but this had been in regard to morality. Machiavelli here changes it to an ability to judge good and bad in terms of *utile*, not *honestum*.[32] Second, the prince must embrace deception himself: 'foxiness should be well concealed: one must be a great feigner and dissembler'.[33] Even the adoption of these more pernicious vices may be less disadvantageous than following their associated virtues, as long as the prince is able to manage the people's perception of his actions, employing *paradiastole*, or rhetorical re-description. The adoption of a vice is only disadvantageous if the people recognise it and are motivated to hatred or contempt by its performance.[34]

Machiavelli's view of prudence and *paradiastole*, then, is notably different from those of the orthodox humanists. For them, prudence had been useful in seeing through re-description; for Machiavelli, it is the virtue which allows one to employ it. Machiavelli suggests that the prince himself must become the master of *paradiastole* in order to hold the esteem of the people. Machiavelli has little trust in the people's ability to see through such deception if it is well executed, for 'men are so naive, and so much dominated by immediate needs, that a skilful deceiver always finds plenty

30 Skinner, *Machiavelli*, 40–1.

31 Machiavelli, *The Prince*, 79. 'the principall point of judgement is in discerning between the qualities of inconvenients, and not taking the bad for the good', Machiavelli, *Machiavel's Prince*, 186.

32 Jacob Soll, 'The Reception of *The Prince* 1513–1700, or Why We Understand Machiavelli the Way We Do', *Social Research* 81, no. 1 (2014): 33–9 gives a history of *phronesis*/prudence and details Machiavelli's redefinition of the term.

33 Machiavelli, *The Prince*, 62. 'it is necessary to understand how to set a good colour upon this disposition, and to bee able to faine and dissemble thoroughly', Machiavelli, *Machiavel's Prince*, 138. Notably, in the translation produced in 1640 by Edward Dacres, this is rendered as putting a 'good colour' on the disposition of the fox, and above, in reference to the seeming nature of virtue and vice, Dacres uses the same term. This connects Machiavelli's advice clearly to the tradition of *paradiastole*, which was often spoken of using the same vocabulary; Quentin Skinner, 'Paradiastole: Redescribing the Vices as Virtues', in *Renaissance Figures of Speech*, ed. Sylvia Adamson, Gavin Alexander and Katrin Ettenhuber (Cambridge: Cambridge University Press, 2007), 149–65, 157. Dacres also explicitly condemns this practice, noting that in these chapters Machiavelli 'descends to particulars, perswading his Prince in the sixteenth to such a supplenese of disposition, as that upon occasion hee can make use either of liberality or miserablenesse as need shall require' and similarly in the other chapters as regards the other virtues and vices, Machiavelli, *Machiavel's Prince*, 141–2. Dacres was not the only one to read Machiavelli this way in the seventeenth century, see Skinner, *Reason and Rhetoric*, 172.

34 See Garver, *Machiavelli and the History of Prudence*, 28 for the analogous relationship between the use of rhetoric in presenting advice and the role of the prince in persuading the people of his reputation.

of people who will let themselves be deceived'.[35] This is a rejection of the Ciceronian use of *decorum* to connect *utile* and *honestum*. For Cicero, *decorum* 'cannot be separated from the honourable [*honestum*]; for what is proper is also honourable and what is honourable is also proper'.[36] *Decorum* 'is perceptible in every virtue' and is 'entirely meshed with virtue', so any action that is comely will also be honest, and any action that is in accordance with virtue will also accord with *decorum*.[37] As *decorum* rests in the opinion of those around us, speaking and living in accordance with *decorum* will produce a good reputation.[38] This is the basis for the connection between *honestum* and *utile*; for Cicero, honest actions will be useful, because they will always incur good repute. Machiavelli rejects this idea: sometimes honest actions will produce a bad reputation, and sometimes dishonest ones a good reputation. Cicero was wrong to suggest an essential link between them.

For Machiavelli, prudence is also essential to navigating the changing winds of Fortune.[39] This means that, despite the definition he gives in Chapter XXI, it is almost impossible to define what exactly *constitutes* prudence – what activities or behaviours define prudent action or the prudential person – for it varies with the times.[40] The path that Machiavelli endorses involves using both virtues and vices as tools, according to the variation in circumstances: 'he must be prepared to vary his conduct as the winds of fortune and changing circumstances constrain him and, as I said before, not deviate from right conduct if possible, but be capable of entering upon the path of wrongdoing when this becomes necessary'.[41] Machiavelli's view of the virtues is thus dependent on an understanding of fluctuations of circumstance and necessity.

This discussion of necessity is dependent on Machiavelli's engagement with the tradition of *kairos*.[42] In addition to the rhetorical traditions of *kairos* – both the sophistic understanding implying moral flexibility and the Plutarchan view enabling *parrhesia* (adopted by Elyot) – *kairos* could also be understood

[35] Machiavelli, *The Prince*, 62. 'men are so simple and yeeld so much to the present necessities, that hee who hath a mind to deceive, shall always find another that will be deceived', Machiavelli, *Machiavel's Prince*, 138.

[36] Cicero, *De Officiis*, I.94. [37] Cicero, *De Officiis*, I.95. [38] Cicero, *De Officiis*, I.97.

[39] Garver, *Machiavelli and the History of Prudence*, 7; Stacey, *Roman Monarchy*, 282–5.

[40] Garver, *Machiavelli and the History of Prudence*, 10, 12: prudence, understood in this way, is 'easier to accomplish than to explain . . . easier to perform than to account for'.

[41] Machiavelli, *The Prince*, 62. 'it behooves [the prince] to have a mind so disposd as to turne and take the advantage of all winds and fortunes; and as formerly I said, not forsake the good; while he can, but to know how to make use of the evill upon necessity', Machiavelli, *Machiavel's Prince*, 140.

[42] See Paul, 'The Use of *Kairos*', 43–78.

as a theory of political action. This understanding was built upon the same temporal view of *kairos*, denoting both the character of a time – as in a season – as well as a rare opportunity or occasion to be taken advantage of.[43] For this, Plutarch was once again the model, as *kairos* is one of the most important factors in determining the success of political actions in his *Lives*. He gives the example of Cato, whose qualities, admirable though they were, did not accord with his times. He 'fared just as fruits do which make their appearance out of season [*kairos*]', as his qualities were 'look[ed] upon . . . with delight and admiration' but did not lead to success.[44] Likewise, political leaders must make use of the opportunities presented to them, as Caesar, who 'took advantage of the favourable instant . . . and thereby . . . in a brief portion of one day he made himself master of three camps'.[45] By contrast, Philopoemen 'threw away his life . . . by hastening to attack Messene before occasion offered'.[46] The lesson of Plutarch's *exempla* is that 'it is [*kairos*] which gives the scales their saving or their fatal inclination'.[47] This urge to act, whereby an actor can assert his agency against the press of *chronos*, often slips into a reverse relationship, whereby *kairos* forces action, and thus becomes strongly connected to a consideration of necessity, leading to the same sort of moral relativism presented by the sophists. For example, Plutarch writes that Titus' 'natural gift of leadership' led him to realise that he should not only rule 'in accordance with the laws' but must also 'when [*kairos*] required it' know 'how to dominate the laws for the common good'.[48] Echoing the sophists, Plutarch writes that 'honourable action has its fitting time and season: nay, rather, it is the observance of due bounds that constitutes an utter difference between honourable and base actions', a sentiment echoed in his *Moralia*: 'every natural virtue produceth the effect to which it is ordained better or worse, according as its season is more or less proper.'[49] In Plutarch, *kairos* not only defines political success, but also defines the bounds of necessity and right action.

Machiavelli's use of this tradition is expressed through his emphasis on *occasione*, most notably in the sixth chapter of *The Prince*.[50] Like Plutarch,

[43] See James Kinneavy, 'Kairos: A Neglected Concept in Classical Rhetoric', in *Rhetoric and Praxis: The Contribution of Classical Rhetoric to Practical Reasoning*, ed. Jean Dietz Moss (Washington, DC: Catholic University of America Press, 1986), 79.

[44] Plutarch, *Plutarch's Lives with an English Translation*, trans. Bernadotte Perrin, vol. 2 (Cambridge, MA: Harvard University Press, 1914), 8:151.

[45] Plutarch, *Lives*, 7:505 [46] Plutarch, *Lives*, 10:389. [47] Plutarch, *Lives*, 2:521.

[48] Plutarch, *Lives*, 10:392. [49] Plutarch, *Lives*, 5:101; Plutarch, *Moralia*, 5:495.

[50] Plutarch's *Lives* were prevalent and available in Machiavelli's Florence; see Marianne Pade, *The Reception of Plutarch's Lives in Fifteenth-Century Italy* (Copenhagen: Museum Tusculanum Press, University of Copenhagen, 2007), 15, 343–4, 347; Joseph Geiger, 'Lives and Moralia: How Were Put

Machiavelli sets out examples of 'remarkable men' to be imitated.[51] In these exemplary cases, the leaders were dependent on Fortune only for the opportunity or occasion to demonstrate their *virtù*: 'they owed nothing to luck [*fortuna*] except the opportunity [*occasione*] to shape the material into the form that seemed best to them'.[52] Machiavelli sets out a mutually supportive relationship between *occasione* and *virtù*; neither can be realised without the other: 'If they had lacked the opportunity, the strength [*virtù*] of their spirit [*animo*] would have been sapped; if they had lacked ability [*virtù*], the opportunity would have been wasted.'[53] *Occasione* for Machiavelli, as for Plutarch, functions as a rare opportunity in chronological time, which only the truly prudent can recognise and take hold of: 'These opportunities [*occasioni*], then, permitted these men to be successful, and their surpassing abilities [*virtù*] enabled them to recognise and grasp these opportunities; the outcome was that their own countries were ennobled and flourished greatly.'[54] *Virtù* is limited and defined by the knowledge of opportunity.

Machiavelli was well aware of the tradition and iconography of *kairos*/*occasio*. In his 'Tercets on Fortune', Machiavelli describes *occasio* as living in the paths between the wheels as a 'tousel-haired and simple maiden' who 'frisks about', followed by her companion 'Penitence'.[55] Likewise, in his poem 'Occasion', *Occasio* is a beautiful woman who stands on a wheel and, for that reason, 'never can be still'.[56] The back of her head is bald, so that she cannot be grasped once she has passed, and she wears a veil so 'in passing I be recognized by none'.[57] She is accompanied by Penitence, and 'He does keep her who cannot capture me!'.[58] Those who 'chattering ...

Asunder What Plutarch Hath Joined Together', in *The Unity of Plutarch's Work*, ed. Anastasios Nikolaidis (Berlin: Walter de Gruyter, 2008), 5–12.

51 Machiavelli, *The Prince*, 19.

52 Machiavelli, *The Prince*, 20. 'it will not appeare, that they had other help of fortune, than the occasion, which presented them with the matter wherein they might introduce what forme they then pleas'd', Machiavelli, *Machiavel's Prince*, 35.

53 Machiavelli, *The Prince*, 20. 'without that occasion, the vertue of their mind had been extinguish'd; and without that vertue, the occasion had been offer'd in vaine', Machiavelli, *Machiavel's Prince*, 35–6.

54 Machiavelli, *The Prince*, 20. 'These occasions [gives examples] therefore made these men happy, and their excellent vertue made the occasion be taken notice of, whereby their country became ennobled, and exceeding fortunate.' Machiavelli, *Machiavel's Prince*, 36. As Skinner and Price, 'Introduction', 107 point out, Cesare Borgia also stands as an exemplar of a leader who knows and takes advantage of *occasione*.

55 Niccolò Machiavelli, 'Tercets on Fortune', in *Machiavelli: The Chief Works and Others*, ed. Allan Gilbert (Durham; London: Duke University Press, 1989), 747.

56 Niccolò Machiavelli, 'Occasion', in *An Anthology of Italian Poems, 13th-19th Century*, ed. Lorna de'Lucchi (New York: Alfred A. Knopf, 1922), 117.

57 Machiavelli, 'Occasion', 117. 58 Machiavelli, 'Occasion', 117.

waste time so rare,/ Immersed in matters vain and manifold' miss *occasio*, and she 'slip[s] our of your hold!'.[59] It takes a rare individual to know and grasp *kairos*, and in *The Prince* Machiavelli imagines this strong figure who is able to grasp her.

These lessons regarding *kairos* and *virtù* are applied in the final chapter of *The Prince*. Like the opening epistle, this chapter is addressed to Lorenzo de' Medici and draws directly on a work of Isocrates – in this case his *Panegyricus*, which urges the people of Athens to take up arms against the barbarian invaders. Echoing Chapter VI, Machiavelli rhetorically ponders whether 'the present time is appropriate for welcoming a new ruler', as 'there is matter that provides an opportunity [*occasione*] for a far-seeing [*prudente*] and able man [*virtuoso*] to mould it into a form that will bring honour to him and benefit all its inhabitants'.[60] The moral rectitude of the act is based on the consideration of its necessity (he quotes Livy on this),[61] and the Medici are forced into action, for 'Circumstances are now very favourable indeed, and the difficulties cannot be very great when the circumstances are propitious, if only your family will imitate the men I have proposed as exemplars'.[62] Machiavelli ends his chapter, and his book, by concluding that 'this opportunity [*occasione*] . . . must not be missed'.[63] Machiavelli counsels that *kairos* demands action from Lorenzo de Medici, never mind the usual expectations of virtuous action.

When it comes to the counsellor himself, Machiavelli is conflicted, but ultimately distrustful, which is perhaps unsurprising in a vision where human nature leads us to consider only our own self-interest, and where prudential counsellors will constantly and actively be changing their allegiances. Princes must be wary of a servant who 'is thinking more about his own affairs than about yours' and whose 'actions are designed for his own interests', for such a man 'will never make a good minister, and you can never trust him'.[64] In the figure of the counsellor Machiavelli finds a conflict

[59] Machiavelli, 'Occasion', 117.

[60] Machiavelli, *The Prince*, 87. 'the times might serve to honour a new Prince', as 'there were matter, that might minister occasion to a wise and valorous prince, to introduce such a forme, that might doe honour to him', Machiavelli, *Machiavel's Prince*, 212.

[61] Machiavelli, *The Prince*, 88.

[62] Machiavelli, *The Prince*, 88. 'Here is an exceeding good disposition thereto: nor can there be, where there is a good disposition, a great difficulty, provided that use bee made of those orders, which I propounded for ayme and direction to you', Machiavelli, *Machiavel's Prince*, 215.

[63] Machiavelli, *The Prince*, 91. 'this occasion [*occasione*] should not bee let passe', Machiavelli, *Machiavel's Prince*, 220.

[64] Machiavelli, *The Prince*, 80. 'stud[ies] more for his owne advantage than thine, and that in all his actions, hee searches most after his owne profit . . . [he] shall never prove a good servant, nor canst thou ever relie upon him', Machiavelli, *Machiavel's Prince*, 189–90.

between the humanist theories that he is willing to jettison and those which he desires to retain. He clings to the view that the counsellor must be selfless in classically humanist terms: 'a man who governs a state should never think about himself or his own affairs but always about the ruler, and concern himself only with the ruler's affairs'.[65] He, however, has placed this figure in a world which makes selflessness impossible, or at least inadvisable.

As a remedy to his redefined problem of counsel, Machiavelli makes two suggestions. First, the prince ought to keep a counsellor's loyalty by 'honouring him, enriching him, attaching him to himself', so that the prince's and counsellor's interests are united.[66] In other words, to make him more servile by making him dependent on the prince's will. Of course, Machiavelli was distrustful of such tactics when applied to mercenaries, so it is unclear whether he actually thought such a strategy would work when applied to counsellors.[67]

We might be inclined to think not, because he goes on to suggest, second, an inversion of the model of counsel proposed by orthodox humanists in an effort to bind royal counsellors to the prince. Whereas for his predecessors the prudence of the counsellor determines the prudence of the prince, Machiavelli's distrust of counsellors leads him to suggest that the influence should work in the other direction: 'Although many hold that a ruler may be properly considered shrewd [*prudente*] because of the high quality of his advisers [*consigli*], and not because he himself is shrewd, this is undoubtedly a mistaken view.'[68] In a rare generalisation, Machiavelli suggests instead that 'it is an infallible rule that a prince who is not himself wise [*savio*] cannot be soundly advised [*consigliato bene*]'.[69] The exception to this is if the prince 'happens to put himself in the hands of a man who is very able [*uomo prudentissimo*] and controls everything',[70] but in such an instance, Machiavelli points out, 'such a governor [*governatore*] would

[65] Machiavelli, *The Prince*, 80. In some ways the 1640 translation comes closer to the original '*lo Stato di uno in mano*': 'he that holds the sterne of the State in hand, ought never call home his cares to his owne particular, but give himselfe wholly to his Princes service', Machiavelli, *Machiavel's Prince*, 190.

[66] Machiavelli, *The Prince*, 80. 'honouring him, enriching, and obliging him to him', Machiavelli 1640, p. 190.

[67] On mercenaries see Machiavelli, *Machiavel's Prince*, 43–51.

[68] Machiavelli, *The Prince*, 82. 'some men have thought, that a Prince, that gaines the opinion to bee wise, may be held so, not by his owne naturall indowments, but by the good counsells hee hath about him; without question they are deceivd', Machiavelli, *Machiavel's Prince*, 194.

[69] Machiavelli, *The Prince*, 82. 'is a generall rule and never failes, that a Prince who of himselfe is not wise [*savio*], can never bee well advisd', Machiavelli, *Machiavel's Prince*, 194.

[70] 'unlesse he should light upon one alone, wholly to direct and governe him, who himselfe were a very wise man', Machiavelli, *Machiavel's Prince*, 194.

soon deprive him of his state'.[71] Counsel would shift into command. The other alternative is to rely on the prudence of a group of wise counsellors, but this would lead to confusion, for the prince 'will always hear conflicting opinions, and will be incapable of reconciling them', as – once again – the counsellors will follow their 'own interests' and the prince 'will not understand this tendency or be able to control them'.[72] Machiavelli rejects both models whereby the prince's prudence is gleaned from external counsel, because in such cases the prince cannot control his counsellors, leading to their manipulation of him for their own interests. Machiavelli concludes 'that good advice, from whomsoever it may come, must have its source in the shrewdness [*prudenzia*] of the ruler; the ruler's shrewdness [*prudenzia*] cannot derive from sound advice'.[73] Machiavelli thus utterly rejects the traditional humanist view of the ends and means of counsel, based on the suggestion that the counsellor will inevitably counsel according to his own interests, and not those of the prince.[74] A counsellor who is wiser – and thus more powerful – than the prince, usurps the reins of government. This might not have seemed such a problem to the humanists, who were often keen to have a counsellor rule the prince, but for Machiavelli it is a result to be avoided, at least from the point of view of a Medici prince.

When it comes to republics, discussed in Machiavelli's later *Discourses on Livy*, there are other solutions to the problems of counsel he had set out in *The Prince*. First, the people are more likely to be persuaded to change with the times; a republic 'is better able to adapt itself to diverse circumstances

[71] Machiavelli, *The Prince*, 82. 'for that governour in a short time would deprive him of his State', Machiavelli, *Machiavel's Prince*, 194.

[72] Machiavelli, *The Prince*, 82. 'each one of the counsellers, probably will follow that which is most properly his owne; and hee shall never finde the meanes to amend or discerne these things', Machiavelli, *Machiavel's Prince*, 195.

[73] Machiavelli, *The Prince*, 82. 'that counsells from whencesoever they proceed, must needs take their beginning from the Princes wisdome, and not the wisdome of the Prince from good counsells'. Machiavelli, *Machiavel's Prince*, 195. It is one of the rare occasions that Machiavelli actually refers to a *consigliere*, either in *The Prince* or the *Discourses*, usually referring instead to *ministri*, as he does in Chapter XXII of *The Prince* or '*che consigliano*' (those that counsel) as he does through much of the *Discourses*. It may be worth noting that Machiavelli's comments on the suspicion of the counsellor mark the only occasion where Dacres commends Machiavelli's text, going as far as to say that 'our Author will make him amends for his other errours by his good advice in his 22 Chap whether I referre him', *Machiavel's Prince*, 197–8.

[74] As James Hankins, 'Machiavelli, Civic Humanism, and the Humanist Politics of Virtue', *Italian Culture* 32, no. 2 (2014): 98–109, 105 suggests, Machiavelli's work 'constituted a subversion of the central premises of the politics of virtue' associated with Renaissance humanism, 'because Machiavelli rejects the solution of the ancient Greek philosophers to political instability and infelicity, which is to empower a political elite consisting of the wise and virtuous'.

[*diversità de' temporali*] owing to the diversity found among its citizens [*diversità de' cittadini*] than a prince can do'.[75] The people are also more open to correction than the prince; they are 'capable of grasping the truth and readily yields when a man, worthy of confidence, lays the truth before it [*da uomo degno di fede è detto loro vero*]'.[76] A 'Grave Man [*uomo grave*]' has 'Influence ... in restraining an Excited Crowd' for 'nothing is more suitable to restrain an excited crowd than respect for some man of gravity and standing [*uomo grave e di autorità*]', who brings them back to an understanding of where their actual good lies.[77] This is in contrast to a prince, who is not as good a judge of character and who will 'often err where his passions are involved, as these are much stronger than those of the populace' without the remedy of counsel.[78] In Chapter 58 of Book I, Machiavelli argues that, whereas the prince will prove obstinate to good counsel, the people will submit: 'A licentious and turbulent populace, when a good man [*un uomo buono*] can obtain a hearing, can easily be brought to behave itself; but there is no one to talk to a bad prince, nor is there any remedy but the sword.'[79] Just as a prince should be 'warned by his advisers [*chi lo consigliasse*]', so to the people ought to have the same failsafe, in the case that they too might err.[80] He concludes that 'when [the people] can get advice [*consigliati*] as a prince can, it makes few mistakes than does a prince'.[81] In short, counsel has far more likelihood of success when given to a people than to a prince.

Machiavelli suggests that even the suspicions he had had about self-interested counsellors are assuaged in a republic. First, just as with every member of the republic, the counsellor's interests are likely to be in line with those of the whole, without the need for bribery. He is, after all, a *cittadino*, and thus will be just as likely as any other citizen to want to bring about the maintenance of liberty within the republic. It is true, Machiavelli suggests in his chapter on conspiracies, that the familiars of a prince should not be trusted, for 'a prince ... should fear those on whom he has conferred excessive favours', but no equivalent warning is given regarding the counsellors of the people.[82] This may be related to a second point: this counsellor is an orator, whose words and character will be judged by the people more perceptively than the prince, as Machiavelli had established in Chapter 34 of Book III. We must as well consider

75 Niccolò Machiavelli, *The Discourses* (London: Penguin Books, 2000), 431.
76 Machiavelli, *The Discourses*, 115.
77 Machiavelli, *The Discourses*, 242.
78 Machiavelli, *The Discourses*, 255.
79 Machiavelli, *The Discourses*, 256.
80 Machiavelli, *The Discourses*, 499.
81 Machiavelli, *The Discourses*, 500.
82 Machiavelli, *The Discourses*, 404.

Machiavelli's dedication to the rhetorical writings of Quintilian. For Quintilian, the good orator is by definition a good man, and hence would not be likely to lead the people astray.[83] Machiavelli seems to assume the same in the *Discourses*: the figure in question is an *uomo buono*, an *uomo grave*, an *uomo degno di fede*. The orator will not convince the people unless his words and character are reflective of truth and worth. The people will only be persuaded by someone who has their own interests at heart. Both 'the advisers of a republic and the counsellors of a prince [*che quegli che consigliano una republica, e quegli che consigliano uno principe*] are undoubtedly in a difficult position', but it is only the former who will avoid the two problems Machiavelli had set out in *The Prince*.[84]

In the context of a republic, then, the counsellor is not such a mistrusted figure, and can take a role more like that assigned to him by the English humanists: guiding and even leading the sovereign (in this case the people) to right action. Whereas those humanists had used a powerful counsellor to inject monarchy with republican principles, for Machiavelli, it is only in a republic that a counsellor can be expected to uphold those principles. It is not, however, the republican model of counsel from Machiavelli which gains traction in the following decades and becomes associated with 'Machiavellianism'.[85]

ii Machiavelli in England

Upon its reception in England in the sixteenth century, Machiavelli's *Prince* becomes understood as presenting advice not only to princes, but also to counsellors, and so the history of Machiavellianism becomes inseparable from a history of the role of political counsel. Although the first publication of an entire Machiavellian text in English does not occur until the 1562 translation of the *Arte of Warre*, and *The Prince* and the *Discourses* are not printed in English until much later, there was an active English readership of Machiavelli's works even within the first decade of their publication in Italian.[86] In fact, of the small number of examples of

[83] Garver, *Machiavelli and the History of Prudence*, 148 also points out that in *The Discourses* 'the relevant moral and intellectual qualities are dimensions of rhetorical excellence'.

[84] Machiavelli, *The Discourses*, 500.

[85] Machiavelli's views are not necessarily consistent with 'Machiavellianism'. Machiavellian thought is marked by 'the observable appropriate of Machiavelli's vocabulary and theoretical framework used to deal with the unpredictable, the contingent in political life', Keith David Howard, 'Fadrique Furió Ceriol's Machiavellian Vocabulary of Contingency', *Renaissance Studies* 26, no. 5 (2012): 642.

[86] Felix Raab, *The English Face of Machiavelli: A Changing Interpretation, 1500–1700* (London: Routledge & K. Paul, 1964); Sydney Anglo, *Machiavelli – The First Century: Studies in*

articulated responses to Machiavelli in the first half of the sixteenth century, most address an English context, and the first attempts to apply his theories to political analysis were by English writers.[87] These responses were intimately connected to the discourse of counsel and the figure of the counsellor. For example, in 1539 Henry Parker, Lord Morley wrote to Thomas Cromwell recommending both the *Istorie Florentine* and *Il Principe* to the high-profile counsellor, suggesting that the latter 'ys surely a very speciall good thing for youre Lordschip, whiche are ny aboughte oure Soueraigne Lorde in Counsell'.[88] It would seem that other prominent counsellors thought the same, as there are records of the purchase or ownership of *Il Principe* by the likes of Thomas Smith, William Thomas and William Cecil.[89]

Large selections of Machiavelli's texts were printed as part of other works, and these too were specifically dedicated to counsellors. Perhaps the greatest example of such selective use of Machiavelli is presented in the 1590 translation of Francisco Sansovino's *The Quintensence of Wit* by soldier and writer Robert Hitchcock. Although Sansovino had originally dedicated his precepts to the Holy Roman Emperor Rudolph II, Hitchcock dedicates his to Robert Cecil, who in the same year had been made Secretary of State, emerging as one of the leading counsellors in Elizabeth's court. Taken from Sansovino's *Concette Politici* published in 1578, and including the added *concetti* of the 1583 amended *Propositioni . . . di cose di Stato*, Hitchcock faithfully translates all 805 of Sansovino's listed maxims, including the 186 directly derived from Machiavelli's works.[90] Notably, although this represented the largest contribution to the *Quintensence* from any single author, Machiavelli is not listed among the 'names of those Authors and writers' from whom 'the conceites of this

Enthusiasm, Hostility, and Irrelevance (Oxford: Oxford University Press, 2005); Petrina, *Machiavelli in the British Isles*; Alessandra Petrina, 'Reginald Pole and the Reception of the *Principe* in Henrician England', in *Machiavellian Encounters in Tudor and Stuart England: Literary and Political Influences from the Reformation to the Restoration*, ed. Alessandro Arienzo and Alessandra Petrina (New York: Routledge, 2016), 14. See particularly Petrina, *Machiavelli in the British Isles*, 15: 'There is ample evidence for the circulation of Machiavelli's books in England, and for an articulate readership that dates back as far as the 1530s.'

87 Anglo, *Machiavelli – The First Century*, 102.

88 Henry Ellis, *Original Letters, Illustrative of English History* (London: Harding, Triphook, and Lepard, 1824), 66. The dating of the letter as 1539 is given by Petrina, *Machiavelli in the British Isles*, 15, although Ellis, *Original Letters*, 63 and Anglo, *Machiavelli – The First Century*, 97 date the letter to 1537.

89 Anglo, *Machiavelli – The First Century*, 20; Petrina, *Machiavelli in the British Isles*, 20.

90 See Vincent Luciani, 'Sansovino's *Concetti Politici* and their Debt to Machiavelli', *PMLA* 67, no. 5 (1952): 839. Luciani provides a meticulous account of the influence of Machiavelli on the *Concetti*, including a list of the Machiavellian precepts and their sources.

present booke be gathered'.[91] Nevertheless, educated English readers would have known where most of these precepts were coming from, perhaps even more intimately and with more immediacy than modern-day readers. For example, John Donne, poet and secretary to the Lord Keeper of the Great Seal, correctly identified the passages drawn from Machiavelli in his 1588 copy of the *Propositioni*, and there is no reason to think that Hitchcock's talented and educated patron, the counsellor Robert Cecil, would lack the ability to do the same.[92]

With the exception of the 1562 translation of the *Arte of Warre*, when Machiavelli's works were published in English, translators consistently dedicated such works to counsellor-figures. Thomas Bedingfield's translation of *The Florentine Historie* was dedicated to Sir Christopher Hatton, Lord Chancellor of England, as it contained matters for 'such as be called to consultation of publike affaires & gouernment'.[93] In the same way, Edward Dacres' later translations of the *Discourses* and *The Prince* are both addressed to James, Duke of Lennox, prominent councillor and cousin to the king. Dacres notes that Machiavelli's work will be especially of use to him whose 'neereness of bloud, as affection and favour, his Sacred Majestie may most probably imploy in this ship of State near the helme'.[94]

The English connection between Machiavelli's works and the role of the counsellor was first established by one of the earliest English responses to Machiavelli, Reginald Pole's *Apologia ad Carolum Quintum* of 1539 (the same Reginald Pole who appeared in Starkey's *Dialogue*). The use of Machiavelli by Pole is only incidental to his purpose: an attack on the Henrician Reformation, which Pole argues can be blamed on a lack of good counsel in the court of Henry VIII.[95] Pole suggests that it is the timidity of the majority of Henry's council, combined with the vicious forwardness of one – Thomas Cromwell – which is to blame for Henry's actions in the Break with Rome. He then suggests that Cromwell got his ideas from another satanic counsellor, Machiavelli in his *Prince*, and

[91] 'The historie of *Florence*' is listed, although only 25 of the 186 Machiavellian precepts come from this work; Luciani 1952: 836. It has been suggested that this had to do with the papal ban on place against Machiavelli's works; see Luciani, 'Sansovino's *Concetti Politici*', 823, 839; Paul F. Grendler, 'Francesco Sansovino and Italian Popular History 1560–1600', *Studies in the Renaissance* 16 (1969): 163.

[92] Grendler, 'Francesco Sansovino', 163.

[93] The letter is dated 1588, seven years before the translation is published, and three years before the death of Hatton. It is unclear why Bedingfield waited until after Hatton's death to publish the work, although we may speculate that was related to the reputation of Machiavelli at the time.

[94] Niccolò Machiavelli, *Machiavels Discovrses*, trans. Edward Dacres (London, 1636), A, 4^{v}.

[95] Anglo, *Machiavelli – The First Century*, 155; Petrina, 'Reginald Pole', 18.

proceeds to offer up his own impassioned critique of the text.[96] Machiavelli is 'an enemy of the human race' who seeks to destroy 'religion, piety and every natural inclination of virtue'.[97] According to Pole, Cromwell had personally recommended *The Prince* to him, although did not send him the text as he later 'regretted having exposed to much of his policies in my company'.[98] Machiavelli's book is presented as pernicious counsel, which will lead to the downfall of any prince who follows its lessons.[99]

Although he addresses himself to princes (to rulers and their sons, to prevent their 'swallow[ing] this most evil and pernicious doctrine'),[100] Pole's subject is counsellors, for he suggests that Machiavelli 'concedes this splendid battleground to all counsellors of princes [*Principnm* [sic] *Consiliariis*], for them to exercise their talents on, so that they continually invent specious arguments borrowed either from religion or from some other pretence of virtue [*virtutis similtudine*]', suggesting that Cromwell himself used this as the basis for his own 'doctrine [*doctrina*]'.[101] Connecting the language of *paradiastole* with that of *kairos*, Pole suggests that Cromwell 'thought that it was easy to extract arguments from the attendant circumstances [*illis circumstantiis*] which, so to speak, clothe each and every matter before it can acquire the name of virtue [*antequam virtutis nomen habere possit*].'[102] For Pole, Machiavelli requires the counsellor to be the one to 'lend some semblance of virtue to any desire whatever of a prince, along with some pretence of those things which contribute to the realization of virtue', otherwise they are 'unworthy to be summoned to [the prince's] advisory councils [*Principis consilia*]'.[103] This is, as we may note, inconsistent with what Machiavelli actually says; he gives the prince the role of turning vice into virtue as necessary. Machiavelli's comments regarding the role of counsellors are short, and he gives them little power over the prince. Contrastingly, in Pole's reading of Machiavelli, counsellors are still very much at the prince's command, but have the power to 'poison' him with Machiavellian principles, and it is they – not the prince – who are to become the masters of the moment and *paradiastole*.

96 Petrina, 'Reginald Pole', 25.

97 Reginald Pole, 'Apology', in *Cambridge Translations of Renaissance Philosophical Texts: Volume 2*, ed. Jill Kraye (Cambridge; New York: Cambridge University Press, 2010), 275.

98 Pole, 'Apology', 275. One of these 'policies' is that the counsellor ought to obey the will of the prince, but that the prince is not constrained by ordinary morality, precisely the reversal noted at the end of the previous chapter.

99 Pole suggests that, based on what he heard upon his recent trip to Florence, Machiavelli actually wrote the text in order to give bad advice to the Medici in the hopes of their downfall, Pole, 'Apology', 285.

100 Pole, 'Apology', 275. 101 Pole, 'Apology', 276. 102 Pole, 'Apology', 276.

103 Pole, 'Apology', 276.

iii The Machiavellian Counsellor

Consistent with this reception history, in the sixteenth century Machiavelli's advice becomes not only the content of political counsel to the prince, but also advice to counsellors regarding how they ought to frame their own speech and actions, a trend borne out by the English translation and adoption of Machiavellian texts on the subject.[104] The clearest example of such reception is provided by the translation of the Spanish writer Fadrique Furió Ceriol's Machiavellian work on the counsellor by the prominent English humanist Thomas Blundeville, a writer and translator from Norfolk, in 1570.[105] Furió Ceriol studied at Louvain in the 1550s and then joined the court of Philip II in the 1560s.[106] His short *El concejo y consejeros de príncipes* was published in Antwerp in 1559 and borrows extensively from Machiavelli's *Prince.*[107]

Blundeville's English translation, or rather abridgement – *A very brief and profitable treatise declaring howe many counsells and what maner of counselers a prince that will gouerne well ought to haue* – is intended to be read and adopted by counsellors, not princes. In contrast to Furió Ceriol's original dedication of the text to Philip II, Blundeville's is dedicated to the prominent counsellor, Robert Dudley, Earl of Leicester, and is meant to be 'a glasse' of the 'vertues and qualities that . . . ought to raigne in euery other good counseler'.[108] In addition, he removes much of the explicitly Machiavellian content; Furió Ceriol's original text contained near word-for-word quotations from *The Prince*, which Blundeville does not translate, claiming to have cut 'all superfluous talke' in his abridged translation.[109] That being said, the Machiavellian themes still persist, even where the verbatim passages have been removed.

Some elements of the text appear to be drawn from a more traditional discourse of counsel. The need for counsel remains couched in the usual terms – 'bicause the Prince can not heare all, see al, knowe all, and prouide

104 Teresa Bałuk-Ulewiczowa, *Goslicius' Ideal Senator and His Cultural Impact Over the Centuries: Shakespearean Reflections* (Krakow: Polska Akademia Umiejętności, 2009), 26, 42.

105 See Howard, 'Machiavellian vocabulary of contingency', 1–17; Tessa Beverley, 'Blundeville, Thomas (1522?–1606?)', Oxford Dictionary of National Biography, October 2009, www.oxforddnb.com/view/article/2718.

106 Howard, *Reception of Machiavelli*, 52. As Fernández-Santamaria, *The State*, 274–5 points out, when it comes to theological matters, Furió Ceriol was a follower of Erasmus.

107 Howard, *Reception of Machiavelli*, 52–5.

108 Fadrique Furió Ceriol, *A Very Briefe and Profitable Treatise Declaring Howe Many Counsells, and What Maner of Counselers a Prince That Will Gouerne Well Ought to Haue*, trans. Thomas Blundeville (London, 1570), sig. A, 2r.

109 Furió Ceriol, *A Very Briefe and Profitable Treatise*, sig. A, 2v; see Howard, 'Machiavellian vocabulary of contingency', 4.

for all, alone of himself', he needs counsel[110] – and these counsellors do have a traditional Plutarchan role of admonishment: 'friendly requireing him, ya, and straightlye charging him to admonishe hym, and with all due reuerence to correct him, when hee seeth it needefull, and in anye wise to be playne with him, and to tell him the truth'.[111] The prince ought to be willing, 'to heare the truth modestly tolde, and in due tyme, at his counselers handes'.[112]

Virtue, however, appears only as part of the Machiavellian adaptation to circumstances. The counsellor ought to be well versed in moral philosophy and the virtues, not in order to instruct his prince, but rather to recognise vice in others. For instance, under the requirement that the counsellor 'bee a good Morall Phylosopher', is included that he 'perfitely knowe the end and true vse of euery vertue' so that he does not 'accompt rudeness & ignoraunce to be plaine dealing, pride to bee magnanimitie, modestye to be cowardlynesse, and foolishe hardinesse to be fortitue, and to be short, doe take vertue for vice, & vice for vertue', in other words, does not fall for the tricks of *paradiastole*.[113] Counsellors do need to determine if what they consult on 'be honest or not' as well ensuring they appoint 'offices to meete persons', but it is not required, as it was for the earlier humanists, that they in any way counsel the prince to virtue.[114]

Furió Ceriol insists, like Machiavelli, that there ought to be a number of counsellors from which the prince takes his advice; this ensure that the prince, once again, always has someone to 'serue his turne' as well as mitigating the issues of delays and of self-interested counsellors.[115] On this, the text is in line with earlier writings on the counsellor: he must place good of the commonwealth before his own. If anything, it is stated more clearly in this text than in earlier ones, drawing a clear line between these public and private concerns. The counsellor 'is a publique person, and therefore ought to bee voyde of all priuate affection'.[116] Those who are not, may 'vnder the colour of Iustice, reuenge his priuate wrong, with the publicke sworde'.[117] This renewed emphasis comes about because the

110 Furió Ceriol, *A Very Briefe and Profitable Treatise*, A, v^{r}. Furió Ceriol's original is more explicit on this point: a prince needs to be 'good' in terms of skill, not morality. The former is furnished by prudence. See Fernández-Santamaria, *The State*, 276–7.

111 Furió Ceriol, *A Very Briefe and Profitable Treatise*, P, 3^{r}.

112 Furió Ceriol, *A Very Briefe and Profitable Treatise*, P, 3^{v}.

113 Furió Ceriol, *A Very Briefe and Profitable Treatise*, F, 3^{r}.

114 Furió Ceriol, *A Very Briefe and Profitable Treatise*, F, 3^{r-v}.

115 Furió Ceriol, *A Very Briefe and Profitable Treatise*, N, 3^{r}, D, i^{r}.

116 Furió Ceriol, *A Very Briefe and Profitable Treatise*, I, i^{r}.

117 Furió Ceriol, *A Very Briefe and Profitable Treatise*, I, 2^{r}.

counsellor is a figure of suspicion, thanks to probable self-interest and ability to identify and use *paradiastole*.

Both counsellors and councils are required to be plentiful, for Furió Ceriol and Blundeville, as they are there to address the various circumstances that a prince may encounter. With seven councils – each with their own offices – there will always be a council to 'serue the turne'.[118] A council, in Blundeville's words, is defined as 'an assembly of wise and discreete persons chosen by the Prince to counsell him in all his affayres', and a counsellor 'a suffie[n]t person, chosen by the Prince, meete to serue in some one of the foresaide counsels, and able to discharge his dutie therein'.[119] The prince's choice of counsellors is crucial, and the short book treats both the qualities of the counsellors and how the prince makes his choice of them; at no point is it suggested that a prince might not have the right to choose his counsellors.

Possible limits to the prince's authority are only treated in terms of the advice offered in the treatise itself, as it is clear that the counsellors – as they are described in it – do not in any way encroach upon the prince's power. Blundeville agrees that a prince 'is free, & that he maye giue & dispose his offices as him pleaseth best', rather than listening to the advice given by Furió Ceriol. It is on this objection that Blundeville (paraphrasing Furió Ceriol) repeats the standard humanist response that the prince is in fact more free when he is ruled by reason: 'mine author answereth that the freedom or libertie of the Prince is no freedome, when it passeth the bounds of reason, and that in preferring will before reason, he ought rather to be called a tyrant than a Prince'.[120] He appears not to be suggesting that it is the counsellors that keep the prince in reason – as earlier writers had – but rather that choosing to follow this advice regarding the choice of counsellors is what is liberating. Furió Ceriol accepts the Machiavellian model of counsel whereby the prince clearly rules his counsellors, and his prudence determines the quality of their counsel, rather than their counsel determining the level of his prudence. As Blundeville writes, 'it seemeth that my Author supposeth, the Prince to be endued wyth all these qualities hymselfe, for otherwise I see not how he should bee able ryghtlye to iudge of them'.[121] Blundeville seems surprised by Furió Ceriol's approach to the relationship between prince and counsellors, but he accepts it.

118 Furió Ceriol, *A Very Briefe and Profitable Treatise*, B, ii^{r}. Blundeville here is quite close to the original, see Fernández-Santamaria, *The State*, 284.

119 Furió Ceriol, *A Very Briefe and Profitable Treatise*, B, i^{r}, D, ii^{r-v}.

120 Furió Ceriol, *A Very Briefe and Profitable Treatise*, Q, 2^{v}- Q, 3^{r}.

121 Furió Ceriol, *A Very Briefe and Profitable Treatise*, D, iv^{r-v}.

It is also worth noting the special emphasis given to prudence in this text, and how it is understood. Prudence is not a virtue in the traditional sense. Blundeville lists prudence as one of the five 'qualities of the mind' needed by the counsellor.[122] Whereas Furió Ceriol's original inventory had been a straightforward list, Blundeville describes them under the headings of the four cardinal virtues, plus science. However, prudence, even in Blundeville's translation, has little to do with virtue, and more to do with evaluating the utility of actions in a given political circumstance. Under this heading he includes the expectation that the counsellor be wise, 'politique', well-travelled, and expert in contemporary affairs ('to knowe the force as well of hys Prince, as of his enymies and neyghbours').[123] Being a 'pollitike counseler', for Furió Ceriol and Blundeville, means being able to answer questions from his prince such as:

> whyther it be better to builde a Citie in a fertyll or barren soyle? which winds are to be barred from an habitation or dwelling place? how manye wayes a state or kingdome is woont to bee lost? by what meanes the good gouernement of anye common wealth is decayed? of what causes seditions and rebellions doe spring? how they may be oppressed? wherin the power of a Prince doth consist? whyther in riches, or in good Souldiers?[124]

We may recognise most of these questions (and the others in his list) as being dealt with in the *Discorsi*, most even being rough translation of chapter titles. If the counsellor can 'rightly and readily answere' these and like questions, the section concludes, 'he is worthy to bee called a pollitike counseler'.[125] To be politic, therefore, is to have knowledge of the important circumstances and realist considerations of the Machiavellian tradition. It is, in other words, to be prudent, in this new and Machiavellian use of the word.

Another text written in the same year as Furió Ceriol's *El concejo y consejeros de príncipes* connects this discussion of prudence and counsellors directly with the language and imagery of *kairos*. Bartolome Felippe's *Tractado Del Conseio y de los Conseieros de los Principes*, written in 1559 and translated in 1589 by John Thorius, also seeks to set out the ideal counsellor. Felippe followed in the tradition of Furió Ceriol; Modesto Santos López refers to him as Furió Ceriol's 'fiel discípulo' – faithful disciple.[126] Little is

122 For the role of prudence in Furió Ceriol's original, see Howard, *Reception of Machiavelli*, 57.

123 Furió Ceriol, *A Very Briefe and Profitable Treatise*, sig. D, 3^{r}.

124 Furió Ceriol, *A Very Briefe and Profitable Treatise*, sig. G, 3^{r-v}.

125 Furió Ceriol, *A Very Briefe and Profitable Treatise*, sig. G, 4^{r}.

126 Modesto Santos López, 'El pensamiento realista y liberal de Bartolomé Felippe, el fiel discípulo de Fadrique Furió', *Cuadernos constitucionales de la Cátedra Fadrique Furió Ceriol*, no. 56 (2006): 5–24.

known about his life; what is known comes from his own book dedications: that he was born in Portugal in 1480 and was a professor of law in the Universities at Lisbon, Salamanca and Coimbra.[127] Thorius was a London translator, who dedicated his work to John Fortescue, a member of Elizabeth I's Privy Council, as he has been employed 'in this time which requireth extraordinarie habilitie and wisedome'.[128]

Timing is prevalent throughout this text and intimately connected to the role of the counsellor. Felippe, drawing on a maxim of Charles V, suggests that 'the affaires of Princes . . . consist in two things: in counsell and excecution', where the latter requires 'haste' the former needs 'slownes' and 'both of the[m] together' constitute 'the *Quintessence* of wise Princes'.[129] As a prince is unlikely to be able to do both himself, counsellors are required. The prudence required of the counsellor consists in being aware of such occasions and opportunities, as the 'singuler wit and rare iudgment, and the putting of matters in execution' required by counsel, 'demaunded fit opportunitie, with occasion proportionable, and much fidelitie'.[130] Due to the nature of their subject matter – that which is particular and unpredictable – 'Countsellers for the most part, depend vpon the occasions and circumstances.'[131] Counsellors therefore must judge how long they ought to stay in consultation, for 'whilst the Counsellors are consulting what is to be doone, the occasion passeth which was offered'.[132] Those who let occasion pass are 'very hurtful vnto the Common-wealth'.[133] Like Isocrates (especially Elyot's reading of Isocrates), Felippe suggests that a good counsellor above all requires a knowledge of *kairos*.

Felippe explicitly connects this discussion with the ancient tradition of *kairos*, writing that 'in ancient times past, the Image of opportunitie [*occasion*] was set vp in many places, that men might remember to let no

[127] Biography from López, 'El pensamiento', 16–17.

[128] Howard Jones, 'Thorius, John (b. 1568)', Oxford Dictionary of National Biography, 2004, www.oxforddnb.com/view/article/27335. Bartolome Felippe, *The Counseller. A Treatise of Counsels and Counsellers of Princes*, trans. John Thorius (London, 1589), sig. A, 2^{v}. Much of Felippe's text reads like a commonplace book, where he sets out the views of other writers on the topic in *utrumque partem* before giving his own view. I have endeavoured in what follows to highlight Felippe's own views, and where he endorses the arguments given by others, though there remains some ambiguity and contradiction. He often references Charles V, who wrote a series of *instrucciones* to his son between 1539 and 1548 (one from 1555 is considered to be a fabrication); see Fernández-Santamaria, *The State*, 237–46. Charles V was also familiar with Machiavelli's work; see Howard, 'Machiavellian Vocabulary of Contingency', 641.

[129] Felippe, *The Counseller*, 4. Felippe here makes reference to Sansovino.

[130] Felippe, *The Counseller*, 4. [131] Felippe, *The Counseller*, 43. [132] Felippe, *The Counseller*, 8.

[133] Felippe, *The Counseller*, 7.

occasion slip, which might be to their commoditie when opportunitie was offered'.[134] Felippe goes on to describe the ancient personification of *occasio* in detail:

> they painted her on a wheele, because she neuer standeth still, nor remaineth in one place, with wings on her feete, because she passeth away swiftly, her face couered with the haire of her forehead, because she lets none know her, but such as be verie attentiue to looke on her: with a raser in her hande, because shee cuts of their hope that take no heede of her but let her passe: with the hinder part of her head balde, because if she once be gone, no man can catch hold of her, and with a Maid that waits vpon her which is called *Poenitentia*, for repentance doth accompanie them that cannot tell how to reape profit by occasion.[135]

For Felippe, the important consideration of the prudent counsellor is not whether an action *ought* be done, but rather *when* it should be done: 'many things in mans life are mard, not for that they ought not to be doone, but because they be not doone in time and place'.[136] The pertinent question to the counsellor is not one of morality, nor even of capability, but of timing.

More importantly, Felippe draws on his Machiavellian principles to re-articulate the strong division between counsel and command. Undoubtedly, the model he presents is of the Machiavellian kind: diverse minds and opinions from which the prince – already wise – chooses the best course of action. Felippe, with reference to Charles V, illustrates two scenarios for counsel which demonstrate his acceptance of this model. In both the prince is counselled by 'learned men', but in one he is 'vertuous' in the other he is 'wicked and lewde'.[137] In the former case, the counsel is 'expedient and profitable' for the prince, in the second, it is 'dangerous and hurtful', because these learned men 'For to euery thing which the Prince will doo, they find either a Law or an History to allow and approue the same'.[138] In neither case can the learning and experience of the counsellors change the quality of the prince, for 'there neuer wanted men of great

[134] Felippe, *The Counseller*, 8. Both the English translation and the original reference Erasmus' *Adagia* in the margins for the source of this image, see Bartolome Felippe, *Tractado Del Conseio y de Los Conseieros de Los Principes* (Turin [London], 1589), 7. Unlike Blundeville's abridgement of Furió Ceriol, Thorius' translation of Felippe is very close to the original. Notably, Machiavelli is named in the list of authors cited in both the original and in Thorius' translation, however, references to him in the margins of the text itself tend to come from the *Discourses*, and relate primarily to the nature of the commonwealth (for instance on 41, 132, 137, 146, 166, 170, 173). Anglo, *Machiavelli – The First Century*, 175 fn25 also gives details of the print history of Felippe's text, as well as his Machiavellian influence.

[135] Felippe, *The Counseller*, 8. [136] Felippe, *The Counseller*, 9. [137] Felippe, *The Counseller*, 13.

[138] Felippe, *The Counseller*, 13.

learning, who contrarie to all reason and iustice, iustified and approoued that which their Prince purposed and appointed to doo'.[139] As with Machiavelli, it is the goodness and wisdom of the prince which determines that of the counsel, not the other way around.

This Machiavellian model is clear when Felippe addresses the recurring question of 'whether it be more profitable to the Common-wealth, to haue a good Prince, and ill Counsellers, or an ill Prince, and good Counsellers'. After considering the views of the ancients on the subject, Felippe concludes, in contradistinction to the earlier humanists, that 'it is farre better and more profitable for the Common-wealth, that the Prince should be good, and the Counsellers naught, then that the Counsellers should be good, and the Prince wicked' because 'all men endeuour to imitate the Prince'.[140] The merit in having good counsellors is not to make the prince wise, but to *show* that he is wise: 'If a Prince haue good Counsellers, though he doo amisse, yet will no man beleeue it: but if his Counsell be not good, though we see the Prince doo well, yet can we not beleeue it, or we thinke that it was doone by chaunce.'[141] Counsellors cannot actually change the quality of the prince, but they can change the perception of that quality.

Felippe also outlines clearly the problem of counsel:

> The Counsellers of Princes are subiect vnto two great inconueniences. The first is, that if they counsaile not theyr Princes to doo that which they thinke to be most profitable for the Common-wealth, without hauing any respect vnto theyr owne profit, or any other thing; then they discharge not their dutie. The second is, that if they doo counsaile their Princes, to doo that which they will not doo, then they incurre daunger of their liues.[142]

To overcome this problem, Felippe does not advise rhetoric, *parrhesia* or diminishing the king's power with councils, the answers given by the Henrician humanists, but rather quite the opposite. They are to use 'great modestie' so that if the prince 'follow their aduice, he may doo it willingly of his own accord', so that he is not 'drawne or forced to doo it, by the importunitie of him that giueth the counsaile'.[143] By embracing modesty, the counsellor avoids blame for counsel that turns out badly, as well as the anger of the prince, should he not like it. Rather than imposing their counsel on the prince, counsellors ought to take a backseat in order to avoid the problem of counsel. Felippe's counsellor is more Harpocrates than Pasquil.

[139] Felippe, *The Counseller*, 14.
[140] Felippe, *The Counseller*, 87.
[141] Felippe, *The Counseller*, 88–9.
[142] Felippe, *The Counseller*, 125.
[143] Felippe, *The Counseller*, 126.

Importantly, counsellors need to avoid the use of persuasive rhetoric in their counsel, for this too crosses the line between counsel and command. True counsel is employed by those who 'counsell a man to doo any thing, and dooe onely shew him a reason why they counsell him to doo so'.[144] These men simply 'make him acquainted with the reasons which mooue them to give such counsell'.[145] This is *exhortatio*, or simple encouragement, and does not 'bind, or by any necessitie force him to whom the counsell is giuen, to follow their counsell'.[146] Such counsel is given simply and straightforwardly, without use of rhetorical persuasive techniques. This is distinct, Felippe suggests, from those who 'commaund and perswade a man to doo a thing'.[147] To command and to persuade are *both* indications of a bad counsellor, for 'they that command will haue that doone which they commaund: and they that perswade, vrge the execution of that which they perswade'.[148] Persuasion, in fact, is even worse than command in the hands of a counsellor. Quoting the Roman jurist Ulpian, Felippe writes that 'it is more to perswade one to commit some offence, then to compell or constraine him to dooe it: for mens mindes are more mooued by perswasion, then by compulsion or commandement'.[149] Felippe ends this argument by turning the rhetoricians' own arguments for the efficacy and potency of oratory against themselves: 'therefore *Cornelius Tacitus* and *Plato* saie, that the Arte which teacheth men to perswade, is the most excellent and noble Arte of al Artes' and he quotes *De inventione* directly: 'for that which by mans force could not be atchieued, hath oftentimes beene obtained by eloquence'.[150] This is precisely the power of rhetoric – extolled by classical writers – that Felippe draws attention to and questions; if to sway a monarch by force is not permissible, why is it acceptable to use an even stronger method?[151] As Francis Bacon writes in a letter of advice to the Earl of Rutland in 1595, shortly after Felippe's text was translated, rhetoric 'makes yow raigne ou*er* the wills and affecc*i*ons of men, which is the greatest sou*er*aignitye that one man can haue over an other.'[152]

[144] Felippe, *The Counseller*, 70.
[145] Felippe, *The Counseller*, 70–1.
[146] Felippe, *The Counseller*, 71.
[147] Felippe, *The Counseller*, 70.
[148] Felippe, *The Counseller*, 71.
[149] Felippe, *The Counseller*, 71.
[150] Felippe, *The Counseller*, 71.
[151] As Markku Peltonen, *Rhetoric, Politics and Popularity in Pre-Revolutionary England* (Cambridge: Cambridge University Press, 2013), 13 makes clear, the orator was widely understood in sixteenth-century England to be a man of 'exceptionally wide powers of mythical and divine potency' and whose rhetoric 'wielded enormous power, much more so than even the mightiest sword'.
[152] Francis Bacon, 'Second Letter of Advice to the Earl of Rutland', in *The Oxford Francis Bacon I: Early Writings 1584–1596*, ed. Alan Stewart and Harriet Knight (Oxford: Oxford University Press, 2012), 658–70.

Rhetorical counsel, then, the great tool of the humanist counsellor, is soundly rejected. To use it is to blur the all-important line between counsel and command.

We can, then, identify eight related elements of the Machiavellian approach to counsel: seven of which are present in Machiavelli's *Prince*, and one that is added by those that adopt his ideas (though their exact articulation may vary). The first three regard the model of counsel, the relationship between prince and counsellors. First, the prince rules his counsellors. It is his prudence that determines the quality of their counsel (rather than their counsel determining the quality of his prudence). Second, the prince's counsellors are not to be trusted, being too likely to be swayed by self-interest. Third, and relatedly, the prince ought to consult many counsellors, rather than depending on one (who is likely to usurp power). The following three elements relate to the content of counsel. First, counsellors should counsel according to what the prince *can* do, not what he *ought* to do. This means, second, they should counsel him to use deception (and *paradiastole*) when necessary. Finally, their counsel and the prince's actions should vary with circumstance. The final two elements speak to the larger vocabularies of counsel. Prudence is redefined: related to *utile* not *honestum*. Last, rhetoric becomes suspect, as a means of counsellors illegitimately commanding their prince. The Machiavellian discourse of counsel, then, critiques the humanist discourse not only for its inutility, but for its willingness to place counsel above command. Where in the humanist worldview this was essential to good governance, for Machiavellians it runs precisely contrary to it.

CHAPTER 4

Political Prudence

In the Machiavellian literature on counsel, the distinction between private and public prudence becomes more pointed, leading to a distinction between a private sphere ruled by morality, and a public sphere in which moral flexibility, or even amoralism, is appropriate.[1] As Machiavellian principles spread, such a view became accepted even amongst self-described anti-Machiavellians, especially in considering 'policy' and political deliberation. Counsellors must weigh both private and public expectations, offering advice that takes into account necessity and advantage politically but with an awareness of traditional expectations, embracing the skill of re-description when occasion, still in the tradition of *kairos*, calls for the employment of vice. Not only does this re-definition of prudence establish a separate sphere of morality (or lack thereof) for politics, it also introduces a language of contingency and exceptionalism, which becomes associated with the counsellor. In contrast with earlier writings on the topic, in this tradition the counsellor must mitigate not the tyranny of the prince, but of fortune.

i Anti-Machiavellian Machiavellians

Even those who reject Machiavellianism find themselves conceding that under certain circumstances (usually expressed in the vocabulary of 'occasion') deception is necessary. This is especially notable in the French anti-Machiavellian works from the 1570s onwards. Robert Bireley has suggested that all anti-Machiavellian works, by definition, attempted to meet Machiavelli 'on his own terms, that is, on the level of practice' and thus accepted the Machiavellian end for political discourse: the preservation of

[1] Reginald Pole had drawn attention to the re-definition of prudence as early as his *Apologia*, noting to Charles V that 'You see, therefore, the prudence of this doctrine and where it leads', Pole, *Apology*, 279.

the state.[2] So while these authors refute Machiavelli's pessimism, and attempt to once again reconcile *utile* and *honestum* in political counsel and practice, they still had to focus on the achievement of *utilitas* primarily, and often accepted political practices not traditionally in line with *honestum*.[3]

For instance, the French writer and ambassador Matthieu Coignet's *Politique Discourses upon Trueth and Lying*, originally published in 1584 and translated into English by Edward Hoby in 1586, contests Machiavelli's counsel, on the grounds that princes who follow it 'haue had most miserable endes, after hauing beene made a laughing stocke vnto their enemyes.'[4] To ensure that his own advice does not lead to such an unfortunate result, Coignet is forced to soften what is otherwise a complete rejection of deception.[5] He concedes in his chapter on 'faining and dissembling' that he does not mean 'that euerie one, nor at al times, nor of euerie matter, should speake what he thinketh', allowing not only for selective silence, but outright deception.[6] For although 'euerie counterfaiting done to the ende to deceiue an other is reprooued . . . if it bee to conceale a good counsell, fearing lest it might be preuented, then is it not to bee blamed'.[7] In particular this applies to those in politics, for 'hee who cannot dissemble, shall neuer raigne prosperously'.[8] Deception might normally be condemned, but it is essential for those who rule.

Coignet provides a similar defence of promise-breaking – another variety of deception – in select circumstances. Although it is to be rejected and reproved, 'neuerthlesse he ought not to bee accused for a lyar, who maye not lawfully keepe [his promise] for some iust occasion [*iuste occasion*]'.[9] So it is that '*Necessitie is the mother of dispensation* [*necessité est mere des dispenses*]' and he suggests that failure to keep promises is 'likewise excusable, if any preiudice, or interest [*interests*] happen not thorough [sic]

[2] Robert Bireley, *The Counter-Reformation Prince: Anti-Machiavellianism or Catholic Statecraft in Early Modern Europe* (Chapel Hill: University of North Carolina Press, 1990), 27.

[3] Bireley, *The Counter-Reformation Prince*, 28–30.

[4] Matthieu Coignet, *Politique Discourses upon Trueth and Lying* (London, 1586), 120. Edward Hoby was the son of Thomas Hoby, translator of Castiglione; Andrew Hadfield, 'Literature and the Culture of Lying Before the Enlightenment', *Studia Neophilologica* 85, no. 2 (2013): 135. Coignet was Master of Requests under Catherine de Medici's regency, a regime often accused of Machiavellian practices, according to his own description in the open pages of *Instruction aux Princes pour garder la foy* (Paris, 1584), sig. a, i^r. See also *Dictionnaire genealogique, heraldique, chronologique et historique*, vol. 1 (Paris, 1757), 503.

[5] Hadfield, 'Literature and the Culture of Lying Before the Enlightenment', 140–1 suggests that Coignet 'argued that lying was never permissible', but as we shall see, this is not quite the case.

[6] Coignet, *Politique Discourses*, 11. [7] Coignet, *Politique Discourses*, 11.

[8] Coignet, *Politique Discourses*, 11.

[9] Coignet, *Politique Discourses*, 29. French from 1584 *Instruction aux Princes*, 41.

the not accomplishing of a promise'.[10] Coignet, in discussion of these issues, notes that 'Here I could alledge the opinion of an *Athenian* embassador recited by *Thucidides*, that a Prince ought somtime to be a friend, somtime an enimie, & to ply himselfe according to occurents [*occurréces*]'; 'occurents' is *kairos* in Thucydides' original Greek.[11] This flexibility is associated with policy and prudence; Hoby identifies this maxim with the marginal note 'Policie in a Prince', where the original had read '*Prudence d'vn Prince*'.[12] Despite elsewhere denigrating the 'Italian Prudence' that he sees recently emerged in Europe, Coignet finds a place for it in his theory.[13]

The French soldier and statesman Jacques Hurault de Cheverny's *Politicke, Moral, and Martial Discourses*, translated by Arthur Golding in 1595, is also written in refutation of Machiavelli, but he too makes concessions, namely in acknowledging that certain circumstances require exceptions.[14] Despite objecting at length to the idea that princes should be held to different standards of morality, Harault admits – with reference to Machiavelli – that the prince should 'be skilfull both in playing the lion to encounter such as will assaile him, and in playing the fox to saue himselfe from the trains and snares that are layd for him'.[15] Dissimulation can be used as a defensive strategy, and he supports this with the same maxim that Coignet had, that 'he which can no skill to dissemble can no skill to reign'.[16] In order to defend this position, he makes a distinction between deceit and dissimulation. Deceit is 'to pretend to be a man of honestie, and to promise that which he intendeth not to performe', which Hurault rejects completely.[17] Dissimulation, on the other hand, 'commeth of Wisedome [*sagesse*]', for 'to dissemble in time and place [*temps & lieu*], is great wisedome'.[18] As others had done, he equates the role of such wisdom

10 Coignet, *Politique Discourses*, 29.

11 Coignet, *Politique Discourses*, 35; Thucydides, *Peloponnesian War*, 1.36.

12 Coignet, *Politique Discourses*, 35; *Instruction aux Princes*, 50.

13 Coignet, *Politique Discourses*, 36, 71.

14 Hurault was a councillor of Henri III of France, Golding a prominent and well-known translator with connections to the Cecil family; Christine Sukič, '"A True Sign of a Readie Wit": Anger as an Art of Excess in Early Modern Dramatic and Moral Literature', *XVII-XVIII. Revue de La Société D'études Anglo-Américaines Des XVIIe et XVIIIe Siècles*, no. 71 (2014): 85–98; John Considine, 'Golding, Arthur (1535/6–1606)', Oxford Dictionary of National Biography, 2004, www.oxforddnb.com/view/article/10908.

15 Jacques Hurault, *Politicke, Moral, and Martial Discourses*, trans. Arthur Golding (London, 1595), 92–3; 'trains' here has the meaning of 'treachery, guile, deceit, trickery'.

16 Hurault, *Politicke, Moral, and Martial Discourses*, 100.

17 Hurault, *Politicke, Moral, and Martial Discourses*, 102.

18 Hurault, *Politicke, Moral, and Martial Discourses*, 100–1. French from Jacques Hurault, *Trois livres des offices d'estat* (Lyon, 1596), 119.

to the skill of a navigator: 'it is as much to say, as that a man must strike saile, apply himselfe to the wind like a good pilot, & take good heed to the seasons [*saisons*]'.[19] In other words, it is the skill which allows a prince to change with the times and fortunes as he encounters them. 'Such dissimulation', rather than being vicious, 'is needfull for a king'.[20]

Perhaps the best-known anti-Machiavellian work of this period was the *Discours sur les moyens de bien gouverner et maintenir en bonne paix un Royaume ou autre Principauté, Divisez en trois parties; asavoir du Conseil, de la Religion et Police que doit tenir un Prince. Contre Nicolas Machiavel Florentin,* written by Innocent Gentillet in 1576 and widely read in England even before its 1602 translation by Simon Patrick.[21] Gentillet was a Huguenot, and his anti-Machiavellianism was related to his opposition to French Catholic rule, a refutation of the ideas that Gentillet held to be behind the events of the St Bartholomew's Day Massacre four years before.[22]

Gentillet's main purpose, as he states in the preface, is to show 'that *Nicholas Machiavell* ... understood nothing or little in this Politicke science [*science Politique*] ... and that he hath taken Maximes and rules altogether wicked, and hath builded upon them, not a Politicke, but a Tyrannical science'.[23] Gentillet opens by noting that the 'Maximes and general rules of the Politicke Art' are useful, they are not 'so certaine as the Maximes of the Mathematicians' and are even 'dangerous, yea, pernitious' if they are applied without attention to the 'circumstances, dependences, consequences, and the antecedents' of a given affair, which are always 'divers and contrarie', to the point that 'although two affairs be like, yet must not men therefore conduct and determine them by one same rule or Maxime.'[24] Thus, those who 'deale in the affaires of publicke estate' need

[19] Hurault, *Politicke, Moral, and Martial Discourses*, 101.

[20] Hurault, *Politicke, Moral, and Martial Discourses*, 101.

[21] See Victoria Kahn, 'Reading Machiavelli: Innocent Gentillet's Discourse on Method', *Political Theory* 22, no.4 (1994): 539–60; Randall Martin, 'Anne Dowriche's The French History and Innocent Gentillet's Contre-Machiavel', *Notes and Queries* 44, no. 1 (1997): 40–2; N. W. Bawcutt, 'The "Myth of Gentillet" Reconsidered: An Aspect of Elizabethan Machiavellianism', *The Modern Language Review* 99, no.4 (2004): 863–74; Anglo, Machiavelli – The First Century, 282–324. Patrick's manuscript translation may have circulated before 1602, see Bawcutt, 'The "Myth of Gentillet" Reconsidered', 863–74.

[22] Antonio D'Andrea, 'The Political and Ideological Context of Innocent Gentillet's Anti-Machiavel', *Renaissance Quarterly* 23, no.4 (1970): 397–411; C. Edward Rathé, 'Innocent Gentillet and the First "Anti-Machiavel"', *Bibliothèque d'Humanisme et Renaissance* 27, no. 1 (1965): 186–225.

[23] Innocent Gentillet, *A Discovrse Vpon the Meanes of Wel Governing* (London, 1602), A, ii^{r}. French from Innocent Gentillet, *Discovrs svr les moyens de bien govverner & maintenir en paix vn royaume, ou autre principauté: divisez en trois parties: a sauoir, du conseil, de la religion, & de la police que doit tenir un prince*, 1579, 3.

[24] Gentillet, *A Discovrse Vpon the Meanes of Wel Governing*, A, i^{v}–A, ii^{r}.

to know not only the rules, but also how they can 'prudently [*sagement*]' apply the rules in the given context, 'yea sometimes to force and bend them to serve to the present affaire'.[25] The 'science singular and excellent' required, thus, is the 'science and habit of knowing well to weigh and examine the accidents and circumstances of affaires, and then to be able handsomely to apply unto them, their rules and principles'.[26] Gentillet thus finds himself somewhere between the Henrician humanist emphasis on *praecepta* over *decreta* and Machiavelli's attention to *occasione*.

It is in discussion of the maxim 'A Prince ought to follow the Nature of the Lyon, and of the Foxe: not of the one without the other' that Gentillet presents a re-definition of the concept of prudence.[27] Rather than suggesting that resorting to beastly behaviour is unbecoming of a prince, or that the deceptive nature of the fox is always to be eschewed, Gentillet's argument is over the definition of the terms. He wants to ensure that *lawful* deception, when 'in warre a man may lawfully use subtilties against his enemies', is disassociated from such beastly vocabulary. These actions are 'not called foxlike subtiltie, or unlawful deceiving, but ought to be called militarie prudence'.[28] This prudence, 'to use subtiltie, fraud and militarie sharpenesse of wit (for all those names may be well used)', Gentillet emphasises, 'is not to counterfeit the beast, nor to play the Fox'.[29] For Gentillet, there is a type of prudence, associated with policy, which involves the use of a type of legitimate deception and fraud.[30]

Despite such concessions, Gentillet attacks the Machiavellian model of counsel in favour of a more traditional one. He acknowledges that Machiavelli's maxim that '*A Princes good Councell ought to proceed from his owne wisedome: otherwise, he cannot be well counselled*' appears, 'At the first shew' to 'haue some appearance of truth', but when it is 'well examined' it is clear that 'it is pernitious and of wicked consequence'.[31] It is true, he admits, that the best case scenario is a prince who is 'of himself wise and prudent', like Plato's philosopher-king.[32] Such 'good commanding' will lead to good obedience and a well-functioning commonwealth.[33] That being said, counsel is still necessary: 'For a Prince, how prudent

[25] Gentillet, *A Discovrse Vpon the Meanes of Wel Governing*, A, ii^{r}.
[26] Gentillet, *A Discovrse Vpon the Meanes of Wel Governing*, A, ii^{r}.
[27] Gentillet, *A Discovrse Vpon the Meanes of Wel Governing*, 222.
[28] Gentillet, *A Discovrse Vpon the Meanes of Wel Governing*, 224.
[29] Gentillet, *A Discovrse Vpon the Meanes of Wel Governing*, 224.
[30] See Gentillet, *A Discovrse Vpon the Meanes of Wel Governing*, 294–6.
[31] Gentillet, *A Discovrse Vpon the Meanes of Wel Governing*, 1.
[32] Gentillet, *A Discovrse Vpon the Meanes of Wel Governing*, 2.
[33] Gentillet, *A Discovrse Vpon the Meanes of Wel Governing*, 2.

[*prudent*] soever he be, ought not so much to esteeme of his own wisedome [*prudence*], as to despite the counsell of other wise men [*sages*].'[34] Against Machiavelli's doctrine, Gentillet strongly asserts the traditional humanist model of counsel in which counsel – in a sense – rules the prince. As he writes, the prince 'ought to conform his opinion to that of the men of his Counsell, which are wise, and ought not stubbornely to resist their advise, but to follow it, and hold his owne for suspected'.[35] He gives the example of Marcus Antonius, who followed the advice of his council, even when he disagreed, and the Emperor Antonius, who held that 'many eyes see clearer than one eye alone' and that 'Experience also teacheth vs, That things determined and resolved by many braines, are alwayes wise, safer, & better ordered, than the resolutions of one alone.'[36] Machiavelli too had warned against relying too heavily on a single counsellor; however, whereas his concern had been such a one usurping power, Gentillet suggests that a single strong counsellor will 'go out of the bonds of reason' and become the subject of 'great envies'.[37] The wiser the prince is, Gentillet goes on to say, the more he will be suspicious of his own wisdom and follow the advice of others. The better maxim for a prince to hold, according to Gentillet, is 'To govern himselfe by good counsell, and beleeve it, and have in suspition his own wisedome.'[38] If he is governed by reason, then his counsellors will 'easily fall to his advise'.[39] It is the prince who must convince his counsellors – ideally – of the wisdom of his advice, not the other way around.

That is because Gentillet adopts a traditional humanist view of the counsellor as more capable and powerful than the prince, rejecting Machiavelli's model. If 'the Princes Counsell is compounded of good and capable men, which have ever before their eyes the service and utilitie of their Prince, which is no other thing but the Commonweale', if they are 'wicked' then the affairs of the prince are doomed, whether or not he is wise.[40] Against Machiavelli, who Gentillet states holds the 'cleane contrary' maxim, Gentillet asserts that 'it is more expedience to the Commonweale, that the Prince be wicked and his Counsell good, than that the Prince be good, and his Counsell good, than that the Prince be good, and his Counsellors wicked'.[41] Like the earlier humanists,

[34] Gentillet, *A Discovrse Vpon the Meanes of Wel Governing*, 3–4, *Discovrs svr les moyens de bien govverne*, 21.
[35] Gentillet, *A Discovrse Vpon the Meanes of Wel Governing*, 4.
[36] Gentillet, *A Discovrse Vpon the Meanes of Wel Governing*, 4.
[37] Gentillet, *A Discovrse Vpon the Meanes of Wel Governing*, 62.
[38] Gentillet, *A Discovrse Vpon the Meanes of Wel Governing*, 4.
[39] Gentillet, *A Discovrse Vpon the Meanes of Wel Governing*, 4.
[40] Gentillet, *A Discovrse Vpon the Meanes of Wel Governing*, 5.
[41] Gentillet, *A Discovrse Vpon the Meanes of Wel Governing*, 5.

Gentillet asserts that 'many good Counsellors may well supplie the want of wisedome that is in a Prince, and moderat his unbrideled and undiscreet appetites' whereas a prince cannot hope to do the same to 'so many evill Counsellors, which will feed their Prince with smoke and lies, and will hide from him such things as he ought to know for the Commonweale'.[42] He demonstrates this with examples of princes who have 'small wisedome and vertue' yet ruled well with the advice of their council, mostly those who came to the crown in their minority.[43]

There remains the issue, Gentillet notes, of how a prince lacking in wisdom can choose good counsellors, considering that there are 'great hypocrisies and dissimulations' and a 'mutabilitie of manners' in so many men.[44] The three rules he sets out are: (1) to choose princes of the blood to the council, (2) retain the counsellors of the prince's predecessor and (3) the three estates provide counsellors to the prince. On this note, Gentillet goes on to specify that his comments thus far have pertained to the Privy Council, but there is 'another Counsell' which the Romans called the Senate, and the French the Parlement or Estates General (depending on the period of history).[45] By such a council, Gentillet explains, laws gain their legitimacy, and the best rulers depend on it as they do their Privy Council, even allowing it to appoint their Privy Councillors.[46] It is the Estates General who steps forward when a king cannot rule himself (whether 'under age', 'not well in his wit and understanding', 'prisoner or captive' or 'that the kingdome have urgent necessitie of a generall reformation').[47] Whereas the Privy Council is also subject to such inconveniences, the Estates 'can never faile, because it consisteth not in *Individuals* and certain particular persons, but it standeth in *Specie*, being a body immortal (as al the French nation is immortall)'.[48] The Estates, alongside the absolute power of the prince (which is limited by God and the law) and the law itself, make up the three pillars of the commonwealth. The prince's absolute power ought also to be limited, Gentillet states, by his civil power, 'which is guided by prudence and good Counsell'.[49] It is always better to use civil rather than absolute power, Gentillet states, but the prince does reserve the right to use the latter, and subjects must obey. In

[42] Gentillet, *A Discovrse Vpon the Meanes of Wel Governing*, 6.
[43] Gentillet, *A Discovrse Vpon the Meanes of Wel Governing*, 7.
[44] Gentillet, *A Discovrse Vpon the Meanes of Wel Governing*, 8–9.
[45] Gentillet, *A Discovrse Vpon the Meanes of Wel Governing*, 15.
[46] Gentillet, *A Discovrse Vpon the Meanes of Wel Governing*, 16–17.
[47] Gentillet, *A Discovrse Vpon the Meanes of Wel Governing*, 21.
[48] Gentillet, *A Discovrse Vpon the Meanes of Wel Governing*, 21.
[49] Gentillet, *A Discovrse Vpon the Meanes of Wel Governing*, 19, 27.

short, he ought to rule through and according to his councils. Gentillet's account of counsel is a clear restatement of the traditional position, directly opposed to Machiavelli's inversion of the same.

He makes a similar restatement in regards to the issue of flatterers, opposing Machiavelli's assertion that a prince should only take advice when he solicits counsel, 'forbidding and inhibiting them to speak to him of any thing but of that whereof he himself hath begun the talke', then choosing the 'Counsell that he shall find best'.[50] This is, in fact, he contends, the secret to flattery, for the 'principall dutie of a good and faithfull Counsellor to his Prince' is to 'declare unto him the abuses committed by his subjects', which the prince cannot know (and therefore ask about) without the counsellor first reporting them.[51] The success of flatterers, Gentillet repeats from Plutarch, is owed to the self-love of the prince, which is easily persuaded by the paradiastolic practices of the flatterer: 'the flatterer adornes his language in such sort, that he will alwaies praise his Princes vice by the resemblance of some vertue nie thereunto' and he does the same with his own vices, 'to cover his owne faults and vices with the visage and likenesse of some vertue nie unto them'.[52] Rhetoric, however, is not entirely to be scorned. The good counsellor will also 'use gentle and civile talke and persuasions', rather than 'taunts and bitter biting speeches'.[53] Persuasion is, once again, the means by which the counsellor leads his prince, rather than the prince taking control of his counsellors, as in Machiavelli. Gentillet re-states the traditional model of counsel but, nevertheless, re-defines prudence in Machiavellian terms.

ii Lipsius and Prudence

The re-definition of prudence, and its connection to changing notions of the role of counsel, is made clearest by Justus Lipsius in his *Politicorum sive Civilis doctrinae libri sex*, translated by William Jones in 1594.[54] The

[50] Gentillet, *A Discovrse Vpon the Meanes of Wel Governing*, 30

[51] Gentillet, *A Discovrse Vpon the Meanes of Wel Governing*, 31.

[52] Gentillet, *A Discovrse Vpon the Meanes of Wel Governing*, 33–4.

[53] Gentillet, *A Discovrse Vpon the Meanes of Wel Governing*, 35. As Kahn, 'Reading Machiavelli', 539–60 points out, Gentillet's critique of Machiavelli related to the method of his rhetoric, not the fact that he used rhetoric.

[54] Soll, 'The Reception of *The Prince*', 52 suggests that 'Lipsius had the greatest effect in disseminating a positive interpretation of Machiavelli's civil science' and his *Politica* defended 'Machiavelli's idea of prudence'. For Lipsius and reason of state see Peter Burke, 'Tacitism, Scepticism, and Reason of State', in *The Cambridge History of Political Thought 1450–1700*, ed. J. H. Burns (Cambridge: Cambridge University Press, 1991), 485–6.

Politica, published in 1589, was produced as a sequel to Lipsius' *De constantia*; whereas the *De constantia* was intended to equip 'citizens for endurance and obedience', *Politica* instructed 'those who rule [*imperant*] for governing [*regendum*]'.[55] The book is a compendium of classical authors, a patchwork of common-places, but with its own central arguments and aims.[56] Jones's translation is based on the 1590 edition, and is generally close to the original, though as Jan Waszink has suggested, he diminishes the 'commonplace-book nature of the text' and renders it less 'dialectical' than the original.[57]

As Waszink has pointed out, the six books of the *Politica* can be separated into two halves: the first three presenting a traditional notion of the political, the second three taking a 'realist' approach.[58] The overall aim is to generate a theory that encapsulates both these dimensions of the political. This bifurcation of form and aim may be why scholars have such difficulty categorising Lipsius into Machiavellian or anti-Machiavellian camps. For example, Bireley lists Lipsius as one of the founders of anti-Machiavellian discourse in Europe, a position countered by Adriana McCrea.[59] Waszink chooses to label him either a '*moderate* Machiavellian or a *moderate* anti-Machiavellian', in other words: neither.[60] Lipsius' intent was not to associate with either tradition exclusively, but rather to fuse them together.[61]

55 Justus Lipsius, *Politica: Six Books of Politics or Political Instruction*, ed. Jan Waszink (The Hague: Uitgeverij Van Gorcum, 2004), 231. On the relationship between Lipsius' political texts see Bireley, *The Counter-Reformation Prince*, 75.

56 David Martin Jones, 'Aphorism and the Counsel of Prudence in Early Modern Statecraft: The Curious Case of Justus Lipsius', *Parergon* 28, no. 2 (2012): 55–85 comments on Lipsius' style and its relationship to political counsel.

57 Waszink, ed., *Politica*, 197. Not much is known of William Jones, though his dedicatory letter to Lord Puckering suggests that he might have been related to – or perhaps even was – the Edward Jones who served Sir John Puckering between 1592 and 1596.

58 Waszink, ed., *Politica*, 82.

59 Bireley, *The Counter-Reformation Prince*; Adriana McCrea, *Constant Minds: Political Virtue and the Lipsian Paradigm in England, 1584–1650* (Toronto: University of Toronto Press, 1997), xxiii.

60 Waszink, ed., *Politica*, 102.

61 This view is in opposition to that presented by Harro Höpfl, 'History and Exemplarity in the Work of Lipsius', in *(Un)masking the Realities of Power: Justus Lipsius and the Dynamics of Political Writing in Early Modern Europe*, ed. Erik Bom, Marijke Janssens and Toon van Houdt (Leiden: Brill, 2010), 64 who suggests that Lipsius' 'definition of prudence was entirely conventional', even 'bland and non-committal', and that he was uninterested in the 'fraught relationship between prudence and virtue'. On the other hand, McCrea, *Constant Minds*, xxvii suggests that Lipsius took 'a number of key humanist concepts – "constantia", "prudentia", and "similitudo temporum"' and 'infused them with new meaning, and re-presented them as tools with which to confront the contemporary situation' as a way to counter the 'perceived threats' to the Ciceronian dedication to the *vita activa*. See also Christopher Brooke, *Philosophic Pride: Stoicism and Political Thought from Lipsius to Rousseau* (Princeton: Princeton University Press, 2012), 59–75.

There is no question, given this preoccupation, that the *Sixe Bookes* is a work which comments at length about the nature and aims of counsel. Lipsius draws the reader's attention to this theme from the outset, noting in his opening letter to 'Emperovr. Kings. Princes' the role and importance of counsel to such rulers. Despite these royal addressees, Lipsius also speaks directly to counsellors in the epistle, writing that 'to deserue well of the Common-wealth, we ought to deserue well of our Prince: that is, we ought to guide and direct him, to this marke of the common profit'.[62] Jones further emphasises these themes in his translation, for where Lipsius had exhorted his royal addressees not to 'despise our counsels, because you are above *iussa*' – above commands – Jones here adds an absent possessive pronoun to render the passage: 'because you are above our commandements': i.e. the commandments of his counsellors.[63] Jones's translation appears to be clearer about the relationship between counsel and command, but there remains ambiguity.

Lipsius states that there are two directors that every man should be attentive to: prudence and virtue. Immediately we must take note that Lipsius presents these two distinctly: prudence is not to be counted among the virtues, but instead holds equal weight with all other virtues in the determinations of daily life.[64] Prudence is the guide of these virtues, it 'not onlely ruleth your self, but vertue likewise, yea it directeth it'.[65] It also stands as a counter to fortune, for '*All things yeeld obedience vnto Prudence, euen Fortune her selfe*'; the wise man, like Machiavelli's man of *virtù*, '*frameth his own fortune*'.[66] Virtue and prudence each have their own jurisdictions as well: virtue is what is required to be a good man, prudence to be a good citizen; virtue is the director of the private sphere, prudence of the political.[67]

Lipsius explicitly addresses political prudence in the third book: 'the vse of *Prudence* is necessarie in all worldly affaires': it is especially required in government and is the '*onely proper vertue belonging to a Gouernour*'.[68] He

62 Justus Lipsius, *Sixe Bookes of Politickes or Civil Doctrine*, trans. William Jones (London, 1594), sig. A, v^r.

63 Lipsius, *Sixe Bookes of Politickes*, sig. A, v^r.

64 As Diana Stanciu, 'Prudence in Lipsius's *Monita et Exampla Politica*: Stoic Virtue, Aristotelian Virtue or Not a Virtue at All?', in *(Un)masking the Realities of Power: Justus Lipsius and the Dynamics of Political Writing in Early Modern Europe*, ed. Erik Bom, Marijke Janssens and Toon van Houdt (Leiden: Brill, 2010), 234 points out, he does at times in the *Politica* define prudence as a virtue, though in the *Monita* he does not.

65 Lipsius, *Sixe Bookes of Politickes*, 11.

66 Lipsius, *Sixe Bookes of Politickes*, 12.

67 G. Remer, 'Justus Lipsius, Morally Acceptable Deceit and Prudence in the Ciceronian Tradition', *History of Political Thought* 37, no.2 (2016): 238–70 suggests that Lipsius' understanding of prudence is drawn from Cicero's account of *decorum*.

68 Lipsius, *Sixe Bookes of Politickes*, 42. The use of 'virtue' here having the meaning of 'quality'.

immediately equates prudence with counsel, suggesting that 'the euent of all ages hath, and will euer instruct vs, that *in the managing of waighties affaires, more things are brought to passe by good aduise and counsell, then by force of armes*'.[69] He notes that it is most commendable for a man to be able to '*foresee all things to come*', but that '*he in like manner doth derserue great praise, that can follow the wise aduise of others*'.[70] In line with traditional views of counsel, Lipsius suggests that counsellors are necessary to supplement the prudence of the prince, but his definition of prudence is more in line with that of Machiavelli and those who follow him. Prudence must take into account the ability to vary with circumstance, for 'he is *truly prouident* [*prudens*] *and wise, that keepeth not alwayes the same pase* [sic], *but the same way. And he is not therefore to be esteemed variable, but rather applyable, and fitting things to the purpose*'.[71] Lipsius concludes that the prudent man is he 'who holdeth not one, and the same course, though he tend, to one and the same hauen'; prudence consists in a variability and adaptability when it comes to ways and means, but a constancy in intended ends.[72] The counsellor supplements the prudence of the prince, but the prudence he provides is Machiavellian.

In the second – more Machiavellian – half of the text, Lipsius carries this acceptance of adaptability into a discussion of dissimulation and deception. He begins the 'new preface' to the work by making clearer his views on 'proper prudence' or 'that which is requisite to be in a Prince'.[73] Such prudence, he suggests, has three main characteristics. First, it is 'diffused' and '*concerneth particular matters*', for which reason precepts are not enough to teach such a skill.[74] Second, it is 'confused', for it is 'imploied about things vncertaine'.[75] Because of these characteristics, prudence itself has no static form:

> if the things themselues are vncertaine, *Prudence* it selfe likewise must of necessitie be so, and so much the rather, because it is not onely tied to the things themselues, but to their dependents, hauing regard vnto the times, the places, and to men and for their least change, she changeth her selfe, which is the reason why she is not in all places alike, no nor the same in one and the selfe same thing.[76]

Having presented 'the best and purest wine' of prudence in the first three books, Lipsius wonders if, based on this new understanding of prudence,

[69] Lipsius, *Sixe Bookes of Politickes*, 42. [70] Lipsius, *Sixe Bookes of Politickes*, 43.

[71] Lipsius, *Sixe Bookes of Politickes*, 47–8. [72] Lipsius, *Sixe Bookes of Politickes*, 48.

[73] Lipsius, *Sixe Bookes of Politickes*, 59; see Waszink, *Politica*, 81. McCrea, *Constant Minds*, 16 suggests that this section holds the 'key to [the] argument' of the *Sixe Bookes*.

[74] Lipsius, *Sixe Bookes of Politickes*, 59. [75] Lipsius, *Sixe Bookes of Politickes*, 59.

[76] Lipsius, *Sixe Bookes of Politickes*, 60.

'it be lawfull for me to mingle lightly, and ioyne with it some dregs of deceipt?'[77] He decides that it would indeed be allowable, based on the conditions of 'this age, and the men that liue therein', suggesting that those who oppose this position '*giue their opinion, as if they liued in the common wealth of Plato, and not in the dregs of the state of Romulus*'.[78] We may recognise this line from Plutarch's discussion of *kairos* in his life of Cato; Lipsius applies it to the question of stretching the definition of prudence to allow for deception, concluding with Machiavelli that since 'we conuerse . . . with craftie and malicious persons, who seeme *to be made of fraude, deceipt and lying*', especially princes, who 'although they shewe themselues to be like Lyons, *yet are they in their corrupt hearts dissembling Foxes*', we ought to adopt the same practices, in order to match our actions to the conditions of the times.[79] Lipsius' view of correct political action borrows the circumstantial flexibility of Machiavelli's.

A prince '*hauing to deal with a foxe*' must sometimes '*play the foxe*', especially in cases where 'the good and publike profit' – synonymous with '*the benefit and profit of the Prince*' – is concerned.[80] Such a cause changes the very moral value and appellation of an action: '*that which is commonly reputed dishonest for this cause, will not be so*'.[81] Thus a prince will 'intermingle that which is profitable, with that which is honest'.[82] Prudence does not change 'albeit a few drops of deceipt bee mingled therewith'.[83] He makes the connection that this argument has to Machiavelli explicit by defending him at the close of this chapter. Lipsius refers to him as the 'Italian *faulte-writer*', identified by name in the margin, whose 'poore soule is layde at of all hands' and whom an experienced man will not condemn for the recognition that '*there is a certain honest and laudable deceipt.*'[84]

In the following chapter Lipsius informs the reader of what this honest deceit consists. It is, he writes, 'a *subtile counsell, which swarveth from vertue or the lawes for the good of the Prince and the estate*'.[85] He sets out three levels of such honest deceit – light, middling and great – claiming that 'the first sort of deceipt I persuade, the second I tollerate, and the third I condemne', although he does not denounce any form absolutely, even the gravest, for there is always an occasion when it may be necessary.[86]

77 Lipsius, *Sixe Bookes of Politickes*, 112.
78 Lipsius, *Sixe Bookes of Politickes*, 112.
79 Lipsius, *Sixe Bookes of Politickes*, 112–13. Plutarch, *Lives*, 8:150.
80 Lipsius, *Sixe Bookes of Politickes*, 113.
81 Lipsius, *Sixe Bookes of Politickes*, 113.
82 Lipsius, *Sixe Bookes of Politickes*, 113.
83 Lipsius, *Sixe Bookes of Politickes*, 114.
84 Lipsius, *Sixe Bookes of Politickes*, 114.
85 Lipsius, *Sixe Bookes of Politickes*, 115.
86 Lipsius, *Sixe Bookes of Politickes*, 115.

The first, 'light' type of deceit '*paceth not farre from vertue*' and is only '*slightly watered with the dewe of euill*', involving practices such as distrust and dissimulation.[87] He repeats the oft-quoted maxim that '*he knew not wel how to beare rule, that knew not how to dissemble*'.[88] In fact, for Lipsius dissembling is *only* allowable when it comes to rulers, for 'it ought not to bee amongst priuat persons' but when it comes to governors 'they shall neuer gouerne well, who know not how to couer well'.[89] This dissembling is not just in relation to 'strangers, or their enemies' but 'likewise towards their owne subiects' and princes must do it '*cunningly*'.[90]

He defines middling deceit as 'when for thy profit thou intisest another by an error or false tale' and, although it is not allowed to those who use such means *against* princes, he argues that it 'be lawfull in a Prince ... *for the commoditie of their subiects ... to vse lying and deceipt*', for '*to deceiue in time and place is wisedome*'.[91] He suggests that such strategies are often stronger and more effective than force, and notes that 'oftentimes *by pollicie of counsel* [princes] *atchieue that*, which the necessitie of affaires, *and want of time doth denie them*', deceiving in speech, letters and through their ambassadors.[92] This 'pollicie of counsel', he suggests, albeit is not to be praised, is certainly necessary and justifiable 'if you enter into a consideration of humane prudence'.[93]

He classifies great deceit under the headings of '*Trecherie* and *Iniustice*'.[94] Even in this discussion, however, Lipsius redefines many otherwise dubious actions in order to make them allowable for princes, for '*it is necessarie to be a little withdrawn from iustice, in matters of small importance*, to the end they may keepe it in waightie matters'.[95] Thus, if a prince commits 'some small iniustice' and it is 'kept secret' then it might be allowable, particularly if it is '*for the commoditie of the common wealth*'.[96]

87 Lipsius, *Sixe Bookes of Politickes*, 115. 88 Lipsius, *Sixe Bookes of Politickes*, 117.
89 Lipsius, *Sixe Bookes of Politickes*, 117. 90 Lipsius, *Sixe Bookes of Politickes*, 117, 118.
91 Lipsius, *Sixe Bookes of Politickes*, 119. 92 Lipsius, *Sixe Bookes of Politickes*, 119.
93 Lipsius, *Sixe Bookes of Politickes*, 119. It is worth noting that this is not the only time that such strategies are described as 'counsel'. In the final book addressing warfare, Lipsius acknowledges that the power of occasion, which 'hath power in all humaine affaires, but especiallie in matter of warre' necessitates the use of not only '*direct counsels*', which '*march in the beaten way of warre*' but also '*indirect counsels, which passe by the secret path of fraud and deceipt*' (*Sixe Bookes of Politickes*, 167). Direct counsels involve attention to the temporal forces so important in war: 'times and seasons', 'the moment of occasion' and 'necessitie' (*Sixe Bookes of Politickes*, 171). He devotes an entire chapter to the consideration of indirect counsels, or what is referred to in the chapter title as 'Politicke Counsels, or strategemes' (*Sixe Bookes of Politickes*, 175). These 'crooked and couert' counsels', consisting in 'art, and pollicie' are not only 'of great profit' in warfare, 'but honorable likewise' (*Sixe Bookes of Politickes*, 175).
94 Lipsius, *Sixe Bookes of Politickes*, 120. 95 Lipsius, *Sixe Bookes of Politickes*, 122.
96 Lipsius, *Sixe Bookes of Politickes*, 122.

In such cases, Lipsius suggests that the prince might employ his skills of re-description, for '*A happie and prosperous mischeife is called vertue*'.[97] For Lipsius, virtue is only one part of the consideration of political success, the other consists of a view of prudence quite removed from its place as one of the cardinal virtues, which allows, based on temporal considerations, for the use of devious practices within the political sphere.[98] For princes, the lightest sort of deceit is necessary and even the worst allowable in certain circumstances. The prudent political actor will know the difference, and act or counsel accordingly.

iii The Essayists and Political Counsel

The creation of a flexible morality based on prudential evaluation of diverse circumstances which is proper to politics, as opposed to private affairs, is even more clearly outlined in the works of the essay writers of the late sixteenth and early seventeenth centuries, whose reflexive and subjective medium causes them to consider not just the theatre of politics, but the nature of the actors involved. Those involved in politics must engage in actions associated with vice. The fact of their position does not render those actions virtuous, but it does make them permissible. Politics is a sphere in which typically vicious action is rendered allowable, even necessary, by those who participate in it.

This tendency, and the essay-writing genre itself, originates with Michel de Montaigne, whose *Essais* were translated into English in 1603 by John Florio, a noted translator and writer in London.[99] Montaigne's work is intimately connected to that of Lipsius: Lipsius himself wrote of Montaigne that 'I have found no one in Europe whose way of thinking about things is closer to my own' and Montaigne described Lipsius as 'the most sufficient and learned man now living'.[100] Montaigne, like Lipsius, has been variously declared both a Machiavellian and anti-Machiavellian by turns, most likely because his intention was also to form a synthesis of the two.[101]

97 Lipsius, *Sixe Bookes of Politickes*, 122. 98 Waszink, ed., *Politica*, 100.

99 Desmond O'Connor, 'Florio, John (1553–1625)', Oxford Dictionary of National Biography, 2004, www.oxforddnb.com/view/article/9758.

100 Richard Tuck, *Philosophy and Government 1572–1651* (Cambridge: Cambridge University Press, 1993), 45.

101 See Ullrich Langer, *The Cambridge Companion to Montaigne* (Cambridge: Cambridge University Press, 2009), 122–5; Biancamaria Fontana, *Montaigne's Politics: Authority and Governance in the* Essais (Princeton: Princeton University Press, 2008), 57–8.

The first edition of the *Essays* was produced in 1580; two revised and extended versions were published in 1588 and 1595 (though the last was produced after Montaigne's death in 1592). Although Montaigne professes that he had originally set out to collect sources on many of the questions Machiavelli, Lipsius and others had tackled – such as 'the role of chance in military and political undertakings [and] the stability of regimes' – he had found the results to be contradictory, and hence gave up the task of producing a cohesive political treatise in the style of his predecessors.[102] Instead, he published a series of '*essais*', attempts to grapple with these questions, with no claim to success, objectivity or conclusion. In fact, the entire collection may present a rejection of such notions. It is the intention, Montaigne's *essai*, that counts.[103]

This emphasis on intention is present in the essays themselves, for Montaigne claims that it is intention that 'iudgeth our actions'.[104] In fact, 'nothing is truely in our power', he suggests, 'except our will'.[105] Thus it is the will which should be the subject of all discussions of morality: '*It is no parte of a well-grounded iudgement, simplie to iudge our selves by our exterior actions*'.[106] With such emphasis on the will, deception becomes the worst sort of immoral act; it is 'an ill and detestable vice' and Montaigne 'hate[s] it to the death'.[107] He declares it 'a vaine and servile humour, for a man to disguise and hide himselfe vnder a maske, and not dare to shew himselfe as he is'.[108] Thus in truth-telling, as in all things, Montaigne professes to choose the course whereby he can defend his intentions, and leave the rest to fortune: 'I apply my selfe to ingenuitie, and ever to speake truth and what I thinke, both by [my] complexion and by [my] intention; leaving the successe thereof vnto fortune'.[109]

The same applies to counsels – it is the intention that matters: 'our counsels go astray, becayse they are not rightly addressed, and have no fixed end'.[110] Such considerations come before any other thought of means: 'a skilfull archer ought first to know the marke he aimeth at, and then apply

102 Fontana, *Montaigne's Politics*, 11–12.

103 As Langer, *Companion to Montaigne*, 3 points out, 'the term *essai* in sixteenth-century French does not refer to a delineated segment of text, but instead retains the senses of "attempt," "trying-out," .... [Montaigne's] book is full of all sorts of "attempts". He tries out all sorts of judgments, of observations, of reflections, and of arguments. But ... they are not meant to be the final word on the matter'.

104 Michel de Montaigne, *The Essayes, or Morall, Politike, and Millitarie Discourses*, trans. John Florio (London, 1603), 14.

105 Montaigne, *The Essayes*, 14.

106 Montaigne, *The Essayes*, 197.

107 Montaigne, *The Essayes*, 16.

108 Montaigne, *The Essayes*, 376.

109 Montaigne, *The Essayes*, 377.

110 Montaigne, *The Essayes*, 197.

his hand, his bow, his string, his arrow and his motion accordingly'.[111] Whether or not he hits his mark is inconsequential: '*counsels ought not to be iudged by the events*' for 'events are but weake testimonies of our worth and capacity'.[112] Just as it is 'folly to thinke, that humane wisedome may acte the full part of fortune', 'vaine is his enterprise, that presumeth to embrace both causes and consequences'.[113] Thus there are two parts that make up correct action and counsel for Montaigne: that the intention has the right aim and that it is in accordance with one's own nature. The power of Fortune will determine the rest.

Unlike for Lipsius, for Montaigne prudence does not have the power to combat Fortune, and so it is that one will see 'Divers events from one selfe same counsell'.[114] 'So vaine and frivolous a thing is humane wisedome [*prudence*]' he declares, 'and contrary to all projects, devises, counsels, & precautions: fortune doth ever keep a full sway and possessions of all events'.[115] Fortune's abilities far outstrip man's; she 'sometimes addresse[s] and correct[s] our counsells' for she 'hath better advise than wee' and 'in hir directions exceedeth all the rules of humane wisedome'.[116] This is even more the case in the political realm: '*publike innouations, depend more on the conduct of fortune*' than private ones.[117] As Fortune 'seldome wil yeeld, or never subject her-selfe vnto our discourse or wisedome', the great power of prudence is humbled by her incomprehensibility.[118]

All of these themes are brought together in the essay, 'Of profit and honestie'.[119] Whereas other writers had rejected the concerns of *honestum/utile* based on particular temporal concerns, Montaigne's objections are based on another particularity. He makes clear in this essay that both the traditional and Machiavellian arguments about *honestum* and *utile* have one weakness in common: a universality that does not take into account the nature of the individuals involved.[120]

111 Montaigne, *The Essayes*, 197.
112 Montaigne, *The Essayes*, 559.
113 Montaigne, *The Essayes*, 560.
114 Montaigne, *The Essayes*, 57.
115 Montaigne, *The Essayes*, 57.
116 Montaigne, *The Essayes*, 110.
117 Montaigne, *The Essayes*, 564.
118 Montaigne, *The Essayes*, 155.
119 Montaigne, *The Essayes*, 475.
120 Thus this argument finds itself between those, such as Skinner, *Foundations*, 253 and Tuck, *Philosophy and Government*, who suggest that Montaigne was advancing arguments for reason of state and those, such as Robert J. Collins, 'Montaigne's Rejection of Reason of State in "De l'"Utile et de L'honneste', *The Sixteenth Century Journal* 23, no.1 (1992): 71–94 and Fontana, *Montaigne's Politics*, 18, who suggest that he was critiquing this view. Montaigne's point, I suggest, was not to take either side, but rather to suggest that both had a fundamental flaw in that they prescribed universalities; either moral system *could* be viable, depending on the particulars. In this way it is aligned with the argument in Fontana, *Montaigne's Politics*, 138: 'on Montaigne's terms, acting prudently, in the private as in the public domain, meant something quite different in each individual case', as 'prudent conduct' consisted of 'following nature'.

He begins the essay with an acknowledgement of the logical consistency of the Machiavellian argument that vices must, at least on occasion, be profitable. This is presented in the form of a simple syllogism. As (P_1) 'there is nothing in nature vnseruiceable, no not invtilie itselfe, nothing thereof hath beene insinuated in this huge vniuerse, but houdeth forme fit place [*place opportune*] therein'[121] and (P_2) 'our essence is symented with crased qualities; ambition, jealousie, enuie . . . ', therefore (C) even these baser and seemingly unnatural qualities must have a purpose and utility.[122] He notes that this is especially true in regards to 'policy': 'in a mater of policie [*police*]-likewise, some necessary functions are not onely base but faultie: vices find therein a seat, and employ themselues in the stitching vp of our frame: as poisons in the preseruation of our health'.[123] That being said, even if some deplorable actions 'become excusable, because we have need of them', that does not mean, Montaigne makes clear, that such actions are to be performed by all men.[124] An action might be excusable because it is necessary, that still does not make it good, and one's conscience may still suffer for it. It therefore should be performed only by those individuals who are suited to it. As he had remarked in his tenth essay, actions ought to be matched to the nature of the individual performing them. When he suggests that '*The way to trueth is but one and simple*', Montaigne is not suggesting a universal moral system, but quite the opposite, for the ruling maxim is '*that becomes euery man especially, which is his owne especially*'.[125] Taking this into consideration, Montaigne can make allowance for what he terms 'lawfull vices'.[126] It is true, he says, that real justice would never allow such things, but we must refer to an 'especiall, and nationall iustice' which is 'restrained and suted to the neede of our pollicies'.[127] It falls upon those required to take such extraordinary action to suffer the consequences of them.

In fact, especially when it comes to princes, the performance of vicious actions may be divinely mandated punishment. Princes may have to conduct themselves immorally, suffering the damage this does to their conscience, for some previous sin:

> When an vrgent circumstance, or any violent and vnexpected accident, induceth a Prince for the necessity of his estate, or as they say for state

[121] 'Les Essais de Montaigne', accessed 10 August 2017, http://artflsrv02.uchicago.edu/philologic4/montessaisvilley/navigate/1/5/2/.
[122] Montaigne, *The Essayes*, 475–6.
[123] Montaigne, *The Essayes*, 476.
[124] Montaigne, *The Essayes*, 476.
[125] Montaigne, *The Essayes*, 478.
[126] Montaigne, *The Essayes*, 478.
[127] Montaigne, *The Essayes*, 478; '*justice speciale, nationale, contrainte au besoing de nos polices*'.

> matters, to breake his worde and faith, or otherwise forceth him out of his ordinarie dutie, he is to ascribe that necessitie vnto a lash of God's rod: It is no vice, for he hath quit his reason, vnto a reason more publike, and more powerfull, but surelie t'is fortune.[128]

For a prince, Montaigne suggests, there is no remedy to this ill fortune: 'were he trulie rackt between these two extreames . . . he must haue done it'.[129] However, if he is a different sort of person, 'one of so tender or cheverall a conscience, to whome no cure might seeme worthie of so extreame a remedie' then his choice *not* to take the vicious action is likewise justifiable: 'I should prise or regarde him no whit the lesse'.[130] This is because, for private men, dedication to the well-being of their country does not have to come above private concerns, such as conscience or family. It is part of our nature as humans to have such bonds, and overriding them fragments that fundamental unity: 'Let vs bereave wicked, bloodie and trayterous dispositions, of this pretext of reason [more publike]; leave we that impious and exorbitant [nationall] justice, and adhere vnto more humane imitations'.[131] It is these individual and particular relationships which define us, both as individuals and a human community, and trump all concerns of either honesty or utility. Thus, he concludes:

> Falselie doe we argue honour, and the beautie of an action, by it's [sic] profit: and conclude as ill, to thinke every one is bound vnto it, and that it is honest, if it be commodious.
> *Omnia non pariter rerum su[n]t omnibus opta.*
> All things a-like to all,
> Doe not well-fitting fall.[132]

Princes are required to transgress the bounds of what is usually assumed to be virtue in order to protect the state. There is a higher expectation of them, given by their position, which does not apply to private men. The demands of necessity, fortune and occasion demand immoral action of such public figures.

[128] Montaigne, *The Essayes*, 480; '*Le Prince, quand une urgente circonstance et quelque impetueux et inopiné accident du besoing de son estat luy faict gauchir sa parolle et sa foy, ou autrement le jette hors de son devoir ordinaire, doibt attribuer cette necessité à un coup de la verge divine: vice, n'est-ce pas, car il a quitté sa raison à une plus universelle et puissante raison, mais certes c'est mal'heur*'.

[129] Montaigne, *The Essayes*, 480. To this first, more morally flexible, prince, Montaigne ascribes limits. First, he must keep in mind that 'they are dangerous examples, rare and crased exceptions to our naturall rules' and that they should be approached with 'great moderation, and heedie circumspection' (*The Essayes*, 481). Second, that 'no priuate commoditie' justifies such actions, neither are they justifiable based on 'the encrease and profit of the publike revenues' (*The Essayes*, 481).

[130] Montaigne, *The Essayes*, 480. [131] Montaigne, *The Essayes*, 482.

[132] Montaigne, *The Essayes*, 482–3.

Even before their translation into English, Montaigne's *Essais* were widely read in English intellectual circles, and – as with the Machiavellian tradition – once again we see a greater emphasis on counsel when this genre is brought into the English context. Montaigne's emphasis on the character of the actor, especially the political actor, as determining the morality of an action gives the English essayists a distinction between private advice and public counsel, the latter of which has different rules of morality (or perhaps none at all). Its purpose is not to combat princely tyranny, but that of fortune.

One of the earliest writers within the English essay genre was William Cornwallis, whose *Essayes* were first published in 1600, with a second half added the following year. Cornwallis's father was Sir Charles Cornwallis, a diplomat and court official well connected to Robert Cecil.[133] Sir William Cornwallis (knighted in 1599) was only about 20 when he wrote his *Essayes*, a few years before he joined the privy chamber of James I. Cornwallis's essays have often been overlooked in favour of those of Bacon, and the early twentieth-century interest in Cornwallis's work has not been maintained.[134] Intimately acquainted not only with the works of Lipsius and Montaigne, but also with the real-world politics of counselling, Cornwallis's essays reflect a fusion of these influences.[135]

His first essay sets this tone, reflecting on the need for politic flexibility to circumstances. 'Of Resolution' begins with a reflection on his own thoughts and views, before turning his evaluating gaze outward – first to society, and then to the political. Touching on the themes of adaptation to occasion, he uses an example from Plutarch's *Lives* – Alexander's decision to wear the clothes of the 'barbarians' he had conquered – declaring that he is 'not of their mindes that tax *Alexanders* putting on the habit of the Persians', for this was a 'a politicke inte[n]t, he ioyned the[m] to him, by that yeelding'.[136] In this case, 'Fantasticknesse lent wisdome to Pollicy'.[137] He thus allows that 'some actions, if they be not wholely vicious,

133 Arthur Kincaid, 'Cornwallis, Sir William, the Younger (c.1579–1614)', Oxford Dictionary of National Biography, 2004, www.oxforddnb.com/view/article/6345, accessed 13 Nov 2017.

134 R. E. Bennett, 'Sir William Cornwallis's Use of Montaigne', *PMLA* 48, no. 4 (1933): 1080–89; Alfred Harbage, 'Essayes by Sir William Cornwallis the Younger (Review)', *Modern Language Quarterly* 9, no. 1 (1948): 107–8; P. B. Whitt, 'New Light on Sir William Cornwallis, the Essayist', *The Review of English Studies* 8, no. 30 (1932): 155–69. The exceptions include Sophie Butler, 'Sir William Cornwallis the Younger (c1579–1614) and the Emergence of the Essay in England' (Phd Thesis, University of Oxford, 2013).

135 See R. H. Bowers, 'Introduction', in *Discourses Upon Seneca the Tragedian (1601)* (Gainesville: Scholar's Facsimiles, 1952), v. Bennett, 'Sir William Cornwallis's Use of Montaigne', 1080–89 gives a full account of the influence of Montaigne on Cornwallis.

136 William Cornwallis, *Essayes* (London, 1600), sig. B, 6^{r-v}.

137 Cornwallis, *Essayes*, sig. N, 2^{v}.

humanitie and good nature shall make [them] sociable'.[138] Taking on the clothes of the barbarians might not be honourable, but it is necessary and 'politique'.

This sort of adaptation is particularly necessary in politics. In the essay 'Of Suspicion', Cornwallis addresses the issue of necessary vicious actions done by princes and makes the argument, like Montaigne, for the separation of private and political moralities. Princes, he writes, are fundamentally different from private men, as 'vppon this state dependes the common good', and so 'among these States, Suspicion and Dissimulation are to be allowed' as they are the 'Handmaydes of Pollicie'.[139] He agrees with Hurault that princes 'ought to be conuersant' in such practices 'not to offend, but to defend'.[140] Taking Montaigne's suggestion that morality should be based on the individual involved, Cornwallis founds his separation of private and public morality on the state of the person acting. Princes in Cornwallis's estimation are fundamentally different from private men; they are allowed actions usually considered dishonest 'not in respect they are men, but in regard they are princes'.[141] Beneath them, these actions 'are not to be allowed, not dissimulation at all'.[142]

Cornwallis goes further than Montaigne in making the suggestion that the moral valuation of these actions is fundamentally changed based on the consideration of who is performing the deed, for 'things [are] different in name and nature, according to the possessor'.[143] Thus 'to a lowe fortune belongs simply the vse of Vertue', but to princes '[virtue] must be often chaunged, not into vice, but not to looke alwayes like Vertue'.[144] Combining this doctrine with that of Lipsius, he tells his reader that the private man need only walk a straight and simple path, but the navigations of princes are more diverse and complex: 'couersant with multitude, [he] must sometime goe about & seek by wayes, which in him may bee vertuous, though in the other it would be termed dishonest'.[145] Virtue and vice are necessarily re-described when speaking of princes. The prince need not employ *paradiastole*; he is the living embodiment of it.

Turning to the controversial topic of dissimulation, Cornwallis connects it directly to the discussions of variable circumstance, calling dissimulation 'a skillfull manager of time'.[146] It is thus 'tollerable; in some courses necessarie' to dissimulate, as Alexander did with his barbaric Persian

138 Cornwallis, *Essayes*, sig. B, 6ᵛ.
139 Cornwallis, *Essayes*, sigs. D, 5ᵛ; D, 6ʳ.
140 Cornwallis, *Essayes*, sig. D, 6ʳ.
141 Cornwallis, *Essayes*, sig. D, 6ʳ.
142 Cornwallis, *Essayes*, sig. D, 6ᵛ.
143 Cornwallis, *Essayes*, sig. D, 6ᵛ.
144 Cornwallis, *Essayes*, sig. D, 7ʳ.
145 Cornwallis, *Essayes*, sig. D, 7ʳ.
146 Cornwallis, *Essayes*, sig. Nn, 7ᵛ.

attire.[147] These cases are defined, as they were for Plutarch and Machiavelli, by an understanding of *kairos*: 'Time in it selfe is alwayes one, but Occasion runs Diuision vpon Time, her note is not alwayes one, which ought to be noted by them which are not negligent of their Time'.[148] Recalling the important connection between *kairos* and counsel, Cornwallis suggests that this attention to occasion must be especially embraced by counsellors, for 'it is the duty of a faithfull seruant to tell his maister of his faultes . . . but he must watch fit oportunity'.[149] This means ensuring that the counsel comes before the event itself, and Cornwallis is clear that such 'servants' are to be chosen by the prince himself as he thinks 'meet' for his 'wisdome'.[150]

Advice is essential to every man, Cornwallis suggests in his second essay 'Of Advice', for 'if the end of life be to be good', and 'if the safest purchase of goodnesse bee counsayle', then 'why eschew wee the blessing of Aduise?'[151] In line with the Aristotelian tradition, Cornwallis suggests that it is advice which is 'the medium transporting' the rays of reason, the means by which we can control the affections and passions.[152] This is especially pertinent in political considerations, for he 'see[s] nothing more decay the fairest branches of our Commonwealth, then this neglect; either wee will not endure Aduise, or not beleeue it'.[153] He ends this essay with an exhortation to political counsel: 'let vs then infranchize Aduise, and perswade our eares to become good common-wealth men, to respect the generall profit: Counsell, and Aduise, are the parents of Gouernment'.[154] Advice is a co-parent of government with counsel, but not synonymous with it.

It is in his essay, 'Of Counsaile', published in the second half of the collection, that he elaborates on his distinction between 'counsel' – proper to politics – and private advice: 'aduice fitteth friend to friend: counsaile counsailours to states, the first priuate, the other publike'.[155] Advice does

[147] Cornwallis, *Essayes*, sig. Nn, 7[r].

[148] Cornwallis, *Essayes*, sig. N, 2[v]. Compare with William Thomas's discussion of occasion and music in the 1550s: 'Trulie as the musicien useth sometime a flatt and sometime a sharpe note, sometime a short and sometime a longe to make his songe perfect, so saieth Macchiavegli ought man to phrame his proceadings unto his tyme' (William Thomas, *The Works of William Thomas*, ed. Abraham D'Aubant (London: J. Almon, 1774), 134) and 'ffor as there is nothing more pleasaunt than the concorde of musicke: nor nothing more displeasaunt than the discorde therof, so whan doinges and tyme agree there is nothing more happie, nor whan they disagree nothing more unhappie: having in them much more variacion than twenes in musicke have' (*Works of William Thomas*, 144). It is perhaps also worth noting that the printer's mark for Edmund Mattes, which adorns the front page of the *Essayes*, is a representation of *kairos*.

[149] Cornwallis, *Essayes*, sig. Mm, 2[v].

[150] Cornwallis, *Essayes*, sig. Mm, 2[v].

[151] Cornwallis, *Essayes*, sig. C, 1[v].

[152] Cornwallis, *Essayes*, sig. C, 5[r].

[153] Cornwallis, *Essayes*, sig. C, 2[r].

[154] Cornwallis, *Essayes*, sig. C, 6[r-v].

[155] William Cornwallis, *Essayes* (London, 1610), sig. Bb, 5[v].

indeed use reason to counter passion, but political tyranny comes in another form, to which counsel is the answer: 'cha[n]ce chalengeth vnpremeditated actions; what more tyrannous?' and so 'must we admit counsaile'.[156] Counsel, specifically *political* counsel as opposed to *personal* advice, is thus transformed from a remedy to the passions of a prince to the counter to the whims of capricious fortune. He concludes that 'counsell then vpholds states, and to Counsaile, and to bee counsailed, fittes a states man'.[157] Cornwallis thus accepts the humanist model of counsel, but renames it 'advice' and relegates it to the private sphere. Counsel is understood in more Machiavellian terms, and is proper to a politics where, thanks to *kairos*, the expectations of morality do not always apply.

These themes are also considered by the best-known of the English essayists, Francis Bacon, who sets out two kinds of prudence: a traditional variant suited to the common man and another for those who must adapt to political circumstance. Bacon's *Essayes* were first published in 1597, followed not long after by one of his best-known works, *The Twoo Bookes of Francis Bacon. Of the Proficience and Aduancement of Learning, Diuine and Humane*. This text sets out not only the case for learning and inquiry, but also attempts to catalogue the varieties of human understanding, including a politic wisdom.

In the *Aduancement of Learning*, Bacon presents two forms of wisdom: a 'wisedome of counsell' and a 'wisedome of pressiing [sic] a mans own fortune'.[158] These two forms of wisdom 'doe sometimes meet, and often seuere'.[159] Like Lipsius, Bacon imposes a division between the wisdom required for political counsel (the wisdom of fortune) and that which brings success in day-to-day affairs (that of 'counsell'): 'many are wise in their owne ways, that are weak for gouernmente or Counsell'.[160] The wisdom of fortune, he writes, must be acknowledged by those with public roles for 'great Pollitiques indeede euer ascribed their successes to their felicitie; and not to their skill or vertue'.[161] Bacon feels the need to set out a doctrine for fortune's disciples, 'for *fortune* layeth as heauy impositions as vertue, and it is as harde and severe a thinge to be a *Pollipolitique* as to be truely moral'.[162] It is his task to ascribe a curriculum for this 'Architecture

156 Cornwallis, *Essayes* (1610), sig. Bb, 4^{v}–5^{r}.
157 Cornwallis, *Essayes* (1610), sig. Bb, 5^{r}.
158 Francis Bacon, *The Twoo Bookes of Francis Bacon. Of the Proficience and Aduancement of Learning, Diuine and Humane* (London, 1605), Aaa, 3^{v}.
159 Bacon, *Aduancement of Learning*, Aaa, 3^{v}.
160 Bacon, *Aduancement of Learning*, Aaa, 3^{v}. This can be blurred when it comes to domestic espionage, see Samuel Garrett Zeitlin, 'Political and Moral Vision in the Thought of Francis Bacon', *Journal of Intellectual History and Political Thought* 1, no. 1 (2012), 49.
161 Bacon, *Aduancement of Learning*, Aaa, 3^{v}–4^{r}.
162 Bacon, *Aduancement of Learning*, Aaa, $4^{r–v}$.

of fortune', for although many will not esteem him for doing it, 'neuerthelesse fortune as an organ of vertue and merit deserueth the consideration'.[163] Bacon intends instruction in this kind of wisdom to those in 'gouernment or Counsell' – politicians and, importantly, counsellors.[164]

He sets out eleven precepts for the education of the architect of fortune, most of which will now be familiar to us. For instance, such a man must know the nature and ends of those around him and learn to mistrust them as unfaithful dissimulators. He must be able to embrace the tools of rhetoric, and specifically *paradiastole*, in order to provide 'flourishes and inhansements of vertue', and for 'the couering of defects . . . by *Caution*, by *Colour*, and by *Confidence*'.[165] From this, Bacon makes clear that the disciple of fortune must also know how to recognise and take hold of *kairos*, to 'frame the mind to be pliant and obedient to occasion', for 'nothing hindereth mens fortunes so much' as to lack the ability to change with the times.[166] Politicians especially must have this skill, for 'nothing is more pollitique then to make the wheels of our mind concentrique with the wheels of fortune'.[167] Like Felippe and Cornwallis, Bacon maintains that the counsellor must especially be attuned to the workings of time and circumstance.

Bacon attempts to make a clear distinction between his brand of temporally based counsel and that associated with Machiavellianism, which he makes a point to deride.[168] Bacon assures his readers that his

[163] Bacon, *Aduancement of Learning*, Aaa, 4^{v}.

[164] As Stephen Gaukroger, *Francis Bacon and the Transformation of Early-Modern Philosophy* (Cambridge: Cambridge University Press, 2001), 52, 55 points out, Bacon's natural philosopher, whose training is set out in the *Twoo Bookes*, would lead an active life in the service of the crown.

[165] Bacon, *Aduancement of Learning*, Ccc, 2^{r}. Bacon had alluded to the use of such techniques in his *Coulers of good and euill*, first published in 1597, noting that 'In deliberatiues the point is what is good and what is euill' and so 'the perswaders labor is to make things appeare good or euill . . . by coulers, popularities and circumstances' (Francis Bacon, *Coulers of Good and Euill* (London, 1597), fo. 17^{r}).

[166] Bacon, *Aduancement of Learning*, Ccc, 3^{r}.

[167] Bacon, *Aduancement of Learning*, Ccc, 3^{r}.

[168] He had set out a similar character to his architect of fortune in the entertainment provided for Elizabeth's Accession Day in 1595. The play itself is a series of orations by counsellors to the Earl of Essex on how to win favour with the queen, each representing a specific type of counsellor-figure. The second such character is the Secretary, whose title and oration identify him immediately with the Machiavel. The Secretary tells Essex that if his end is 'to make the Prince happie whom he serves' he ought to 'make himself cunning . . . in the humors & drifts of persons' and always 'haue an eye rather to the by [sic] circumstance then to the matter itself'; Francis Bacon, 'Essex's Device', in *The Oxford Francis Bacon I: Early Writings 1584–1596*, ed. Alan Stewart and Harriet Knight (Oxford: Oxford University Press, 2012), 714. In the end, however, the Secretary's advice is rejected, and he is chided for thinking that he can 'governe the wheele of fortune', for no man can make 'his own cunning & practices (without regard of religion, honour, & morall honesty) his foundation'. Such an 'vntrue Politique' is the 'truest bondman to *Philautia*' for trying to 'binde occasion, & to ouer-worke fortune'; 'Essex's Device', 718.

instructions are '*Bonae Artes*' and to be distinguished from 'euill arts', which consist in 'that principle of *Machiauel*: *That a man seeke not to attain vertue it selfe: But the apparance only thereof*'.[169] This flexibility and willingness to embrace re-description on occasion should not, Bacon makes clear, replace the desire to attain true virtue.

Bacon also repeats these sentiments in his essay 'On Counsaile', first published in the edition of the *Essayes* of 1612, connecting them to the debate over the relative power of counsel and command. Describing counsel as the 'greatest trust' that can exist between men, Bacon emphasises what is at stake in taking the counsel of another; whereas 'in other confidences men commit the partes of their life', in counsel 'they commit the whole'.[170] This is not to say, however, that for princes it presents 'any diminution to their greatness ... to rely vpon counsell', quite the contrary. Counsel is precisely what protects a prince from the vicissitudes of time and 'the waues of *Fortune*'.[171] Whereas the earlier humanists had made the case that counsel did not diminish sovereignty (even if counsel ruled the prince) because it freed princes from enslavement to the passions, Bacon argues that counsel does not take away from the power of the prince because it mitigates the influence of fortune, which would otherwise enslave him.

Counsel is also clearly subjugated to command in Bacon's vision, which offers a slight revision to the Machiavellian model. Bacon uses the mythic union of Jupiter and Metis, and the birth of Minerva/Pallas, as a metaphor for the marriage that should exist between 'Soueraignty or authority' and counsel – suggesting that counsel serves to support the sovereignty of the king, as long as it occurs within the proper limits.[172] Jupiter impregnated Metis, and then ate her, growing their child, Pallas, out of his own head. Likewise, first kings 'ought to referre matters to [the Counsell of state]' and then, when 'their counsel ... grow ripe' they ought to 'take the matter back into their own hand, & make it appeare to the world, that the decrees and final directions ... proceede from themselues'.[173] Whereas Machiavelli had noted the importance of appearances in politics, he had nevertheless

[169] Bacon, *Aduancement of Learning*, 105.
[170] Francis Bacon, *Essayes* (London, 1612), 56.
[171] Bacon, *Essayes*, 57, 58. In his *Historie of the reign of King Henrie the Seuenth*, published in 1622, Bacon emphasises the relationship between a king and his time. He writes of Henry that 'No doubt, in him as in all men (and most of all in *Kings*) his *Fortune* wrought vpon his *Nature*, and his *Nature* vpon his *Fortune*'; Francis Bacon, *The Historie of the Reigne of King Henry the Seuenth* (London, 1629), 245.
[172] Bacon, *Essayes*, 59. This is taken from Bacon's 1609 *De Sapientia Veterum*.
[173] Bacon, *Essayes*, 60, 61.

insisted that the prince rule the counsel in reality, as well as in appearance. Bacon adds this awareness of outward appearances to the relationship between prince and counsellors. In both cases, however, the prince clearly rules his counsellors, and only takes counsel on matters he has first referred to them.

The separation between private and public prudence provides the foundation for a new idea of political counsel, which is rendered clearly distinct from private advice. The latter requires adherence to traditional moral rules, the former does not, although the expectation on behalf of some may require the use of re-description from time to time. The counsellor is no longer expected to lead the prince to virtue to ensure he avoids tyranny, but instead he must mitigate the effects of fortune by learning what he can about contingency and opportunity. This view of counsel – one that is suspicious of counsellor, reliant on the power of the prince and sceptical about virtue – collides with the traditional model in the context of late Tudor England and the rule of three monarchs deemed to be incapable of either ruling for themselves or defending themselves against the tyrannous rule of their counsellors.

CHAPTER 5

Late Tudor Counsellors

By abandoning the focus on virtue and replacing it with a focus on preservation by means of occasional deception, the Machiavellian discourse casts suspicion on the role of the counsellor, and especially problematises his powerful role over the monarch. This is especially the case in late Tudor England, ruled by monarchs perceived to be 'weakened' by their age or gender. Historians, most notably Patrick Collinson, John Guy, Stephen Alford and A. N. McLaren, have thoroughly investigated the way in which 'queen-in-parliament' became the dominant model for governance, based on the need to constrain the monarch with counsel.[1] These works bring to light the perceived 'weaknesses' of young and female monarchs, and the special pressures these placed on the functioning of political counsel. The Machiavellian tradition, however, has received less attention, as has the way in which the individual – and potentially self-interested – counsellor came to be seen as a threat to monarchical sovereignty, especially in such a context.[2] It is essential to understand the

[1] See Patrick Collinson, *Elizabethan Essays* (London: Bloomsbury, 1994); John Guy, ed., *The Reign of Elizabeth I: Court and Culture in the Last Decade* (Cambridge: Cambridge University Press, 1995); McLaren, 'Delineating the Elizabethan Body Politic', 224–52; Stephen Alford, *Kingship and Politics in the Reign of Edward VI* (Cambridge: Cambridge University Press, 2004); McLaren, *Political Culture*; Colclough, *Freedom of Speech*; Alice Hunt, 'The Monarchical Republic of Mary I', *The Historical Journal* 52, no.3 (2009): 557–72. Stephen Alford, *The Early Elizabethan Polity: William Cecil and the British Succession Crisis, 1558–1569* (Cambridge: Cambridge University Press, 1998), 210 suggests that this trend is traceable to the 1530s and the work of Elyot and Starkey. See also Mayer, 'Thomas Starkey', 201–27.

[2] The works cited above each only contain one mention of Machiavelli, and never in direct reference to any of his texts. Alford, *Early Elizabethan Polity*, 211 notes that Philip Sidney had read Machiavelli while travelling Italy; Alford, *Kingship and Politics*, 23 mentions the connection between the works of William Thomas and *The Prince*; Guy, *The Reign of Elizabeth I*, 69 references 'Machiavellian manoeuvres' in the negotiation of Elizabeth's marriages and McLaren, *Political Culture*, 91–6 treats Stephen Gardiner's 'Machiavellian Treatise'. In addition, Stephen Alford, *Burghley: William Cecil at the Court of Elizabeth I* (New Haven: Yale University Press, 2008), a biography of William Cecil, does not mention Machiavelli at all, and Stephen Alford, *The Watchers: A Secret History of the Reign of Elizabeth I* (New York: Penguin UK, 2012) makes only passing references to the accusation of Machiavellianism. The exception to this is Lake, *Bad Queen Bess?*, which explores the accusation of

interplay between theoretical debates (humanist versus Machiavellian models of counsel) and practical political ones (who should rule in the case of a 'weak' monarch) which determines the institutional remedies presented during the Elizabethan regime. Whereas the Henrician humanists had advocated counsellors who ruled their princes, the threat of Machiavellianism and weak monarchs renders such arguments threatening, and the counsellor falls under greater suspicion for his perceived usurpation of power.

At the same time – and by contrast – there is a view that such weak monarchs require strong counsel to guide them. If this cannot come from individuals, as they are likely to be self-interested, then it must come from different, 'dis-interested', sources. Whereas single private counsellors will be self-interested and thus ought not to rule a monarch, especially a female one, assemblies such as parliament will guide the prince according to the good of the commonwealth. For this reason, they need to have a share in the government. Command becomes 'bridled' by this source of counsel. The perceived weaknesses of the final Tudor monarchs expose the tensions in the discourse of counsel and lead to the establishment of theoretical and institutional precedents in regard to the relationship between advice and sovereignty. In short, Tudor England showcases the conflict between the humanist and Machiavellian models of counsel and the inherent tension in the counsel / command divide.

i Weak Monarchs

Although the increasing roles of the Privy Council and Parliament have been noted in scholarship on each of the three reigns which make up the later Tudor period, Alford has called for more work to unpack the 'literature of English conciliarism' that runs through them.[3] In order to understand this tradition, and its associated themes, it is important to appreciate that all three regimes can be, and were, seen as presenting a 'species of interregnum' to which a council was the given answer. As we've seen, using counsel as a remedy for weak monarchs was nothing new,

Machiavellianism in Protestant, Puritan and Catholic polemics under Elizabeth I. Even here, however, little attention is given over to how these accusations relate to a Machiavellian model of counsel.

3 Alford, *The Early Elizabethan Polity*, 210. McLaren, *Political Culture*, 87. As Watts, 'Counsel and the King's Council', 68, 85 demonstrates, from the middle of the fourteenth to the middle of the sixteenth centuries, there was an increase in the institutionalisation and formalisation of counsel-giving.

either in theory or in practice, but it does take on a renewed force in the late Tudor period, thanks to the age and gender of Henry VIII's three children and heirs: Edward VI, Mary I and Elizabeth I.

Most writers on the topic of counsel, from the classical to the early modern period, agreed that counsel ought to be given by older men, and was best if it were given to them as well.[4] The traditional cautionary tale on this account in the Christian tradition was of Rehoboam, the king who, according to the Old Testament 'forsook the counsel of the old men, which they had given him, and consulted with the young men that were grown up with him' (King James, 1 Kings 12:8). Scripture warns against the rule of youths, 'Woe to thee, O land, when they king is a child' (Ecclesiastes 10:16)[5] and drew a connection between the governorship of children and women: 'As for my people, children are their oppressors, and women rule over them' (Isaiah 3:12). The 1572 *Treatise of Treasons*, considered below, likewise suggests that the rule of women, children and the democratic multitude are all as anarchic as the other, condemning the Protestant religion which is ruled by 'a mo[n]struous Policratie of so many heads, as there are Princes, yea of women Heades, of children Heades and of popular heades . . . as if it were lauful, to have as many diuers fourmes of regiment in the Church of God'.[6] To have a woman or youth rule was as ridiculous as giving rule over to the uneducated mob. Each of these would be more likely to be ruled by their passions, and thus their self-interest, becoming tyrants.[7]

The key was prudence, which, as we've seen, was the principle virtue of the counsellor and was required for good governance. As it was drawn, at least in part, from experience, youthful counsellors would not be in possession of it, and young rulers would require elder prudent counsellors to impart it upon them. Writers on the education of princes, such as

[4] Boccaccio's *Fall of Princes* makes this lesson clear 'Howe kynge Roboam for gyuenge faythe to yonge counsayle lost the beneuolence of his people', a chapter that directly follows the contrary example 'how Saule kyng of Jerusalem borne of lowe degre as longe as he loued god and drad him and was obedyent to his lawes & ruled by good counsayle' (Giovanni Boccaccio, *The Fall of Princes*, trans. John Lydgate (London, 1527), fol. xlv^{r}). This was the example cited by Christine de Pisan in her *Book of the Body Politic* (translated as *The Body of Polycye* in 1521), and the frontispiece to the 1521 translation shows a king crowned by assembled men, presumably counsellors. It is also used in the 'book of advice' given to the rebels during the Pilgrimage of Grace in 1536, which also appealing also to the memory of Edward II and Richard II; John Guy, 'The King's Council and Political Participation', in *Reassessing the Henrician Age: Humanism, Politics and Reform, 1500–1550*, ed. Alistair Fox and John Guy (Oxford; New York: Blackwell Pub, 1986), 121–2.

[5] The verse continues 'and the princes eat in the morning!', which recalls the discussions of right-timing from Chapter 2.

[6] *Treatise of Treasons* (Louvain, 1572), 141^{v}; see Lake, *Bad Queen Bess?*, 74.

[7] McLaren, 'Elizabethan Body Politic', 235.

Erasmus and Christine de Pisan, agreed that young princes ought to be given over to the guidance of a wise tutor.[8] Pisan in particular describes 'one older knight of great authority'. It is by them that 'the sons of princes and lords ought to be governed'.[9] Furthermore, prudence was the virtue missing from women, as Aristotle had suggested, making them unfit for political rule.[10] In the words of perhaps the best-known opponent of sixteenth-century female rule (or at least Catholic female rule), John Knox, women's 'sight in civile regiment, is but blindness: their strength, weaknes: their counsel, foolishenes'; they lack both 'the spirit of counsel and regiment'.[11] Counsel could provide the remedy for the weaknesses of both youths and women.[12]

Whereas female kings, especially unmarried ones, were essentially unheard of in English history in the sixteenth century, monarchical precedent was peppered with examples of minority reigns, most recently Henry VI and Edward V; Henry VIII himself had barely made the age of majority before his own father had died in 1509.[13] As with these two most recent examples, Henry VIII sought to establish a regency council for his young son's rule after his death. In the case of Henry VI this had been largely successful; in the case of Edward V it had not, with first the rise of the Woodvilles and then the usurpation of the Lord Protector as Richard III.[14] This worry had been on Henry's mind since at least 1536, when

[8] See Chapter 1. [9] Pisan, *Body Politic*, 9.

[10] Leah Bradshaw, 'Political Rule, Prudence and the "Woman Question" in Aristotle', *Canadian Journal of Political Science* 24, no.3 (1991): 557–73. Women could be, and often in the medieval tradition were, sources of personal counsel: see Deist, *Gender and Power*; M. Schieberle, *Feminized Counsel and the Literature of Advice in England, 1380–1500* (Turnhout: Brepols Publishers, 2014); McLaren, *Political Culture*, 14.

[11] John Knox, *The First Blast of the Trumpet against the Monstruous Regiment of Women* (Geneva, 1558), 9–10; see McLaren, 'Elizabethan Body Politic', 224–52. Although prevalent, there were a multiplicity of ways of interpreting female rule, as pointed out by Victoria Smith, '"For Ye, Young Men, Show a Womanish Soul, Yon Maiden a Man's": Perspectives on Female Monarchy in Elizabeth's First Decade', in *Gender and Political Culture in Early Modern Europe, 1400–1800*, ed. James Daybell and Svante Norrhem (London; New York: Routledge, 2016), 143–57. See also Hannah Coates, 'The Moor's Counsel: Sir Francis Walsingham's Advice to Elizabeth I', in *Queenship and Counsel in Early Modern Europe*, ed. Helen Matheson-Pollock, Joanne Paul and Catherine Fletcher (Cham: Springer International Publishing, 2018), 187–214.

[12] McLaren, 'Elizabethan Body Politic', 244.

[13] Charles Beem, 'Woe to Thee, O Land! The Introduction', in *The Royal Minorities of Medieval and Early Modern England*, ed. Charles Beem (New York: Palgrave Macmillan, 2008), 2. For the etymological issues with 'queens' regnant, see Charles Beem, *The Lioness Roared – The Problems of Female Rule in English History* (New York: Palgrave Macmillan, 2006), 2–3.

[14] Ralph Alan Griffiths, *The Reign of King Henry VI: The Exercise of Royal Authority, 1422–1461* (Berkeley: University of California Press, 1981), 22–4, 38–46; Michael Hicks, 'A Story of Failure: The Minority of Edward V', in *The Royal Minorities of Medieval and Early Modern England*, ed. Charles Beem (New York: Palgrave Macmillan, 2008), 197–210.

the Second Act of Succession 'empowered the king to compose a council of regency to rule for a minor'.[15]

Henry's will acted on this, establishing a 'council of regency', which gave 'full powre and authorite unto our sayd Counsaillours that they . . . may make, devise and ordeyn what thing soever they . . . think meet, necessary or convenient'.[16] Edward is to be 'ordred and ruled both in his marriage and also in ordering of th[']affaires of the Realme as wel outward as inward[,] and also in all his oun priuate affayres[,] and in gyving of offices of charge by th['] advise and counsail of our right entierly beloved Counsaillours'.[17] It is they who have the 'the gouvernement of our moost deere sonne prince Edward and of all our Realmes, dominions and Subgectz[,] and of all th[']affayres publicq and private'.[18] They are awarded full and unchallengeable sovereignty, for the 'thinges devised made or ordeyned by them . . . shall and may Laufully' be executed 'by their discretions . . . In as large and ample maner as if we had or did expresse unto them by a more sp[e]call commission under our great Seale of Englande'.[19] In short, they alone rule with the authority of the king of England.

Although Henry first sets out that this is to be the case until Edward 'shall have fully accompleted the eightenth year of his age', he later gives a second condition for the termination of this conciliar rule: 'until our sayde sonne and heyre shalbe bestowed and maryed by their advise'.[20] The importance placed upon marriage is explicitly expressed in the case of Henry's daughters, Mary and Elizabeth. Henry, in establishing the order of the succession to the crown, notes that Mary would inherit after Edward and his heirs 'upon condition that . . . [she] shall not mary ne take any personne to her husbande without the assent and consent of the pryvey consaillours and others appoincted by us to be of counsail', and the same condition is placed upon Elizabeth.[21] To act in opposition is to sacrifice the right to the throne: 'if our sayd doughter Mary do mary without the consent and agreement of the pryvey Counsaillours and others appointed by us to be of the counsail to our sayd sonne . . . the sayde imperial croun and other the premisses shall holly remayn be and cum to our sayd doughter Elizabeth . . . as though our sayd

[15] Charles Beem, '"Have Not Wee a Noble Kynge?" The Minority of Edward VI', in *The Royal Minorities of Medieval and Early Modern England*, ed. Charles Beem (New York: Palgrave Macmillan, 2008), 215.

[16] E. W. Ives, 'Henry VIII's Will – a Forensic Conundrum', *The Historical Journal* 35, no. 4 (1992): 779–804, 801; Suzannah Lipscomb, *The King Is Dead: The Last Will and Testament of Henry VIII* (London: Head of Zeus, 2015), 85–90, 113–16, 123–4, 193.

[17] Lipscomb, *The King Is Dead*, 189–92.

[18] Lipscomb, *The King Is Dead*, 192.

[19] Lipscomb, *The King Is Dead*, 193–4.

[20] Lipscomb, *The King Is Dead*, 192, 194.

[21] Lipscomb, *The King Is Dead*, 181, 182.

doughter Mary wer thenne dead'.[22] Only by the advice and consent of the Privy Council can the heirs of Henry VIII, especially the female heirs, be married and still maintain their right to rule. As women, they were to be subordinate to their husbands, which presented the opportunity for a strong, prudent influence on the queens regnant, but also the opportunity for England's subjection to a foreign power.[23]

The regency council only lasted eight weeks into the reign of Edward VI before the rise of the king's uncle, the Duke of Somerset, as Protector and effective ruler of Edward and England. Despite (or perhaps because of) this, more often than not the official propaganda legitimising the young king's reign still played on the image of his being 'ruled' by others' counsel.[24] For instance, the court preacher Hugh Latimer choose as his theme during a court sermon in Lent 1549 the quotation from Ecclesiastes noted above, decrying a land ruled by a child. Any criticisms, he said, were not to be levelled at Edward himself, for 'The Kynge is a chyld' and 'knoweth not of it', but rather at his leading counsellors.[25] The same year Somerset wrote to Reginald Pole that 'you fear because the king is a child. But, with the help of God and faithful councilours and subjects, he has defended his own ... Josias and Solomon at his best were not old.'[26] As Alford has shown, the presentation of Edward VI ruling with his council became central to the appearance of the reign as legitimate and godly.[27] Nevertheless, the strict barrier between counsel and command must not be destroyed; in Alford's words 'counsel could not be turned into compulsion'.[28] Edward himself distinguished between the rule of a king under fourteen, who would need others to rule on his behalf, and a king between the ages of fourteen and eighteen, who would rule in conjunction with his council, the model that appears to have been adopted through much of his reign.[29] He reflected privately that he would 'seme to be in bondage' to his need to call his council before enforcing his will.[30] The paradox of counsel thus sat at the centre of Edward's reign, as it

[22] Lipscomb, *The King Is Dead*, 184.

[23] Allyna E. Ward, *Women and Tudor Tragedy: Feminizing Counsel and Representing Gender* (London: Rowman & Littlefield, 2013), 38–9; see Thomas Becon, *The Golden Boke of Christen Matrimonye* (London, 1543).

[24] See McLaren, *Political Culture*, 15–6 for the image of Edward as a counselled Josiah.

[25] Edward Hall, *The Union of the Two Noble and Illustre Families of Lancastre and Yorke* (London, 1548), sig. A, i^{r-v}, quoted in Alford, *Kingship and Politics*, 50; see also Beem, 'The Minority of Edward VI', 226.

[26] TNA Sp. 10/7 n. 28; quoted in Beem, 'The Minority of Edward VI', 226.

[27] Alford, *Kingship and Politics*, 51. [28] Alford, *Kingship and Politics*, 63.

[29] Alford, *Kingship and Politics*, 4, 43, 171. His own father had been seventeen when he'd come into full rule and his cousin James V of Scotland had been fourteen.

[30] Alford, *Kingship and Politics*, 160.

would for his two sisters: Edward – as a minor – needed to be controlled, but he could not be compelled. This 'inherent weakness' undermined the reign.[31] The recourse to Edward Seymour, duke of Somerset as *alter rex* did little to solve the problem, especially as he himself was frequently unreceptive to good counsel.[32] Seymour's refusal to rule according to the advice of the council was given priority in the justifications of his downfall.[33] Whereas Edward VI had received the education for rule that detailed the complicated and ultimately contradictory relationship between king and counsel, Edward Seymour had not, and he had failed to acquire or heed the lessons in practice.[34]

With Somerset's fall, the regime reverted to the conciliar programme of Henry VIII's will, with John Dudley, (from 1551) Duke of Northumberland assuming the role of leader, though not Protector.[35] Northumberland appears to have been more receptive to counsel, responding to William Cecil's reminder of Proverbs 11:14 – *ubinon sont consilia cadit populus* – that it was 'often had in mynde emonge us'.[36] Under Northumberland, Edward slowly took more of the reins of power himself, though in conjunction with the Privy Council.[37] In 1552, a 'counsel for the [e]state' was established, either to ease Edward's transition into majority or to 'streamline' the work of the Privy Council, or both.[38] Edward VI's early death in 1553 put an end to any plans to free him from the 'bondage' of counsel in his maturity.

Given the experience under Edward VI, it is no surprise that with the accession of Mary I, a lone female ruler of England, counsel was once again seen as a viable way to control the passions of a ruler who could not be trusted to rule herself. Mary's marriage to Philip II of Spain, though controversial, did provide some comfort to those who were concerned about the unbridled nature of this female monarch.[39] However, Philip's physical proximity to the helm of the state was necessary for such assurances, for when this was absent, an institutionalised council once again was proposed to fill the power vacuum. Before departing from England in 1555, Philip established a 'select council' to represent and replace him in the

[31] Alford, *Kingship and Politics*, 64. [32] Alford, *Kingship and Politics*, 49, 71–2.
[33] Alford, *Kingship and Politics*, 72–3. [34] Alford, *Kingship and Politics*, 46–8.
[35] Beem, 'The Minority of Edward VI', 230. [36] Alford, *Kingship and Politics*, 136.
[37] Beem, 'The Minority of Edward VI', 231. [38] Beem, 'The Minority of Edward VI', 232.
[39] Glyn Redworth, '"Matters Impertinent to Women": Male and Female Monarchy under Philip and Mary', *The English Historical Review* 112, no.447 (1997): 597. Records show that Philip, despite the restrictions placed upon him by statute, played an active role in the governance of England, attending Privy Council meetings twice weekly and playing a personal role in determinations of office; see Redworth, 'Male and Female Monarchy', 597–613.

governance of England.[40] This institution was established to be a permanent presence at court, reporting its proceedings to Philip three times a week, communicating with other councillors weekly, and even taking the place of the Privy Council in Mary's consultations.[41] Mary's reign was defined by constant and careful negotiations with her councils: 'leaving the daily affairs of the kingdom to her advisers, Mary maintained a veto-like power in those concerns which really mattered to her', primarily religion and her marriage.[42] In 1558, at the end of Mary's reign, the Protestant clergyman Christopher Goodman in his *How Svperior Powers Oght* [sic] *to be Obeyd*, suggested that the 'Counsellors . . . office is to brydle the affectio[n]s of their Prince a[n]d Gouuernours, in geui[n]g such counsele as might promote the glorie of God, a[n]d the welthe of their co[n]trie'.[43] A queen such as Mary needed to be controlled by good counsel.

We see the same negotiation between the power of council and crown played out in the much longer reign of Mary's sister, Elizabeth.[44] Unlike Mary, who acquiesced to conciliar rule in the form of her husband's select council late in her reign, Elizabeth's rule demonstrated an opposite tendency, beginning with a powerful Privy Council who saw their role as limiting and controlling the prerogative of the ruler and ending with a severe reduction of conciliar control and a markedly imperial rule by Elizabeth.[45] Much has been written on Elizabeth's relationship with her councils and with counsel.[46] In particular, it has been noted how the ongoing succession crisis under Elizabeth I yielded a number of proposals for regency councils. The 'Brief Discourse', most likely written by one of Elizabeth's councillors, sets out a plan for conciliar aristocratic rule in the case of an interregnum.[47] This 1563 document establishes that it is 'very necessary beside the ordynary government of the Realme' there should remain after Elizabeth's death 'a Counsell of estate' which is 'usually named a privee Counsell'.[48] This council is awarded the governance of all things domestic and international, spiritual and temporal until a new monarch is found. Notably, like Starkey's council (Chapter 2), this council

40 See Joanne Paul, 'Sovereign Council or Counselled Sovereign: The Marian Conciliar Compromise' in *The Birth of a Queen: Essays on the Quincentenary of Mary I*, edited by Sarah Duncan and Valerie Schutte (New York: Palgrave Macmillan, 2016), 135–53.

41 See Redworth, 'Male and Female Monarchy', 601–2.

42 Paul, 'Sovereign Council', 136.

43 Christopher Goodman, *How Svperior Powers Oght to Be Obeyd of Their Subiects* (London, 1558), 34; for the language of 'rule' of counsellors, see McLaren, *Political Culture*, 42–3.

44 McLaren, *Political Culture*, 99–100.

45 Alford, *Early Elizabethan Polity*, 3.

46 See those noted above, especially McLaren, *Political Culture*.

47 Lake, *Bad Queen Bess?*, 162–72.

48 Transcribed in Alford, *Early Elizabethan Polity*, 225.

is instituted by parliament, which also has the power to dissolve it once the new monarch is 'declared'. Parliament is awarded the power to both transfer royal imperial power to the council as well as to 'find' and 'declare' a new successor.[49] This clause endured, revived in the 'Elizabethan Exclusion Crisis' of the 1580s, when further proposals were made for 'headless conciliar government'.[50] As Lake has shown, despite the failures of these interregnum plans, they continued throughout Elizabeth's reign, growing in scope and elaboration into the 1580s.[51] Likewise, a scheme for instituting a citizen militia in the hands of Elizabeth's counsellors has been connected to the rising republicanism of the reign.[52] One answer, thus, to the perceived weakness of Elizabeth I and her half-siblings was a strong conciliar presence, either through the governance of a single counsellor or a group, formally or informally, a reflection of the traditional humanist model of counsel.[53] However, this model, as we've seen, had already received a convincing challenge from the Machiavellian discourse, and so too the conciliar control of the late Tudor monarchs is subject to Machiavellian opposition.

ii Tyrannous Counsellors

From one perspective, these conciliar measures were seen as important ways of 'bridling' monarchs sorely in need of it; from another, they were 'power grabs' from Machiavellian counsellors out to secure their own power and self-interest, regardless of what damage it did to monarch and country.[54] This perspective problem certainly had a great deal to do with religious allegiances, as Lake demonstrates, but was also facilitated by the tension between the traditional humanist and Machiavellian models of counsel.[55] In the second half of the sixteenth century, the idea that weak monarchs needed to be ruled by counsel came up against a growing fear of Machiavellian counsellors, who would take advantage of an incapable monarch to seize power for their own interests. Machiavellian counsellors were too willing to place *utile* over *honestum*, or policy over religion, and constituted a real threat to the realm with a weak monarch on the throne. Machiavelli's solution was a prudent prince, but the context had not

[49] Alford, *Early Elizabethan Polity*, 112. [50] Collinson, *Elizabethan Essays*, 43, 42.
[51] Lake, *Bad Queen Bess?*, 207.
[52] Neil Younger, 'Securing the Monarchical Republic: The Remaking of the Lord Lieutenancies in 1585', *Historical Research* 84, no. 224 (2011): 249–65.
[53] McLaren, 'Elizabethan Body Politic', 236–7. [54] Lake, *Bad Queen Bess?*, 173–4.
[55] Lake, *Bad Queen Bess?*, 108.

provided one, especially when Elizabeth refused to marry. As such, an alternative source of counsel would need to be found, one that avoided the problems of self-interest highlighted by the Machiavellian discourse.

Machiavellianism, as we've seen, had entered an elite English consciousness by the 1530s. Both Edward VI and Mary I received 'Machiavellian' advice. The Privy Council clerk William Thomas wrote a series of secret Machiavellian counsels to Edward VI, suggesting that in cases of relations with other (devious) princes, 'policie is no vice' and 'crafte' and 'subtiltie' are 'rather honourable than otherwise'.[56] Likewise, a manuscript *Discourse on the Coming of the English and Normans to Britain* given to Mary I and Philip II notes, with Machiavelli, that 'Our purpose at present is not to show what a prince is permitted to do and what he is not permitted to do, but only to show by what ways and means a prince can maintain or lose his state' and so 'I do not blame such cruelty when a prince is all but forced to do it, in order to maintain his state.'[57] That being said, the spectre of the 'Machiavel' only fully manifests under Elizabeth I, and it is during her reign that concerns of tyrannous counsellors taking advantage of a weak monarch are most clearly articulated.

The definition of Machiavellianism is given by the 1571 *Treatise of Treasons*: 'a Machiauellian State & Regime[n]t' is 'where Religion is put behind in the seco[n]d & last place: wher y^t^ ciuil Policie ... is preferred before it'; this is 'a Machiauellian defined'.[58] The author does not seek to criticise Elizabeth, but like others we shall see, writes against what he perceives as the *real* power behind the throne – her counsellors, in particular two unnamed men (William Cecil and Nicholas Bacon)[59] to whom he attributes 'what so euer of importance commeth foorth vnder [Elizabeth], or hath bene sene in her time'.[60] Prioritising policy over religion and using the rhetorical arts of persuasion, these counsellors have transgressed the line between counsel and command: 'of these two men, I say, and of none other, am I to be vnderstanden in this Treatise, when I vse any terme, that may seeme to touche Authoritie: bycause I meane none other Authority, then of

[56] Thomas, *The Works of William Thomas*, 139, 143.

[57] Peter S. Donaldson, ed., *A Machiavellian Treatise* (Cambridge: Cambridge University Press, 2009), 138, 141.

[58] *Treatise of Treasons*, sig. a, 5^r^. This text is usually attributed to the Scottish bishop and humanist John Leslie; Margaret Beckett, 'The Political Works of John Lesley, Bishop of Ross (1527–96)' (PhD, University of St Andrews, 2002), 163–93 demonstrates convincingly that this was most likely not the case, although Leslie may have been involved in a collaborative effort with a number of other authors; see Lake, *Bad Queen Bess?*, 70–93.

[59] Lake, *Bad Queen Bess?*, 73.

[60] *Treatise of Treasons*, sig. a, 7^v^.

them two only'.[61] They are the tyrants, ruling for 'their own private before the common profit' and the queen is only so 'but in name'.[62] Likewise, John Stubbs's *Discoverie of a Gaping Gulf*, for which its author, a Protestant writer and member of Lincoln's Inn, would lose his hand, reproached those who place profit before honesty: 'In all deliberations of most private actions, the very heathen are wont first to consider honesty and then profit', but there is a 'strange Christianity of some men in our age, who in their state consultations have not so much respect to honesty as they had to profit', who 'use the word of God with as little conscience as they do Machiavelli, picking out of both indifferently what may serve their turns'.[63] Although concerned with negotiations over the French marriage in particular, Stubbs makes clear from the outset that the tract is in fact about counsel in general. The 'gaping gulf' of the title, in which 'England is Like to be Swallowed' refers directly to the deficit of good counsel in the English court:

> some English mouths professing Christ are also persuaders of the [marriage] . . . alas, this ship of unhappy load hath among us and of ourselves (I would, not in prince's court) those who with all their might and main help to hale it in, and . . . our own men walk on this shore and lay to their shoulders with fastened lines and cables to draw it in. This is our mischief, this is the swallowing gulf of our bottomless destruction; else might we think ourselves impregnable.[64]

These counsellors, Stubbs suggests, are not only self-interested, and thus to the extent that they are in power are tyrants, but are also convincing Elizabeth to pursue her self-interest, crafting her into a tyrant as well. More than just a tactic to avoid a direct attack on the monarch (as the text did not avoid this in any case), this critique of counsellors was part of an opposition to Machiavellianism in the court, and a genuine concern about its influence.[65]

The paranoia about the power of these Machiavellian counsellors is drawn from the weakness of rule presented by the queen's gender. The

[61] *Treatise of Treasons*, sig. a, 8^r.

[62] *Treatise of Treasons*, sig. c, 4^r; fol. 29^v; Lake, *Bad Queen Bess*, 78–9.

[63] John Stubbs, *Gaping Gulf, with Letters and Other Relevant Documents*, ed. Lloyd E. Berry (Charlottesville: University Press of Virginia, 1968), 3, 12; see Peltonen, *Rhetoric, Politics, and Popularity*, 117–27; See Mears, 'Counsel, Public Debate, and Queenship', 629–50; Lake, *Bad Queen Bess?*, 99–103.

[64] Stubbs, *Gaping Gulf*, 4.

[65] Lake, *Bad Queen Bess?*, 72 treats the 'mask of evil counsel' in *Treatise of Treasons*.

problem of sole monarch, clear in the classical and humanist works, becomes re-worked as a problem of sole *female* monarch under Elizabeth. Speaking of 'the chief of these two Machiauellians', the *Treatise*'s author suggests that even before Elizabeth came to the throne, he, 'finding that he had a yong Ladie in hand, that was vnexpert in matters of State', had worked his way into her trust and also introduced to her counsel his 'confederate', the second counsellor in question.[66] These counsellors, as Stubbs puts it, are 'not Satan in body of a serpent, but the old serpent in the shape of a man, whose sting is in his mouth, and who doth his endeavour to seduce our Eve'.[67] Stubbs reminds his readers that these pernicious counsellors are even more worrying in England's present state of female rule, 'because [our Eve] is also our Adam and sovereign lord or lordly lady of this land, it is so much more dangerous'.[68] William Allen, an exiled English Cardinal, writes in his 1584 *A true, sincere and modest defense of English Catholics*, that the Protestant counsellors who persecute Catholics in England have 'abused [Elizabeth's] weak sex and former years of her youth'.[69] Elizabeth is a woman, and this 'infirmary' made her easy to 'seduce'.[70] The 'more gentle or innocent' the sovereign is, the more 'violent' the government, 'through the abuse of their simplicity by the tyranny of such as occupy under them the principle authority'.[71] *A declaration of the True Causes of the Great Troubles Presupposed to be Intended against the Realm of England* of 1592, a short tract based on a Latin text written by the Jesuit Robert Parsons, compares Elizabeth to Eve and Leicester to the serpent. As in Allen, Leicester has 'abused the sex and capacity of his princess' in leading her astray.[72] Parsons himself, in *Newes from Spayne and Holland*, published a year later, likewise held that the 'chiefest grownde' of the Machiavellian rule of Lord Burghley 'hath bin the Queenes being a sole woman, who therby hath bin enforced to giue her selfe wholy into his handes'.[73]

66 *Treatise of Treasons*, 86^{v}, 86^{r}.

67 Stubbs, *Gaping Gulf*, 3. See also *A Declaration of the True Causes of the Great Troubles Presupposed to Be Intended against the Realm of England* (Antwerp, 1592), 8–9 for Elizabeth as the tempted Eve; Lake, *Bad Queen Bess?*, 345.

68 Stubbs, *Gaping Gulf*, 3–4.

69 William Allen, *The Execution of Justice in England, by William Cecil; and A True, Sincere, and Modest Defense of English Catholics, by William Allen*, ed. Robert MacCune Kingdon (Ithaca: Cornell University Press, 1965), 107; see Lake, *Bad Queen Bess?*, 137.

70 Allen, *Modest Defense*, 141.

71 Allen, *Modest Defense*, 141; see below for a discussion of the 'tyranny' of counsellors.

72 'Abuse, V.', in *OED Online* (Oxford University Press), www.oed.com/view/Entry/822: 'abuse, v.: To use (something) improperly, to misuse; to make a bad use of; to pervert; to take advantage of wrongly.'

73 Robert Parsons, *Newes from Spayne and Holland* (Antwerp, 1593), 35^{r}.

Returning to the important relationship between counsel and marriage, these problems may have been averted if the queen had married, but as it was, this was 'the state and condition, in which your Prince, a yong Ladie, and sole Virgin, without help of Husband, entered & was setled in her Crowne and Dominion, & toke to her seruice this couple of Counsailers'.[74] The *Treatise* advises the queen that she ought to free herself from such influences, for 'wisedome (I wene) yea and Machiauell him self' would recommend that she ought to 'cast both them and their Counselles, out of her credit and Courte'.[75] Here, the author seems to make reference to Chapter XXIII of *The Prince*, in which Machiavelli treats the case of a monarch whose own wisdom is not enough to rule over his counsellors, in England's case a woman without prudence to guide her. Stubbs takes the same approach; he addresses Elizabeth directly: 'we instantly beseech you, to keep this sin far from you by admitting no counsel that may bring it near to you ... [and to] stop your Majesty's ears against those sorcerers and their enchanting counsels'.[76] Like Machiavelli and the author of the *Treatise*, he accepts that it is the prince who must be prudent enough to control his counsellors, not the other way around, and so he prays that she be given a 'principle spirit' to 'sift counsels that you may smell a flatterer from a loyal counsellor, prove all and approve the best'.[77]

The recourse to Machiavelli as a way to counter Machiavels is most clearly seen in *Leicester's Commonwealth*, which began circulating in 1584.[78] Written in reply to Burghley's *True Execution of Justice in England*, which condemns the treasonous nature of the Catholic population of England, this anonymous dialogue puts forward the argument that the far greater threat to England comes from closer to the crown, namely the ambitious Earl of Leicester, whose influence 'hath done more hurt to his common-wealth than if he had murdered many thousands of her subjects or betrayed whole armies to the professed enemy'.[79] The dialogue's participants agree with the premise of Burghley's *True Execution*, that there is a 'degree' of treason which 'want[s] but occasion or ability to break into the second [degree]'; in other words all it lacks is the right moment to be put into

[74] *Treatise of Treasons*, 87^{r}. [75] *Treatise of Treasons*, 169^{v}, 171^{r-v}. [76] Stubbs, *Gaping Gulf*, 30.

[77] Stubbs, *Gaping Gulf*, 30.

[78] Originally circulated with the title *The Copy of a Letter Written by a Master of Art of Cambridge*, it almost immediately became known as *Leicester's Commonwealth*; see D. C. Peck, 'Introduction', in *Leicester's Commonwealth: The Copy of a Letter Written by a Master of Art of Cambridge (1584) and Related Documents* (Athens, OH: Ohio University Press, 1985), 3–5.

[79] D. C. Peck, ed., *Leicester's Commonwealth: The Copy of a Letter Written by a Master of Art of Cambridge (1584) and Related Documents* (Athens, OH: Ohio University Press, 1985), 79; see Peck, 'Introduction', 5.

execution.[80] However, there is a 'cause or circumstance [which] may stay' the Catholics from such treason 'when they shall have ability and opportunity': the fear of servitude to other countries.[81] Leicester's treason, on the other hand, lacks only opportunity – the queen's death – an event which he himself could orchestrate and which is, in the end, inevitable.

In general, the author writes, there is a danger posed by any counsellor who crosses the line between counsel and command, for it 'it cannot be but prejudicial and exceeding dangerous unto our noble prince and realm that any one man whatsoever . . . should grow to so absolute authority and commandry in the Court'.[82] For this reason, Leicester, like other controlling counsellors is a 'tyrant'.[83] Playing on the idea that the prince ought to be 'bridled' by good counsel, the author suggests that such a man 'cast[s] nets and chains and invisible bands about that person whom most of all he pretendeth to serve, [and] he shutteth up his prince in a prison most sure, though sweet and senseless', while other counsellors watch on silently.[84] The main speaker of the dialogue comments on how 'many even of the best and faithfullest subjects of the land do yield to the present time and do keep silence in some matters that otherwise they would take it for duty to utter'.[85] Leicester, on the other hand, will use time to his advantage, for having learned from 'Seignor Machiavel my Lord's counsellor', Leicester waits until the moment when 'occasion serve[s]' to move against the queen; 'Such is the variable policy of men that serve the time, or rather that serve themselves of all times, for their purposes'.[86]

Notably, the solution proposed in *Leicester's Commonwealth* is to adopt the same attitude to time and expediency as the traitorous Leicester. Traditional justice is too confining, for it waits until the treasonous act has been committed. Instead, one must accept the use of pre-emptive justice; it may not be honourable, but it is necessary to the safety and well being of the state: 'Perhaps the consultation of this affair is not what were convenient but what is expedient: not what ought to be done in justice, but what may be done in safety'.[87] The typical demands of justice must be dispensed with in the name of expediency. Thus, although the author remarks against Leicester's use of Machiavelli, he is forced to accept that the only way to fight fire is with fire – to pre-empt Machiavellianism by using it first.[88]

[80] *Leicester's Commonwealth*, 68. [81] *Leicester's Commonwealth*, 68.
[82] *Leicester's Commonwealth*, 93.
[83] *Leicester's Commonwealth*, 72, 73, 78, 102, 186, 189; see Lake, *Bad Queen Bess?*, 118–20, 122.
[84] *Leicester's Commonwealth*, 93. [85] *Leicester's Commonwealth*, 99.
[86] *Leicester's Commonwealth*, 132, 154. [87] *Leicester's Commonwealth*, 192.
[88] Philip Sidney points out this recourse to Machiavelli in his *Defense of Leicester* written against *Leicester's Commonwealth*: '[only] when [the author of the *Commonwealth*] plays the "statist," wringing very unluckily some of Machiavel's axioms to serve his purpose, then indeed he triumphs';

iii The Counsel of the Dead

Counsellors thus become tyrants if they cross the divide between counsel and command and rule in their own self-interest. Furthermore, there was a recurrent concern about the way in which this counsel crossed another divide: that between public and private. Whereas private counsel was advocated by More, who condemned public counsel, increasingly in the latter half of the sixteenth century private counsel is viewed with suspicion, if not seen as necessarily treasonous. The fear of the contamination of public interest with private, condemned throughout this discourse, becomes connected with a denunciation of private counsel.[89] Counsel in the public interest will be given in public; the counsel that hides in the shadows must necessarily be privately interested. As unmarried female monarchs like Elizabeth were perceived as being simply incapable of controlling counsellors, a source of counsel that was public and publicly interested would have to be sought.

There are at least two solutions proposed to this problem. First, for many, to find a disinterested, honest, prudent source of counsel, one only need open up a book. In Francis Bacon's essay on counsel, he encounters three inconveniences of counsel. The first we have already treated, that counsel subjected the crown, a problem he solves with the tale of Jupiter and Metis. The second is that soliciting counsel has the potential for 'the reuealing of affaires'.[90] In response, he states that princes are not compelled to disclose secrets of state nor 'it is necessarie, that hee that consulteth what hee should doe; should declare what he will doe'.[91] We shall come back to this issue of secret-keeping in the next chapter. Bacon's third inconvenience, 'that men will counsel with an eie to themselues', he treats as having the most significance.[92] He gives a number of suggestions as to how princes can remedy this problem, but concludes that the best solution is to avoid living counsellors altogether. He ends his essay: 'It was truly said; *Optimi Consiliarij mortui*' for 'Books will speake plain, when *Counsellors* Blanch'.[93]

Although the source is Erasmus (see Chapter 1), this adage is used often throughout this period as a remedy to the suspicion of the Machiavellian counsellor. Lipsius employs this phrase in his treatment of history and counsel in the *Sixe Bookes*. Although experience, '*The knowledge of worldly*

Philip Sidney, 'Defense of Leicester', in *Leicester's Commonwealth: The Copy of a Letter Written by a Master of Art of Cambridge (1584) and Related Documents*, ed. D. C. Peck (Athens, OH: Ohio University Press, 1985), 254.

89 Lake, *Bad Queen Bess?*, 83 connects this to the language of 'policy'.

90 Bacon, *Essayes*, 62.

91 Bacon, *Essayes*, 63.

92 Bacon, *Essayes*, 64–5.

93 Bacon, *Essayes*, 68–9.

matters which we haue either seene or had the handling of, is far more valuable than memory, '*the like knowledge of those things, we haue eyther heard or read*', experience is more problematic as it is 'not learned by precepts, but taught by time'.[94] It is only old men who can possess such knowledge, and the lessons will die with them. Experience is conquered by time, rather than standing triumphant above it. Thus, 'the memorie of things, or of a historie' is the easier approach 'not onely to attain vnto prudence, but to goodnesse likewise'.[95] It 'bringeth more things that are profitable both to prudence, and beside to more persons then vse doth'.[96] Here we see the Machiavellian shift in the meaning of prudence linked to a preference for knowledge gleaned from histories, based in large part on its applicability to particular circumstances. In its contingency, such knowledge is universally valid; it 'agreeth with all men, and fitteth all times, and seasons'.[97] History is what provides us with the knowledge to recognise and seize *kairos*. Quoting Cicero, Lipsius notes that history is the '*preseruer of the vertue of worthy personages*', a '*benefactresse to all mankind*', the '*light of truth, the mistresse of life*' and a 'glasse' in which one may '*behold, all maner of instruction and examples*'.[98] Just as he had argued that experience 'principally ... conduceth vnto Ciuill policy', Lipsius suggests that this 'more safe, and assured' way to prudence 'is most necessarie in this part of Ciuill life' and 'Directeth those that haue publike authoritie'.[99] Furthermore, histories in particular 'are in matter of publike counsell ... *most profitable*' and 'in consultation ... holdeth the chiefest place'.[100] This is not to say that they should be wielded by counsellors, but rather that they should replace such figures altogether, for he ends by declaring that 'the best counsellors are the dead, that is ... authors, which are without dissimulatio[n]', meaning 'the bookes, and treaties of histories'.[101]

Lipsius appeals to the counsel of the dead as a superior means of the counsellor acquiring prudence, according to his definition of it. Others turn to history's counsel as a means of avoiding the taint of self-interest. Matthew Coignet, for example, employs the adage in his 1586 *Discourses upon Trueth and Lying*, questioning the reliability of counsellors to present the king with frank and truthful advice, either due to the decorous demands of rhetoric, or their own self-interest. He supports his argument –

94 Lipsius, *Sixe Bookes*, 12. 95 Lipsius, *Sixe Bookes*, 13. 96 Lipsius, *Sixe Bookes*, 13.

97 Lipsius, *Sixe Bookes*, 13.

98 Lipsius, *Sixe Bookes*, 14; See A. J. Woodman, *Rhetoric in Classical Historiography* (Portland: Taylor & Francis, 2003), x, 78–97; Matthew Fox, *Cicero's Philosophy of History* (Oxford: Oxford University Press, 2007), 136, 140, 165.

99 Lipsius, *Sixe Bookes*, 14. 100 Lipsius, *Sixe Bookes*, 14. 101 Lipsius, *Sixe Bookes*, 14.

that princes should thus turn instead to literary counsel – with the advice of Demetrius to King Ptolomy: to 'diligently reade such bookes, as intreated of the gouernmentes of kingdomes and segnuries, to the end he might be instructed in those thinges, which men dare not so freelie, deliuer them selues to princes'.[102] Coignet concludes that 'the penne is of a more free condition then the tongue' and thus it is best 'To take cou[n]sell of the deade'.[103] A living counsellor, armed with dissimulation and burdened by self-interest, cannot be trusted as much as a dead one.

We can identify this tradition in the dedications of histories in the period, which are framed as more worthwhile counsel than can be gleaned from dubious living counsellors. The 1549 *Epitome of Chronicles*, written by Thomas Lanquet and finished by Thomas Cooper, a theologian and later bishop of Winchester, stresses the role that history should play in replacing the counsellor.[104] Cooper's dedicatory address is written to 'the ryghte hyghe and myghtye Prynce, Edward', by whom he means not Edward VI, but rather his protector, the Duke of Somerset, the 'gouernour of the kynges maiestees most royall person, and protectour of all his hyghnesse realmes dominions, and subiectes'.[105] His address to Somerset stands as a striking example of the way in which history could serve as a replacement to living counsellors. He begins by praising (in the manner of Erasmus' panegyric) the Duke for his openness to receiving counsel. As all people of all degree 'maye at all conueniente times haue free access' to Somerset, Cooper thinks it likely that 'the true knowledge of the state and condicion of the weale publike, is at all tymes to your grace reueled & opened'.[106] He goes on, however, to question this assumption, for in all commonwealths of the past there have been those who have 'hindered *true report*'.[107] He thus worries about those who through 'flatterye and dissimulacion' may 'abuse your godly gentlenesse', leading Somerset and England to ruin.[108] Cooper does away with this traditional model of counsel, replacing it with one built on history. Since 'of all other it is a thinge mooste difficile and harde to rule well, and for a chiefe magistrate and gouernour to be truly and without dissimulacion informed in euerye case', he suggests that 'the best and most sure way for a noble gouernour . . . is to reade such bookes as most wittily and pithilye treat of the states of common weales, and namely

[102] Coignet, *Politique discourses*, 69. [103] Coignet, *Politique discourses*, 69–70.

[104] See Anna R. Beer, '"Left to the World without a Maister": Sir Walter Ralegh's "The History of the World" as a Public Text', *Studies in Philology* 91, no. 4 (1994): 448–52.

[105] Thomas Lanquet, *Epitome of Chronicles* (London, 1549), sig. A, ii^{r}.

[106] Lanquet, *Epitome of Chronicles*, sig. A, ii^{r}. [107] Lanquet, *Epitome of Chronicles*, sig. A, ii^{r}.

[108] Lanquet, *Epitome of Chronicles*, sig. A, ii^{r}.

histories'.[109] Not only will true counsel be guaranteed through such means, but 'in bookes shall [the prince] lerne to know the wilie flattering foxes, from his sure and trustye friends: good and faythfull ministers, from false feigning dissemblers'.[110] Furnished with such knowledge, the duke will have no need of any external counsel, for 'he shall learne out of bookes to bee him selfe to him selfe, the best the truest and the surest counsaylour'.[111]

The clearest articulation of this idea comes in the 1571 translation of Pierre Boaistuau's *A most excellent Hystorie, Of the Institution and First Beginning of Christian Princes* by James Chillester. The original French text purports to have been a translation from the work of Chelidonius Tigurinus, but there is no other record of such a person, and it has been suggested instead that Boaistuau obtained his material from the 1519 *De regis officio opusculum* by Josse van Clichtove, the ascription to a fictional Chelidonius being a deliberate fabrication.[112] Boaistuau tells his readers that the original work fell short of his expectations; 'Chelidonius' neglected to write on several topics typical of the classical advice-to-princes genre. To make up for this, Boaistuau adds a number of treatises of his own construction, including an elaborate treatise on flattery, which serves as his prologue. Like Coignet, Lipsius and Bacon, he emphasises the truth-telling potential of history over and above living persons, based on the temporal constraints faced by the latter: 'Bookes do always franckly & with all libertie admonish vs of those things which our Friends (commonly giuing place to time) do suppresse and keepe in silence'.[113] It is worth quoting Boaistuau's articulation of this idea at length:

> Bookes are as Iudges without feare, which neuer are ashamed to shewe the truth, nor neuer stay themselues for the dyspleasure or indignation of any King, Prince, or Magistrate, but folowing their free nature and condition, with sharp and nypping wordes to disclose mens corrupt manners, rebuking them sharply, that there is no sworde more to bee feared than the Learned pen.[114]

The living counsellors of the court, on the other hand, Boaistuau describes as 'flattering and mealy mouthed friends', who 'oftentymes did stoppe their eares, become mute and dumbe, and passe vnder consent the enormities

109 Lanquet, *Epitome of Chronicles*, sig. A, iii^r.
110 Lanquet, *Epitome of Chronicles*, sig. A, iii^v.
111 Lanquet, *Epitome of Chronicles*, sig. A, iii^v.
112 H. Tudor, 'L'Institution Des Princes Chrestiens: A Note on Boaistuau and Clichtove', *Bibliothèque d'Humanisme et Renaissance* 45, no. 1 (1983): 103–6.
113 *A Most Excellent Hystorie, of the Institution and First Beginning of Christian Princes* (London, 1571), 4.
114 *A Most Excellent Hystorie*, 4.

and abuses they see ... nothwithsta[n]ding they know and see very well, their Princes and Lordes want greatly admonition and councell'.[115] Thus, princes 'want nothing but frank and discrete mouthes that should tel them the truth', a role which Boaistuau would give to philosophers, who would act as 'a dog, that shal bee capable of reason, and shall bark agaynst all men, yea euen against your owne selfe if ye shal do any thing worthy of reprehensio[n], and shal vse with al wisdom & discretio[n], and haue regard to the time & season when and how he ought to do his office', in other words, the traditional humanist figure of the counsellor.[116] However, the time for such a figure has passed. Thus, 'there is no medicine more meete' for the diseases of princes 'than the continuall reading of Bookes, which do the office of Iudges and refourmers, and giue them knowledge of their offences'.[117] In the context of the post-Machiavellian court, princes are best to avoid counsellors altogether, and learn directly from histories.[118]

When histories are aimed at counsellors, as the source for their counsel, they replace moral philosophy as the proper raw material for the counsellor. Blundeville's translation of Furió Ceriol (which we explored in Chapter 3), for example, shifts emphasis to the necessity of histories for princes by writing that 'nothing is more necessary for a counseler, than to bee a diligent reader of Hystories', and Felippe repeats a similar lesson: 'The Counsellers of Princes, ought to haue attentively read, both ancient and newe Histories'.[119] This model is expressed in most detail by Blundeville in his 1574 *The true order and methode of wryting and reading hystories*, dedicated to the Earl of Leicester. In his opening epistle Blundeville tells Leicester that his purpose in writing such a work is 'to gather thereof such iudgement and knowledge as you may therby be the more able, as well to direct your priuate actions, as to giue Counsell lyke a most prudent Counseller in publyke causes'.[120] Within the work, he stresses the role of the historian to present the truth in its entirety, so that those who read it – counsellors like Leicester – can apply lessons to their present context. He also highlights history as the means to acquire the ability to navigate occasion; it is the 'skill' of the individual in history which 'causeth him to take occasion when it is offered, and to vse the meetest meanes to bring it to passe'.[121] This role is echoed by

[115] *A Most Excellent Hystorie*, 5. [116] *A Most Excellent Hystorie*, 6.
[117] *A Most Excellent Hystorie*, 9.
[118] Another of Boaistuau's added treatises addresses the importance of marriage, aimed, almost certainly, at Elizabeth I.
[119] Furió Ceriol, *A very Briefe and Profitable Treatise*, sig. F, 1^v-2^r; Felippe, *The Counseller*, 45.
[120] Thomas Blundeville, *The True Order and Method of Writing and Reading Histories* (London, 1574), sig. A, ii^r.
[121] Blundeville, *Writing and Reading Histories*, sig. B, ii^v.

the reader of history, who by its knowledge gains 'better knowledge of the opportunitie of affayres' of his own time, and is thus better prepared to bring his own endeavours to success.[122] In addressing 'What Profite hystories doe yeelde', Blundeville makes clear that the application of history is political, replacing moral philosophy as the proper raw material for the counsellor. Although 'the way to come to that peace [of the commonwealth] wherof I speake, is partly taught by the Philosophers in generall precepts and rules', it is 'the Historiographers' that 'doe teache it much more playnlye by perticular examples and experiences', especially if they write in the way he prescribes.[123] Such 'perticular examples' allow the reader to see the chain of causes and effects which bring political situations into being: 'the three generall actions of any Citie, Prince, or common weale' – peace, sedition and war – 'we ought diligently to obserue in histories with such considerations, as we may learne thereby, how one selfe effect springeth of one selfe cause'.[124]

In the Elizabethan period there is also a growing sense that the multitude or people might have privileged access to the knowledge of recent history, having lived through it.[125] Anne Dowriche's *The French Historie* of 1589 places the onus of a political role of spectatorship and counsel on the Protestant multitude, due to the untrustworthiness of traditional counsellor-figures who have adopted Machiavellian tactics and are, in the most crucial event of the history, represented by a weak queen (in this case the French queen mother Catherine de' Medici).[126] Dowriche establishes these themes in her address to the reader, writing that her 'onelie purpose in collecting & framing this worke was to edifie, comfort and stirre vp the godlie mindes vnto care, watchfulnesse, zeale & feruentnesse'.[127] In contrast with these weak counsellors, seduced by Machiavellianism, Dowriche calls upon the English Protestant multitude to 'watchfulness'. There is, however, a further role, as Elaine Beilin has demonstrated, for the Protestant multitude, which is to 'speak to and advise the ruler', largely through the extension of free speech in Parliament.[128] Given the failure of

[122] Blundeville, *Writing and Reading Histories*, sig. B, iv^r.

[123] Blundeville, *Writing and Reading Histories*, sig. D, iii^v-iv^r.

[124] Blundeville, *Writing and Reading Histories*, sig. E, iii^v.

[125] Lee, *Popular Sovereignty*, 171.

[126] See Randall Martin, 'Anne Dowriche's "The French History", Christopher Marlowe, and Machiavellian Agency', *Studies in English Literature, 1500–1900* 39, no. 1 (1999): 69, 75–81 for the characterisation of Catherine de Medici as 'an ambitious Machiavel'.

[127] Anne Dowriche, *The French Historie* (London, 1589), sig. A, 3^v.

[128] Elaine V. Beilin, '"The World Reproov'd": Writing Faith and History in England', in *Culture and Change: Attending to Early Modern Women*, ed. Margaret Mikesell and Adele F. Seeff (Newark; London: University of Delaware Press, 2003), 266–80.

both counsellors and their female ruler, the (godly) people are left as the only legitimate source of good counsel.[129]

This brings us to the second solution tentatively presented to the problem of the counsellor raised above: the discourse described by A. N. McLaren, in which the queen is bridled by good counsel, especially that of parliament.[130] As McLaren has shown, during Elizabeth's reign, parliament is increasingly seen as a way of providing control over Elizabeth, largely through counsel. Central to the legitimacy of Elizabeth's reign, as articulated primarily by John Aylmer, was the concept of the 'mixed constitution', which reassured readers that Elizabeth would rule by the law, parliament and her male counsellors.[131] Aylmer writes that because England has been 'of late . . . a lytle maymed', 'it is necessary for al good men, & the dutie of all faithfull Subiectes to haue an eye to it, that it runne not vpon the rockes, and make shipp wrake', vocabulary which is reflected in Dowriche's *Historie*.[132] Aylmer presents a 'new species of obedience', in which loyalty is given to the queen, 'insofar as she has been counselled – and counselled by men who are themselves godly', which requires a further opening out of the concept of counsel.[133] For instance, John Hooker in his *Order and Usage*, published in the 1570s, defines counsel – in McLaren's words – as 'geographically extensive and potentially socially inclusive', embodied in parliament.[134] But Hooker also tinges Aylmer's vision with a hint of pessimistic realism. For Hooker, the monarch held parliament in order to seek 'aduise and counsel of all the estates of his Realme' in times of 'necessitie', but it was entirely bound to the prince's will, 'without this his authoritie: no parlement can properly be summoned or assembled'.[135]

For this reason, if the prince was seduced by Machiavellian counsel, there was little that parliament could do in opposition to this, as John Stubbs points

[129] See Mihoko Suzuki, 'Warning Elizabeth with Catherine De' Medici's Example: Anne Dowriche's French Historie and the Politics of Counsel', in *The Rule of Women in Early Modern Europe*, ed. Anne J. Cruz and Mihoko Suzuki (Urbana: University of Illinois Press, 2009), 174–93; Beilin, 'The World Reproov'd', 266–80; Micheline Monica White, '"Cunning in Controversies": English Protestant Women Writers and Religious and Literary Debates, 1580–1615' (Ph.D., Loyola University Chicago, 1998); Elaine V. Beilin, '"Some Freely Spake Their Minde": Resistance in Anne Dowriche's The French Historie', in *Women, Writing, and the Reproduction of Culture in Tudor and Stuart Britain*, ed. Mary Elizabeth Burke et al. (Syracuse: Syracuse University Press, 2000), 119–40.

[130] McLaren, 'Elizabethan Body Politic', 237–52; McLaren, *Political Culture*; see also Guy, 'Rhetoric of Counsel', 301 for parliament as a 'locus of *consilium*' during the reign of Elizabeth I.

[131] McLaren, *Political Culture*; Ward, *Women and Tudor Tragedy*, 31–2.

[132] John Aylmer, *An Harborowe for Faithfull and Trewe Svbiectes* (London, 1559), B^{r}.

[133] McLaren, 'Elizabethan Body Politic', 245. [134] McLaren, *Political Culture*, 164–8.

[135] John Hooker, *The Order and Vsage of the Keeping of a Parlement in England* (London, 1575), 20^{r}; see Guy, 'Rhetoric of Counsel', 303–4.

out in regard to Elizabeth's marriage.[136] It may have theoretically been a mixed constitution, but in reality, parliament had little power even to offer counsel unless Elizabeth was willing to hear it. And it certainly could offer no governance over her. Holinshed's history makes clear that parliament's counsel must occur within the strictures of the counsel / command distinction. As Annabel Patterson has pointed out, the *Chronicles* put forward parliament as the most important political institution in England, and the compilers of the later editions, which included John Hooker, 'added material that ... was probably recognizable as the vehicle of a clear and ideologically potent theory, a theory of Parliament's role as the emblem (if not the guarantor) of limited monarchy'.[137] For this reason, freedom of speech within parliament is essential to communicate their advice to the monarch; for Holinshed, parliament is a place of both counsel and consent.[138] Despite these strong parliamentary themes, Holinshed also iterates Elizabeth's demarcation of the difference between counsel and command in the context of parliament.[139] Upon receiving a petition in regard to her marriage, Elizabeth tells the representatives that she 'doe lyke' the 'maner' of their counsel and she 'take[s] it in good part', as 'it is simple, and contayneth no lymitation of place or person' – they have counselled within their bounds – but she also takes this opportunity to issue a warning regarding the division between counsel and command.[140] Elizabeth tells them that if they overstepped themselves by attempting to command or force her, she 'must haue mislyked it verie much, and thought in you a verie great presumption, being vnfitte and altogither vnmeete, to require them that may commaunde, or those appoynt, whose partes are to desire or such to binde and limitte, whose duties are to obey: or take vpon you to draw my loue to your lykings, or to frame my wil to your fancies'.[141] Elizabeth includes any attempts to 'draw [her] loue to [their] likings, or to frame [her] will to [their]

[136] Lake, *Bad Queen Bess?*, 102–3; see Guy, 'Rhetoric of Counsel', 302.

[137] Annabel Patterson, *Reading Holinshed's Chronicles* (Chicago: University of Chicago Press, 1994), 99. Hooker's *Order and Vsage* was published alongside the 1587 edition of the *Chronicles*; see Patterson, *Reading Holinshed's Chronciles*, 126.

[138] Patterson, *Reading Holinshed's Chronicles*, 108, 122–3.

[139] This was, as it had been in Marsilius of Padua, expressed in a divide between temporal and spiritual powers. The Anglican bishop, Thomas Bilson, set out in his 1585 *The true difference between Christian obedience and unchristian rebellion* that the clergy have an important role in giving counsel, but hold no power to command a sovereign: the importance of 'asking counsel' of holy men is demonstrated in the Bible, but the priest 'hath no further authority', whereas the king can 'command'; Thomas Bilson, *The True Difference between Christian Obedience and Unchristian Rebellion* (Oxford, 1585), sig, A, viii^v; Lake, *Bad Queen Bess?*, 196–8. The 'rule' of a physician, Bilson goes on to say, does not imply actual 'jurisdiction' over their patients; the same is true of counsellors; Bilson, *The True Difference*, 165, see also 127, 339.

[140] Raphael Holinshed, *Chronicles of England, Scotlande, and Ireland* (London, 1577), 1777.

[141] Holinshed, *Chronicles*, 1777.

fancies' as equally inappropriate as attempts to bind her, echoing Felippe's equation of persuasion with force, on the grounds that they are just as bad as (if not worse than) attempts to command the prince.

The political situation of late Tudor England exposes the tension in the discourse of counsel between humanist and Machiavellian models. A 'weak' monarch, like the young King Edward VI, or Queens Mary I and Elizabeth I, ought to be 'bridled' by counsel according to the humanist tradition. Yet Machiavelli's work was sufficiently widely read that it was also acknowledged that counsellors would often be self-serving and could easily use such influence to rule through such a monarch. As a result, some writers put forward a mixed-monarchy model, whereby the legitimate advice of parliament and Privy Council would bind the queen, and (ideally) overrule the advice of private extra-institutional counsellors. Despite limits to this vision, the advice of the people – bound by the counsel / command divide – gains prominence and power.

PART III

CHAPTER 6

Reason of State and the Counsellor

As we have seen, by the latter half of the sixteenth century the Machiavellian challenge to the orthodox humanist discourse of counsel had decisively shaped the political culture of the late sixteenth century. Both this tradition and the answer to it come to be articulated, by the turn of the century, in the language of 'reason of state'. Because of its ties to Machiavellianism, most reason of state writers adopted Machiavelli's model of counsel, in which the problem of self-interest requires the monarch to assert his supremacy over his advisers, in contrast to the traditional humanist model examined in Chapters 1 and 2. Furthermore, as reason of state emphasises the knowledge of contemporary affairs as essential to good government – over and above, for instance, moral philosophy or the study of history – the counsellor becomes little more than a transmitter of (presumably) accurate information, instead of a guide to correct action. This model suited Stuart monarchs well, who sought to re-assert a strong monarchical control of government in the face of late Tudor conciliar solutions to their 'weakened' monarchs.

Reason of state discourses see a renewed preoccupation with the divide between public and private. Even as there is an increased understanding of the need to keep state secrets, there are likewise increasing attempts to peer into hearts and minds of rulers. At the centre of this tension is the counsellor, whose position between public and private remains in contention. It is the emerging language of 'interests' which shows this tension most clearly. The counsellor is to advise according to the interest of the state, and not his own private interest. The more public a counsellor can be, the more likely he is to give advice in line with this state interest. Three problems emerge from this model, however. First, how can the counsellor be both secretive and public? Second, how can a private individual abandon his personal interests? And, third, a recurring issue, what if the counsellor knows the state's interests better than the monarch: should his counsel then become command? These are the issues which come to the fore in the mid-seventeenth century, born of tensions apparent in the reason of state tradition.

i Botero and Reason of State

The phrase 'reason of state' cannot be said to have any definitive or uncontested meaning in the early modern period.[1] We can, however, explore its use in two early seventeenth-century conciliar discourses.[2] The first is the 'Machiavellian' tradition, in line with what we have explored in the previous chapters. This is reason of state as associated with the tenets of Machiavellian counsel to princes, particularly the dissociation of *utile* and *honestum*, which becomes rearticulated – as we've seen – as a tension between 'policy' and the word of God.[3] However, little direct evidence of this Machiavellian reason of state exists; our knowledge of it proceeds almost entirely from the critiques which make up the second discourse of reason of state, which seeks to advance 'true' reason of state against the Machiavellian variant.[4] Primarily articulated by Jesuit writers, this view suggests that true reason of state and policy are not in contradiction to divine law, for following God's law is in fact what is beneficial to the state.[5] In other words, these writers sought to undo the Machiavellian separation of *utile* and *honestum*, restoring the Ciceronian ends of counsel, by reconciling the state's advantage with religious concerns. Their willingness, however, to engage with concepts and terminology borrowed from their opponents, and to make their arguments for *honestum* from a concern for *utile*, mark their work as fundamentally different from that of Cicero

[1] See Burke, 'Tacitism', 479–80; Harro Höpfl, 'Orthodoxy and Reason of State', *History of Political Thought* 23, no.2 (2002): 211; G. Baldwin, 'Reason of State and English Parliaments, 1610–42', *History of Political Thought* 25, no. 4 (2004): 623–4; Noel Malcolm, *Reason of State, Propaganda, and the Thirty Years' War: An Unknown Translation by Thomas Hobbes* (Oxford: Oxford University Press, 2010), 105; Conal Condren, 'Reason of State and Sovereignty in Early Modern England: A Question of Ideology?', *Parergon* 28, no. 2 (2012): 13; Noah Millstone, 'Seeing like a Statesman in Early Stuart England', *Past and Present*, 2014, 81. Harro Höpfl, *Jesuit Political Thought: The Society of Jesus and the State, c.1540–1630* (Cambridge: Cambridge University Press, 2004), 84 gives a full breakdown of the term and its possible meanings. See Thomas M. Poole, *Reason of State: Law, Prerogative and Empire* (Cambridge: Cambridge University Press, 2015), 2–3 for the various meanings of 'Reason of State' across time and space.

[2] Malcolm, *Reason of State*, 98. [3] Malcolm, *Reason of State*, 93.

[4] As Höpfl, 'Orthodoxy', 211 points out, it was in fact those writing in opposition to this utility-based reason of state 'who *constructed* the identity "reason of state" for others as well as for themselves', and thus, as he suggests in Harro Höpfl, 'Thomas Fitzherbert's Reason of State', *History of European Ideas*, Pact with the Devil: the Ethics, Politics and Economics of Anti-Machiavellian Machiavellism, 37, no. 2 (2011): 95, 'the confrontation between "Anti-Machiavellians" and "Machiavellians" was in considerable measure a rhetorical ploy'. See Burke, 'Tacitism', 480–1.

[5] See Höpfl, 'Orthodoxy', 211–37.

and the orthodox humanists and closer to the 'false' reason of state they were attempting to discredit.[6]

In order to understand the concept of 'reason of state' and its role in the relationship between command and counsel in this period, one must begin with Giovanni Botero's *Ragione di Stato*, originally published in Italian in 1589, while acknowledging that Botero himself claims he is not the first to comment on the subject. Like many of his contemporaries and predecessors, including Machiavelli himself, Botero was a counsellor, most importantly for Cardinal Frederick Borromeo.[7] It was during his time in Borromeo's service that Botero produced his major political works, largely gleaned from his experience in the papal court in Rome.[8] *Ragione di Stato*, like *The Prince*, is a piece of political advice and adopts both traditional humanist models and Machiavellian vocabularies.[9]

Botero makes explicit that his goal is to counter the rise of Machiavellianism in the 'government and counsels [*consigli*] of princes'.[10] Such rectification, however, does not mean that he disagrees with the Machiavellian idea that the preservation of the state should be the ultimate goal of such policy and counsel, but rather suggests that the means by which

6 As Burke, 'Tacitism', 483 puts it 'the problem . . . was that, much as they might dislike Machiavelli's recommendations, they could not do without his ideas'. As a result, 'What they produced may be described, according to taste, as a more Christian or simply a more hypocritical version of Machiavelli'.

7 P. J Waley and D. P Waley, 'Introduction', in *The Reason of State and The Greatness of Cities*, (London: Routledge & Kegan Paul, 1956), viii; Harald E. Braun, 'Knowledge and Counsel in Giovanni Botero's *Ragion Di Stato*', *Journal of Jesuit Studies* 4, no. 2 (2017): 273.

8 Braun, 'Knowledge and Counsel', 271–2, 273.

9 Waley, 'Introduction', viii; Braun, 'Knowledge and Counsel', 273, 274. As Braun, 'Knowledge and Counsel', 271 points out, scholarship is moving past a view of Botero as simply falling into Machiavellian and/or anti-Machiavellian camps, and instead seeing the richness of Botero's 'intellectual universe'. There is a manuscript abridged translation of *Ragione di Stato*, produced by Richard Etherington (BL Sl. MS 1065). The text is dedicated to Sir Henry Hobart, who served as Lord Chancellor to Prince Charles as well as Chief Justice of Common Pleas from 1613 until his death in 1625. The dedication to Hobart dates the writing of the manuscript to between his appointment (or more likely his re-appointment in 1617) and the death of James I in March 1625. Etherington was a prominent member of Lincoln's Inn in the 1580s, which is probably where he met Hobart. His fortunes fell in the first decades of the seventeenth century, and the text may have been written after 1621, when he was outlawed for debt, in an attempt to gain Hobart's assistance; Joanne Paul, 'Counsel and Command in Anglophone Political Thought, 1485-1651' (PhD Thesis, Queen Mary, University of London, 2013), 331, manuscript transcription, 333–56. Etherington provides an abridgement of this epistle under the heading 'Law of State and Conscience one': 'Some haue grounded their reason in litle conscience. Some haue mantled their tyranny with a cloke of barbarous lawe of Ma[jes]^{tie}, and yet both accounted famous Statists or Idœaes of State, as though there were one law of State another of conscience: when as such as take away consciences Iurisdiction more in publique then in priuate thinges haue neither Soule nor God' (Sl. MS 1065, fo. 5^{r}).

10 Giovanni Botero, *Botero: The Reason of State*, ed. Robert Bireley (Cambridge: Cambridge University Press, 2017), 2.

this preservation will come about ought to be in line with *honestum*. In other words, he rejects the type of reason of state that has been propagated, but not the aims of it. He writes in his dedicatory epistle that 'If all animals have a natural instinct that inclines them to what is useful [*vtili*] and holds them back from what is harmful, should the light of reason and the dictates of conscience given to man to know how to discern the good and the evil, be blind in public affairs and defective in matters of importance?'[11] The 'light of reason' and 'dictates of conscience' – reason of state and God's word – should and will be united in the achievement of *utile*. The end of the political for Botero, therefore, remains profit, but this profit can only be achieved through means which are in line with *honestum*.

Botero defines reason of state as 'knowledge [*notitia*]' of such means by which one may 'found, conserve and expand' dominion.[12] Reason of state is not the end of the political – this remains the security of the state – but rather the knowledge of the means by which to reach this end. This is usually understood as 'knowing when and how to violate the legal, constitutional, and ethical norms for pragmatic political reasons'.[13] Notably, for Botero preservation is more important than expansion, and scholars have drawn attention to the way in which reason of state recognises and furthers the development of the modern territorial state.[14]

As for Machiavelli, the security of the state rests in the achievement of *virtù* and the maintenance of the prince's reputation. In Chapter 8, Botero notes that the most important element of a state's preservation is the 'peace and quiet of the subjects', best gained by establishing the prince's *riputatione* among the people.[15] As the people only give the right of governance to those 'in whom they recognize valor and *virtù*', *virtù* is essential to maintaining stable governance over a people: 'The fundamental principle of every state is the obedience of the subjects to its superior, and this is based on the eminence of the prince's *virtù*'.[16]

11 Botero, *Reason of State*, 2.

12 Botero, *Reason of State*, 4. It is unclear if *notitia* here carries the meaning of knowledge as a set of rules or principles, akin to a science, or rather a general awareness. Its relation to 'intelligence' and 'news' in the period suggests a connection to the knowledge of contemporary affairs, which Botero and others emphasise in relation to reason of state. Etherington renders this passage 'Iudgement of state is a notive of meane actions to found, conserue and enlarge gouernment or dominyons' (Sl. MS 1065, fo. 5[r]). Although no dictionary entry exists for 'notive', it is probably related to 'notition' meaning 'knowledge, information, intelligence'.

13 Braun, 'Knowledge and Counsel'; see also Höpfl, *Jesuit Political Thought*, 86.

14 Braun, 'Knowledge and Counsel', 271 n.5, 274–5.

15 Botero, *Reason of State*, 13.

16 Botero, *Reason of State*, 14, 15. Etherington retains the essence of this passage: 'Reputation ... [is] desireable in Prynces, for that the foundations of euery State, is the obedience of ye Subiect to the Superior, wch is grounded vpon the eminency of the vertue of the Prynce' (Sl. MS 1065, fo. 6[v]).

In Chapter II Botero provides his explanation of this crucial term.[17] Whereas Machiavelli had dissociated *virtù* from the classical taxonomy of virtues, Botero reiterates this connection, placing the classical virtues into three categories.[18] In the first are those virtues which inspire love among the people and are associated with justice and liberality, such as *humanità*, *cortesia* and *clemenza*. Although Botero provides a lengthy treatment of both justice and liberality in the chapters that follow, he makes it clear that they are of lesser importance when it comes to political leadership, for they are more likely to inspire love than *riputatione*, and it is the latter which will ensure the security of the state. It is the second category of virtues which inspire the reputation of the prince, and thus are more important. These include *fortezza*, military and political skills, *constanza*, *il vigor dell'animo* and *la prontezza dell'ingengo*, summarised under the headings of prudence and valour.[19] The final category contains temperance and religion, which support the achievement of the other virtues.

Despite his declared attention to the *consegli* of princes, Botero says little about the role of the counsellor in relation to reason of state. As had classical writers, Botero associates prudence with counsel and valour with military expertise, suggesting that the two must go hand-in-hand for any successful political leadership: 'Prudence serves the prince as his eye, valor as his hand ... Prudence aids counsel and valor power. The former commands, the latter executes'.[20] Prudence is to be differentiated from 'astuteness'. Though both 'seek and recover suitable means to reach the goal', prudence takes into account *honesto*, whereas astuteness 'takes account only of interest [*interesse*]'.[21]

Like Machiavelli and others, Botero 'takes the prevalence of political self-interest simply as a given'.[22] For this reason, prudence is better learned from the dead than the living.[23] Botero is keen to downplay the role of the living

[17] See Bireley, *Counter-Reformation Prince*, 54.

[18] Botero's list of the key virtues is almost identical to the four cardinal virtues, with the substitution of liberality for temperance, which is removed from the list of principle virtues and placed alongside religion in the third category. This may have to do with Machiavelli's specific treatment of liberality in Chapter XVI of *The Prince*.

[19] Etherington: 'Reputation by fortitude, Art military, policye, constancy, vigor of mynde, readines of witt, wch are reduced to prudence and valour' (Sl. MS 1065, fo. 6^{v}).

[20] Botero, *Reason of State*, 34.

[21] Botero, *Reason of State*, 48. This discussion of prudence and astuteness is in the 1589 edition but removed from the 1598.

[22] Braun, 'Knowledge and Counsel', 287.

[23] Botero, *Reason of State*, 37. Botero, too, makes reference to the adage from Demetrius Phalerius: 'that he would find many secrets in books that no one would dare to tell to him', Botero, *Reason of State*, 44.

counsellor for the same reasons that Machiavelli and those who followed him had been: they cannot be trusted. Counsellors must not have 'interests' that differ from those of the ruler, for it will corrupt their advice: 'Do not admit to your council of state any person dependent upon another prince because the advice of one who has at heart the interest of another cannot be sincere.'[24] This issue of interest is crucial to the problem of counsel for Botero, for 'in the deliberation of princes interest overcomes every other consideration.'[25] A prince should not appear to be dependent on any other man's advice, and should appear to rule alone.[26] Counsel, however, remains essential. In seeking advice of the living, the prince should take time to consider the consequences of the plan chosen, which means that advice from 'practical men' should be esteemed no less than that of 'the learned'.[27] To learn what is necessary for rule, the prince should 'have near him persons scarce in every profession', a very different model of counsel than the traditional humanist one.[28]

In considering the potential success of counsel, the primary consideration is its relationship to temporal concerns. As Höpfl has suggested, 'The salient feature of political reality, according to reason of state, is unpredictability (*fortuna*).'[29] One of Botero's 'maxims of prudence' is that a ruler must 'recognize the proper time [*occasioni*] for campaigns and for negotiations and embrace the right moment. Nothing is of greater importance than a certain period of time which is called opportunity'.[30] Using the classical language of *kairos*, Botero describes '*oppotunità*' as a *periodo di tempo*, a 'combination of circumstances that facilitates an endeavor that before or after that point would be difficult'.[31] Like Machiavelli, Botero agrees that rulers who have been called 'great' have usually been so thanks to their attention to *occasione*, rather than their valour alone.[32] Given the definition of reason of state given above, it is perhaps no surprise that the language of occasion is given such a prominent role. We may recall that in the Greek literature the notion of *kairos* was used to justify immoral action in achieving one's ends. So, too, is reason of state. This variability of affairs in reason of state, although increasing the need for a diversity of sources of information, also furthers the desire to centralise political control in the hands of one: ideally a single prince, who has control over his counsellors, just as in the Machiavellian tradition.[33] Botero is no exception to this.[34]

24 Botero, *Reason of State*, 46. 25 Botero, *Reason of State*, 41. 26 Botero, *Reason of State*, 55.
27 Botero, *Reason of State*, 50. 28 Botero, *Reason of State*, 36.
29 Höpfl, *Jesuit Political Thought*, 88. 30 Botero, *Reason of State*, 45.
31 Botero, *Reason of State*, 45. 32 Botero, *Reason of State*, 60.
33 Höpfl, *Jesuit Political Thought*, 88.
34 On all points described, Höpfl, *Jesuit Political Thought*, 90 describes Botero as 'prototypical'.

Botero's acceptance of the Machiavellian tradition means that he adopts its view of the counsellor as well. The counsellor should be held in suspicion, advice should be taken from a multitude of sources – largely from those with practical knowledge – and all must be done with an eye to the opportune moment, which determines the outcome of such counsel. To this, however, Botero adds the explicit language of reason of state, as well as its associated terms: policy and interest, which become interwoven with these ideas.

ii Interests

The phrase 'reason of state' appears in England before the 1589 publication of Botero's text, and its greatest early proponent in English is the Jesuit Robert Parsons, who first uses the phrase in 1582.[35] His 1593 *Newes from Spayne and Holland* criticises the 'councelles' of Lord Burghley for being lacking in 'iustice or co[n]science' as well as in 'humane wisdome and pollycy set downe by Machauel him selfe'.[36] Parsons demonstrates that it is 'a great ouersight in reason of state' for Elizabeth to have made 'so vniuersal a change of religion'.[37] The tract known as *Leicester's Commonwealth* (see Chapter 5) also connects reason of state to Machiavellian language: 'For as the Prince whom you signifie, wil not faile (by al likeliehood) to pursue his title wyth al forces that he can make, if occasion were offered, so reason of state and pollicie wil enforce other Princes adioyni[n]g, to let & hinder him therein what they can'.[38]

By the end of Elizabeth's reign, reason of state is present not only in published writings, such as those of Parsons, but has entered into quotidian political parlance as well.[39] In a letter ascribed to Francis Bacon from the

[35] Robert Parsons, *A Defence of the Censure* (Rouen, 1582), 10; see also Robert Parsons, *A Christian Directorie* (Rouen, 1585), 17^{v}; Robert Parsons, *A Temperate Ward-Word, to the Turbulent and Seditious Wach-Word of Sir Francis Hastinges Knight* (Antwerp, 1599), 30, 49, 127; Robert Parsons, *A Manifestation of the Great Folly and Bad Spirit of Certayne in England Calling Themselues Secular Priestes* (Antwerp, 1602), 97^{v}; Robert Parsons, *The Warn-Word to Sir Francis Hastinges Wast-Word* (Antwerp, 1602), 6^{v}, 81^{v}. See also from the same press and probably under Parson's influence: *A Conference about the next Succession to the Crowne of Ingland* (Antwerp, 1595), 122, 140, 148, 207, 217, 264. See Höpfl, 'Thomas Fitzherbert's Reason of State', 94, 96. 'Reason, n.1', in *OED Online* (Oxford University Press), accessed 17 January 2019, www.oed.com/view/Entry/159068 suggests that the first appearance of the phrase is in Parson's text in 1585, a text responding to Edmund Bunny, *A Briefe Answer, Vnto Those Idle and Friuolous Quarrels of R.P. against the Late Edition of the Resolution* (London, 1589), which had used the phrase as well (99).

[36] Parsons, *Newes from Spayne and Holland*, 22.

[37] Parsons, *Newes from Spayne and Holland*, 22. [38] *Leicester's Commonwealth*, 127.

[39] See Joanne Paul with Valerie Schutte, 'The Tudor monarchy of counsel and the growth of reason of state', in *The Routledge History of Monarchy*, ed. Elena Woodacre et al. (London: Routledge, 2019), pp. 655–667.

1580s, the author suggests that the queen ought to determine 'in all reason of state' what to do about the Catholics, who threaten her rule, noting he does not see how 'either in conscience' or 'in policy' she will be able to make them content.[40] Likewise, in a 1597 letter to the Earl of Essex, William Lylle[41] tells him how 'in reason of state' princes 'ought to seek peace to assure their estates',[42] and in Essex's 1599 letter from Ireland to the Privy Council, he notes that 'reason of state doth teach that a difficult war cannot be successfully managed by a disgraced minister'.[43] By 1601, the Privy Council is judging a matter to do with the Lord Mayer 'according to the reason of state and good government'.[44] The 1603 speech to the new king, James I, includes the suggestion that 'when necessary reason of state shall bend your Maiesties Counselles' to an enterprise against France.[45] As this last example suggests, reason of state vocabulary becomes essential to the discourse of counsel in the opening decades of the sixteenth century. Those writing in the English context, once again, go further in exploring the theme of counsel than the originally continental tradition. In doing so, they occasionally use the phrase 'reason of state', but more often they employ associated vocabularies, most notably 'interest'.

The English Catholic priest Thomas Fitzherbert takes the anti-Machiavellian discourses of policy and reason of state and translates them into 'general rules or aduises no lesse pious then politic, for the instructio[n] of such as desire to mannage affairs of state', especially those 'aduanced by his princes fauor to be of his *Councel*' in his *The First Part of a Treatise Concerning Policy, and Religion* printed in 1606.[46] Fitzherbert addresses Machiavellians as political counsellors, who have failed in their duty to give advice in line with both God's law and reason of state. Even if God is taken out of the equation, the damage done to a prince's reputation by embracing Machiavellian policies ensures his downfall. Thus whether

40 [Francis Bacon?], '[Letter of Advice to Queen Elizabeth I]' in *The Letters and Life of Francis Bacon*, ed. James Spedding (London: Longman, Green, Longman, and Roberts, 1861), 47, 48. For Bacon and reason of state see Vera Keller, 'Mining Tacitus: Secrets of Empire, Nature and Art in the Reason of State', *BJHS* 45, no. 2 (2012): 189–212.

41 I have not been able to conclusively establish the identity of William Lylle.

42 William Lylle, 'William Lylle to Earl of Essex', in *Calendar of the Manuscripts of the Most Hon. the Marquis of Salisbury, Preserved at Hatfield House, Hertfordshire*, ed. R. A. Roberts, vol. 5 (Dublin, 1894), 447.

43 SP 63/205 fol. 210, July 17 1599.

44 PC 2/26 fol. 493, 1601.

45 Richard Martin, *A Speach Deliuered, to the Kings Most Excellent Maiestie in the Name of the Sheriffes of London and Middlesex* (London, 1603), sig. A, iv^{v}.

46 Thomas Fitzherbert, *The First Part of a Treatise Concerning Policy, and Religion* (London, 1606), 304, 318. Fitzherbert, a contact of Robert Parsons, had published on reason of state in a tract published from the same Antwerp printer that Parsons used: Thomas Fitzherbert, *A Defence of the Catholyke Cause* (Antwerp, 1602), 3^{v}, 28^{r}, 31^{r}–34^{r}, 42^{v}–43^{r}. Fitzherbert became a Jesuit in 1614.

one is concerned for the prince's conscience, reputation or commodity, the advice ought to be the same:

> Therfore I conclude that whereas commodity, conscience and reputation, are to be respected in al deliberations concerning princes affairs, conscience ought euer to predominate, and to serue for the touchstone and rule, as wel of reputation as of temporal commodities; and therein a councellour shal wel discharge his duty, if in al his consultations he hold the knowne axiome of Cicero for his ground, to wit, that *Nihil est vtile quod non sit honestum. Nothing is profitable which is not honest.*[47]

Fitzherbert revives the Ciceronian unification of *utile* and *honestum* based on a consideration of reason of state in the role of the counsellor. It is reason of state that, rather than justifying Machiavellian principles, serves to discredit them: 'the absurdity of *Macchiauel*, is most manifest in true reason of state, seeing that in councelling princes to wickednes and tiranny, vpon confidence of humane force and policy, he exposeth them to an assured danger, and doth not geue them any assured or probable remedy but rather heapeth danger vpon danger'.[48] Machiavellians fail as counsellors as they do not preserve the life of prince or state.

Fitzherbert ascribes the deviation from true reason of state to the personal motives of evil counsellors. Even Machiavelli himself, Fitzherbert suggests, was guilty of this; he argues that Machiavelli *intentionally* counselled against true reason of state in order to overthrow the Medici regime.[49] Thus Fitzherbert underlines his requirement that counsellors should be free from 'passion, and particular affection', or else they too will put forward advice that will bring about their own designs and not the good of the prince.[50]

Of course we've seen this concern regarding the fear that private concerns may interfere with the accomplishment of a public duty in the role of the counsellor before. It was this issue which underpinned the concern over the role of the Machiavellian counsellor, felt so powerfully in England in the second half of the sixteenth century. In the early years of the

[47] Fitzherbert, *Treatise*, 362. [48] Fitzherbert, *Treatise*, 402.

[49] Fitzherbert, *Treatise*, 412: 'some Florentines of no meane iudgement [Machiavelli's] owne cuntrymen, and frends, who in their ordinary discourses concerning his pollicies, doe not stick to confesse that he him selfe knew theym to be contrary to true reason of state, and pernicious to princes, & that neuerthelesse desiring to ouerthrow those of the house of the *Medices* which opprest the commonwelth of *Florence* in his tyme, he published his pestilent doctrin, hoping that they wold embrace it & ruine theymselues by the practise therof, wherby the state of *Florence* might returne to the ould *Democracy* or popular gouernment wher in it had continued many yeres before.' Reginald Pole had suggested the same; see Chapter 3.

[50] Fitzherbert, *Treatise*, 327.

seventeenth century, to the requirements of the good counsellor is added the language of 'interest', which allows those writing on the topic to express these concerns in more straightforward ways, articulating a dichotomy between the private interests of the counsellor and the public interests of the prince or state.[51] For example, in *Of Wisdome*, translated in 1608, the Catholic theologian Pierre Charron adds to the need for 'honesty, and sufficiency' in counsellors 'a third, and that is, that neither they nor their neerest and inward friends haue any particular interest in the business'.[52]

This concern with interest is expressed in the continued publication of works in the advice-to-counsellors genre. *The Counsellor of Estate*, written by the French administrator and diplomat Philippe de Béthune in 1633, and translated by Edward Grimston a year later, combines the work of several noted authors, including Felippe, Lipsius and Botero, in addressing the office of the counsellor. In his chapter on 'the setling of a Councell of Estate, and of the quallities and number of Councellors' Béthune adds Botero's language of interest to Felippe's account of the qualities of counsellors, stating that 'it is likewise certayne, that in affaires where we haue no interest, we iudge much better, then when as we put our interest in Ballance with our opinions in Councells'.[53] Béthune uses the metaphor of gamblers to demonstrate this point, writing that 'he that lookes ouer Gamesters, and is not possest neyther with the hope of gayne, nor the feare of losse, will giue a better iudgment of the carriage of the game then he that playes' and so likewise 'he that in Councell hath not any feare to lose his Estate, and who brings neyther affection nor passion, will alwayes take the most honourable party'.[54] He makes clear that this 'affection' and 'passion' is synonymous with interest, for 'he which hath any interest preuented by his owne opinion and feare, will willingley incline to that side by the which he thinks to saue himselfe'.[55] He questions how likely it is that such disinterested counsellors are to be found, for he writes that 'the Councellors of Princes are accompanied with iealousie one against another; and tending all to one end, they finde out many times publique Councels, and make them serue to their owne

[51] Burke, 'Tacitism', 482; Lionel A. McKenzie, 'Natural Right and the Emergence of the Idea of Interest in Early Modern Political Thought: Francesco Guicciardina and Jean de Silhon', *History of European Ideas* 2, no. 4 (1981): 277–98. Höpfl, *Jesuit Political Thought*, 86. See also Malcolm, *Reason of State*, 9–5.

[52] Pierre Charron, *Of Wisedome*, trans. Samson Lennard (London, 1608), 324. For Charron's place in the reason of state tradition, and especially as a sceptic and follower of Montaigne, see Burke, 'Tacitism', 496–7.

[53] Philippe de Béthune, *The Counsellor of Estate*, trans. Edward Grimeston (London, 1634), 55, 59.

[54] Béthune, *The Counsellor of Estate*, 59.

[55] Béthune, *The Counsellor of Estate*, 59.

priuate interests'.[56] Thus it is the prince who must outwit his own counsellors, even by spying on them, as the Grand Seignior, who views his counsellors through a secret window in the council chamber.[57] Turning to the second type of interest – that of the state – Béthune makes reference to it via his translation of Botero's first maxim of prudence: 'Interest is the part and reason which preuailes, and makes the resolutions, bend to that side where it shewes it selfe: And therefore [the prince] must neither trust to Friendship, alliance, league, nor any other Bond, if there be no interest'.[58] Béthune expresses a need for the prince to rule over and be distrustful of his counsellors, supported by the language of interests.

Notably, these texts also express a clearly defined distinction between counsel and command. Béthune writes that 'in Estates, whereas Councellors commaund that which they Councell, they may not onely be termed Councellors but Souereignes' and 'in regard of the Councels power, it ought onely to consist in giuing Councell, and not to command, Commandment being inseparable with the Souereignty'.[59] The Jesuit Fray Juan de Santa Maria had likewise condemned the conflation of counsel and command in his *Policie vnveiled*, first published in English in 1632. He notes that a king must have about him 'iust, prudent, & dis-interessed persons, to aduise them'.[60] Such disinterest consists in an 'vnderstanding ... tearme[d] the Will' which is 'free and disincumbranced of affection, or particular passions, as well in asking, as giuing Counsaile', but all are inclined to 'tread in one and the same steps ... of their owne black and fowle Interest'.[61] He condemns those counsellors who 'cloath themselues with the Kings royall command, as with a garment, and beare themselues too insolently-high vpon the Title of their Offices; and vnder colour and zeale to the seruice of their Kings, will make themselues their Tutors, Masters of their libertie, Lords, ouer their vassalls, and sole Commanders of the whole Kingdome' as being 'like vnto that great *Leuiathan,* or huge Whale in the Sea'.[62] The concern about interests encourages these writers to reinforce the distinction between counsel and command.

In opposition to personal interest, counsellors ought to be ruled by the state's interest, which runs counter to the passions. Jean-Louis Guez de

56 Béthune, *The Counsellor of Estate*, 67–8. 57 Béthune, *The Counsellor of Estate*, 8.
58 Béthune, *The Counsellor of Estate*, 261. 59 Béthune, *The Counsellor of Estate*, 64.
60 Fray Juan de Santa Maria, *Policie Vnveiled*, trans. J. M. (London, 1650), 55.
61 Santa Maria, *Policie Vnveiled*, 271, 64. Santa Maria concludes based on this that 'Princes ought to peruse Histories' for 'Onely Histories, without feare or dread, speake plaine language to Kings' (273).
62 Santa Maria, *Policie Vnveiled*, 138.

Balzac, a French epistolary writer, directly connects this state interest with the proper ends of counsel in his *Prince*, composed in eulogistic praise of Louis XIII in 1631, and translated into English in 1648.[63] Writing against those who 'mingle God among their passions, who ingage him in their Interests, and who employ him upon all occasions', de Balzac writes that true interest leads us to honest action, for 'we must be honest men of necessity and out of Interest, when we cannot be by Inclination nor will; since evill is as unprofitable as dishonest'.[64] He praises Louis's clemency as it demonstrates that 'he moves only by the line of Reason . . . [and] that the Interest of his State retain in him this day, the place of the passions of his soul'.[65]

Importantly, following interest can also lead to preventative action that runs contrary to the dictates of mercy, such as in the case of the traitor who 'mingled his own Interests with those of the State' so that 'none but the King could separate them'.[66] This man's death was 'excusable severity' as it was used 'to divert misfortunes which threaten the state'.[67] Balzac uses this example of mingled interests to praise 'that punctuall and scrupulous Justice' which preventatively prosecutes crimes before they take place.[68] This 'extream right' would be 'extream injustice' if prudence did not 'ease Justice in many things' such as this.[69] For 'Justice is exercised only upon the Actions of men, but *Prudence* hath a right over their thoughts, and secretest Intention . . . she respects the publicke Interest'.[70] Prudence leads one to uncover the state's true interest, which can serve to justify the overthrow of justice through pre-emptive action.

Balzac applies the pre-emptive defence of state interest to the question of the '*Monster*' of Europe: the Spanish 'design of the Universall *Monarchie*'.[71] This 'monster' is a perversion of the relationship between counsel and command, for Balzac 'accuse[s] that Counsel which fights against the good nature of the *Prince*, which will command its own Master; and this is the *Monster* of which I speak'.[72] It is 'at the[ir] perswasion' that the 'Emperour himself so wise and vertuous' has plotted against his fellow Christian princes, so that the actions of Spain are 'but a part of the Actions and Thoughts of this *Monster*'.[73] The Spanish Council of State embraces

[63] See Pierre Watter, 'Jean Louis Guez de Balzac's *Le Prince*: A Revaluation', *Journal of the Warburg and Courtauld Institutes* 20, no. 3/4 (1957): 215–47.

[64] Jean-Louis Guez de Balzac, *The Prince*. Translated by H. G. (London, 1648). This is paralleled in Balzac's *Aristippe*, first published in French in 1658: 'Our reason must not withdraw itself from our immediate interests and the business at hand'; quoted in Watter, 'Balzac's *Le Prince*', 216.

[65] Balzac, *The Prince*, 82. [66] Balzac, *The Prince*, 147. [67] Balzac, *The Prince*, 151, 152.

[68] Balzac, *The Prince*, 153. [69] Balzac, *The Prince*, 153. [70] Balzac, *The Prince*, 154.

[71] Balzac, *The Prince*, 175, 174. [72] Balzac, *The Prince*, 175. [73] Balzac, *The Prince*, 179–80, 183.

'Machiavellian' counsels: 'that Truth of it self is not better than falsehood, and that we ought to measure the value of the one and of the other, by the profit which comes from them' and that 'vertue may be sometimes dangerous, but its appearance alwayes necessary'.[74] These counsellors have 'renounce[d] all hope of *Paradice* for the smallest Interest' and have 'give[n] certain vices the names of vertues, which are neer unto them'.[75] In other words, Balzac paints the Spanish counsellors as the worst of Machiavellians. This inversion of what Balzac considers to be the proper order of things results in something truly monstrous, and the only answer to it – according to reason of state – is to move against it, before it is too late.

Perhaps the greatest illustration of the seventeenth-century view of interest and its role in counsel comes from the Italian satirist Trajano Boccalini, whose *Ragguagli di Parnaso* was translated as *The New-Found Politicke* by William Vaughn in 1626, but is better-known as the *News-sheet from Parnassus.* Boccalini takes particular aim at those who espouse Machiavellian reason of state as well as those who are willing to see the state's interest (albeit aligned with morality) as the guiding star of the political counsellor. The book opens with a discussion of the 'publick Shop in *Parnassus*' which has been set up by the 'Corporations of *Politicians*', selling various tools of their trade, for instance (critiquing redescription associated with *kairos*) 'most excellent Pencils for those *Princes*, who in their vrgent occasions, are often enforced to paint white for black vnto their people'.[76] Also sold in this shop are 'certain *Compasses* . . . of the pure interesse of the most fine *reputation*'.[77] These compasses 'measure a mans owne proper actions' far better than those of 'fantasticke conceit, of self-will, or of meere interresse'.[78]

'Interresse' receives a resounding critique in the *New-sheet.*[79] In Boccalini's allegory of the flight of Fidelity from Parnassus, Fidelity states that it is 'that infamous Interesse', which 'tyrannizeth ouer the minds of all the best Nations', that has 'banished me from out the heart of men, which in former times were wholly mine'.[80] The metaphor of the compass returns again in Boccalini's analysis of Spain, in which he writes that 'they who measuring all the Actions and proceeding of those which reigne among Princes, by the onely compasse of priuate interesse, doe seldome admit any manner of piety towards God, much lesse of charity towards men' and that

[74] Balzac, *The Prince*, 188. [75] Balzac, *The Prince*, 198, 235.
[76] Boccalini, *The New-Found Politicke*, 1, 2. [77] Boccalini, *The New-Found Politicke*, 4.
[78] Boccalini, *The New-Found Politicke*, 4. [79] See Burke, 'Tacitism', 490–1.
[80] Boccalini, *The New-Found Politicke*, 9–10.

Spain knows well 'how vnder her rich robe of cloth of gold to paliate her priuate interesse, be it neuer so diabolicall'.[81] The country is in trouble, however, as 'the ministers and officers of Spaine are continually interessed in their priuate profit'.[82] Both kinds of interest – public and private – are corrupting, though the latter is still at the heart of a country's problems.

Following this analysis of the ministers of Spain, Boccalini treats those 'seruants, that with their prodigious ambition, and artificial tricks (altogether diabolical) vndertake to rule and gouerne their Lord and Master' and who 'are without charity towards their Princes welfare, or priuate interesse' in favour of their own.[83] Like Balzac, Boccalini seems to especially condemn those counsellors who with their 'tricks' rule over their unwitting princes. It is satirically suggested in one passage that the best way to combat the self-interest of such counsellor-figures is to adopt the German method 'of excessiue quaffing of Wine'.[84] Counsellors in Germany, 'did most exquisitely well aduise & counsell their country ... by means of the good store of wine that they had drunk, hauing therein drowned all priuate interesses'.[85] Getting them steaming drunk was one option, but beyond that there seemed to be little to be done about the issue of self-interest amongst counsellors.

iii Travel and Observation

The language of interests also presented a challenge to the suggestion that books of history offered a source of unbiased counsel, which we saw in Chapter 5. Nicholas Popper has noted the shift from the moral lessons of history to those of 'observation', history being used as background to current affairs, to impart lessons regarding statecraft and contingency, or to as test one's ability to discern rhetorical tricks.[86] Even as writers like Botero and de Balzac continued to praise the importance of histories, others were not so certain.[87] Despite writing in praise of Tacitus,

[81] Boccalini, *The New-Found Politicke*, 65, 72.
[82] Boccalini, *The New-Found Politicke*, 93.
[83] Boccalini, *The New-Found Politicke*, 93, 95.
[84] Boccalini, *The New-Found Politicke*, 51.
[85] Boccalini, *The New-Found Politicke*, 51.
[86] Nicholas Popper, *Walter Ralegh's 'History of the World' and the Historical Culture of the Late Renaissance* (Chicago: University of Chicago Press, 2012), 3–6, 210. See Elizabeth Williamson, 'A Letter of Travel Advice? Literary Rhetoric, Scholarly Counsel and Practical Instruction in the Ars Apodemica', *Lives and Letters* 3, no.1 (2011): 1–22; Noah Millstone, *Manuscript Circulation and the Invention of Politics in Early Stuart England* (Cambridge: Cambridge University Press, 2016), Chapter 6.
[87] As Braun, 'Knowledge and Counsel', 288-9 has pointed out, Botero's *Ragione* explicated new forms of political knowledge, combining these with the more traditional. In particular, the reference to

Bolognese aristocrat and prolific political writer Virgilio Malvezzi details the corruptions common to historians in his *Discourses*, printed in English in 1642, connecting this theme with the language of interests. He writes that historians have most difficulty with the 'persons interessed' in their histories, 'which are either Princes, or Common-wealths'.[88] Malvezzi seeks to determine what kind of historian is 'most worthy to be credited': those who write of times past or those who write of present events – both of whom he describes as 'historians' – taking into consideration as well the difference between those who write as witnesses and those who use the accounts of others.[89] He concludes that it is 'historians' of present events who are most credible, as in 'writing of their owne time, they are not tied to stand to the bookes of others, who never agree with one another'.[90] Malvezzi suggests that it is this present historian who relies on accounts, rather than having witnessed the event himself, who will be the most reliable; for although 'it appeares there is more credit to be given to an Historian that writes of his owne time, and of those things at which he hath himselfe been present', he who writes of events he did not witness will be 'voyd of those affections, which make Historians speake lesse truth'.[91] Thus for Malvezzi it is the historian of contemporary affairs, not present at the events that he relates, who is the most reliable source; historians who speak of present events which they witnessed themselves are second-most credible, and it is the historian of past events who is the least trusted to relate the truth.

Malvezzi drives this point home in his own history of present events: *The Pourtract of the Politicke Christian-Favourite*, translated in 1647. He provides an account of the life of Count Gaspar de Guzmán, Duke of Olivares. As Guzmán was still alive at the time of its composition, 'the book is not yet finished', containing 'not All that the Duke hath done, nor all that hee will doe'.[92] It is, thus, very much a present history, and Malvezzi explicitly positions himself as the historian most to be credited, noting that what he writes is 'onelie a little that I came to heare of', not that which he was present at himself.[93] Thus his 'actions are without policies' for he is 'without interest' in the affairs he relates.[94] The main body of the work echoes

practical concerns, a sort of science of politics that went beyond Aristotelian typologies was novel to the reason of state discourse; see Millstone, 'Seeing Like a Statesman', 106-11.

88 Virgilio Malvezzi, *Discovrses Upon Cornelius Tacitus*, trans. Richard Baker (London, 1642), 68.

89 Malvezzi, *Discovrses*, 77. 90 Malvezzi, *Discovrses*, 77. 91 Malvezzi, *Discovrses*, 77.

92 Virgilio Malvezzi, *The Pourtract of the Politicke Christian-Favourite*, trans. Thomas Powell (London, 1647), sig. A, 8r.

93 Malvezzi, *Pourtract*, sig. A, 8r-v. 94 Malvezzi, *Pourtract*, sig. A, 5r.

these themes, further discrediting the verity of histories of past events. In his 'State Maxims, and Pollitical observations on the actions of Count Olivares', Malvezzi notes especially that 'the relation of things past, is like the painting of a picture, and some oddes there is, in relating things past, and present'.[95] Like many painters, historians opt for flattery in their portrayal of their subject: 'the Actions of Predecessours that they may be praised, require no more then to bee flourishingly related' and so, like a portrait, 'if they be but master-like painted, no consideration is had, whether the Actions be true' for, being in the past (and as 'the space of an hundred yeares, is the bredth of the channell of the river of forgetfulesse'), no one can determine for certain whether or not they occurred as reported.[96] Instead, he concludes that 'it is profitable to Register the egregious performances of men in being', rather than those in the past.[97]

Malvezzi uses this distrust of historical accounts to mount an attack on Machiavelli. '*Machiavell*', he writes, was 'deceived in believing, that the helpe of history did consist in the making use of example; and from this errour, as from the Root, come all his failings in policy'.[98] One must turn to the present, not to the past, to guide our choices and actions: 'As in Astrologie, the observation that is nearest, is least false, so in pollicy, is that example, which is most moderne'.[99] He who, like Machiavelli (or Malvezzi's interpretation of Machiavelli), 'believes that after he hath read a laudable example of our Predecessours, that he is able by and by, to put it in practice, is deceived; he should have need first to change all the world'.[100] Political knowledge of reason of state is more context-specific and particular, and thus requires an understanding not of moral principles nor past events, but of contemporary affairs.[101]

The use of historical example, Malvezzi goes on, does not properly take into account the workings of chance and fortune. The attempt to form rules for action from historical study is undermined by the variable of fortune in history.[102] He does not wish to suggest that history be done away with altogether – 'I blame not by this the reading of history, for I commend it' – but rather the way that it is used.[103] He suggests that just as 'Statues are no use to Sculptours, but for good delineation' and not for imitation, 'So

95 Malvezzi, *Pourtract*, n.p. 'Odds' here having the meaning of 'The amount by which one number or quantity differs from another, or by which one thing exceeds or surpasses, or falls short of or below another; amount in excess or defect; difference'.

96 Malvezzi, *Pourtract*, 3–4. 97 Malvezzi, *Pourtract*, 3. 98 Malvezzi, *Pourtract*, 93.

99 Malvezzi, *Pourtract*, 91. 100 Malvezzi, *Pourtract*, 92.

101 Maurizio Viroli, *From Politics to Reason of State: The Acquisition and Transformation of the Language of Politics 1250–1600* (Cambridge: Cambridge University Press, 1992), 241.

102 Malvezzi, *Pourtract*, sig. A, 6^r. 103 Malvezzi, *Pourtract*, 93.

Histories are little helpfull to Polititians, but only for the setling of a good judgement. *For they are not to operate according to the examples, but according to the judgement that they have raised upon the reading of the examples*'.[104] In other words, those in politics should use histories to sharpen their prudence – their ability to discern truth from falsehood – rather than to adopt rules or lessons. For this former task, the biases of historians and the influences of fortune are actually perfectly suited.

If the examples of the past cannot be trusted, from where ought counsel be drawn? Certainly Malvezzi points us in the right direction – observation of present events is best, whether this comes from eyewitnesses or collected second-hand accounts. The clearest answer, however, is provided by Botero, not in the *Ragione di Stato* but in the *Relationi universali*, an account of the relations between the major nations of the world. The *Ragione* had no contemporary English print translation; however, the *Relationi* was translated by the essayist Robert Johnson in 1601, going through six editions in the years from 1601 to 1616, followed by a further edition in 1630.[105] Johnson took great liberty with Botero's text and each edition was different, as he constantly amended and added to the work, keeping it up-to-date with the changing times, as the subject matter itself demanded.[106] Johnson's background also contributed to his desire to update his *Relations* often. Johnson was part of a powerful anti-Spanish

[104] Malvezzi, *Pourtract*, 94.

[105] Robert Shackleton, 'Botero, Bodin and Robert Johnson', *The Modern Language Review* 43, no. 3 (1948): 405:

(1) 1601 *The Travellers Breviat, or an Historical Description of the most famous Kingdoms in the World*. pp. 180. Dedication signed 'Robert Iohnson'.

(2) 1601 *The Worlde, or an Historical Description of the most famous Kingdoms and Commonweales therein*. pp. 222. Dedication signed 'I.R.'

(3) 1603 *Historical Description of the most famous Kingdoms and Commonweales in the Worlde*. pp. 268. Dedication signed 'I.R.'

(4) 1608 *Relations of the most famous Kingdoms and Common-weales* .... pp. 330. Dedication signed 'R.I.'

(5) 1611 *Relations of the most famous Kingdoms and Common-weales* .... [same title as 1608] pp. 437. Dedication signed 'Rob. Ihonson'.

(6) 1616 *Relations of the most famous Kingdoms and Common-weales* .... pp. 437. Dedication signed 'Rob. Iohson'.

Those behind the 1630 edition of the text – *Relations of the most famous kingdomes and commonwealths thorowout the world discoursing of their situations, religions, languages, manners, customes, strengths, greatnesse, and policies* – are not identified, but were certainly not Johnson; see Peltonen, *Classical Humanism*, 293.

[106] As Andrew Fitzmaurice, 'The Commercial Ideology of Colonization in Jacobean England: Robert Johnson, Giovanni Botero, and the Pursuit of Greatness', *The William and Mary Quarterly* 64, no. 4 (2007): 794 suggests, Johnson's editions are 'translation[s] only in the most liberal sense' and ought to be seen as political treatises in their own right.

faction amongst London merchants, which used Botero's ideas in an effort to influence English policy.[107] Each of Johnson's editions are produced because of a particular political debate in which he seeks to intervene, and all express an anti-Spanish sentiment.[108] This more topical aim runs along-side Johnson's developing articulation of the trend towards observation of contemporary affairs as the primary political knowledge necessary to good government.

Johnson's first edition, *The Travellers Breviat, OR An Historicall Description of the Most Famous Kingdoms in the World*, directly translates Botero's survey of the most powerful nations of the world from the *Relationi*. It is 'a generall description of the World', and little else. In the same year, however, Johnson also published an extended edition of the text, *The Worlde*, adding the details of countries not included in the first.[109] This version also contained a new introductory section taken from Botero's *Relationi*: 'Of the World, and the greatest Princes therein', which explains to the reader that it is not enough to know 'those occurances which daily passe in the world' – as was contained in the first edition – but in order to deserve 'the commendation of wit and iudgement' one must be able to determine 'the true reasons, whereby one kingdome or state becommeth greater than other'.[110] Both Botero and Johnson understood that the *Relationi* contained the source material necessary for determining reason of state, which is why it had to be kept up-to-date.

The 1611 and 1616 editions most clearly outline how the knowledge contained in the *Relationi* was to inform reason of state, replacing both moral philosophy and the reliance on histories.[111] In 1611, Johnson added a section, 'Of Observation', which opens the first book of the text. Here, he makes clear the subject matter of the work, and its relationship to the overall purpose:

107 Details from Joanne Paul and Kurosh Meshkat, 'Johnson's *Relations*: Visions of Global Order, 1601–1630', *Journal of Intellectual History and Political Thought*, no. 2.1 (2013): 108–40.

108 Paul and Meshkat 'Johnson's *Relations*', 108–40.

109 As Paul and Meshkat, 'Johnson's *Relations*', 112–15 point out, this was produced on the heels of a debate over the East India Company Charter.

110 Giovanni Botero, *The Worlde, or an Historical Description of the Most Famous Kingdoms and Commonweales Therein*, trans. Robert Johnson (London, 1601), 1.

111 See Paul and Meshkat, 'Johnson's *Relations*', 115–20 for treatments of the 1603 and 1608 editions, which contained explicitly anti-Spanish content, but less emphasis on the theoretical reflections contained in the later editions. Paul and Meshkat, 'Johnson's *Relations*', 120–1 suggest that this may have been caused by the growth of the anti-Spanish faction in the court, under the direction of Prince Henry. The 1616 edition also contains new content; Paul and Meshkat, 'Johnson's *Relations*', 126–7.

> Being to relate of the *Customes*, *Manners*, and *Potencies* of *Nations* and great *Princes*; my Scope shall neyther be, to trouble your Readings with such obsolete Authors, as are to be accounted verie ancient (for of these Themes they were ignorant, by reason of indiscouerie:) Neyther will I wholly refer you to Histories, because their Caueats being infinite; some are growne out of vse, some are temporarie, some opposite, and others mutable; eyther of themselues, or by the pleasure of Princes; whereof no profitable vse can be expected.[112]

With this, Johnson rejects outright the two sources of counsel we encountered previously: classical philosophy and history. Instead, he wishes 'to lay downe some few obseruations' in order to make clear 'the reasons, which giue occasions to one Prince to excell another'.[113] It is 'observation' and not ancient authors or histories which will relate the essential knowledge for politics.

Such observations are of two kinds, Johnson suggests. The first are 'stable and are never changed', describing the character and behaviour of men according to their climate and place on the globe.[114] For this he borrows not from Botero, but from Jean Bodin. In his *Methodus ad facilem historiarum cognitionem*, first printed in 1566 and with no contemporary English print translation, Bodin establishes that there is good reason to 'impugn history, or to withhold agreement' for 'those who ought to have had the highest standards' have not always 'had regard for truth and trustworthiness' and so we find 'disagreement among historians' and even that they 'contradict themselves'.[115] To determine which histories are to be trusted, and how best to interpret them, Bodin seeks to 'make some generalizations as to the nature of all peoples or at least of the better known, so that we can test the truth of histories by just standards'.[116] These generalisations cannot be learned from classical or historical sources, for on this 'the ancients could write nothing' and so they were forced to judge 'by inferences of probability', rather than fact.[117] Johnson takes Bodin's treatment of the various peoples of the globe, set out to evaluate history, and presents it to his audience as a superior method for the establishment of historical knowledge. He expresses these ideas in his *Essaies, or Rather Imperfect Offers*, first published in 1601, with further editions in 1607 and

112 Giovanni Botero, *Relations of the Most Famous Kingdoms and Common-Weales*, trans. Robert Johnson (London, 1611), 1.

113 Botero, *Relations* (1611), 1.

114 Jean Bodin, *The Method for the Easy Comprehension of History*, trans. Beatrice Reynolds (New York: W.W. Norton & Co., 1969), 110.

115 Shackleton, 'Botero, Bodin and Robert Johnson', 408; Bodin, *Method*, 110.

116 Bodin, *Method*, 110.

117 Bodin, *Method*, 110.

1613. In his seventh essay, 'Of Hystories', he first commends the profit of reading history, and especially those of a Tacitean nature, for they contain 'most necessarie thinges, that can be warned vs'.[118] However, like Bodin and later Malvezzi, he also cautions regarding the application of history, for such knowledge 'only enformes a likelyhoode' and so to 'gouerne our counselles by it' requires 'a concurrance of the same reasons, not onelie in generall, but also in particularities'.[119] Thus the use of history is dependent on observation, for 'In making iudgement of Historie, and considerately applying it to our present interestes, wee must speciallie regard the dispositions of the agentes, and diligentlie remarke how they are affected in minde'.[120] History, like moral philosophy, can give some general rules, but in order to determine if they apply in the particular circumstances, one has to know what those circumstances are.

This leads us to consider Johnson's second kind of observation, defined by its ability to vary with the times, keeping up with the rise and fall of great states.[121] This is the knowledge of 'the greatest Princes and Potentates, which at this day sway the world', the section taken from Botero which Johnson had included since the second 1601 edition.[122] The key to achieving this knowledge is given by Johnson in the seventh, and final, added chapter to *Of Obseruation*: 'Of Trauell'. Here, Johnson once again discredits the use of ancient knowledge, replacing it with first-hand observation of other states. As tradition is 'A Sandy foundation either in matter of Science, or Conscience', there is 'nothing fitter' than travel for 'the bettering of our vnderstanding', both by 'hauing a conference with the wiser sort in all sorts of learning, as by the Eie-sight of those things, which otherwise a man cannot attain vnto but by Tradition'.[123] Rather than Botero or Bodin, Johnson is here quoting from Robert Dallington's *Method for Trauell* of 1605, in which he notes that, for any traveller, 'the end of his *Trauell* is his ripening in knowledge; and the end of his knowledge is the seruice of his countrie' which is 'done by *Preseruation* of himself and *Obseruation* of what he heares and sees in his trauelling'.[124] Once again these ideas are also evident in Johnson's essays, which include a section 'Of Trauell', in which he sets out that 'this obseruation' gleaned from travel is 'most powerfull to inspire vs with ciuill wisedome, and inable our iudgement for any actiue employment'.[125]

118 Robert Johnson, *Essaies, or Rather Imperfect Offers* (London, 1601), sig. C, 8^{v}.
119 Johnson, *Essaies*, sig. D, 5^{r}.
120 Johnson, *Essaies*, sig. D, 5^{r}.
121 Botero, *Relations* (1611), 14.
122 Botero, *Relations* (1611), 14.
123 Botero, *Relations* (1611), 23.
124 Robert Dallington, *A Method for Trauell* (London, 1605), sig. B, 1^{r}.
125 Johnson, *Essaies*, sig. E, 3^{r}.

The connection between the knowledge gained by travel and 'ciuill wisedome' is brought out most clearly by the editors of the 1630 version of the text, produced, it seems, after Johnson's death.[126] The editors of this edition ascribe the entirety of the text – drawn from the 1611 and 1616 editions – to Botero, and write that 'Our Author deserves rather to bee numbred among the Politicians, than amongst the Historians or *Geographers*'.[127] They expand upon Johnson's argument in 'Of Obseruation', noting that the 'Observations, Rules, and Caveats' of 'obsolete Authors' are 'nothing so certaine as ours of these lightsomer times' and were 'neither so pleasant nor so useful as these more assured & more moderne Relations'.[128] The constant flux of political affairs has made past knowledge redundant, for 'Time and the Warres have altered much since *Aristotle* and *Ptolomies* dayes; whose Rules and Observations have since growne partly out of use; and beene partly bettered'.[129] Although 'tis true' that knowledge alone cannot advance a state, 'yet . . . by observing of some naturall and casuall advantages' – the two types of observation laid out by Johnson – one can learn to 'make a small towne to become a great Citie, and to sowe greatnesse to posteritie'.[130] For this reason, the editors once again update the text with recent events (most notably the raids of Gabriel Bethlen against the Habsburgs).[131]

The idea that political counsel could be gleaned from the writings of travellers was not new in 1630, nor indeed in 1603, having been articulated as early as 1578 by William Bourne's *Treasure for Traueilers*.[132] Although primarily a text describing the instruments of navigation, the mathematician Bourne also outlines for his readers the purpose of travel. As 'euery gentleman' ought to 'defend the common weale, or els to profyt it some otherway . . . as well in their counsel, and also in their acts and deeds', so travellers are 'very necessary members in the common weale' for they are able 'to geue iudgement by his owne Countrie of other' – to compare the elements of the state in much the way that Botero's *Relationi* does.[133] Such knowledge is 'very necessarie to bee knowne vnto to nobilitie' in order to

[126] Paul and Meshkat, 'Johnson's *Relations*', 127.

[127] Giovanni Botero, *Relations of the Most Famovs Kingomes and Common-Wealths Throrowout the World* (London, 1630), sig. A, 3^{v}; Shackleton, 'Botero, Bodin and Robert Johnson', 408. It is this oversight which may have led to the neglect of Johnson's work, even in modern scholarship; see Fitzmaurice, 'Commercial Ideology', 795; Paul and Meshkat, 'Johnson's *Relations*', 127.

[128] Botero, *Relations* (1630), 1. [129] Botero, *Relations* (1630), 1. [130] Botero, *Relations* (1630), 21.

[131] Paul and Meshkat, 'Johnson's *Relations*', 127–9. In this they are actually out of date, as they pray for Bethlan's 'recovery' despite the fact that he had died the year before.

[132] See Millstone, 'Seeing Like a Statesman', 101-4; for travel as counsel see Williamson, 'A Letter of Travel Advice?', 1–22.

[133] William Bourne, *A Booke Called the Treasure for Traueilers* (London, 1578), iii^{r}.

'prouide them selues, and their Countrie for their better safetie'.[134] Travel is presented as a duty for elites, which contributes to the well-being of the commonwealth.

Thomas Palmer's *Essay of the Meanes how to Make our Trauailes, into Forraine Countries, the More Profitable and Honourable* of 1606, an imitation of Theodor Zwinger's *Methodus apodemica* of 1577, repeats this sentiment in the address to the reader. He tells his audience that 'of all voluntarie Commendable actions that of trauailing into forraine States ... is the most behoueable & to be regarded in this Commonweale'.[135] Palmer, a courtier and member of the king's Privy Chamber, dedicated his work to the young Prince Henry, who despite having a great interest in the affairs of other countries, was limited by his station and unable to travel, thus relying on others to bring him the information essential to his training for rule.[136] Palmer seeks to demonstrate 'the means how to make the trauailes of other men ... somewhat more profitable and honorable' to him.[137] In a world where travel is the best way to acquire the knowledge necessary to statecraft, yet the prince is limited within his realm, traveller-counsellors become essential in relaying this information.

Observation is the basis of this political knowledge. In the second part of the essay, which details 'what is meete' for these purposes, Palmer relates that the 'sixt and last generall duetie which is the very point which euery Trauailer ought to lay his witts about' is 'To get knowledge for the bettering of himselfe and his Countrie'.[138] Such knowledge is 'the meanes whereon all policie is grownded' and the 'vtensils, and materialls of States men'.[139] The acquisition of this wisdom marks the difference between 'the home States man ... & the compleate Trauailer' for the former 'is fed by aduertisements only, and is ledde by other mens eyes'.[140] Drawing on the critique of philosophy we have already seen, Palmer suggests that such difference is like that between the soldier, who has real experience, and the theorist, 'whose booke rules, in accidentall things, faile many times as in

134 Bourne, *Treasure for Traueilers*, iii^{v}.

135 Thomas Palmer, *An Essay of the Meanes How to Make Our Trauailes, into Forraine Countries, the More Profitable and Honourable* (London, 1606), sig. A, 1^{r}.

136 Michelle O'Callaghan, '*Coryats Crudities* (1611) and Travel Writing as the "Eyes" of the Prince', in *Prince Henry Revived: Image and Exemplarity in Early Modern England*, ed. Timothy Wilks (Seattle: University of Washington Press, 2007), 85, 87, 89. Palmer was likely well aware of Henry's desire to travel, given that his son, Roger, was the prince's cup-bearer; O'Callaghan, '*Coryats Crudities* (1611)', 101 fn. 1.

137 Palmer, *An Essay*, sig. A, 2^{v}.

138 Palmer, *An Essay*, sig. 52–3.

139 Palmer, *An Essay*, sig. 53.

140 Palmer, *An Essay*, sig. 53.

particular motions'.[141] Direct observation is the key: 'For, the eye hath a more perfect sense in iudgement then the eare'.[142] In other words, this sort of observation avoids the perils associated with rhetoric, allowing the traveller to see for himself, rather than being convinced of something which may or may not be true.

It is worth noting that travellers were not universally acknowledged to be good sources of advice, either because of their potential for falsity or because of the corrupted morals they may have picked up along the way. The gentleman traveller William Parry notes in his 1601 edition of *The Trauels of Anthony Sherley*, whom he accompanied, that the idea that '*Trauellers may lie by authority*' had already become 'prouerbiall speech' by the turn of the century, and so he makes clear that he gives the 'true relation of what mine eies saw . . . contenting my selfe with the conscience of the truth'.[143] Although some 'entiteling themselues Trauellers' do indeed 'take authoritie to vtter lies', likewise 'many honest and true Trauellers, speaking the truth . . . are concluded liers for their labour'.[144] Parry uses the allegory of the cave to explain away accusations of falsity, for 'how could a man, from his birth confined in a dungeon or lightlesse Caue, be brought to conceiue, or beleeue the glorie and great magnificence of the visible, celestiall, and terrestriall globes'?[145] Travellers will often be mistrusted because of the exoticism of what they report, but just like philosophers, they need to be believed.

Benjamin Fisher repeats the same metaphor in the address to the reader to his *Profitable Instructions Describing what Speciall Obseruations Are to Be Taken by Trauellers* of 1633, a book which contained papers and letters relating to the subject from Robert Devereux, the Earl of Essex, Elizabeth I's secretary, William Davidson and Philip Sidney. Arguing against those who have 'lately maintained . . . That the best travailing is in maps and good Authors', Fisher suggests that such a view is a 'pleasing opinion for solitary prisoners, who may thus travell ouer the world, though confined to a dungeon'.[146] This 'sedentary Traueller' only passes for a wise man if he 'converseth either with dead men by reading; or by writing, with men absent', but as soon as he must 'enter on the stage of publike imployment' it becomes clear that he is 'vnfit for Action'.[147] Just as the philosopher had

141 Palmer, *An Essay*, sig. 53. 142 Palmer, *An Essay*, sig. 53.

143 William Parry, *The Trauels of Anthony Sherley* (London, 1601), 2.

144 Parry, *The Trauels of Anthony Sherley*, 1–2. 145 Parry, *The Trauels of Anthony Sherley*, 2.

146 Benjamin Fisher, *Profitable Instructions Describing What Speciall Obseruations Are to Be Taken by Trauellers* (London, 1633), sig. A, 1^r–A, 2^r.

147 Fisher, *Profitable Instructions*, sig. A, 2^v–A, 3^r.

been the ideal figure to provide political counsel for the orthodox humanists in the light of his knowledge of moral philosophy, so now does the traveller take his place on the political stage because of his better understanding of world affairs.

Fisher's 'sedentary Traueller' is 'innocent', for he has escaped the 'corruptions' that are risked by travel, 'but withall is Ignorant' of the knowledge essential for governance.[148] The expert traveller and writer Fynes Moryson had made this trade-off between innocence and experience clear in his *Itinerary* of 1617, emphasising that it had more to do with the original condition of the traveller than the influence of travel itself, for 'if an Asse at *Rome* doe soiourne, An Asse he shall from thence returne'.[149] Nevertheless, for Moryson, such an ass is still better advanced than those 'graue Vniuersity men' who are 'sharpe sighted in the Schooles' and yet are 'often reputed idiots in the practice of worldly affaires'.[150] Those who 'discourage the affects of these great rewards' to be gained from travel 'are not vnlike the Sophisters, who perswade that blindnesse, deafenesse, and the priuations of other senses, are not to be numbred among euils, because we see many vnpleasing things, often heare that which offendeth the eares, and for one good smell draw in twenty ill sauors'.[151] Such opinions, Moryson suggests, have led to travellers being denied their rightful place as informants to 'Counsellours of States, and Peeres of Realmes', who instead 'desire to haue dull and slothful companions, then those that are wise and ambitious'.[152] Thus he intends to 'write especially in this place to the Humanist', meaning 'him that affects the knowledge of State affaires, Histories, Cosmography and the like'.[153]

These themes are brought together in the popular *Coryat's Crudities*, first published in 1611.[154] Dedicated to Prince Henry, the prince sponsored the book, and his copy is still extant in the British Library. Thomas Coryate, a traveller and unofficial jester in the prince's court, writes in his address that he was encouraged 'to present these my silly Obseruations' by the hope that they would spur 'many noble and generose yong Gallants' of Henry's court 'to trauell into forraine countries', enriching themselves 'partly with the obseruations, and partly with the languages' of the regions that they

[148] See O'Callaghan, '*Coryats Crudities* (1611)', 88.

[149] Fynes Moryson, *An Itinerary* (London, 1617), 3. [150] Moryson, *Itinerary*, 3.

[151] Moryson, *Itinerary*, 8. [152] Moryson, *Itinerary*, 8. [153] Moryson, *Itinerary*, 9.

[154] Andrew Hadfield, *Literature, Travel, and Colonial Writing in the English Renaissance, 1545–1625* (Oxford: Clarendon Press, 1998), 59 labels this text 'the first self-consciously styled work of English travel writing'. For the novelty of this work see Hadfield, *Literature, Travel, and Colonial Writing*, 59-66; O'Callaghan, '*Coryats Crudities* (1611)', 86–7, 93.

visit, 'seeing thereby they will be made fit to doe your Highnesse and their Country the better seruice'.[155] Coryate uses the vocabulary of observation throughout this dedication, playing on its relation to the language of travel in his sign-off: 'By him that trauelleth no lesse in all humble and dutifull obseruance to your HIGHNESSE then he did to Venice and the parts abouementioned, Your Highenesse poore Obseruer, Thomas Coryate, Peregrine of Odcombe'.[156]

Before relating his travels to Henry, Coryate includes an oration from the German philosopher Hermann Kirchner, 'That young men ought to Trauell', in which Kirchner argues that 'there can be no nearer way to the attayning of true wisedome and all experience of a ciuill life, no speedier way to aspire to the gouernement of a Commonweale . . . then trauell'.[157] Knowledge cannot be gleaned from the 'mute sounds of books', but rather 'we must go unto those learned men, know & search for many things, and gather many things by our eye and sight'.[158] Kirchner suggests that all sciences, especially history, are predicated on such observation, declaring:

> For good God, what Historiographer can you exemplify vnto me, of what credite, knowledge, or experience soeuer he was, that hath not for the most part beene personally present at those matters, which hee hath thought good to commit . . . that hath not with his owne eyes seene those places whereof he maketh a description to others, that hath not obserued the manners and behauior of those men, who he eyther praiseth or dispraiseth?[159]

The knowledge gleaned from travel 'doth impart farre greater benefits to Common-weales' than simply to the traveller himself.[160] There is no one more suited to be 'aduanced to the sterne of a Common weale' then such a traveller.[161] Kirchner goes as far as to combine this figure with that of Plato's philosopher-king, asserting that 'surely this is the man whom *Plato* doth call a Philosopher, who before hee came to the administration of the Common-weale, disputed not at home in his halfe-mooned chaire . . . but, which by trauersing the Common-weales of many Nations, hath searched out all the wayes and meanes that pertaine to a ciuill life, and the gouerning of a humane society'.[162] Combining this with the language of reason of state, Kirchner suggests that it is such a one who will know 'what doth weaken, disipate and ouerthrow a Kingdome, and what again doth

155 Thomas Coryate, *Coryats Crudities* (London, 1611), sig. a, 4^{v}–5^{r}; see O'Callaghan, '*Coryats Crudities* (1611)', 86.

156 Coryate, *Coryats Crudities*, sig. b, 1^{v}.

157 Coryate, *Coryats Crudities*, sig. B, 1^{r}; B, 2^{r}.

158 Coryate, *Coryats Crudities*, sig. B, 3^{r}; see O'Callaghan, '*Coryats Crudities* (1611)', 90.

159 Coryate, *Coryats Crudities*, sig. B, 3$^{r\text{-}v}$.

160 Coryate, *Coryats Crudities*, sig. B, 8^{r}.

161 Coryate, *Coryats Crudities*, sig. B, 8^{r}.

162 Coryate, *Coryats Crudities*, sig. B, 8^{r}.

strengthen, establish & preserue it'.[163] 'O happy that Common-weale', he declares, 'which hath from aboue gotten some such ruler'.[164] However, in those kingdoms where God has not been so kind to institute this travelling-philosopher as king, then this figure ought to be the counsellor, as 'what other Counsellor can a Prince chuse himselfe [?] . . . For this Counsellor is like that opticke Glasse, wherein not onely the space of three or tenne miles, but also of a whole Prouince, yea and of the whole world it selfe may be represented'.[165] This is the new model of the ideal counsellor, inspired by the needs of reason of state: a clear and pure transmitter of the world's affairs.

The wide-spread acceptance of reason of state in the writers of the late sixteenth and early seventeenth centuries, with its emphasis on variable circumstances, real-world affairs and interests, leads to the predominance of a different sort of essential political knowledge to be communicated through counsel. This knowledge is gained not through study of moral philosophy or history, but through travel, and is not to be communicated using rhetoric, but straightforwardly presented. The counsellor becomes the transmitter of this information – the 'eyes' of the prince. In no way, then, ought the counsellor to lead or rule over the prince, further diminishing his role in relation to the sovereign power of the prince. It is a political knowledge that lends itself to subjection to, rather than rule over, the prince.

163 Coryate, *Coryats Crudities*, sig. C, 1^{r}.
164 Coryate, *Coryats Crudities*, sig. B, 8^{v}.
165 Coryate, *Coryats Crudities*, sig. C, 2^{r}.

CHAPTER 7

Counsel, Command and the Stuarts

It would be an understatement to suggest that the early Stuarts had a difficult and uncomfortable relationship with counsel. This was caused by an unfortunate confluence of personal preference and cultural change. Whereas both James VI/I and Charles I increasingly relied heavily on close favourites to advise them, this mode of counsel was, in a sense, outdated and seen to be suspicious.[1] There remained a tension – even an irony – in the relationship between counsel and command. Both these Stuart monarchs had a preference for a strong central monarchy; their reliance on personal advisers was seen by others to weaken this, though they saw the affront to their power coming from the suggestion that they abandon their personal counsel. In response, counsel was increasingly vested in the parliament over and above the Privy Council, encroaching upon kingly authority.[2] Parliament was seen to be more transparent and resolve the 'problem of interest' that we've encountered in the previous chapter. If one accepts the Machiavellian/reason of state assumption that all counsellors are self-interested, and that this conflicted with advice-giving in the interests of the state, then, many reasoned, the obvious solution was to rest the responsibility of giving counsel in an institution wherein self-interest was

[1] As Alan R. Macdonald, 'Consultation, Counsel and the "Early Stuart Period" in Scotland', in *The Politics of Counsel in England and Scotland, 1286–1707*, ed. Jacqueline Rose (Oxford: Oxford University Press, 2017), 193–210 points out, James VI began his reign as king of Scotland seeking 'an unprecedented level of formal consultation' that actually went against what he said on the topic in his written works, but this was significantly reduced in 1603 and continued to dwindle under the pre-eminence of Buckingham.

[2] It is worth noting that a number of sixteenth-century texts on the subject of counsel were printed or re-printed in this period, including George Buchanan, *Tyrannicall-Government Anatomized* (London, 1642), subtitled 'A discovrse concerning evil-councellors being the life and death of John the Baptist'. It had originally been written in the 1540s; see George Buchanan, *A Critical Edition of George Buchanan's Baptistes and of Its Anonymous Seventeenth-Century Translation Tyrannicall-Government Anatomized*, ed. Steven Berkowitz (New York: Garland Publishing Inc, 1992). Roper and Cavendish's biographies were also published at this time, as was Edmund Dacre's translations of Machiavelli's *Prince* and *Discourses*.

synonymous with the interests of the state. The Stuarts, however, resisted this conclusion, seeing themselves as the state, and the choice of counsellors solely resting with themselves.

There are a multiplicity of ways to assess the causes and motivations behind the English Civil War, especially when one considers its place in the wider War of the Three Kingdoms.[3] The role of the discourse of counsel, however, has been underemphasised, despite its clear centrality in the sources.[4] Alan Cromartie has rightly drawn attention to the way in which debates over the role of the law, and thus Parliament's place as the highest 'Court' in the realm, played a part in the debates of the English Civil War. As with counsel, the issue was – in the words of one MP – 'If the judges may judge the imposition by the legall power, then the absolute power is controllable by the legall power. And therefore he may not sett it by his absolute power'.[5] There was a similar issue at hand in regard to Parliament's role as a source of counsel. Parliamentarians, such as Henry Parker, asserted that especially in crisis moments, such as when the king is seduced by 'evil counsel', parliament's role as a conciliar institution granted it the right to command. Those defending the rights of the crown countered that a distinction was needed between counsel and command, or else there was no clear sovereign. This debate had the effect of reinforcing a focus on sovereignty: parliamentarians made the argument that the central conciliar institution was in fact a locus of sovereignty;[6] royalists sought to reduce the power and relevance of counsel. For this reason, the

[3] It is impossible to try to summarise these causes, or the scholarship which details them. See Ann Hughes, *The Causes of the English Civil War* (Basingstoke: Palgrave Macmillan, 1998); Conrad Russell, *The Causes of the English Civil War: The Ford Lectures Delivered in the University of Oxford, 1987–1988* (Oxford: Clarendon Press, 1990); Christopher Hill, *Intellectual Origins of the English Revolution – Revisited* (Oxford: Clarendon Press, 1997); Lawrence Stone, *The Causes of the English Revolution 1529–1642* (London: Routledge, 2017).

[4] There are mentions: see Glenn Burgess, *Absolute Monarchy and the Stuart Constitution* (New Haven: Yale University Press, 1996), 52–60; 'The Impact on Political Thought: Rhetorics for Troubled Times', in *The Impact of the English Civil War* (London: Collins & Brown, 1991), ed. John Stephen Morrill and Glenn Burgess, 68–74; Hughes, *The Causes of the English Civil War*, 85–90; Kevin Sharpe, *Faction and Parliament: Essays on Early Stuart History* (Clarendon Press, 1978), 37–42 Millstone, *Manuscript Circulation*, 200; Rose, 'Sir Edward Hyde and the Problem of Counsel', 249–69.

[5] Quoted in Alan Cromartie, 'Parliamentary Sovereignty, Popular Sovereignty, and Henry Parker's Adjudicative Standpoint', in *Popular Sovereignty in Historical Perspective*, ed. Richard Bourke and Quentin Skinner (Cambridge: Cambridge University Press, 2016), 151.

[6] As Rose, 'Sir Edward Hyde and the Problem of Counsel', 249 put it: 'counsel provided a useful tool by which parliament first criticised the policies of the 1630s Personal Rule, then levered itself into position as the dominant element within the mixed constitution, and ultimately claimed sovereignty'.

English Civil War sees the end of the 'monarchy of counsel' and the turn to a politics focused on theories and expressions of sovereignty.[7]

i Sovereignty and Parliament

The early Stuart period saw a strong and widespread re-articulation of the distinction between counsel and command, largely drawn from the work of Jean Bodin. Although written in 1576, Bodin's *Les Six livres de la République* only had a meaningful effect on English political thinking in the late sixteenth century, and had a profound impact following the accession of the first Stuart in 1603 (the text was translated and published in 1606).[8] Although recent scholarship has shown Bodin to be less of an absolutist than he was long thought to be, Stuart commentators were happy to read him as such.[9]

Bodin, famously, gives a clear and unequivocal definition of sovereignty: 'that absolute and perpetual power vested in a commonwealth [*République*]'.[10] Against those who used the reason of state emphasis on contingency and the relationship between counsel and *kairos* to suggest that counsellors were those best poised to deal with moments of emergency, Bodin maintains that such exigent moments reveal the location of sovereignty, and this cannot be in a council unless it itself is sovereign.[11] By definition, if anything commands the sovereign authority, it usurps its sovereignty, even (or especially) in exceptional moments.

Bodin recognises that counsellors have been left in an – as Daniel Lee has put it – 'undefined interstitial space between sovereignty and subjection', thanks to Aristotle's conflation of *concilium* and *imperium* (as well as *iurisdictio*).[12] Part of his purpose, then, is to correct this issue. The king is, he makes clear, not 'bound' to take the advice of any conciliar body, whether the Three Estates or the English parliament. Although the prince's

[7] See Rose, 'Sir Edward Hyde and the Problem of Counsel', 249–69.

[8] Lee, *Popular Sovereignty*, 273–4: 'Bodin would quickly become one of the central authorities invoked by English royalists in the heat of constitutional debates in the Stuart monarchy'; see also McLaren, *Political Culture*, 44; Sharpe, *Faction and Parliament*, 29–30. As Johann P. Sommerville, 'Introduction', in *King James VI and I: Political Writings* (Cambridge: Cambridge University Press, 1995), xxviii points out, James had Bodin in his library as a youth, and their 'political theories plainly belong to the same family'.

[9] Lee, *Popular Sovereignty*, 159–253; Richard Tuck, 'Democratic Sovereignty and Democratic Government', in *Popular Sovereignty in Historical Perspective*, ed. Richard Bourke and Quentin Skinner (Cambridge: Cambridge University Press, 2016), 115–41.

[10] Jean Bodin, *Bodin: On Sovereignty: Six Books of the Commonwealth*, trans. M. J. Tooley (Massachusetts: CreateSpace Independent Publishing Platform, 2009), 49.

[11] Lee, *Popular Sovereignty*, 179. [12] Lee, *Popular Sovereignty*, 177–8.

'majesty' is most expressed in such an assembly, that institution has no power of 'commanding or determining, or any right to a deliberative voice'.[13] There is nothing ambiguous about Bodin's articulation of the distinction between counsel and command: 'A council is instituted to advise those who exercise sovereign authority in the commonwealth ... the council in any well-ordered commonwealth should have no power of action [*comma[n]der*]', and this is even clearer in the accompanying marginal note: '*Le Senat establi seulement pour donner aduis, & non pour commander*'.[14] If the council could enforce its advice, it would become sovereign itself, 'the councillors would rule ... This would not be without the diminution or even destruction of the sovereign majesty'.[15]

Councils are not necessary, in fact, to the 'continued existence' of the commonwealth, for the king may be wise enough to rule without them.[16] This leads Bodin to consider the recurring hypothetical dilemma of the discourse of counsel: 'whether it is better to have a foolish prince who is well-advised or a wise man who eschews good counsel'.[17] Both options are, he says, best rejected as 'unreal'. A wise man is not in need of good counsel anyway, and a stupid prince cannot possibly recognise it. As such, Bodin appears at first to adopt a Machiavellian model: the prudence of the prince rules his counsellors, not the other way around. As he says 'the majesty of a prince is best displayed when he can, and his prudence when he knows how to, weigh and appraise the advice of his council, and decide according to the opinion of the wiser part, rather than the opinion of the greater part'.[18]

Yet Bodin adopts a more traditional answer to this question, one that appears to assume – in a traditional humanist vein – that a prince is ruled by his counsellors who correct the misfortunes of his birth: 'since the gift of wisdom is vouchsafed only to the very few, and we are bound in obedience to all such princes as it pleases God to bestow upon us, the best thing we can hope for is that he may have wise counsel.' Sounding very much like Erasmus, Bodin continues that 'it is much less dangerous to have a bad prince who is well-advised than a good one who is ill-advised'. The prince

[13] Bodin, *On Sovereignty*, 71.

[14] Bodin, *On Sovereignty*, 119. 'that the Senat is established to giue aduise and councell to them which haue the soueraigntie in euerie Commonweale ... the Senat in a well ordered Commonweale, ought not to haue power to commaund', Jean Bodin, *The Six Bookes of a Commonweale*, trans. Richard Knolles (London, 1606), 272.

[15] Bodin, *On Sovereignty*, 120. 'the councellors of the estate, in stead of councellors should ther of become maisters ... a thing impossible to be done, without the impairing, or to say better the vtter subuersion of all soueraigntie and maiestie', Bodin, *Six Bookes*, 277.

[16] Bodin, *On Sovereignty*, 342. [17] Bodin, *On Sovereignty*, 342. [18] Bodin, *On Sovereignty*, 119.

ought to be 'guided' (in the 1606 'ought to follow', the original has '*conduit*') his counsellors' advice in all things. As in the reason of state tradition, however, this is done for reasons of image and reputation, to give an air of legitimacy to all decrees and to ensure obedience; we may recall that Felippe makes a similar statement (see Chapter 3). The prince, Bodin makes clear, must rule his counsellors, and in doing so, can take benefit from them. Responding to the objection that because 'many heads are better than one' (or 'many men see better than one', '*plusieurs voyant mieux*'), Bodin reiterates that 'there is a great difference between counsel and command'.[19] In counsel, it is indeed better to hear the opinions of many, but 'for taking a decision and issuing an order, one is always better than many' and thus 'it is necessary that there should be a sovereign prince with power to make decisions on the advice of his counsel'.[20]

The Stuarts repeated this Bodinian distinction between counsel and command in their interactions with parliament, in much stronger terms than had Elizabeth I in Holinshed's account. The members of the House of Commons had used the language of 'counsel' in describing their public function since at least the 1570s, fuelled by the 'species of interregnum' encountered in Chapter 5.[21] This was not uncontentious, however, for, as David Colclough has shown, 'at various times both James I and Charles I (as well as members of both Houses) would argue either that they were not first and foremost called to counsel the monarch or that they were failing to counsel well'.[22] As Sharpe has pointed out, in many regards Parliament was ill-suited to give counsel, as it – or rather its members – did not conform to the expectations of wise and grave men, propounded by many writers on counsel.[23] However, as we have seen, there was another perspective on counsel, growing through the sixteenth and seventeenth centuries, that advocated for counsel as transmitting the voice of the people and observation of contemporary affairs; parliament was particularly well suited to communicate this sort of advice.

James's experience of personal monarchy in Scotland, however, differed from this situation in England. As he told his first parliament: 'Precedents in the times of minors, of tyrants, or women or simple kings [are] not to be credited.'[24] Part of the struggle of the Stuarts in

[19] Bodin, *On Sovereignty*, 237. [20] Bodin, *On Sovereignty*, 237.

[21] Levy Peck, 'Kingship, Counsel and Law', 98. Colclough, *Freedom of Speech*, 131–8 gives a longer history, since Thomas More's time as Speaker in 1523, though this evidence comes from Roper's biography of More, and may not be completely accurate. For its appearance in the 1570s, see McLaren, *Political Culture*, 161.

[22] Colclough, *Freedom of Speech*, 120–1, see also 138–49. [23] Sharpe, *Faction and Parliament*, 39.

[24] Quoted in McLaren, *Political Culture*, 6; see Levy Peck, 'Kingship, Counsel and Law', 99.

attempting to establish themselves as monarchs in the truest sense was to dismantle the scaffolding which had kept the Elizabethan regime standing, and which had now become an indelible part of the political landscape.[25] The result was that James got off on the wrong foot with his first parliament, called in 1604.[26] Parliament responded with the Form of Apology and Satisfaction, in which they expressed their concerns and grievances according to their role as counsellors to the king.[27] Although blessed with a king of 'such understanding and wisdom', it remains that 'no human wisdom, how great soever' can know all the particularities that the king must know – a restatement of the single prince problem evidenced from the Middle Ages onwards.[28] The king has been 'misinformed' and thus has turned against his parliament.[29] In particular, he has been misled as to the purpose of parliament, which stands as an eternal corrective to the potential tyranny of changeable monarchs. This gives members various powers and liberties, which they iterate. To end, they remind the king that this includes a liberty of speech, which is threatened by outside counsels: 'Let no suspicion have access to [the people's] fearful thoughts, that their privileges, which they think by your Majesty should be protected, should now by sinister information or counsel be violate or impaired'.[30] The parliament should have the ability to speak freely to the king, especially regarding 'abuses'.[31] After all, 'The voice of the people in things of their knowledge is said to be as the voice of God.'[32] If the king hears the petitions of the people voiced through parliament, he is sure to have their love forever. They do not state explicitly what will happen if he does not.

James's response to such claims was to reiterate the submissive nature of counsel to command. In the 1606 session, James informed his parliament that they were 'Subjects' though they were 'specially called to be Counsellors of the Kingdom', and 'the Thought of the One must not

[25] Robert Filmer, for instance, writing under Charles I, must contend with the Elizabethan mixed constitution in establishing his theory of supreme monarchy, derived in large part from Bodin; Robert Filmer, 'Patriarcha', in *Filmer: 'Patriarcha' and Other Writings*, ed. Johann P. Sommerville (Cambridge: Cambridge University Press, 1991), 40, 52–3, 57–60; see Levy Peck, 'Kingship, Counsel and Law', 108.

[26] As Sharpe, *Faction and Parliament*, 43 suggests, 'Perhaps one of the most striking features of the problems that beset James I is the speed with which they materialized'.

[27] Colclough, *Freedom of Speech*, 143: 'the Apology is itself couched in terms of frank but honest counsel'.

[28] J. P. Kenyon, ed., *The Stuart Constitution, 1603–1688: Documents and Commentary* (Cambridge: Cambridge University Press, 1986), 29.

[29] Kenyon, ed., *The Stuart Constitution*, 29.

[30] Kenyon, ed., *The Stuart Constitution*, 35.

[31] Kenyon, ed., *The Stuart Constitution*, 35.

[32] Kenyon, ed., *The Stuart Constitution*, 35.

make them forget the Consideration of the other'.[33] In 1610, he opposed the parliament's view of itself as a necessary source of counsel, instead suggesting that he consulted them only for 'convenience' and to make his work as king 'seem more glorious'.[34] After the breakdown of the addled parliament in 1614, James reminded his parliament that they were not his only source of counsel: although 'there is not in the world so great a counsel as [that of the parliament], both in the quantity and quality', he also had wise and experienced counsellors which he had retained from Elizabeth's reign, who were advising him contrary to the counsel of parliament; it must be parliament that is mistaken.[35]

By the time of James's death in 1625, evil counsel had become a headline issue with most of the attention centred on the figure of the Duke of Buckingham.[36] Many of the critiques focused on the fact that Buckingham was a singular source of counsel: the best counsel came from a multitude of counsellors.[37] The king's counsel, as William Walter put it, 'rides upon one horse', causing many ills to the realm.[38] The 'private' nature of his advice was also deeply problematic. As the MP George Wilde suggested, 'the refusing of the cordial counsel of parliament' was one of the causes of kingdom's great evils, and although it is not right to judge counsel by its outcome, 'when great things are manged by single counsel or private respects, they are to be looked into'.[39] The MPs maintained their right to censure the counsel of the king, based on historical precedent and their need to give the king counsel themselves.[40]

Charles's response to this demand was to once again reiterate firmly the distinction between counsel and command. The Lord Keeper, Thomas Coventry, told both Houses that 'his Majesty does not forget that the parliament is his council and therefore it ought to have the liberty and freedom of a council, but his Majesty also understands the difference between counselling and controlling'.[41] Parliament was doing the latter, though subtly. This approach was 'dishonourable and full of distrust', 'for

[33] 'House of Commons Journal Volume 1: 16–18 November 1606', in *Journal of the House of Commons: Volume 1, 1547–1629* (London, 1802), 314–15, www.british-history.ac.uk/commons-jrnl/vol1/pp314-315; see Colclough, *Freedom of Speech*, 145–6.

[34] Quoted in Colclough, *Freedom of Speech*, 155–6.

[35] Quoted in *Freedom of Speech*, 165.

[36] Colclough, *Freedom of Speech*, 185.

[37] Colclough, *Freedom of Speech*, 187–8, see also Thomas Frankland, ed., *The Annals of King James and King Charles the First: 1612–1642* (London, 1681), 242.

[38] Quoted in Colclough, *Freedom of Speech*, 190.

[39] Quoted in Colclough, *Freedom of Speech*, 189.

[40] Colclough, *Freedom of Speech*, 188.

[41] William B. Bidwell and Maija Jansson, eds., *Proceedings in Parliament 1626, Volume 2: House of Commons* (New Haven: University of Rochester Press, 1997), 392.

though you have avoided the literal words of a condition' it has the 'effect' of such, which is not 'a parliamentary way to deal with kings'.[42] Charles reminded them that 'parliaments are altogether in my power for calling, sitting and continuance of them. Therefore as I find the fruits either good or evil they are to continue or not to be'.[43]

When the 1629 parliament came to an end, ushering in the Personal Rule, it was with a strongly worded objection to 'new counsels' – counsel from sources other than parliament – read out while the Speaker was forcibly and physically restrained in his seat.[44] Colclough has suggested that this led 'to the almost inconceivable notion that Parliament was arguing that all Englishmen could be counsellors, and speaking frankly to the king'.[45] Although this might not have been entirely acceptable, there was a broadening of political interest and expertise, which fuelled the notion that the king ought to open himself to political counsel from a wider segment of the population.[46] This was not distinct from the changes in political knowledge brought about by the reason of state tradition. After all, if valuable political knowledge is nothing but observation, then there is no reason that it should remain the purview of the privileged.

ii Most Secret Instructions

This broadening of counsel via the parliament cannot be separated from other ways in which politics was opened to the people in this period. Taciteanism had highlighted the role of the *arcana imperii* (secrets of the state) largely by – as Boccalini was keen to point out – exposing them. The essential relationship between secrets and reason of state had been outlined by Botero, who – like others before him – quotes the popular maxim *qui nescit (dis)simulare, nescit regnare.*[47] Santa Maria, in his *Policie Vnveiled,* notes too that it is to 'Ministers, and Secretaries of State . . . [that] secrecie more properly belongs', a fact which is clear even in their titles, 'for out of that obligation which they haue to be secret, they are called Secretaries, and are the Archiues and Cabinets of the secrets of the King, and the

[42] Bidwell and Jansson, eds., *Parliament 1625, Volume 2*, 395.

[43] Bidwell and Jansson, eds., *Parliament 1625, Volume 2*, 395.

[44] Colclough, *Freedom of Speech*, 194. Conrad Russell, *Parliaments and English Politics 1621–1629* (Oxford: Oxford University Press, 1979), ebook. For more on the history of 'new counsels' see Hughes, *The Causes of the English Civil War*, 85–90.

[45] Colclough, *Freedom of Speech*, 194.

[46] Millstone, 'Seeing Like a Statesman', 83.

[47] Braun, 'Knowledge and Counsel', 286.

kingdom'.[48] He ends with an exhortation to such persons: 'Let Priuie-Counsellours (I say) and Secretaries of State, bridle their tongues; If not, let Kings, if they can, restraine them'.[49] The importance of secrets of state furthers the Machiavellian inversion of the traditional model of counsel, with princes bridling and controlling their counsellors, rather than the reverse.

Boccalini highlights the inherent irony: the proliferation of reason of state and its warnings about secret-keeping made it even more difficult to keep them. The lessons of Tacitus, intended 'onely for the benefit of Princes', have been 'imbraced and cherished with such insatiate greedinesse, by priuate and meane subiects' who 'shew not themselues more cunning in any profession than of State policy'.[50] The publication and proliferation of Tacitus' work fundamentally altered the political environment: '*Tacitus* with the seditious argument of his *Annals*, and of his Histories, hath framed a kinde of spectacles, that work most pernitious effects for Princes', for 'being put vpon the noses of silly and simple people, they so refine and sharpen their sight, as they make them see and prie into the most hidden and secret thoughts of others', including princes.[51] Importantly, although the people ought not to be allowed these 'spectacles', they are to be retained by 'Secretaries, and vnto Priuy Counsellors of States to Princes' so that they might 'facilitate vnto them the good and vpright gouernment of the people'.[52] Counsellors have the crucial role of manipulating both truth and falsehood in the negotiation of state secrets and reason of state.

The counsellor's role in advising and keeping state secrets is demonstrated and usurped in a set of popular texts of the 1620s known as the *Secretissima Instructio* works.[53] These texts purport to be missives written to the Elector Palatine, Frederick V, from his counsellor, advising him on his present position, possible actions and the probable outcomes. Such fabricated insights were becoming 'ordinarie practise' in the period, and it was often difficult for statesmen to tell the difference between real intercepted correspondence and fabrication.[54] They open up the discourse between counsellors and princes in a partly-factual, partly-imagined propagandistic genre, drawing on the reason of state tradition to fuel the suspicions of princes and people in an environment of deception and dissimulation.[55] In so doing, both counsellor and prince are presented in a negative light, and

48 Santa Maria, *Policie Vnveiled*, 322. 49 Santa Maria, *Policie Vnveiled*, 326.
50 Boccalini, *The New-Found Politicke*, 20. 51 Boccalini, *The New-Found Politicke*, 29.
52 Boccalini, *The New-Found Politicke*, 32. 53 Millstone, 'Seeing Like a Statesman', 97–8.
54 Millstone, 'Seeing Like a Statesman', 99–100. 55 Malcolm, *Reason of State*, 34, 32.

the communication between them made all the more dubious for its secretive nature.

There are three known texts within this genre, all anonymous: the first published in 1620, the second in 1622 and the third in 1626.[56] Although never printed in English, two of the *Secretissima* texts – the first, the *Secretissima Instructio*, and the third, the *Altera Secretissima Instructio* – were translated into English and circulated in manuscript form. The *Altera* is a longer, more detailed and more sophisticated text, but both follow the same basic outline. They begin with an appeal to the prince from the writer that he accept his counsel. In the *Secretissima*, the counsellor places himself in a position of authority over his prince, describing himself as the prince's 'most faithfull tutor' as well as his 'maistor' who will minister to him 'secret, but serious Councells'.[57] The writer of the *Altera* takes an even stronger position, demanding 'That you will beleeue me I deserue, not aske' for 'you owe it me'.[58] With Bethune and Boccalini in mind, such language increases the suspicion of this counsellor who rules his prince.

The advice given is couched in the air of suspicion, dissimulation and opportunism surrounding reason of state. As the author of the *Altera* writes, 'Neuer aske' what the cause of the variation and infidelity of princes might be, for it is always 'the great cause, cause of causes, *Reason of State*'.[59] Frederick is not to trust any of his friends, who will vary allegiance based on changing circumstances, with only their interests to guide them. In order to counter this, both writers counsel Frederick that he too must adopt such stratagems and plots, or be destroyed. If 'By force, the way is barred' the author of the *Altera* writes, the Elector Palatine has only recourse to 'Prayers and Fraud ... When ye Lions skin is worne out, put on the Foxes case'.[60] Frederick has two tools at his disposal: 'wise Counterfeiting and dissembling; and speedie execution'.[61] The first he has used effectively thus far, but his credit has run out, and so it is 'best to proceed wth the other pollicy ... I meane Celeritie'.[62] Frederick must move quickly in order to act in 'due tyme', before circumstances change.

The counsellor tells Frederick that the other princes of Europe will not hesitate to seize occasion – 'Doe yo^u thinke the *Turke* would refuse so faire an oportunity' to move against him 'if it were offered?' – and so Frederick

56 Malcolm, *Reason of State*, 31, 45, 58. 57 Sl. MS 3938, fo. 2^r.

58 Noel Malcolm, ed., 'Altera Secretissima Instructio', in *Reason of State, Propaganda, and the Thirty Years' War: An Unknown Translation by Thomas Hobbes* (Oxford: Oxford University Press, 2010), 128.

59 'Altera', 144. 60 'Altera', 174. 61 Sl. MS 3938, fo. 16^r. 62 Sl. MS 3938, fo. 17^v.

must be willing to do the same.[63] Echoing Machiavelli and other writers on occasion, the counsellor advises Frederick that there is 'at this present affaire occasion wch offereth it self vnto' him, and if he does not take it, it will be too late.[64] The same emphasis on seizing occasion is expressed, in much stronger terms, by the author of the *Altera*: 'Nothing distresses me more', he tells Frederick, 'I am torn apart in my mind, I am shattered by pain at the thought that we may lose this opportunity [*occasio*]; if those things pass us fruitlessly, I shall hang myself'.[65] By adopting the vocabularies and aims of reason of state, the *Secretissima Instructio* counsellors are presented as dangerous and scheming, especially because they offer their advice privately to the prince.

Although there were only three *Secretissima Instructio* texts, similar writings were prevalent in the period. The most prolific English writer within this genre – he wrote over twenty-five tracts in total – was Thomas Scott, whose anonymously published pamphlets created such a stir in England that he spent most of his literary career in exile on the continent, until his assassination in 1626.[66] Scott was a Puritan divine who had important connections at court; in 1616 he was listed as one of James I's chaplains.[67] His work advocates for anti-Catholic and anti-Spanish policies, as well as articulating humanist ideas regarding civic government, and he uses semi-truthful news despatches and letters to steer public opinion, especially regarding Spanish and hispanophile counsellors.

Scott was fully aware of the tradition with which he was engaging, as he produced a translation of selections of Boccalini's *New-Sheet* in 1622. His most famous work is *Vox Populi, or Newes from Spayne*, also his first published pamphlet, written in Scotland and printed in London in 1620. This work too blends fiction and fact by presenting an imagined meeting of Spanish councillors, convincing enough that many readers took it as a genuine piece of political intelligence, prompting Scott's flight to the Netherlands. The main figure of *Vox Populi* is the Spanish ambassador to Britain, Diego Sarmiento de Acuña, Count of Gondomar. Scott uses him to highlight the devious practices of the Spanish, specifically of its ambassadors and counsellors.

Vox Populi offers counsel to James I by highlighting the advantages that Gondomar thinks Spain has against England. For example, Gondomar tells his fellow counsellors that James 'extreamly hunts after peace' and that

[63] Sl. MS 3938, fo. 4^v^. [64] Sl. MS 3938, fo. 24^r^. [65] 'Altera', 190.
[66] See Peltonen, *Classical Humanism and Republicanism*, 231.
[67] Leticia Álvarez Recio, 'Opposing the Spanish Match: Thomas Scott's *Vox Populi*', *Sederi* 19 (2009): 5–22.

the English 'haue no patience to temporize and dissemble' like the Spanish and so are less suspicious of the plots of the Spaniards, as well as being less likely to move against them.[68] Thus Scott advocates both for war and for more Machiavellian practices through his text; to beat the Spanish – particularly the scheming Spanish counsellors – the English must become more like them.

Scott repeats this problematic distinction between the natures of the English and the Spanish in his sequel, *The Second Part of Vox Populi, or Gondomar Appearing in the Likenes of Matchiauell*, published four years later. In this text, he draws on Bodin and Botero to establish that the Spanish, as they are in the south and thus 'neere to the Sunne', are 'more crafty, politique, and religious', whereas the English in the north, 'howsoeuer goodlier in person', are 'plaine simple' and therefore more easily deceived. Scott works to make the English generally, and James I specifically, aware of the plots of which their innocence makes them ignorant.[69] Like the writers of the *Secretissima* texts, Scott presses James towards a course of action which combines dissimulation and 'temporizing' as these are the tactics which his enemies employ.

Spain, in addition to being adept at dissimulation, is presented in both these works as a state willing at all times to 'followe opportunity close at the heels', for Gondomar's 'very many faithfull and fast friends in *England*' are willing to move against the English, as soon as 'time and occasion be offered'.[70] Scott brings out these themes of time and opportunity in his *Experimental Discoverie of Spanish Practises*, written in 1623, in which he argues in favour of a timely war against the Spanish. The text begins with an address from the publisher to the reader, which notes that, although the text is not yet complete, 'because (as we say in the prouerb) *Delayes are dangerous*, specially in matters of moment' he has 'presumed to publish it as it is'.[71] Although peace is to be preferred to war in most cases, 'yet for that the time agreeing with the necessity', Britain must go to war with Spain.[72] Spain has 'faire opportunityes offered vnto the greatnesse of his desire' and no 'opportunitie . . . would he let slip for the accomplishment thereof'.[73] There is 'no people' who can 'readier finde the occasion, or sooner take, or

[68] Thomas Scott, *Vox Populi, or Newes from Spayne* (London, 1620), sig. B, 1^{v}; B, 3^{r}; see Peltonen, *Classical Humanism and Republicanism*, 257.

[69] Thomas Scott, *The Second Part of Vox Populi, or Gondomar Appearing in the Likenes of Matchiauell* (London, 1624), 12.

[70] Scott, *The Second Part of Vox Populi*, 45, 8.

[71] Thomas Scott, *An Experimentall Discoverie of Spanish Practises* (London, 1623), sig. A, 1^{v}.

[72] Scott, *Experimentall Discoverie*, 1. [73] Scott, *Experimentall Discoverie*, 1.

resolue it, when it is offred' than the Spanish.[74] James must emulate the Spanish and 'make a warre with your enemie, whilst you haue the aduantage in your hands'.[75] He is 'now of more power then any of his Predecessours' and Spain has gone into decline.[76] Danger must be prevented 'in a conuenient season' for 'opportunitie doth not attend upon Captaines and Councellours pleasures, but sheweth it self on a suddaine; and if not imbraced, passeth away without returning'.[77]

Returning to the *Vox Populi* texts, here too Scott is keen to offer counsel on the pernicious effects of Spanish temporising practices, specifically in relation to the respective positions of James, his counsellors and parliament.[78] Gondomar in the first *Vox Populi* claims that 'one of the principle services' he has done to aid the Spanish cause against England is to have worked 'such a dislike betwixt the King and the lower house' that 'the King will never indure Parliament againe'.[79] James will 'rather suffer absolute want then receive conditionall relief from his subjects'.[80] In 1620, when *Vox Populi* was published, parliament had not sat since the eight-week 'addled parliament' of 1614. As Gondomar makes clear, this has put James in a vulnerable position, for 'levying of subsidies and taskes have been the onely use princes haue made of such assemblies'.[81] As it is 'unlikely there should ever be a Parliament' it is 'impossible that the Kings debts should be payed, his wants sufficiently repaired' except by the marriage to Spain, which is but a 'cover for much intelligence'.[82] This has also stopped Britain building its defences and furnishing its navy, weakening it against a possible attack by Spain. The suspension of parliament has been achieved, Gondomar suggests, by an English counsellor – 'that honourable Earle and admirable Engine' who was 'a sure servant to us and the catholike cause while he lived'.[83] It is not just he, however, who stands in the way of

74 Scott, *Experimentall Discoverie*, 6. 75 Scott, *Experimentall Discoverie*, 3.

76 Scott, *Experimentall Discoverie*, 47.

77 Scott, *Experimentall Discoverie*, 4, 6. There is a close connection between the themes of this text and Chapter XXVI of Machiavelli's *The Prince*, as well as Isocrates' *Panegyricus*.

78 See Peltonen, *Classical Humanism and Republicanism*, 238, 257.

79 Scott, *Vox Populi*, sig. B, 3^r. 80 Scott, *Vox Populi*, sig. B, 3^r.

81 Scott, *Vox Populi*, sig. B, 3^v. 82 Scott, *Vox Populi*, sig. B, 1^v.

83 Scott, *Vox Populi*, sig. B, 3^r. The obvious candidate for this 'honorable earl' might be the Earl of Buckingham (not the *Duke* of Buckingham until 1623), who was often accused of being an enemy of parliament. However, he was still alive in 1620, and Scott, especially in the second *Vox Populi*, goes to great lengths to defend him against the accusation of standing in opposition to parliament (although such protestations need not be sincere). Instead, Gondomar is most likely referring to Henry Howard, Earl of Northampton, who had died in 1614. He secretly converted to Catholicism in that year with the help of Gondomar himself and openly declared himself an active supporter of the Spanish match. He wrote to the Spanish ambassador with the details of his advice to James I in regard to parliament, declaring that his advice to the king against the calling of parliament was 'in

the remedy of parliament, for 'there are so many about' the king, 'who blow this cole fearing their owne stakes, if a Parliament should inquire into their actions'.[84] Although there are those 'who preserve the priviledge of subjects against soveraign invasion' and who 'call for the course of the common lawe', the 'lawe proper to their nation', the 'tyme servers cry the lawes down and cry up the prerogative'.[85] In doing so they 'prey upon the subject by suites and exactions' and 'procure themselves much suspition ... & hate'.[86] Scott paints a clear picture of enmity between the favourite counsellors of the king – who follow their own interests – and the parliament, holding up the latter as the mainstay of the state.

The second *Vox Populi* deals even more specifically with these parliamentary and conciliar themes. Published in 1624, it takes place during the 'happy parliament' of 1624–1625. This parliament is praised by Scott, and is placed as the primary cause of the 'tempestuous times' faced by the Spanish.[87] In particular, the 'now-present parliament' of England has uncovered 'in all treatises for the space of these two hundred yeares' how '*Spaine* hath dealt with the English, *fide punica*' to 'serue her necessities for the present'.[88] In other words, it is the parliament who has fulfilled the role of discovering the secret plans and machinations of the Spanish, which Scott had detailed in the first *Vox Populi*. As a result, this parliament is chief of 'the mischeifes' facing the Spanish, for the king has 'wholy referred himselfe' to it, 'not onely for the examination and redresse of all abuses and misdemeanors at home, but for the discussing and searching into all plots and practices of other abroad, that may seeme any way to preiudice the quiet and well gouerned estate of his Kingdomes, without interposition or mediation'.[89] In this way, 'the King and people goe all on and together, with that alacrity and constancy, in prouiding for the good estate of the Kingdome, as the like hath no beene seene these nany [sic] yeeares'.[90] This parliament, Gondomar suspects, will persecute their Catholic agents, weakening their cause and intelligence in England. The work ends with an address 'TO THE ILLVSTRIOVS MAGNIFIQUE AND GRAVE Assembly of the High Court of Parliament in England'.[91] Calling them 'the Most Honorable,

keeping with the good of Christianity and the advantage and service of Spain'; quoted in Pauline Croft, 'Howard, Henry, Earl of Northampton (1540–1614)', Oxford Dictionary of National Biography, 2004, www.oxforddnb.com/view/article/13906.

84 Scott, *Vox Populi*, sig. B, 3ʳ. 85 Scott, *Vox Populi*, sig. B, 3ᵛ. 86 Scott, *Vox Populi*, sig. B, 3ᵛ.

87 Scott, *The Second Part of Vox Populi*, 3. 88 Scott, *The Second Part of Vox Populi*, 13–14.

89 Scott, *The Second Part of Vox Populi*, 24. 90 Scott, *The Second Part of Vox Populi*, 24.

91 Scott, *The Second Part of Vox Populi*, 59.

Great, and Graue *Senate*', Scott encourages them to view 'as in a little glasse' the 'effect of a seauen yeares Treaty with Spaine'.[92] In Scott's work, it is the parliament, *against* James's private counsellors, who 'may plainly see' the plots and practices of the devious Spanish and make steps to oppose them. Parliament fulfils the role which had been given to the counsellor in the reason of state tradition.

Another false text of the period, which was once again accounted by many as genuine, is *The Propositions for your Majesty's Service*, circulated in late 1629 and 1630.[93] Originally derived from a genuine missive by the disgraced illegitimate son of the Earl of Leicester, this text advises Charles that the best way to get around the issues with his parliament is force it into subjection, advice that purportedly came from the Privy Council. It uses Machiavellian language and emphasised its secrecy, to further incriminate its content, just as the *Secretissima* texts had done.[94] In other words, it fed precisely the fear of 'new counsels' generated in James's and Charles's parliaments, and fuelled the opposition between parliamentary and private counsel. The first part of the *Propositions*, which proclaimes to 'secure your state and bridle the impertinency of Parliaments', sets out proposals such as fortresses in chief towns about the realm and oaths to subjects.[95] Circulated towards the end of the 1629 Parliament, the last before the Personal Rule, and the subsequent breakdown of the English political system, the *Propositions* demonstrate the role that related ideas regarding reason of state and the fear of evil counsellors had in the politics of the time.[96] The king's desire to supress the counsel and consent of parliament was portrayed as stemming from evil private counsellors who surrounded him – a fear that was real enough to cause the downfall of more than one of them. As Noah Millstone has pointed out, the *Propositions* function as a piece of widening 'political awareness' while also calling for more public involvement in politics, by presenting a dystopic vision of tyrannical oppression of parliament.[97]

[92] Scott, *The Second Part of Vox Populi*, 59.

[93] All quotes from the *Propositions* as well as details of its circulation and reception from Noah Millstone, 'Evil Counsel: *The Propositions to Bridle the Impertinency of Parliament* and the Critique of Caroline Government in the Late 1620s', *Journal of British Studies* 50, no. 4 (2011): 813–39.

[94] Millstone, 'Evil Counsel', 817. [95] Millstone, 'Evil Counsel', 818.

[96] Millstone, 'Evil Counsel', 839.

[97] A similar approach is taken in the publication of the king's letters in *The King's Cabinet Opened* (London, 1645). The authors note in the opening address that it is 'a great sin against the mercies of God, to conceale those evidences of truth, which hee so graciously (and almost miraculously) by surprizall of these Papers, hath put into our hands'. The main criticism levelled in the pamphlet was that Charles had followed the advice not of his 'Great Councell' but of a much lesser source of

iii Civil War

In the early years of the Civil War, parliamentarians claimed to be protecting both king and country against evil counsellors who sought to rule the king and destroy the commonwealth.[98] For instance, *The Parliaments Kalendar of Black Saints*, published in two parts in 1644, lists counsellors who 'can subert Kingdomes, burne whole Townes, Steale, Ravish, Kill, and say *The King and Queene will have it so*'.[99] They in fact control the crown, for they can '*make his Majestie beleeve any thing, and scrue and wind themselves (as they do the Law) into his Majesties favour*' to the cost of England.[100] Those who oppose such vipers have the law of self-defence at their disposal to resist: 'The law allowes rather to kill, then be killed; *David* was not restrained to defend himself against *Saul*, much lesse against his Evill Counsellors.'[101] The author does not present himself as against the king, but rather in defence of him: 'to redeem his Majestie from Evill Counsellors, to preserve the true and pure Gospel, and to rescue our Lawes and Hereditary rights from the Violence of malignants, Delinquents, papists and others'.[102] It is parliament who has such a defensive role, as they are counsellors themselves, chosen by and trusted with the rights of the people, and acknowledged by the king to be 'his great Councell'.[103] This is the language used by the Parliament's *Declaration or Remonstrance* of 1642. Having 'withdrawn' himself from his proper counsel, the king is 'exposed to the wicked and unfaithfull councells as such as have made the wisdome, and justice of the Parliament dangerous to themselves'.[104] It is the 'duty of the Parliament, to preserve his Majesty, and to fix the guilt of all evill actions and councells'.[105]

Parliament's *Nineteen Propositions* are framed in similar language, and the content prioritises the issue of counsel.[106] The first three propositions

counsel: the queen; see William J. Bulman, 'The Practice of Politics: The English Civil War and the "Resolution" of Henrietta Maria and Charles I', *Past & Present* 206, no. 1 (1 February 2010): 43–79; Laura Lunger Knoppers, *Politicizing Domesticity from Henrietta Maria to Milton's Eve* (Cambridge: Cambridge University Press, 2011), 42–67. Although these texts are authentic – albeit heavily edited – other 'cabinet opened' texts are more difficult to verify, and likely contain fabrications.

98 Burgess, 'Impact on Political Thought', 68.

99 *The Parliaments Kalendar of Black Saints: Or a New Discovery of Plots & Treasons* (London, 1644), 7.

100 *A Nest of Persidious Vipers: Or the Second Part of the Parliaments Kalendar of Black Saints* (London, 1644), 8.

101 *Persidious Vipers*, 8. 102 *Persidious Vipers*, 8. 103 *Persidious Vipers*, 8.

104 *The Declaration or Remonstrance of the Lords and Commons in Parliament* (London, 1642), 2.

105 *Declaration*, 2.

106 Burgess, 'Impact on Political Thought', 68. As Colin Tyler, 'Drafting the Nineteen Propositions, January–July 1642', *Parliamentary History* 31, no. 3 (1 October 2012): 263–4 points out, there was

deal with the issue of counsel. The first seeks to remove all Privy Councillors except those approved by parliament, institute new councillors at the approval of parliament, and subject all to an oath devised by parliament.[107] The second reinforces the divide between public and private advice. Public matters ought not to be 'Concluded or Transacted by the Advice of private men, or by any unknown or unsworn Councellours', but by the king's 'great and supreme Councell': Parliament.[108] Those matters that parliament deems best to be decided by the Privy Council – a council made up of members it has approved of – are enacted only 'by the advice and consent of the major part of your Councell' and not by the 'Royal Authority' alone.[109] And finally, the third proposition states that the major offices of the realm, such as that of Lord High Steward, Lord Chancellor and Lord Keeper, are all to be approved by parliament. The model of politics generated by the first three of the *Nineteen Propositions* is not unlike that proposed by Thomas Starkey over a century before (see Chapter 2), with a king ruled over by a series of hierarchical councils, at the top of which is parliament, the greatest source of counsel.

The king reacted as one might expect; he vehemently reiterated the priority of command over counsel. The parliamentarians were themselves driven with 'private interest' and inspired by 'civil Counsels of ambitious turbulent Spirits'.[110] The propositions would force the king to 'abandon that power' by which he protects the country, and give it instead to others.[111] The demand that Privy Councillors be appointed by parliament is 'but one link of a great Chain . . . by which Our Just, Ancient, Regall Power is endeavoured to be fetched down to the ground'.[112] The same usurpation of authority, Charles goes on, is contained in the second demand, by which he would become but 'the Picture, but the signe of a King', the real power residing in parliament. Charles sensed that within this demand was contained the removal of the king's right to refuse whatever is recommended by parliament, and thus a demand to turn counsel into the right to command. Charles defends his ability of 'discours[ing] with whom We please, of what We please, and informing Our Understanding by debate with any Persons, who may be well able to Inform and Advise Us in some particular', even if

nothing expressly new contained in the *Propositions*, all the demands having been expressed before in parliamentary speeches or documents, but remains an important document because of its timing.

107 *Nineteen Propositions . . . With His Majesties Answer Thereunto* (Cambridge, 1642), 2; this issue of an oath recurs in proposition 11.

108 *Nineteen Propositions*, 2. 109 *Nineteen Propositions*, 2. 110 *His Majesties Answer*, 3.

111 *His Majesties Answer*, 4. 112 *His Majesties Answer*, 6.

they are not fit to be sworn councillors.[113] When Charles calls upon the 'Advices both of Our Great and Privie Councell' he shall 'look upon their Advices as Advices, not as Commands'.[114] His counsellors are not 'Tutours or Guardians' and he is not their 'Pupill, or Ward'.[115] The demands made by the first and second propositions generate 'new-fangled kind of Councellours' whose power is such that they become 'ioynt Patentees with Us in the Regality', and in fact the king relegated, in this partnership, almost no power at all.[116] England is a 'regulated monarchy' and a mixed constitution, but such demands would render it a 'Republick'.[117] Charles's response to the *Nineteen Propositions* contains a wholesale rejection of the humanist tradition of counsel as it had become used by parliamentarians to assert their authority by means of claims to counsel.

One of the most influential writers for the parliamentarian side using these conciliarist arguments was undoubtedly Henry Parker. He presented himself as a counsellor to the people,[118] as well as the 'Observator'; a word that had multiple meanings, including 'a person who observers a law, command principle'; 'a person who keeps watch after something', and also makes reference to the reason of state emphasis on observation.[119] As early as the first tract that can be plausibly attributed to him, the *Divine and Politike Observations* of 1638, Parker embraces the reason of state model of counsel as the transmitter of observation, in order to demonstrate its necessity in governing a prince.[120] Figuring himself as the 'translator' of the piece, Parker explains to the reader that 'great Princes can hardly see any thing, but in such shape as it is represented to them by such of their Courtiers or Councellors as they are pleased to trust', which is why he has 'adventured to translate in English the foresaid Observations'.[121] *Divine*

113 *His Majesties Answer*, 9. 114 *His Majesties Answer*, 9. 115 *His Majesties Answer*, 9.

116 *His Majesties Answer*, 9–10, 13. 117 *His Majesties Answer*, 11–12.

118 For Parker's role as a 'public privado' who 'fashioned his concept of parliament (or more generally, government) in his own image, the image of a counsellor' see Michael Mendle, *Henry Parker and the English Civil War: The Political Thought of the Public's 'Privado'* (Cambridge: Cambridge University Press, 2003).

119 Michael Mendle, 'Parker, Henry [Called the Observator] (1604–1652), Political Writer', Oxford Dictionary of National Biography, 2004, https://doi.org/10.1093/ref:odnb/21307. For Parker's commitment to the idea of 'observation' see Mendle, *Henry Parker*, 9–10, 34; for 'the Observator' see Mendle, *Henry Parker*, 2, 90.

120 Mendle, *Henry Parker*, 8–10. See also Henry Parker, *A Discourse Concerning Puritans* (London, 1641), 43: 'Temporall Counsellors . . . in State affairs' are 'good spectacalls'.

121 Henry Parker, *Divine and Politike Observations* (Amsterdam, 1638), n.p. The king's dependence on counsel is a theme that runs throughout his oeuvre, repeated in Henry Parker, *Jus Populi* (London, 1644), 9–10: 'the Major part of Kings are so farre from being the best Judges, the profoundest Statesmen, the most excellent soldiers, that when they so value themselves they prove commonly most wilfull, and fatall to themselves and others; and that they ever govern best, when they most

and Politike Observations also first establishes his important tri-partite definition of parliament; parliament is the 'honourable Court',[122] the 'representative body of the Kingdome'[123] as well as 'his Majesties most faithfull and least corruptible counsell'.[124]

Parker provides 'three things wherein parliaments excell all other Councells whatsoever' in *Divine and Politike Observations,* which he refines and repeats in his later texts of 1642 – *Some Few Observations* and *Observations upon Some of His Majesties Late Answers and Expresses.*[125] Both texts respond to the issues surrounding the Militia Ordinance of 1642 and the growing sense of 'emergency' in English political culture, and both use the superiority of parliament as an advisory body to argue that parliament should not only step into the 'conciliar breach' left by the growing ineffectiveness of the Privy Council, but also take control of the king's arbitrary sovereign power.[126] Parker's reasons for parliament's superior conciliar authority, in *Some Few Observations,* are: 'first . . . [that] they must in probabilitie be more knowing then any other privadoes; Secondly, in regard of their publike interest, they are more responsible then any other, and lesse to be complayned of in case of errour. Thirdly, they have no private interest to deprave them, nothing can square with the Common Councell but the common good'.[127] It is worth detailing the case Parker makes for each of these, as they bring together the argument from prudence, which had been running through the discourses of counsel for millennia, with the emerging seventeenth-century language of interest.

The first element Parker addresses in making his case is prudence, which as we have seen remained the quintessential virtue of the counsellor. For Parker, this prudential counsel, based in the ability to 'see', is best found in

relye upon the abilities of other good Counsellors and Ministers'. See also *The Declaration*, 15: 'The Wisdome of this State hath intrusted the Houses of Parliament with a power to supply what shall be wanting on the part of the Prince'.

122 For Parker's assertion that Parliament is the highest court in the realm, i.e. the highest arbiter, see Burgess, *Absolute Monarchy*, 177–81.

123 For Parker's view of representation see Quentin Skinner, 'Hobbes on Representation', *European Journal of Philosophy* 13, no. 2 (2005): 155–84.

124 Parker, *Divine and Politike Observations*, 13. See also Parker, *Discourse Concerning Puritans*, 52: 'Parliaments, which are the grand Courts and Counsells of Kingdomes'; Henry Parker, *The True Grounds of Ecclesiasticall Regiment* (London, 1641): 'the best, and highest of all Counsells, *viz.* Parliaments'; Henry Parker, *The Oath of Pacification* (London, 1643), 17: parliament is 'the Common Counsell of all the Land'. See Mendle, *Henry Parker*, 9, 76.

125 Henry Parker, *The Case of Shipmony Briefly Discoursed* (London, 1640), 35. Note once again the use of 'observation' in the titles of these texts.

126 Mendle, *Henry Parker*, 75–85.

127 Henry Parker, *Some Few Observations upon His Majesties Late Answer to the Declaration or Remonstrance* (London, 1642), 5.

parliament. As he writes in *The Case of Shipmony*, 'For wisedome, no advice can bee given so prudent, so profound, so universally comprehending, from any other author' than parliament.[128] The prudence of parliament is so deep, he establishes in his *Discourse Concerning Puritans* a year later, that it issues 'infallible avisoes' which 'are now in all well-governed Countries, the very Oracles of all Policy, and Law', and thus a prince cannot be deceived that is ruled by them.[129]

Parliament's role as representative of the kingdom and the people lies at the foundation of its prudential abilities. It is 'incredible' he writes in *The Case of Shipmony*, that 'an inconsiderable number of Privadoes should see or knowe more then whole Kingdomes'.[130] Parliament is able to bring together the collective prudence of the kingdom as a whole, as he suggests in *Some Few Observations*: '[T]hat which is the judgement of the major part in Parliament is the judgement of the whole Kingdome' and thus it 'is more vigorous, and sacred, and unquestionable, and further beyond all appeal, then that which is the judgement of the King alone, without all Councell' or even 'of the King, with any other inferiour Clandestine Councell'.[131] He supports this view in *Observations* with reference to a popular classical (and, specifically, Aristotelian) metaphor: 'I think every mans heart tels him, that in all publique Consultations, the many eyes of so many choyce Gentlemen out of all parts, see more then fewer'.[132]

Parker's second reason for the superior counsel of parliament is its consistency with the interest of state: 'in regard of their publike interest,

[128] Parker, *The Case of Shipmony*, 35.

[129] Parker, *Discourse Concerning Puritans*, 52; see Mendle, *Henry Parker*, 53–61. Parker's opponents disagreed. The *Answer* to Parker's *Observations* asserted that even if the king's counsellors have 'the absolute faculty', yet nevertheless they ought not to have 'absolute Power to determine' and must 'prostrate the gravity of their wisedome to their Sovereign'; Richard Burney, *An Answer, or Necessary Animadversions, upon Some Late Impostumate Observations Invective against His Sacred Maiesty* (London, 1642), 21.

[130] Parker, *The Case of Shipmony*, 35. See also Parliament, *The declaration*, 22: 'we still desire and hope that his Majesty will not be guided by his own understanding . . . to which he shall be advised by the Wisdome of both Houses of Parliament; which are the Eyes in this Politique Body'. For 'privado' see Mendle, *Henry Parker*, 11–13.

[131] Parker, *Some Few Observations*, 9. This is not just the collective judgment of those sitting in parliament at any given time, however, but a collective memory and prudence, as Parker alludes to in writing against the Leveller John Lilburne. Lilburne's 'exceeding defective, and insufficient' knowledge and judgement ought to bow to the 'Authority of so many Parliaments' and 'the prudence of so many ages', as should all royalists, Henry Parker, *A Letter of Due Censure* (London, 1650), 10.

[132] Parker, *Some Few Observations*, 9.

they are more responsible then any other', which must be considered in conjunction with Parker's third factor, the avoidance of the taint of private interest: 'thirdly, they have no private interest to deprave them, nothing can square with the common Councell but the common good'.[133] Drawing on the writings that we examined in Chapter 6, Parker makes clear that it is only parliament that will be able to assess and represent the public interest successfully in the political arena. As he writes in *The Case of Shipmony*: 'the common body can effect nothing but the common good, because nothing else can bee commodious for them'.[134] By 1642, he had integrated the language of 'interest' to this appraisal, as he does in *Some Few Observations* and *Observations*: the counsel of parliament is superior because of 'the great interest the Parliament has in common justice and tranquillity'.[135] Although the king too may have such an interest, Parker makes clear that he 'is not so much interessed in it as themselves'.[136] Parliament, he writes, 'does not deny the King a true-reall Interest' but affirms that 'the State hath an Interest Paramount' above it, which is represented in the parliament.[137] He that 'confesses, That the King hath a true and perfect interest in the Kingdom' must also accept 'That the Kingdom hath a more worthy and transcendent interest in it self'.[138] In fact, it is one of the two primary functions of parliaments 'not to be attained to by other meanes' that 'the interest of the people might be satisfied', the second being that 'Kings might the better be counsailed'.[139]

Finally, parliament accurately understands and follows the public interest because they, in contrast with the counsellors who surround the king, have no private interests to distract them from it.[140] Already in *Divine and Politike Observations* of 1638, Parker writes that 'Courtiers or Councellors' of princes 'often have private ends or interest for disguysing truths unto them' and he repeats the theme in his *Discourse* three years later:

[133] Parker, *Some Few Observations* 5. See Viroli, *Philosophy and Government*, 228–30 for Parker's need to explain why Parliament rather than the king would be seen as the defender of the 'public interest'.

[134] Parker, *The Case of Shipmony*, 36; see also Parker, *Discourse Concerning Puritans*, 53.

[135] Henry Parker, *Observations upon Some of His Majesties Late Answers and Expresses* (London, 1642), 11.

[136] Parker, *Observations*, 13.

[137] Parker, *Observations*, 33. This is because, for Parker, parliament virtually (in the sense of being a portrait or a picture) represents the state, even *is* the state. This is opposed to Hobbes, who sees the sovereign as the representative of the state (not requiring the sense of virtual representation, but rather authorship); see Skinner, 'Hobbes on Representation', 155–84.

[138] Parker, *Some Few Observations*, 9.

[139] Parker, *Observations*, 5.

[140] In *The Case of Shipmony*, 38 Parker's third reason for the superiority of parliament's counsel is not the element of private interest, but rather its effectiveness: 'because the hearts of the people doe not goe along with any other, as with that', a factor which he compounds in the 1642 *Some Few Observations* with his second point concerning public interest.

'Individualls may have many particular ends, severed from the Princes or the States . . . and have judgement beside apt to be darkened by their owne severall interests and passions'.[141] By his *Observations* in 1642, he can declare it 'a maxime . . . grounded in Nature, and never till this Parliament withstood' that 'a community can have no private ends to mislead it'.[142] The very 'composition of Parliaments . . . takes away all jealousies' so that there is no vying for position or fuelling of ambition.[143] The issue here is, once again and now much more strongly stated, that of private versus public sources of advice. The former is condemned; it includes both the king's 'own private advise' – i.e. internal counsel – and the advice of his private counsellors.[144] Public advice comes from parliament. As Parker writes in *The Danger to England Observed*, 'as we see none but good fruits in this publike Councell, so we see none but bad in its private opposite'.[145] The 'private Councell by which his Majesty is incensed against his generall Councell, obscures itself from the world', as such, one must assume they have something to hide.[146] 'Court-flatters and time-serving Projectors' would like nothing more than to do away with the counsel of parliament altogether.[147] This is a natural antagonism, Parker suggests in *Some Few Observations*; parliament is 'odious to Court parasites' and their machinations, and so it is 'no wonder that the Kings *Favorites* and *Followers* hate Parliaments'.[148] These figures work against parliament, and thereby against the true interests of the state, by 'perswading [the king] first to withdraw himself from his parliament, and then to call away the Members of both Houses'.[149]

For Parker, this indicates a greater emergency than any the king can cite in justification of increased taxes, for instance, in the debate over shipmoney in the late 1630s. Citing the 'emergency' of the Thirty Years War, the king levied taxes – without calling parliament – in order to fund the navy fleet.[150] The opposition to this levy did not deny that the king had such a prerogative, but that it did not apply in this case, 'no emergency required the levy year after year', and that it still required the consent of parliament.[151] The final

[141] Parker, *Divine and Politike Observations*, n.p.; Parker, *Discourse Concerning Puritans*, 53.
[142] Parker, *Observations*, 22. [143] Parker, *Observations*, 23.
[144] Burgess, 'Impact on Political Thought', 71.
[145] Henry Parker, *The Danger to England Observed* (London, 1642), 3. [146] Parker, *The Danger*, 1.
[147] Parker, *Discourse Concerning Puritans*, 58–9.
[148] Parker, *Some Few Observations*, 10, 14. We can see here Parker's debt to Thomas Scott.
[149] Henry Parker, *A Political Catechism* (London, 1643), 5.
[150] Levy Peck, 'Kingship, Counsel and Law', 110–11; documents printed in Kenyon, ed., *The Stuart Constitution*, 98–104.
[151] Levy Peck, 'Kingship, Counsel and Law', 110–11.

decision by the court, supporting the king, did acknowledge that subjects have a 'peculiar interest' in the land, but that the king had the right to judge what constituted an emergency and could levy a tax accordingly without parliament's consent.[152] Parliament was presented as a *concilium* at the king's command to call and dissolve, and whereas the king cannot err, parliament can and does.[153]

Henry Parker deals with this issue in *The Case of Shipmony briefly Discoursed*, published two years after the event. Unlike other writers on the topic, Parker does not oppose the invocation of necessity and reason of state to justify the tax, but rather the *king's* invocation of it.[154] The reason is counsel. Parker writes that one must accept that 'Kings may be bad', and it is in fact 'more probable and naturall, that evill may be expected from good Princes, than good from bad', and so it is that they must receive the best possible counsel.[155]

Evil counsellors use and abuse the logic of reason of state and necessity.[156] Parker accepts 'That the King ought to have aid of his subjects in time of danger, and common aid in case of common danger' as being 'laid down for a ground, and agreed upon by all sides'.[157] Such emergency powers are not limited by the ordinary concerns of either *utile* or *honestum*; they are given 'out of necessity, not honour or benefit' and are essential to the proper functioning and survival of the commonwealth.[158] The issue for Parker is the ability to recognise and declare such crises, for kings, due to 'ill counsell', may 'pretend danger causlesly' in order to do away with the legal constraints on their power, constraints in place to protect the people from the 'jealousies' of precisely these 'flatterers' about the king.[159] Parker suggests that this is the case with regard to ship-money and demands that, in addition to the reversal of the judgement, 'some dishonourable penalty may bee imposed upon those Iudges which ill advised the King herein'.[160] Such crimes against the state cannot go unpunished.

152 Levy Peck, 'Kingship, Counsel and Law', 111; Kenyon, ed., *The Stuart Constitution*, 100.

153 Kenyon, ed., *The Stuart Constitution*, 102.

154 See Mendle, *Henry Parker*, 37–8, 43–8. As Viroli, *Philosophy and Government*, 227 points out, Parker also didn't see that *salus populi* was threatened in this case, but the stronger and more radical argument, I maintain, is that the king does not have the power to judge this question.

155 Parker, *The Case of Shipmony*, 22; see Mendle, *Henry Parker*, 47.

156 For the language of reason of state in these debates see Tuck, *Philosophy and Government 1572–1651*, 222–3.

157 Parker, *The Case of Shipmony*, 2. For the connection between the ship-money debates and the languages of necessity and reason of state see Mendle, *Henry Parker*, 43; Baldwin, 'Reason of State and English Parliaments', 638.

158 Parker, *The Case of Shipmony*, 12.

159 Parker, *The Case of Shipmony*, 23, 25.

160 Parker, *The Case of Shipmony*, 47.

Parker had alluded to this removal of ill counsel in the epigraph of *Divine and Politike Observations*: '*Take away the wicked from before the King, and his Throne shall be established in Righteousnesse*', and it formed one of the fundamental demands of the parliamentarians in the early 1640s, as well as underlying the justification of the Militia Ordinance in 1642.[161] The argument that parliament ought to take up arms to remove the king's counsellors, however, obviously broke through the fundamental barrier between counsel and command, and many recognised it. As Parker records in *Observations* in 1642, the king's response to parliament was to reiterate this fundamental distinction: '*the Lords and Commons . . . Commission and trust . . . is to be Counsellors, not commanders*'.[162]

Parker agrees that the maintenance of the boundary between sovereignty and counsel is indeed the 'ordinary course' in English politics, and he reinforces this traditional distinction in reference to spiritual counsel in his 1641 *True Grounds of Ecclesiasticall Regiment*. Using the example of Peter and Nero, Parker writes that 'If *Nero* forbid *Peter* to preach, contradicting God herein, whose power is still transcendent, this prohibition binds not *Peter*, but if *Nero* use the Sword hereupon against *Peter*, this sword is irresistible'.[163] This is because the sword – command – must always come above persuasion and counsel: 'The use of power is not to intreat, or perswade only, for these may be done without power, but to command, and commands are vaine without compulsion, and they which may not compell, may not command, and they which cannot command, may not meddle at all except to intreat or perswade'.[164] Whomsoever uses compulsion to enforce their words has gone beyond counsel into the realm of command, for 'if *Peter* may doe more then perswade *Nero*, the Scepter is *Peters* not *Neroes*'.[165] Parker writes that 'whethersoever the power of commanding rests, it cannot rest in both, the Scepter cannot be shared, independence cannot be divided'.[166] Parker makes clear that 'that power which is proper, must include not only a right of commanding, but also an effectuall vertue of forcing obedience to its commands, and of subjecting and reducing such, as shall not render themselves obedient'.[167]

Doing away with this 'ordinary course' of politics can be justified, however, according to the language of necessity and emergency. As he writes in *Observations*, there is a 'Crisis of seducement' in the king's

[161] Parker, *Divine and Politike Observations*, 62; Parker, *Observations*, 30.
[162] Parker, *Observations*, 6. [163] Parker, *True Grounds*, 23. [164] Parker, *True Grounds*, 23–4.
[165] Parker, *True Grounds*, 25. [166] Parker, *True Grounds*, 24. [167] Parker, *True Grounds*, 24.

'preferring private advise before publike'.[168] In such an instance, the 'ordinary course cannot be taken for the preventing of publike mischiefes' and so 'any extraordinary course that is for that purpose the most effectuall, may justly be taken'.[169] In other words, 'if the King will not joyne with the people, the people may without disloyalty save themselves'.[170] This involves, first and foremost, as in *The Case of Shipmony*, moving against the pernicious counsellors of the king: 'if Kings be so inclineable to follow private advise rather then publique ... then they may destroy their best subjects at pleasure, and all Charters and Lawes of publike safetie and freedome are voyd' and so 'there must be some Court to judge of that seducement, and some authoritie to inforce that iudgement, and that Court and Authoritie must bee the Parliament'.[171] One may detect a weakness in the argument here – if there is a crisis of counsel, parliament should be given the authority to determine if there is a crisis of counsel – but it does the work that Parker needs it to, supporting the claim that parliament's 'Councell [is] of honour and power about all other, and when it is unjustly rejected, by a King seduced, and abused by private flatterers, to the danger of the Commonwealth, it assumes a right to judge of that danger, and to prevent it'.[172]

It also involves control of the militia, as Parker makes clear in his *Political Catechism* of 1643, a response to the king's retaliation against the *Nineteen Propositions*. Here he reiterates the dangers of self-interested counsellors – the 'most Pernicious Instruments ... of *Faction* and *Division*' – against the interests of state and the superiority of parliament – the 'Great Councel of State'.[173] These counsellors have, as forewarned in *The Case of Shipmony*, used 'the Name of *publick necessity*' to move against their 'Enemies' in parliament and, Parker insists, it is parliament which ought 'to be *Trusted*' in such cases to declare such trickery.[174] The step Parker takes in *Political Catechism* is to note that such theoretical juridical power also translates into concrete military power: 'The Power of both Houses is by Law to raise Arms if need be, for the apprehending of Delinquents'.[175] In such a case, 'the two Houses have Power by the Law to raise not only the *Posse Comitatus* of those Counties where such

[168] Parker, *Observations*, 30. The 1641 *Answer to the Lord Digbies Speech in the House of Commons*, most likely written by Parker (see Mendle, *Henry Parker*, 73–4) had already established that counsel, even when not executed, could constitute treason. See McLaren, 'Elizabethan Body Politic', 244 for the source of the language of 'seduction' in Marian and Elizabethan discourse.

[169] Parker, *Observations*, 16. [170] Parker, *Observations*, 16. [171] Parker, *Observations*, 30.

[172] Parker, *Observations*, 29. [173] Parker, *Political Catechism*, 5.

[174] Parker, *Political Catechism*, 8. [175] Parker, *Political Catechism*, 10.

Delinquents are, to apprehend them, but also the *Posse Regni*, the Power of the whole Kingdom if need be'.[176] In the name of 'their own and the Kingdoms safety' the two houses of parliament 'have Legal Power to *command* the People to this purpose' which is the 'Punishment of *Delinquents*, and for the *Prevention* and *Restraint* of the power of Tyranny'.[177] As had the humanist writers of the early sixteenth century, Parker maintains that counsel has the power to mitigate tyranny, though he gives it much more power than they had.

In *The Contra-Replicant*, also written in 1643, Parker articulates these arguments for parliament's extra-legal action in the language of reason of state and counsel. He reiterates that 'Lawes ayme at *Iustice*, [and] Reason of state aimes at *safety*' and thus the latter 'goes beyond all particular formes and pacts, and looks rather to the being, then well-being of a State . . . by emergent Counsels, and unwritten resolutions'.[178] As 'The Parliament is . . . better regulated and qualified for consultation' than any other body, it is also better able to take the necessary powers dictated by reason of state and to be given 'a kind of a dictatorian power'.[179] Therefore, '*To deny the Parliaments recourse to reason of State in these miserable times of warre and danger* [*is*] *to deny them self-defence*'.[180] Parliament must 'make use of an arbitrary power according to reason of state' rather than 'confin-[ing] themselves to meere expedients of Law'.[181] Such arbitrary power is 'only dangerous in one men or in a few men' but not in parliament, and so 'To have then an arbitrary power placed in the Peers and Comm[ons] is naturall and expedient at all times, but the very use of this arbitrary power, according to reason of state, and warlick [sic] policy in times of generall distresse is absolutely necessary and inevitable'.[182] Parliament, as they

176 Parker, *Political Catechism*, 10.

177 Parker, *Political Catechism*, 11–12; emphasis added to 'command', other emphasis original. Parker had laid the foundations for such an argument in *Some few observations*, 13: because the king 'is now seduced by wicked Councell, and therefore rejects [parliament's] requests, to the danger of the State', the members of parliament 'conceive there is a power in them to secure the State without [the king's] concurrence . . . At other times, when the Kings are not seduced, [parliament] ought to do nothing without [kings'] consent'.

178 Henry Parker, *The Contra-Replicant, His Complaint to His Maiestie* (London, 1643), 18–19.

179 Parker, *The Contra-Replicant*, 19.

180 Parker, *The Contra-Replicant*, 19.

181 Parker, *The Contra-Replicant*, 29. This echoes the Parliament's 1642 *Declaration and Remonstrance*, in which they had stated that: 'in regard of the imminent danger of the Kingdome, the Militia, for the security of his Majesty, and his people, might be put under the command of such noble and faithfull persons, as they had all cause to confide in, and such was the necessity of this preservation, that we declared, that if his Majesty should refuse to joyne with us therein, the two Houses of Parliament being the supreame Court and highest councell of the Kingdome, were enabled by their owne authority to provide for the repulsing of such imminent, and evident danger', *Declaration*, 3.

182 Parker, *The Contra-Replicant*, 29.

proper source of counsel, is also the protector of reason of state and the holder of the powers it justifies.

Parker was not alone in this. The 1642 Parliamentarian pamphlet, *The Aphorismes of the Kingdome*, written by William Prynne but published anonymously, rejects the king's assertion that 'The *Parliament* is merely admitted to counsell the King . . . because they may not command, as if there were nothing in the power of the *Parliament* but either counsell or command.'[183] Prynne goes on to note that counsel and command must go together, tied together by consent: 'The whole Essense lies in the consent of the will, which comes between counsell, and power to command.'[184] Command without counsel is just foolishness, or worse, not command at all, because one cannot will for the thing that one does not understand. The combination of counsel and consent in the parliament, for Prynne, is precisely what makes Law, or 'that the King calls Command'.[185]

The parliament is not just any source of counsel, however, but the ultimate source, which is why it also holds the power to command. Just as, Prynne writes, they have 'no supreme King but one' likewise there is only one 'supreme Councell' and thus just as they refuse to acknowledge any king above their own, he ought not to take counsel from any source but the parliament.[186] And just as the 'King is major singulis, minor universis', so he ought to 'think himself to be lesse than his whole Councell' and his 'subjection' to it not rendering him a 'subject', but a 'servant' to the common good.[187] For Prynne, the king needs to submit to counsels, ratified with the consent of parliament, to avoid breaking the law himself and becoming a tyrant. Consent rests on – or at least alongside – parliament's right to give counsel.[188] Taken in combination, they ground parliament's right to command the king.

Royalist opponents took note of Parker and Prynne's conflation of counsel and command. John Spelman in his *View of the Observations* of 1642 suggests that Parker transgresses the line between counsel and command by supporting the parliament's right to enforce their advice. He has no qualm with Parker's argument that parliament is an important source of

183 William Prynne, *The Aphorismes of the Kingdome* (London, 1642), 3–4.

184 Prynne, *Aphorismes*, 4. Prynne repeats this in the accompanying text, *The Commission of Array*, 49: 'We know in all Councells, sacred and secular, that two things concurre to the essence of a Law, *counsell* and *consent*, and that command follows in the royall authority by way of confirmation and corroboration, which are accidental to the Law, and that in the making of a Law by free votes, there can be no coactive power.' The king's power is 'duly to confirme and corroborate whatsoever in a lawfull Councell is consented unto by the most'.

185 Prynne, *Aphorismes*, 4. 186 Prynne, *Aphorismes*, 8. 187 Prynne, *Aphorismes*, 8.

188 Kenyon, ed., *The Stuart Constitution*, 60–2.

counsel, he 'grant[s] it behoovefull for the King to hearken to His Parliament'; however, he makes it clear that 'we must not understand it so behoovefull, that there should be inevitable necessity laid upon Him that He should follow whatsoever they advise', for to do so would be to 'overthrow the fundamentall Law & frame of Parliaments'.[189] It would suggest that 'The Soveraignty (against all our Oathes and expressions to the contrary) is not in the King but in the people' and 'His will, his understanding, and his power ... is all subjected to the body of the very Subject'.[190] In other words, and echoing Charles I, if counsel becomes command, 'there is really nothing but a meer popular assembly, not of Subjects but Soveraignes ... we are but a Republic'.[191]

Towards the end of the war, in February 1648 (though written as early as 1644), the Royalist propaganda printer Richard Royston published *The Free-Holders Grand Inquest*, 'an outspokenly royalist survey of English constitutional history', which responded directly to Prynne. There is debate as to the author of this anonymous work, though most have attributed it to Robert Filmer.[192] Filmer's best-known work is *Patriarcha*, written in the 1620s but not published until 1680, in which he writes that General Assemblies are 'for Consultation' and 'such Meetings do not Share or divide the Soveraignty with the Prince: but do only deliberate and advise their Supreme Head, who still reserves the Absolute power in himself'.[193] These ideas are even clearer in *Free-Holders*. There he makes his second central argument, written largely against Prynne, 'That the Lords or common council by their rite are only to treat and give counsel in parliament' and have no share in the 'legislative power'.[194] This is because counsel cannot command the king. The problem can be 'easily reconciled' if one appeals to the 'distinction of the schoolmen' that 'the king is free from the coactive power of laws or counsellors, but may be subject to their directive power'.[195] In other words, 'God can only compel' the king, 'but the law and his courts may advise him'.[196] His immediate source is *The*

[189] John Spelman, *A View of a Printed Book Intituled Observations upon His Majesties Late Answers and Expresses* (London, 1642), 16.

[190] Spelman, *View of a Printed Book*, 17. [191] Spelman, *View of a Printed Book*, 17.

[192] There has been debate as to the authorship of this tract. It was published in 1679 alongside a collection of works that were certainly authored by Filmer, and there was no challenge made to this attribution. Johann Sommerville has outlined the argument for the attribution to Filmer on the grounds of consistency and common sources with his other works, and so we will proceed with this attribution. See Sommerville, 'Authorship and Dating', xxxiv–xxxvii for this discussion.

[193] Robert Filmer, *Patriarcha, or the Natural Power of Kings* (London, 1680), 91.

[194] Robert Filmer, 'The Free-Holders Grand Inquest', in *Filmer: 'Patriarcha' and Other Writings*, ed. Johann P. Sommerville (Cambridge: Cambridge University Press, 1991), 72, 74.

[195] Filmer, 'Free-Holders Grand Inquest', 80. [196] Filmer, 'Free-Holders Grand Inquest', 80.

Speech of the Lord Chancellor of England by Thomas Egerton,[197] but Egerton's source is Thomas Aquinas' *Summa Theologica*, where he suggests that the king is exempt from the coercive power of the law.[198] Neither Aquinas nor Egerton's use of him, however, give Filmer the additional 'or counsellors', which makes his point explicit in regards to parliament, though he goes on to say that it is historically only the barons who make up the king's counsellors anyway, even if the king does occasionally ask for the Commons' advice.[199]

Parliament can be divided along these lines: 'the Lords are to treat and to give counsel; the Commons are to perform and consent to what is ordained'.[200] Because the Lords also have a 'judicial power', Filmer, like Bodin before him, has to distinguish between the powers conflated by Aristotle. A judge's office is – unsurprisingly – 'to give judgement' and can also 'command in the place of the king'.[201] He can act as a representative of the king, commanding with a limited power. A counsellor has no such authority, instead his duty is simply to 'advise the king what he himself shall do, or cause to be done'.[202] If they did command, and here Filmer is directly drawing on Bodin, 'that were to take away the sovereignty from their prince, who by his wisdom is to weigh the advice of his council, and at liberty to resolve according to the judgement of the wiser part of his council, and not always the greater'.[203] As it is the prince's wisdom which rules his council (the Machiavellian model), and his sovereignty must be undiminished (Bodin), Filmer reiterates the divide between counsel and command, noting, as Bodin had, that the king does not

197 Thomas Egerton, *The Speech of the Lord Chancellor of England, in the Exchequer Chamber, Touching the Post-Nati* (Societie of stationers, 1609), 106: '*Rex solutus a Legibus quoad vim coactiuam, subditus est legibus quoad vim directiuam propria voluntate.*'

198 See N. P. Swartz, 'Thomas Aquinas: On Law, Tyranny and Resistance', *Acta Theologica* 30, no. 1 (June 2010): 145–57. Filmer was drawing on the long tradition, from Aquinas, and more importantly Marsilius of Padua, that insisted on the advisory power of the Church as apart from the coercive authority of temporal powers. See Richard Crakanthorpe, *The Defence of Constantine* (London, 1621), 42: Christ 'neither gaue; nor left, or committed to Peter, or any of Peters Successours, any *temporall Kingdome*, or *coactive power*, but gaue vnto them onely a *power of direction*, whereby they might guide others to *faith* and *sanctitie* in this life, and to euerlasting *glorie* in the life to come.' The same author repeats the distinction in a work a decade later: Richard Crakanthorpe, *Vigilius Dormitans* (London, 1631), 285.

199 Filmer, 'Free-Holders Grand Inquest', 80–3.

200 Filmer, 'Free-Holders Grand Inquest', 94.

201 Filmer, 'Free-Holders Grand Inquest', 94.

202 Filmer, 'Free-Holders Grand Inquest', 94. Filmer does go on to say that in some circumstances, as decreed by the king, these two roles can be interchangeable, and counsellors can hold the power to command as judges, but it is only when the king so decrees (94–5).

203 Filmer, 'Free-Holders Grand Inquest', 94.

have to resolve according to the advice of his counsel at all, and certainly is under no greater constraints to follow the advice of the majority.

Filmer then applies this distinction to the House of Lords, who are called to be counsellors.[204] It is a 'thing most absurd' he says, 'to make the king assent to the judgements in parliament and make him no part of the consultation'. To do so would be to 'make the king a subject'.[205] In short, 'Counsel loseth the name of counsel, and becomes a command, if it put a necessity upon the king to follow it. Such imperious counsels make those that are but counsellors in name to be kings in fact, and kings themselves to be but subjects'.[206] Filmer articulates the problem of counsel and command, and the need for a distinction between them, clearly and decisively.

This distinction is also repeated as the Civil War came to an end, remaining a foundational tenet of the Royalist camp. It appears in the anonymous *Eikon Basilike*, purported to have been written by the king, though now generally thought to have been compiled by John Gauden, later Bishop of Exeter, from the king's papers.[207] Reinforcing the Bodinian line that the king had put forward while he was alive, the text asserts: 'Sure it ceases to be Councell; when not Reason is used, as to men to perswade; but force and terrour as beasts, to drive and compell men . . . He deserves to be a slave without pitty, or redemption, that is content to have the rationall soveraignty of his Soul, and liberty of his will, and words so captivated'.[208] The author tackles the Aristotelian metaphor referenced by Bodin, calling a democracy a 'many-headed Hydra of Government' for although it is true that the people 'have more eyes to foresee; so they will find it hath more mouthes too, which must be satisfied'.[209] The monarch must have the ability to reject counsel, or else it is an imposition on sovereignty. John Milton takes these arguments head on in his response, *Eikonoklastes*, noting that the no king is 'wiser then all his councel' and that 'Parlament is his Superior' and so he ought to take their advice.[210] To 'reject all their counsels' is to 'dishonour them' so that they become 'frustrated, disappointed, denied and repulsed by the single whiff of a negative, from the mouth of one wilful man', a situation which can only be described as tyranny.[211]

[204] Filmer, 'Free-Holders Grand Inquest', 95. [205] Filmer, 'Free-Holders Grand Inquest', 95.
[206] Filmer, 'Free-Holders Grand Inquest', 95.
[207] Liam Sims, 'Charles I and the Eikon Basilike – Cambridge University Library Special Collections', accessed 31 August 2017, https://specialcollections.blog.lib.cam.ac.uk/?p=6793.
[208] *Eikon Basilike* (London, 1649), 45, see also 19, 23. [209] *Eikon Basilike*, 71.
[210] John Milton, *Eikonoklastes* (London, 1650), 102, 103. [211] Milton, *Eikonoklastes*, 538.

iv Hobbes and the End of Counsel

Whatever else may be said about the work of Thomas Hobbes, it is incontrovertible that his political system sought to avoid the causes of political discord Milton describes. This required, for him, the firm articulation of a distinction between counsel and command.[212] In so doing, he both robs the parliamentarians of their argument for sovereignty from counsel, as well as puts an end to any argument for an influential role for the political counsellor, rejecting the centuries-long tradition we have been exploring.[213]

Hobbes's attack on the use of the discourse of counsel to support the parliamentary position demolishes two of the key pillars upon which that discourse had rested for a least a century, if not several millennia: *kairos* and *phronesis*.[214] Rather than seeking to redefine these concepts, as we've seen others do, Hobbes rejects their political relevance and utility entirely. Hobbes does not make a single reference to *kairos* in his political thought, a silence that, given the centrality of the concept to his predecessors, is both deafening and telling. There can be no question that Hobbes was aware of the term and its history, given his familiarity with a wide variety of sources which deal with it explicitly. One of these is Thucydides, whose *History of the Peloponnesian War* Hobbes translated in the 1620s, and which makes several references to *kairos*. Hobbes provides the usual early modern translations for the term: 'in season', 'the occasion', 'when time served', 'out of season', 'opportunity' and 'unseasonably'.[215] The relevance of *kairos*, as we've seen, relates to a world of variable passions and the whims of fortune, and knowledge of it is drawn from a study of the past in the hope of recognising it in the future. Hobbes rejects all of these

212 Along with, of course, a redefinition of representation, but this has been treated at length elsewhere. See Tuck, *Philosophy and Government*, 328; Skinner, *Visions of Politics: Volume III*, 181–208; Noel Malcolm, ed., *Thomas Hobbes: Leviathan: Editorial Introduction* (Oxford: Oxford University Press, 2012), 15–16.

213 For *Leviathan* as an example of political counsel see Malcolm, *Thomas Hobbes*, 55, 58. For counsel and command in Hobbes see A. P. Martinich, *The Two Gods of* Leviathan: *Thomas Hobbes on Religion and Politics* (Cambridge: Cambridge University Press, 1992), 111–32, 296–7; A. P. Martinich, *A Hobbes Dictionary* (Cambridge: Blackwell, 1995), 70–3; Joanne Paul, 'Counsel, Command and Crisis', *Hobbes Studies* 28, no. 2 (2015): 103–131. For counsellors and corruption see Adrian Blau, 'Hobbes on Corruption', *History of Political Thought* 30, no. 4 (2009): 596–616. Blau has also written on counsel as an analogue for reason, Adrian Blau, A. P. Martinich and Kinch Hoekstra, 'Reason, Deliberation and the Passions', in *The Oxford Handbook of Hobbes* (Oxford: Oxford University Press, 2013), online. See also Gabriella Slomp, 'The Inconvenience of the Legislator's Two Persons and the Role of Good Counsellors', *Hobbes Studies* 19, no. 1 (2016): 68.

214 Skinner, *Reason and Rhetoric*, 259–62.

215 Thucydides, *Eight Bookes of the Peloponnesian Warre*, trans. Thomas Hobbes (London, 1629), 24, 60, 135, 151, 281.

elements as essential parts of his new political philosophy. Hobbes's view of time is, as Skinner has put it, 'duration', which underpins his view that the state must have 'an Artificiall Eternity of life'.[216] This requires 'blocking off' other views of time, including *kairos*, which might subject the state to variation or decay. Even if the future is a fiction, like the person of the state, it is an essential one, when conceived of as durable and peaceful (in contrast to the continual anxiety of the State of Nature).[217] *Kairos* has little place in such a vision of enduring stability.[218]

When Hobbes does use language associated with *kairos*, it is usually marking threats to the stability of the state, for instance in Chapter XVIII, where he notes the importance of the sovereign's ability to draw on citizens 'on any emergent occasion, or sudden need, to resist, or take advantage on their Enemies'.[219] The 'emergent occasion' does need to be taken advantage of, but has come as part of an external disruption. Likewise, in Chapter XXIX Hobbes speaks of the 'great numbers of men' who 'rebel' 'when occasion is presented [*data occasione*]', brought on by the sovereign's refusal to exercise all of the power available to them.[220] The seizing of occasions is not just taken up by internal enemies of the state, but external ones as well, who will see the denial of necessary power on the part of the sovereign as an opportunity to move against them: 'forraign Common-wealths; who in order to the good of their own Subjects let slip few occasions [*opportunitas*] to *weaken* the estate of their Neighbours', and he gives the examples of

[216] Quentin Skinner, 'Why States Need Time' (10 May 2018); Thomas Hobbes, *Thomas Hobbes: Leviathan: The English and Latin Texts*, ed. Noel Malcolm (Oxford: Oxford University Press, 2012), 298; '*Artificialis vita*' in the Latin, 299. See also Katherine Bootle Attie, 'Re-Membering the Body Politic: Hobbes and the Construction of Civic Immortality', *ELH* 75, no. 3 (30 August 2008): 497–530; Christopher Scott McClure, *Hobbes and the Artifice of Eternity* (New York: Cambridge University Press, 2016).

[217] See Loralea Michaelis, 'Hobbes's Modern Prometheus: A Political Philosophy for an Uncertain Future', *Canadian Journal of Political Science/Revue Canadienne de Science Politique* 40, no. 1 (2007): 101–27; Giovanni Fiaschi, 'Hobbes on Time and Politics', *Hobbes Studies* 18, no. 1 (2005): 3–26; Jose Brunner, 'Modern Times: Law, Temporality and Happiness in Hobbes, Locke and Bentham Critical Modernities: Politics and Law beyond the Liberal Imagination', *Theoretical Inquiries in Law* 8 (2007): 277–310; J. G. A. Pocock, *Politics, Language, and Time: Essays on Political Thought and History* (Chicago: University of Chicago Press, 1989), 155–7.

[218] Hobbes does note that 'Irresolution' which results in loss of 'the occasions, and fittest opportunities of action' is a 'manner' to be rejected in the commonwealth, therefore one might assume that resolution to seize opportunity might be a beneficial element of civil life, but this is no part of *political* life or action; Hobbes, *Leviathan*, 156. Notably, the Latin uses only '*tempus*' here; Hobbes, *Leviathan*, 157. 'Occasion' appears more often in the text than 'opportunity', but generally Hobbes uses it in a loose sense, related to causes, with little connection to the vocabulary of *kairos*; see for instance in discussion of 'dieting' in Chapter 24; Hobbes, *Leviathan*, 392.

[219] Hobbes, *Leviathan*, 282. Notably there is no reference to '*occasio*' in the Latin, so although in the English there are connections with the vocabulary of *kairos*, Hobbes may not have had it in mind.

[220] Hobbes, *Leviathan*, 498, 499.

Thomas Beckett, supported by the Pope and the barons' rebellion against King John.[221] Laying off any of the power which the sovereign is meant to hold is what precipitates the emergence of occasion, representing a threat to the State.

Hobbes's dismissal of prudence is related to his rejection of the temporal thinking related to *kairos*, as this rejection is, at least in part, based on his arguments about the unknowable nature of both past and future.[222] His definition of prudence remains consistent with that of previous writers: 'Sometime a man desires to know the event of an action; and then he thinketh of some like action past, and the event therefore one after another; supposing like events will follow like actions . . . Which kind of thoughts, is called *Foresight*, and *Prudence*'.[223] It pertains to the connection between ends and means, and is thus 'When the thoughts of a man, that has a designe in hand, running over a multitude of things, observes how they conduce to that designe; or what designe they may conduce unto'.[224] As one might expect, such knowledge is determined 'by how much one man has more experience of things past, than another'.[225]

It is here that Hobbes levels his critique. If prudence is simply learning from experience, it is an equal and naturally innate attribute, the differences in men arising only from their variable experience, not any difference in ability: 'For Prudence, is but Experience, which equall time, equally bestowes on all men'.[226] Furthermore, it is not a quality to be extolled, for it is not inherently rational or distinctively human, nor does it lead to the 'infallible' results Parker had attributed to the prudence and knowledge of parliament, for 'though it be called Prudence, when the event answereth our Expectation; yet in it its nature, it is but Presumption'.[227] As he had declared in *Elements of Law*, written in 1640, 'PRUDENCE is nothing else but conjecture from experience' and 'Experience concludeth nothing universally'.[228] In the end, the 'best Prophet' is in fact only 'the best guesser; and the best guesser, he that is most versed and studied in the

[221] Hobbes, *Leviathan*, 500, 501. Hobbes uses similar language in speaking of the Jewish people in Chapter XL: 'they took occasion as oft as their Governours displeased them, by blaming sometimes the Policy, sometimes the Religion, to change the Government, or revolt from their Obedience at their pleasure'. This is distinct from a theological understanding of 'occasion' which is also in operation in the second half of *Leviathan*.

[222] See Fiaschi, 'Hobbes on Time and Politics', 3–26. [223] Hobbes, *Leviathan*, 42.

[224] Hobbes, *Leviathan*, 108. [225] Hobbes, *Leviathan*, 42. [226] Hobbes, *Leviathan*, 188.

[227] Hobbes, *Leviathan*, 44.

[228] Thomas Hobbes, *The Elements of Law, Natural and Politic*, ed. Ferdinand Tönnies (London: Barnes & Noble, 1969), 16.

matters he guesses at'.[229] Prudence draws from that animalistic 'Trayn of regulated Thoughts', which seeks 'the causes, or means that produce' a given effect, as opposed to that which seeks 'all the possible effects, that can by it be produced', which is accomplished by man only.[230] Prudence does so by noting the signs, the 'Event Antecedent, of the consequent', and noting these in sequence to attempt to determine what might be the consequences of the action at hand.[231] It is, in short, a backward-looking way of trying to look forward, a conjectural means of determining future effects, and it is neither infallible nor universal.[232]

True philosophy, Hobbes explains, is '*the Knowledge acquired by Reasoning*', not by prudence.[233] The key to this is science, defined as 'the knowledge of Consequences, and dependence of one fact upon another: by which, out of what we presently do, we know how to do something else when we will, or the like, another time'; it is how we observe 'like causes' in order to 'produce the like effects', and thus usurps the place of prudence in achieving the ends of our designs. Science involves the generation of rules which predict outcomes, and Hobbes's project is to generate a moral and civil science analogous to those of figures (geometry) and motion (physics).[234] Although, as he points out, prudence is often synonymous with wisdom (as it is in Parker's work), science is *true* wisdom, and 'as much Experience is *Prudence*, so, is much Science, *Sapience*'. It is the latter, he explains, which is 'infallible', whereas the former, simply 'useful'.[235]

It is clear for Hobbes, then, that science, not prudence, will provide the best sort of counsel – personal or political. When deliberating on an action, Hobbes writes, 'the Appetites and Aversions are raised by foresight and the good and evill consequences, and sequels of the actions whereof we Deliberate'.[236] He who can best connect the 'chain of consequences' is most able to determine what actions are conducive to his appetites: 'so that he who hath by Experience, or Reason, the greatest and surest prospect of Consequences, Deliberates best himself; and is able when he will, to give

229 Hobbes, *Leviathan*, 44. 230 Hobbes, *Leviathan*, 21.

231 Hobbes, *Leviathan*, 22; see also Hobbes, *Elements*, 14–15.

232 See Hobbes, *Elements* I, 4.10, 16; A. V. Houten, 'Prudence in Hobbes's Political Philosophy', *History of Political Thought* 23, no.2 (2002): 266–70; L. van Apeldorn, 'Reconsidering Hobbes's Account of Practical Deliberation', *Hobbes Studies* 25, no.2 (2012): 160.

233 Hobbes, *Leviathan*, 1052.

234 See Noel Malcolm, *Aspects of Hobbes* (Oxford: Oxford University Press, 2002), 146–52.

235 Hobbes, *Leviathan*, 76. It should be clear, that although Hobbes calls the conclusions drawn from science 'infallible', this is meant in the sense of *likely* being true, for he notes elsewhere that 'No Discourse whatsoever, can End in knowledge of Fact' (98) and that science is 'conditionall Knowledge' (100).

236 Hobbes, *Leviathan*, 94.

the best counsell unto others'.[237] Although presented here as two options, it is clear that when it comes to counsel reason once again trumps experience; it is 'Want of Science, that is, Ignorance of causes' which 'disposeth, or rather constraineth a man to rely on the advise, and authority of others'.[238] The office of a counsellor is 'when an action comes into deliberation . . . to make manifest the consequences of it', which is more assuredly done by reason than by prudence.[239]

This is especially the case, Hobbes maintains, in politics. There is a 'skill of making, and maintaining Commonwealths', which 'consisteth in certain Rules, as doth Arithmetique and Geometry; not . . . on Practise onely'.[240] Certainly, experience plays a helpful role in counsel, but it ought to be paired with scientific study of the rules: '*No man is presumed to be a good Counsellour, but in such Businesse, as he hath not onely been much versed in, but hath also much meditated on, and considered.*'[241] Counsel requires both experience *and* science, which Hobbes separates into two fields of requisite knowledge. Knowledge of 'the disposition of Man-kind, of the Rights of Government, and the nature of Equity, Law, Justice, and Honour' is 'not to be attained without study' and thus falls under science; knowledge of 'Strength, Commodities, Places . . . the inclinations, and designes of all Nations that may any way annoy them' – which we may recognise as the content of Botero's reason of state – is 'not attained to, without much experience'.[242] This experience, he later explains, is gathered from '*Intelligences, and Letters*' and the like, such as those which the *Secretissima* literature sought to emulate.[243] This experiential knowledge in political counsel is limited, however, by scientific rule-based knowledge: 'all the experience of the world cannot equall his Counsell, that has learnt, or found out the Rule'.[244] It is only when 'there is no Rule' that he who 'hath most experience in that particular kind of businesse, has therein the best Judgement, and is the best Counsellour'.[245] Prudence is an adequate source of counsel until one is introduced to Hobbesian civil science.

237 Hobbes, *Leviathan*, 94. 238 Hobbes, *Leviathan*, 156. 239 Hobbes, *Leviathan*, 406.

240 Hobbes, *Leviathan*, 322; see also Hobbes, *Leviathan*, 546. Note that in the Latin edition of 1668, Hobbes uses the term '*Scientia*' not '*ars*' for the 'skill' required (Hobbes, *Leviathan*, 323). As has been well established by Skinner, *Reason and Rhetoric*, Hobbes also rejects the humanist contention that moral philosophy might provide the basis for political decision making; see Hobbes, *Elements*, 66; Hobbes, *Leviathan*, 1052–97.

241 Hobbes, *Leviathan*, 406. 242 Hobbes, *Leviathan*, 406.

243 Hobbes, *Leviathan*, 408. Hobbes himself translated the *Altera* into English, as Malcolm, *Reason of State* shows.

244 Hobbes, *Leviathan*, 406. 245 Hobbes, *Leviathan*, 408.

The question becomes, in what sciences ought the political counsellor to be versed? As we saw, Hobbes suggested that three elements make up the knowledge to be gained through science: 'the disposition of Man-kind', 'the nature of Equity, Law, Justice, and Honour' and 'the Rights of Government'.[246] If we look to the Ramist chart of the sciences included in Chapter 9 of *Leviathan*, we see that the 'disposition of Man-Kind', or the 'Consequences from the Qualities of *Men*', becomes divided into two further questions, the 'Consequences from the *Passions* of Men', which is 'ETHIQUES', and 'Consequences from *Speech*'.[247] This, in turn, becomes further subdivided into disciplines including poetry, rhetoric, logic and 'The *Science* of JUST and UNIUST', which also covers Hobbes's insistence that the counsellor understand 'the nature of Equity, Law, Justice, and Honour'.[248]

It seems clear, however, that although the counsellor ought to have *knowledge* of disciplines such as ethics and rhetoric, this is not so that he can use them in the communication of his counsel, as it was for the early humanists, but simply in predicting outcomes; they form part of the 'disposition of Man-Kind', not the skill-set of the counsellor. This is perhaps best demonstrated in his own counsel, intended for Charles I in late 1643 or 1644.[249] Here, he seeks to use knowledge of the situation of other states – namely Scotland and Sweden – to predict future events and consequences. He combines this with an understanding of the passions of men – specifically the Earl of Warwick – to attempt to predict his reaction to a carefully crafted proposal, drawing on the earl's reputation and the promise of honours and rewards to convince him to abandon the parliamentarian cause. Although he suggests that Warwick be subject to persuasive speech and rhetorical arguments, he does not use them himself in his proposal, which is devoid of rhetorical structure – such as an introductory passage establishing the writer's *ethos*.[250]

Regarding 'the Rights of Government', the final aspect of the scientific knowledge which the political counsellor ought to be versed in, Hobbes is quite clear. 'CIVILL PHILOSOPHY' is defined as the 'Consequences from the Accidents of Politique Bodies' and is wholly distinct from natural philosophy, which is 'Consequences from the Accidents of Bodies

246 Hobbes, *Leviathan*, 406.

247 Hobbes, *Leviathan*, 131; see Skinner, *Visions of Politics: Volume III*; Malcolm, *Thomas Hobbes*, 141–5.

248 Hobbes, *Leviathan*, 131.

249 Presented in Noel Malcolm, 'An Unknown Policy Proposal by Thomas Hobbes', *The Historical Journal* 55, no.1 (2012): 146–7.

250 Malcolm, 'An Unknown Policy Proposal', 157; see Skinner, *Reason and Rhetoric*, 127–32.

Naturall' and includes the above-mentioned categories of ethics and rhetoric.[251] When it comes to civil science, there are only two parts, first 'Consequences from the *Institution* of COMMON-WEALTHS, to the *Rights*, and the *Duties* of the *Body Politique*, or *Soveraign*' and 'Consequences from the same, to the *Duty*, and *Right* of the *Subjects*'.[252] Civil science is a topic dealing solely with the duties and rights of sovereignty and of obedience. It is, in short, a science of sovereignty, which is wholly contained in *Leviathan*.[253]

There is no reason, Hobbes insists, to assume that any class or group has a better grasp of this science of politics than any other.[254] 'Good Counsell' Hobbes writes, 'comes not by Lot, nor by Inheritance; and therefore there is no more reason to expect good Advice from the rich, or noble, in matter of State'.[255] Nor is there any reason to expect it more of parliament. As he maintains in *Behemoth*, written following the Civil War, the lords were 'no more skilful in the Publick affairs than the Knights and Burgesses' and both houses were 'prudent and able men as any in the Land, in the business of their Private Estates, which requires nothing but diligence, and a Natural Wit to govern them; but *for the Government of a Common-wealth neither Wit, nor Prudence, nor Diligence is enough, without infallible Rules, and the true Science of Equity and Justice*'.[256] It is not sufficient, he tells us in *Leviathan*, 'onely to be lookers on' in politics.[257] Being the 'Observator' is not enough.

Furthermore, such assemblies are more likely to contain the taint of private interest. In opposition to those such as Parker who maintained that the multitude were more likely than single individuals to do away with private interest and identify and follow the state's interest, Hobbes maintains the reverse. This is clear even in his early works; for instance in his 'Of the *Life* and *History* of *Thucydides*', which accompanied his 1629 translation of *The Peloponnesian War*, Hobbes suggests that '[Thucydides] least of all liked the Democracy'. He provides the same reasons that would later appear in *Leviathan*, most notably 'the emulation and contention of the

251 Hobbes, *Leviathan*, 130. In the Latin of 1668, there is no mention of the science of justice, and civil philosophy is included among the sciences attained by contemplation of the disposition of man: '*Ex contemplatione denique Hominis & Facultatum ejus oriuntur Scientiae* Ethica, Logica, Rhetorica, *& tandem* Politica sive *Philosophia Civilis*' (*Leviathan*, 129).

252 Hobbes, *Leviathan*, 130.

253 Note that Hobbes excludes history completely from the consideration of philosophers, as it is 'The Register of *Knowledge of Fact*' and no part of the knowledge of consequences (*Leviathan*, 124).

254 See Malcolm, *Thomas Hobbes*, 157. 255 Hobbes, *Leviathan*, 546.

256 Thomas Hobbes, *Behemoth, or the Long Parliament* (London, 1679), 69–70.

257 Hobbes, *Leviathan*, 546.

Demagogues . . . the inconstancy of Resolutions, caused by the diuersity of ends, and power of Rhetoric in the Orators'.[258] This theme is also presented in the frontispiece to the work, which contrasts a council-scene of '*hoi aristoi*' with a scene of demagoguery in '*hoi polloi*'.

The same systems are juxtaposed, using the language of interests, in *Leviathan*'s '*Comparison of Monarchy, with Soveraign Assemblies*'. Hobbes notes that 'whosoeuer beareth the Person of the people, or is one of the Assembly that bears it, beareth also his own naturall Person' and although he 'be carefull in his politique Person to procure the common interest' he cannot help but also 'to procure the private good of himself, his family, kindred and friends'.[259] When, inevitably, 'the publique interest chance to crosse the private' Hobbes suggests that such a person 'preferrs the private', as 'the Passions of men, are commonly more potent than their Reason'.[260] Regarding sovereign power, 'in Monarchy, the private interest is the same with the publique' and so the monarch's preference for private interest will not have the same disastrous consequences.[261]

But where does counsel stand in this? Hobbes, in dealing with the '*Differences of fit and unfit Counsellours*', begins by reiterating the importance of experience and science in counsel: 'to the Person of a Common-wealth, his Counsellours serve him in the place of Memory and Mentall Discourse'.[262] However, 'with this resemblance . . . there is one dissimiltude joyned, of great importance'.[263] Whereas for a man, 'the naturall objects of sense . . . work upon him without passion, or interest of their own', the same cannot be said of counsellors, who 'may have, and often have, their particular ends, and passions, that render their Counsells alwayes suspected, and many times unfaithfull'.[264] It is based on this that Hobbes sets down 'for the first condition of a good Counsellour, *That his Ends, and Interest, be not inconsistent with the Ends and Interest of him he Counselleth*'.[265]

[258] Thucydides, *Eight Bookes of the Peloponnesian Warre*, fo. 2^{v}–2, a^{r}. In *Leviathan*, Hobbes gives six reasons for the superiority of monarchy: (1) the 'common interest', (2) the quality and secrecy of the counsel, (3) (in)constancy of resolution, (4) (dis)agreement, (5) favourites and flatterers and (6) usurpation (by regents) (Hobbes, *Leviathan*, 289–94). All but the issue of secrecy appears in this passage of his introduction to *The Peloponnesian War*.

[259] Hobbes, *Leviathan*, 289. [260] Hobbes, *Leviathan*, 289. [261] Hobbes, *Leviathan*, 289.

[262] Hobbes, *Leviathan*, 404. [263] Hobbes, *Leviathan*, 404.

[264] Hobbes, *Leviathan*, 404; for more on the corruption of counsellors, see Blau, 'Corruption', 596–616.

[265] Hobbes, *Leviathan*, 404; see also Hobbes, *Leviathan*, 546. The Latin edition of 1668 is more concerned with a specifically political application than the English, for in place of 'and passions, that render their Counsells alwayes suspected, and many times unfaithfull' the Latin reads '*nec*

In order to ensure that private interest is not interfering with the public, Hobbes gives a prescription completely at odds with that of Parker: 'a man is better Counselled by hearing [counsellors] apart, then in an Assembly'.[266] He provides a number of reasons for this argument, the most important being that in an assembly the voice of one will soon drown out or determine all other voices, and this single voice will almost always be that of one whose interests are not aligned with the public: 'in an Assembly of many, there cannot choose but be some whose interests are contrary to that of the Publique, and these their Interest make Passionate, and Passion Eloquent, and Eloquence draws others into the same advice'.[267] Because interests are associated with the passions, and the passions drive eloquence, the most eloquent and persuasive will be the speaker with the most private interest.[268] It is better, Hobbes suggests, to have no counsel at all, than to take the advice of a multitude in assembly.[269] Countering the Aristotelian metaphor employed by Parker, Hobbes admits that 'although it be true, that many eys see more than one; yet it is not to be understood of many Counsellours', for 'many eyes see the same thing in divers lines, and are apt to look asquint towards their private benefit'.[270]

Hobbes disqualifies assemblies from being viable counsellors, countering the arguments made by Parker and others. Like Bodin and Filmer, he also establishes clearly the distinction between counsel and command, though he goes further than they do in subjugating counsel. He lays out three criteria in his political works – with another added in *Leviathan* – by which one can distinguish between counsel and command: the beneficiary of the counselled action, what reason or justification is given, and whether or not the counsel is understood to be obligatory.

The first, the question of benefit, touches very closely on Hobbes's theory of interest which we have explored. The second criterion – the justification of the counsel – follows from this, and is drawn from Hobbes's rejection of prudence in favour of scientific reasoning. In *The Elements of Law*, Hobbes suggests that counsel ought always to be given in 'provisive'

semper cum scopo Civitatis congruentem' and where it reads '*Ends and Interest of him he Counselleth*' the Latin gives: '*Finibus & Bono publico*' (Hobbes, *Leviathan*, 404, 405).

266 Hobbes, *Leviathan*, 408; Latin: '*Monarchae cui Consiliarii sunt, audire illos satiùs est seorsim unumquemque*' (Hobbes, *Leviathan*, 409).

267 Hobbes, *Leviathan*, 408.

268 See Skinner, *Reason and Rhetoric*, 334–73.

269 Here Hobbes uncharacteristically employs a simile – comparing the relationship of counselled and counsellor to firsts and seconds in a tennis match. Not only does Hobbes retain this analogy in the Latin edition, but he includes '*concilium comparatum ludo pilae*' in his index; Hobbes, *Leviathan*, 410, 412, 1253.

270 Hobbes, *Leviathan*, 412.

(i.e. provisional) language, 'as for example, If this be done or not done, this will follow'; counsel must always 'give the reason of the action it adviseth to'.[271] It demands reasoning on the consequences of actions, which in the case of politics, as we have already seen, requires knowledge of the 'rules' of civil science. When it comes to counsel, 'the expression is Do, because it is best', whereas in law it is 'Do, because I have a right to compel you; or Do, because I say Do'.[272]

This issue of compulsion – the third criterion – is central for Hobbes, addressing precisely the transgression that Parker and the parliamentarians make in seeking to enforce their counsels regarding the 'privadoes' of Charles I. This concern first emerges in *The Elements of Law*, in which Hobbes makes clear that 'the counsel of a man is no law to him that is counselled'.[273] If it were – 'if to counsellours there should be given a right to have their counsel followed' – then they would be 'no more counsellours, but masters of them whom they counsel; and their counsels no more counsels, but laws'.[274] It is a mistake that 'men usually call counselling, by the name of governing' and only do so because they envy those who are called to counsel, a reason that he would later give as a cause of the civil war.[275] *De Cive* repeats these lessons. Those who 'do not scrupulously weigh the force of words' tend to 'confound law with advice' by thinking that 'it is the monarch's duty not only to listen to advisors but also to obey them'.[276]

It is in Chapter 25 of *Leviathan* – 'Of *COUNSELL*' – that Hobbes fully develops this strong distinction between counsel and command. Although the opening marginal note reads '*Counsell what*', Hobbes uncharacteristically does not begin this chapter with a definition but rather opens by railing, as he had in *De Cive*, against those who have conflated the definitions of counsel and command: 'How fallacious it is to judge of the nature of things, by the ordinary and inconstant use of words, appeareth in nothing more, than in the confusion of Counsels, and Commands'.[277] This arises from 'the Imperative manner of speaking in them both',

271 Hobbes, *Elements*, 185, 186.

272 Hobbes, *Elements*, 186. Here we see Hobbes's debt to Felippe, *The Counsellor*, 70–1: 'that they which giue a man counsell, and make him acquainted with the reasons which mooue them to giue such counsell . . . doo not bind, or by any necessitie force him to whom the counsell is giuen, to follow their counsell: but they that will commaund, will haue y[t] doone which they commaund'.

273 Hobbes, *Elements*, 186. 274 Hobbes, *Elements*, 186.

275 Hobbes, *Elements*, 186; see Hobbes 1679, p. 164.

276 Thomas Hobbes, *Hobbes: On the Citizen*, ed. Richard Tuck and Michael Silverthorne (Cambridge: Cambridge University Press, 1998), 153.

277 Hobbes, *Leviathan*, 398.

a reference to his treatment of the types of speech in Chapter 6, in which he had made clear that 'all Passions may be expressed' either '*Indicatively*; as *I love, I fear, I joy, I deliberate, I will, I command*',[278] '*Subjunctively*', which is proper to 'Deliberation' and 'differs not from the language of Reasoning, save that Reasoning is in generall words; but Deliberation for the most part is of Particulars' or, finally, '*Imperative*[*ly*]; as *Do this, forebeare that*'.[279] This last, Hobbes marks, is the language of '*Command*' otherwise it is '*Prayer*, or els *Counsell*'.[280] Whereas in *The Elements of Law* Hobbes had kept imperative speech separate from the 'provisive' speech of counsel, in *Leviathan* he acknowledges the common practice of stating both imperatively, 'for the words *Doe this*, are the words not onely of him that Commandeth; but also of him that giveth Counsell'.[281] The confusion between these types of speech, Hobbes suggests, is not one of mere ignorance, but based on the interests of those making the judgement, for those who 'mistake sometimes the Precepts of Counsellours, for the Precepts of them that Command' do it 'according as it best agreeth with the conclusions they would inferre, or actions they approve'.[282] The confusion between counsel and command can be both intentional and dangerous.

In Chapter 25 he once again repeats the distinctions between counsel and command based on the intended beneficiary and justification of the advice, before coming to the issue of obligation: 'that a man may be obliged to so what he is Commanded . . . But he cannot be obliged to do as he is Counselled'.[283] However, in *Leviathan*, this becomes merely an extension of the idea that 'Command is directed to a mans own benefit, and Counsell to the benefit of another man'.[284] In place of this, Hobbes adds another distinguishing element: 'that no man can pretend to be of another mans Counsell'.[285] For Hobbes in 1651 even pressing the right to give counsel is to cross the boundary between counsel and command. Part of this rests on the sovereign's control of the secrets of state, required for experiential knowledge; its acquisition requires 'hav[ing] seen the archives of the commonwealth' and so 'they who are not called to Counsell, can have no good Counsell in such cases to obtrude'.[286] Hobbes's contention,

[278] Notably, 'I command' is left out of the Latin edition of 1668; Hobbes may have wanted to distinguish it from imperative speech.

[279] Hobbes, *Leviathan*, 94. [280] Hobbes, *Leviathan*, 94. [281] Hobbes, *Leviathan*, 398.

[282] Hobbes, *Leviathan*, 398. [283] Hobbes, *Leviathan*, 400. [284] Hobbes, *Leviathan*, 398.

[285] Hobbes, *Leviathan*, 400.

[286] Hobbes, *Leviathan*, 408. The MS copy held in the British Library (MS Egerton 1910), widely held to be the presentation copy given to Charles II, reads 'they who are not called to Counsell in such cases can have no good Counsell to obtrude' and here, as well as at a number of points in this

however, goes even further than this practical consideration. In *The Elements of Law*, the proscription against uninvited counsel is one of the fundamental Laws of Nature: 'That no man obtrude or press his advice or counsell to any man that declareth himself unwilling to hear the same' because 'there may often be just cause to suspect the counsellor' and so it is a 'breach of peace' and 'against the law of nature to obtrude it'.[287] He abandons this as a law of nature in *Leviathan*, but revives it in marking the distinction between counsel and command.[288]

In *Leviathan* Hobbes also introduces a third category in addition to counsel and command: exhortation.[289] He that exhorts, like he that commands, 'doth not deduce the consequences of what he adviseth' and so does not 'tye himselfe therein to the rigour of true reasoning'.[290] Instead, he appeals to the 'common Passions, and opinions of men' for his reasons, making use of 'Similtudes, Metaphors, Examples, and other tooles of Oratory' in order 'to perswade the Utility, Honour, or Justice of following their advice', advice which is 'directed to his own benefit' and proceeds 'from his own occasions'.[291] This is a pointed and deliberate attack not only on humanist neo-classical rhetoric, but also on public privadoes such as Parker, as 'the use of Exhortation and Dehortation lyeth onely, where a man is to speak to a Multitude because when the Speech is addressed to one, he may interrupt him, and examine his reasons more rigorously'.[292] Such men, 'are corrupt Counsellours, and as it were bribed by their own interest' for, as he explains in the Latin edition, 'men are generally more vehement in their own interests than in those of others'.[293] If it is parliament which can be accused of crossing the line between counsel and command in pressing both the obligation and right of their counsel, it is Parker and his fellow public counsellors who are to blame for exhorting them to do so.

Counsel, especially from parliament and from its counsellors, emerges even more strongly as the causal factor in the outbreak of the civil war in

section on the requirements of counsel, text has been added, and then crossed out, probably in Hobbes's own hand. The original text is rendered illegible by such corrections. See Tuck, 'Introduction', li–lvi; Malcolm, *Thomas Hobbes*, 197–208.

287 Hobbes, *Elements*, 91–2.

288 Hobbes's pressing of the difference between counsel and command may have to do with the connection between counsel and deliberation, and the latter's literal meaning of 'putting an end to the *Liberty* we had of doing, or omitting'; counsellors ought not to deprive anyone, especially the sovereign, of his liberty (Hobbes, *Leviathan*, 92).

289 Hobbes, *Leviathan*, 400; see Felippe, *The Counsellor*, 70–1.

290 Hobbes, *Leviathan*, 400.

291 Hobbes, *Leviathan*, 400.

292 Hobbes, *Leviathan*, 402; see Skinner, *Reason and Rhetoric*.

293 '*homines in suis plerumque rebus vehementiores sint, quam in alienis*' (Hobbes, *Leviathan*, 403). The English is more lengthy and convoluted on this point.

Hobbes's later accounts. In *A Dialogue between a Philosopher and a Student of the Common Laws*, written in the late 1660s, the Philosopher and the Student agree that a king who 'will not Consult with the Lords of Parliament and hear the Complaints and Informations of the Commons . . . sinneth against God'.[294] However, under no circumstances can he be 'Compell'd to do any thing by his Subjects by Arms, and Force'.[295] In fact, the Philosopher makes clear that a king has a right to, and often ought to, 'neglect such advice', for instance 'if the Lords and Commons should Advise him to restore those Laws Spiritual, which in Queen *Maries* time were in Force'.[296] The same is repeated in *Behemoth*, also a dialogue, in which Hobbes notes that men who distinguished themselves according to their military valour were often marked out to be members of the king's council, and so 'Kings of *England* did upon every great occasion call them together by the name of Discreet and Wise men of the Kingdom, and hear their Councils'.[297] Although such men – the Lords – 'gave him Council when he requir'd it' they 'had no Right to make War upon him, if he did not follow it'.[298] As to the Commons, the speakers in the dialogue doubt that they 'were part of the King's Council at all'.[299] Hobbes suggests that he cannot find evidence that 'the end of their summoning was to give advice', but rather 'in case they had any Petitions for Redress of Grievances' to be given to the king.[300] This statement closely echoes the closing passage of Hobbes's treatment of the choice of counsellors in *Leviathan*, in which he writes that 'The best Counsell, in those things that concern not other Nations . . . is to be taken from the generall informations, and complaints of the people of each Province', as long as that stands not 'in derogation of the essentiall Rights of Soveraignty', for without these 'the Common-wealth cannot at all subsist'.[301] The best counsel, then, is simply the expression of petitions or grievances, only voiced when it does not interfere in any way with the operation of sovereign power. Hobbes severely limits the influence of counsel in his attempt to protect sovereignty.[302]

So what do Hobbes and Parker leave us with in terms of a mid-seventeenth century discourse of counsel? For Parker, although he seems to embrace the orthodox humanist model of counsel, the conciliar role of parliament gives

294 Thomas Hobbes, *A Dialogue Between a Philosopher and a Student, of the Common Laws of England*, ed. Alan Cromartie (Oxford: Oxford University Press, 2005), 26.

295 Hobbes, *A Dialogue*, 26. 296 Hobbes, *A Dialogue*, 26. 297 Hobbes, *Behemoth*, 77.

298 Hobbes, *Behemoth*, 77, 78. 299 Hobbes, *Behemoth*, 78. 300 Hobbes, *Behemoth*, 78.

301 Hobbes, *Leviathan*, 548. 302 Coleman, 'A Culture of Political Counsel', 20.

way to a sovereign one whenever the king can be said to be 'seduced' by private counsel, in other words, when the king does not follow parliament's advice. This obligatory parliamentary counsel, as his opponents point out, crosses the line between counsel and command, placing the latter in the hands of parliament, and reducing counsel to nothing more than a cover for sovereign power. Counsel, in Parker's model, becomes command.

Hobbes's attempts to rebuild the distinction between these two concepts are, at least in part, in response to Parker and the events of the 1640s. In reconstructing the barrier between counsel and command, however, Hobbes buries the former beneath the latter. Rejecting the humanist model of counsel built on the persuasive power of rhetoric, the Machiavellian model built on history, as well as the reason of state model built on direct experience, he denies any political body a right to give advice, completely subjecting counsel to the will of the sovereign. For Hobbes, sovereignty takes precedence, overthrowing centuries of political discourse based on the importance of counsel. In either case, sovereignty becomes central to seventeenth-century political theory, and counsel fades into the shadows of political thought.

Bibliography

Manuscript Sources

BL Sl. MS 1065, The British Library, London
BL Sl. MS 3938, The British Library, London
PC 2/26, The National Archives, London
SP 10/7 n. 28, The National Archives, London
SP 63/205, The National Archives, London

Primary Sources

A Conference about the Next Succession to the Crowne of Ingland. Antwerp, 1595.

A Declaration of the True Causes of the Great Troubles Presupposed to Be Intended against the Realm of England. Antwerp, 1592.

A Most Excellent Hystorie, of the Institution and First Beginning of Christian Princes. London, 1571.

A Nest of Persidious Vipers: or the Second Part of the Parliaments Kalendar of Black Saints. London, 1644.

Aeschylus. *Aeschylus, with an English Translation.* Translated by Herbert Weir Smyth. Vol. 2: Libation Bearers. 2 vols. Cambridge, MA: Harvard University Press, 1926.

Allen, William. *The Execution of Justice in England, by William Cecil; and A True, Sincere, and Modest Defense of English Catholics, by William Allen.* Edited by Robert MacCune Kingdon. Ithaca: Cornell University Press, 1965.

Aquinas, Thomas. *Summa Theologiae.* Translated by W. D. Hughes. Vol. 23. Cambridge: Cambridge University Press, 2006.

Aristotle. *Nicomachean Ethics.* Translated by H. Rackham. Cambridge, MA: Harvard University Press, 1926.

Politics. Translated by H. Rackham. Cambridge, MA: Harvard University Press, 1944.

Aylmer, John. *An Harborowe for Faithfull and Trewe Svbiectes.* London, 1559.

Bacon, Francis. *Coulers of Good and Euill.* London, 1597.

Essayes. London, 1612.

'Essex's Device'. In *The Oxford Francis Bacon I: Early Writings 1584–1596*, edited by Alan Stewart and Harriet Knight, 675–722. Oxford: Oxford University Press, 2012.

'Letter of Advice to Queen Elizabeth I'. In *The Letters and Life of Francis Bacon*, edited by James Spedding, 47–56. London: Longman, Green, Longman, and Roberts, 1861.

'Second Letter of Advice to the Earl of Rutland'. In *The Oxford Francis Bacon I: Early Writings 1584–1596*, ed. Alan Stewart and Harriet Knight (Oxford: Oxford University Press, 2012), 658–70.

The Historie of the Reigne of King Henry the Seuenth. London, 1629.

The Twoo Bookes of Francis Bacon. Of the Proficience and Aduancement of Learning, Diuine and Humane. London, 1605.

Balzac, Jean-Louis Guez de. *The Prince*. Translated by H. G. London, 1648.

Becon, Thomas. *The Golden Boke of Christen Matrimonye*. London, 1543.

Béthune, Philippe de. *The Counsellor of Estate*. Translated by Edward Grimeston. London, 1634.

Bidwell, William B., and Maija Jansson, eds. *Proceedings in Parliament 1626, Volume 2: House of Commons*. New Haven: University of Rochester Press, 1997.

Bilson, Thomas. *The True Difference between Christian Obedience and Unchristian Rebellion*. Oxford, 1585.

Blundeville, Thomas. *The True Order and Method of Writing and Reading Histories*. London, 1574.

Boccaccio, Giovanni. *The Fall of Princes*. Translated by John Lydgate. London, 1527.

Boccalini, Trajano. *The New-Found Politicke*. Translated by John Florio. London, 1626.

Bodin, Jean. *Bodin: On Sovereignty: Six Books of the Commonwealth*. Translated by M. J. Tooley. Massachusetts: CreateSpace Independent Publishing Platform, 2009.

The Method for the Easy Comprehension of History. Translated by Beatrice Reynolds. New York: W.W. Norton & Co., 1969.

The Six Bookes of a Commonweale. Translated by Richard Knolles. London, 1606.

Botero, Giovanni. *Botero: The Reason of State*. Edited by Robert Bireley. Cambridge: Cambridge University Press, 2017.

Relations of the Most Famous Kingdoms and Common-Weales. Translated by Robert Johnson. London, 1611.

Relations of the Most Famovs Kingdomes and Common-Wealths Throrowout the World. London, 1630.

The Worlde, or an Historical Description of the Most Famous Kingdoms and Commonweales Therein. Translated by Robert Johnson. London, 1601.

Bourne, William. *A Booke Called the Treasure for Traueilers*. London, 1578.

Buchanan, George. *A Critical Edition of George Buchanan's Baptistes and of its Anonymous Seventeenth-Century Translation Tyrannicall-Government*

Anatomized. Edited by Steven Berkowitz. New York: Garland Publishing Inc, 1992.
Tyrannicall-Government Anatomized. London, 1642.
Bunny, Edmund. *A Briefe Answer, vnto Those Idle and Friuolous Quarrels of R.P. against the Late Edition of the Resolution*. London, 1589.
Burney, Richard. *An Answer, or Necessary Animadversions, upon Some Late Impostumate Observations Invective against His Sacred Maiesty*. London, 1642.
Castiglione, Baldassare. *The Book of the Courtier*. Edited by Virginia Cox. Translated by Thomas Hoby. London: J. M. Dent & Sons Ltd/ Everyman's Library, 1994.
Cavendish, George. *The Negotiations of Thomas Woolsey*. London, 1641.
Charron, Pierre. *Of Wisedome*. Translated by Samson Lennard. London, 1608.
Cicero, Marcus Tullius. *Cicero: On Duties*. Edited by M. T. Griffin. Translated by E. M. Atkins. Cambridge: Cambridge University Press, 1991.
De Inventione. Translated by H. M. Hubbell. Cambridge, MA: Loeb Classical Library, 1949.
'On Invention', *The Orations of Marcus Tullius Cicero*, trans. Charles Duke Yonge, vol. 4. London: H.G. Bohn, 1853.
Coignet, Matthieu. *Instruction aux Princes pour garder la foy promise*. Paris, 1584.
Politique Discourses upon Trueth and Lying. London, 1586.
Cornwallis, William. *Essayes*. London, 1600.
Essayes. London, 1610.
Coryate, Thomas. *Coryats Crudities*. London, 1611.
Crakanthorpe, Richard. *The Defence of Constantine*. London, 1621.
Vigilius Dormitans. London, 1631.
Dallington, Robert. *A Method for Trauell*. London, 1605.
Donaldson, Peter S., ed. *A Machiavellian Treatise*. Cambridge: Cambridge University Press, 2009.
Dowriche, Anne. *The French Historie*. London, 1589.
Egerton, Thomas. *The Speech of the Lord Chancellor of England, in the Exchequer Chamber, Touching the Post-Nati*. Societie of stationers, London, 1609.
Eikon Basilike. London, 1649.
Ellis, Henry. *Original Letters, Illustrative of English History*. London: Harding, Triphook and Lepard, 1824.
Elyot, Thomas. *Of the Knowledeg Whiche Maketh a Wise Man*. London, 1533.
Pasquil the Playne. London, 1533.
The Book Named The Governor. Edited by S. E. Lehmberg. New York: Dent, 1962.
The Dictionary. London, 1538.
The Doctrinall of Princes. London, 1534.
Erasmus. *Erasmus and His Age: Selected Letters of Desiderius Erasmus*. Edited by Hans J. Hillerbrand. New York: Harper and Row Ltd, 1970.
Praise of Folly. Edited by A. H. T. Levi. Translated by Betty Radice. London: Penguin UK, 1993.

The Adages of Erasmus. Edited by William Watson Barker. Toronto: University of Toronto Press, 2001.

The Education of a Christian Prince. Translated by Lisa Jardine. Cambridge: Cambridge University Press, 1997.

Felippe, Bartolome. *The Counseller. A Treatise of Counsels and Counsellers of Princes*. Translated by John Thorius. London, 1589.

Tractado Del Conseio Y de Los Conseieros de Los Principes. Turin [London], 1589.

Filmer, Robert. 'Patriarcha'. In *Filmer: 'Patriarcha' and Other Writings*, edited by Johann P. Sommerville, 1–68. Cambridge: Cambridge University Press, 1991.

Patriarcha, or the Natural Power of Kings. London, 1680.

'The Free-Holders Grand Inquest'. In *Filmer: 'Patriarcha' and Other Writings*, edited by Johann P. Sommerville, 69–130. Cambridge: Cambridge University Press, 1991.

Fisher, Benjamin. *Profitable Instructions Describing What Speciall Obseruations Are to Be Taken by Trauellers*. London, 1633.

Fitzherbert, Thomas. *A Defence of the Catholyke Cause*. Antwerp, 1602.

The First Part of a Treatise Concerning Policy, and Religion. London, 1606.

Foxe, John. *Actes and Monuments*. London, 1570.

Frankland, Thomas, ed. *The Annals of King James and King Charles the First: 1612–1642*. London, 1681.

Furió Ceriol, Fadrique. *A Very Briefe and Profitable Treatise Declaring Howe Many Counsells, and What Maner of Counselers a Prince That Will Gouerne Well Ought to Haue*. Translated by Thomas Blundeville. London, 1570.

Gentillet, Innocent. *A Discovrse Vpon the Meanes of Wel Governing*. London, 1602.

Discovrs svr les moyens de bien govverner & maintenir en paix vn royaume, ou autre principauté: divisez en trois parties: a sauoir, du conseil, de la religion, & de la police que doit tenir un prince, 1579.

Goodman, Christopher. *How Svperior Powers Oght to Be Obeyd of Their Subiects*. London, 1558.

Gower, John. *The Complete Works of John Gower*. Edited by G. C. Macaulay. Vol. 1. Oxford: Clarendon Press, 1901.

Guevara, Antonio de. *The Diall of Princes*. London, 1557.

Hall, Edward. *The Union of the Two Noble and Illustre Families of Lancastre and Yorke*. London, 1548.

Hobbes, Thomas. *A Dialogue Between a Philosopher and a Student, of the Common Laws of England*. Edited by Alan Cromartie. Oxford: Oxford University Press, 2005.

Behemoth, or the Long Parliament. London, 1679.

Hobbes: On the Citizen. Edited by Richard Tuck and Michael Silverthorne. Cambridge: Cambridge University Press, 1998.

The Elements of Law, Natural and Politic. Edited by Ferdinand Tönnies. London: Barnes & Noble, 1969.

Thomas Hobbes: Leviathan: The English and Latin Texts. Edited by Noel Malcolm. Oxford: Oxford University Press, 2012.

Hoccleve, Thomas. *Thomas Hoccleve: The Regiment of Princes*. Edited by C. Blyth. Kalamazoo: Medieval Institute Publications, 1999.

Holinshed, Raphael. *Chronicles of England, Scotlande, and Ireland*. London, 1577.

Hooker, John. *Parliament in Elizabethan England: John Hooker's Order and Usage*. Edited by Vernon F. Snow. New Haven: Yale University Press, 1977.

The Order and Vsage of the Keeping of a Parlement in England. London, 1575.

'House of Commons Journal Volume 1: 16–18 November 1606'. In *Journal of the House of Commons: Volume 1, 1547–1629*, 314–15. London, 1802. www.british-history.ac.uk/commons-jrnl/vol1/pp314–315.

Hurault, Jacques. *Politicke, Moral, and Martial Discourses*. Translated by Arthur Golding. London, 1595.

Trois livres des offices d'estat. Lyon, 1596.

Isocrates. *The Orations of Isocrates Volume 1*. Translated by J. H. Freese. London: George Bell & Sons, 1894.

John of Salisbury. *Policraticus: Of the Frivolities of Courtiers and the Footprints of Philosophers*. Edited by Cary J Nederman. Cambridge: Cambridge University Press, 1990.

Johnson, Robert. *Essaies, or Rather Imperfect Offers*. London, 1601.

Kenyon, J. P., ed. *The Stuart Constitution, 1603–1688: Documents and Commentary*. Cambridge: Cambridge University Press, 1986.

Knox, John. *The First Blast of the Trumpet against the Monstruous Regiment of Women*. Geneva, 1558.

Laertius, Diogenes. *Lives of Eminent Philosophers*. Translated by R. D. Hicks. Cambridge, MA: Harvard University Press, 1972.

Lanquet, Thomas. *Epitome of Chronicles*. London, 1549.

Lipsius, Justus. *Politica: Six Books of Politics or Political Instruction*. Translated by Jan Waszink. The Hague: Uitgeverij Van Gorcum, 2004.

Sixe Bookes of Politickes or Civil Doctrine. Translated by William Jones. London, 1594.

Lydgate, John. *Gouernaunce of Kynges and Prynces*. London, 1511.

Lylle, William. 'William Lylle to Earl of Essex'. In *Calendar of the Manuscripts of the Most Hon. the Marquis of Salisbury, Preserved at Hatfield House, Hertfordshire*, edited by R. A. Roberts, 5:447. Dublin, 1894.

Machiavelli, Niccolò. *Il Principe*. Edited by L. Arthur Burd. Oxford: Clarendon Press, 1891.

Machiavels Discovrses. Translated by Edward Dacres. London, 1636.

Nicholas Machiavel's Prince. Translated by Edward Dacres. London, 1640.

'Occasion'. In *An Anthology of Italian Poems, 13th-19th Century*, edited by Lorna de'Lucchi. New York: Alfred A. Knopf, 1922.

'Tercets on Fortune'. In *Machiavelli: The Chief Works and Others*, edited by Allan Gilbert, 745–9. Durham; London: Duke University Press, 1989.

The Discourses. London: Penguin Books, 2000.

The Prince. Edited by Quentin Skinner and Russell Price. Cambridge; New York: Cambridge University Press, 2000.

Malcolm, Noel, ed. 'Altera Secretissima Instructio'. In *Reason of State, Propaganda, and the Thirty Years' War: An Unknown Translation by Thomas Hobbes*, 124–98. Oxford: Oxford University Press, 2010.

Malvezzi, Virgilio. *Discovrses Upon Cornelius Tacitus*. Translated by Richard Baker. London, 1642.

The Pourtract of the Politicke Christian-Favourite. Translated by Thomas Powell. London, 1647.

Marsilius of Padua. *Defensor Minor and De Translatione Imperii*. Edited by Cary J. Nederman. Cambridge: Cambridge University Press, 1993.

The Defender of Peace: The Defensor Pacis. Edited by Alan Gewirth. New York: Columbia University Press, 1967.

Martin, Richard. *A Speach Deliuered, to the Kings Most Excellent Maiestie in the Name of the Sheriffes of London and Middlesex*. London, 1603.

Milton, John. *Eikonoklastes*. London, 1650.

Montaigne, Michel de. 'Les Essais de Montaigne'. http://artflsrv02.uchicago.edu/philologic4/montessaisvilley/navigate/1/5/2/.

The Essayes, or Morall, Politike, and Millitarie Discourses. Translated by John Florio. London, 1603.

More, Thomas. *The Yale Edition of the Complete Works of St. Thomas More: English Poems, Life of Pico, the Last Things*. Edited by Anthony G. Edwards, Katherine Gardiner Rogers, and Clarence H. Miller. Vol. 1. New Haven: Yale University Press, 1997.

The Yale Edition of the Complete Works of St. Thomas More: History of King Richard III. Edited by Richard S. Sylvester. Vol. 2. New Haven: Yale University Press, 1963.

The Yale Edition of the Complete Works of St. Thomas More: The Apology. Edited by J. B. Trapp. Vol. 9. New Haven: Yale University Press, 1979.

The Yale Edition of the Complete Works of St. Thomas More: The Confutation of Tyndale's Answer. Edited by Louis A. Schuster, Richard C. Marius, and James P. Lusardi. Vol. 8. New Haven: Yale University Press, 1973.

The Yale Edition of the Complete Works of St. Thomas More: Utopia. Edited by Edward Surtz and J. H. Hexter. Vol. 4. New Haven: Yale University Press, 1965.

Moryson, Fynes. *An Itinerary*. London, 1617.

Nineteen Propositions . . . With His Majesties Answer Thereunto. Cambridge, 1642.

Palmer, Thomas. *An Essay of the Meanes How to Make Our Trauailes, into Forraine Countries, the More Profitable and Honourable*. London, 1606.

Paradin, Claude. *The Heroicall Deuises*. London, 1591.

Parker, Henry. *A Discourse Concerning Puritans*. London, 1641.

A Letter of Due Censure. London, 1650.

A Political Catechism. London, 1643.

Divine and Politike Observations. Amsterdam, 1638.

Jus Populi. London, 1644.

Observations upon Some of His Majesties Late Answers and Expresses. London, 1642.

Some Few Observations upon His Majesties Late Answer to the Declaration or Remonstance. London, 1642.
The Case of Shipmony Briefly Discoursed. London, 1640.
The Contra-Replicant, His Complaint to His Maiestie. London, 1643.
The Danger to England Observed. London, 1642.
The Oath of Pacification. London, 1643.
The True Grounds of Ecclesiasticall Regiment. London, 1641.
Parry, William. *The Trauels of Anthony Sherley*. London, 1601.
Parsons, Robert. *A Christian Directorie*. Rouen, 1585.
A Defence of the Censure. Rouen, 1582.
A Manifestation of the Great Folly and Bad Spirit of Certayne in England Calling Themselues Secular Priestes. Antwerp, 1602.
Newes from Spayne and Holland. Antwerp, 1593.
A Temperate Ward-Word, to the Turbulent and Seditious Wach-Word of Sir Francis Hastinges Knight. Antwerp, 1599.
The Warn-Word to Sir Francis Hastinges Wast-Word. Antwerp, 1602.
Peck, D. C., ed. *Leicester's Commonwealth: The Copy of a Letter Written by a Master of Art of Cambridge (1584) and Related Documents*. Athens, OH: Ohio University Press, 1985.
Pisan, Christine de. *The Book of the Body Politic*. Edited by Kate Langdon Forhan. Cambridge: Cambridge University Press, 1994.
Hystoryes of Troye. London, 1549.
Plato, *The Republic*, ed. Paul Shorey. Cambridge, MA: Harvard University Press, 1969.
Plutarch. *Moralia*. Translated by Frank Cole Babbitt. Vol. 1. Cambridge, MA: Harvard University Press, 1927.
Plutarch's Lives with an English Translation. Translated by Bernadotte Perrin. Vol. 2. Cambridge, MA: Harvard University Press, 1914.
The Philosophie, Commonlie Called, the Morals. Translated by Philemon Holland. London, 1603.
Pole, Reginald. 'Apology'. In *Cambridge Translations of Renaissance Philosophical Texts: Volume 2*, edited by Jill Kraye, 274–84. Cambridge; New York: Cambridge University Press, 2010.
Prynne, William. *The Aphorismes of the Kingdome*. London, 1642.
Rachin, Guillaume du. *A Review of the Councell of Trent*. Translated by Gerard Langbaine. Oxford, 1638.
Roper, William. *The Mirrour of Vertue in Worldly Greatness; or, The Life of Sir Thomas More, Knight*. London: De la More Press, 1902.
Santa Maria, fray Juan de. *Policie Vnveiled*. Translated by J. M. London, 1650.
Scott, Thomas. *An Experimentall Discoverie of Spanish Practises*. London, 1623.
The Second Part of Vox Populi, or Gondomar Appearing in the Likenes of Matchiauell. London, 1624.
Vox Populi, or Newes from Spayne. London, 1620.
Seneca, Lucius Annaeus. *L. Annaei Senecae Tragoediae: incertorum auctorum Hercules (Oetaeus), Octavia*. Edited by Otto Zwierlein. Oxford: Clarendon Press, 1985.

Lucubrationes omnes. Edited by Erasmus. Basel, 1515.

Moral Letters to Lucilius (Epistulae Morales Ad Lucilium). Edited by Richard Mott Gummere. 3 vols. Cambridge, MA: Harvard University Press, 1917.

Serres, John de. *A General Inuentorie of the History of France*. Translated by Edward Grimeston. London, 1607.

Sidney, Philip. 'Defense of Leicester'. In *Leicester's Commonwealth: The Copy of a Letter Written by a Master of Art of Cambridge (1584) and Related Documents*, edited by D. C. Peck, 165–77. Athens, OH: Ohio University Press, 1985.

Spelman, John. *A View of a Printed Book Intituled Observations upon His Majesties Late Answers and Expresses*. London, 1642.

Starkey, Thomas. *A Dialogue Between Pole and Lupset*. Edited by Thomas F. Mayer. London: Royal Historical Society, 1989.

Stubbs, John. *Gaping Gulf, with Letters and Other Relevant Documents*. Edited by Lloyd E. Berry. Charlottesville: University Press of Virginia, 1968.

The Declaration or Remonstrance of the Lords and Commons in Parliament. London, 1642.

The King's Cabinet Opened. London, 1645.

The Parliaments Kalendar of Black Saints: Or a New Discovery of Plots & Treasons. London, 1644.

Thomas, William. *The Works of William Thomas*. Edited by Abraham D'Aubant. London: J. Almon, 1774.

Thucydides. *Eight Bookes of the Peloponnesian Warre*. Translated by Thomas Hobbes. London, 1629.

Treatise of Treasons. Louvain, 1572.

Tusser, Thomas. *Five Hundred Points of Good Husbandry*. London, 1580.

Secondary Sources

'Abuse, V.' In *OED Online*. Oxford University Press. www.oed.com/view/Entry/822.

Ahl, Frederick. 'The Art of Safe Criticism in Greece and Rome'. *The American Journal of Philology* 105, no. 2 (1984): 174–208.

Albury, W. R. *Castiglione's Allegory: Veiled Policy in the Book of the Courtier (1528)*. Burlington: Ashgate, 2014.

Alford, Stephen. *Burghley: William Cecil at the Court of Elizabeth I*. New Haven: Yale University Press, 2008.

Kingship and Politics in the Reign of Edward VI. Cambridge: Cambridge University Press, 2004.

'Politics and Political History in the Tudor Century'. *The Historical Journal* 42, no. 2 (1999): 535–48.

The Early Elizabethan Polity: William Cecil and the British Succession Crisis, 1558–1569. Cambridge: Cambridge University Press, 1998.

The Watchers: A Secret History of the Reign of Elizabeth I. New York: Penguin UK, 2012.

Anglo, Sydney. *Machiavelli – The First Century: Studies in Enthusiasm, Hostility, and Irrelevance*. Oxford: Oxford University Press, 2005.

Apeldorn, L. van. 'Reconsidering Hobbes's Account of Practical Deliberation'. *Hobbes Studies* 25, no.2 (2012): 143–65.

Ascoli, Albert Russell. 'Machiavelli's Gift of Counsel'. In *Machiavelli and the Discourse of Literature*, edited by Victoria Ann Kahn and Albert Russell Ascoli, 219–57. Ithaca: Cornell University Press, 1993.

Attie, Katherine Bootle. 'Re-Membering the Body Politic: Hobbes and the Construction of Civic Immortality'. *Attie* 75, no.3 (30 August 2008): 497–530.

Baker-Smith, Dominic. *More's Utopia*. Toronto: University of Toronto Press, 2000.

Baldini, A. Enzo. 'Le De regia sapientia de Botero et De la naissance, durée et chute des Estats de Lucinge'. *Astérion. Philosophie, histoire des idées, pensée politique*, no. 2 (2004).

Baldwin, G. 'Reason of State and English Parliaments, 1610-42'. *History of Political Thought* 25, no.4 (2004): 620–41.

Bałuk-Ulewiczowa, Teresa. *Goslicius' Ideal Senator and His Cultural Impact Over the Centuries: Shakespearean Reflections*. Krakow: Polska Akademia Umiejętności, 2009.

'Goslicius' Treatment of the Idea Senator: The Englishman's Epitome of Polish Republicanism'. *Kultura Polityka* 9 (2011): 89–103.

Baumlin, James S. 'Ciceronian Decorum and the Temporalities of Renaissance Rhetoric'. In *Rhetoric and Kairos: Essays in History, Theory and Praxis*, edited by Phillip Sipiora and James S Baumlin, 138–64. New York: State University of New York Press, 2002.

Bawcutt, N. W. 'The "Myth of Gentillet" Reconsidered: An Aspect of Elizabethan Machiavellianism'. *The Modern Language Review* 99, no. 4 (2004): 863–74.

Beckett, Margaret. 'The Political Works of John Lesley, Bishop of Ross (1527–96)'. PhD Thesis, University of St Andrews, 2002.

Beehler, Sharon A. '"Confederate Season": Shakespeare and the Elizabethan Understanding of Kairos'. In *Shakespeare Matters: History, Teaching, Performance*, edited by Lloyd Davis, 74–88. Newark; London: University of Delaware Press; Associated University Press, 2003.

Beem, Charles. '"Have Not Wee a Noble Kynge?" The Minority of Edward VI'. In *The Royal Minorities of Medieval and Early Modern England*, edited by Charles Beem, 211–48. New York: Palgrave Macmillan, 2008.

The Lioness Roared – The Problems of Female Rule in English History. New York: Palgrave Macmillan, 2006.

'Woe to Thee, O Land! The Introduction'. In *The Royal Minorities of Medieval and Early Modern England*, edited by Charles Beem, 1–16. New York: Palgrave Macmillan, 2008.

Beer, Anna R. '"Left to the World without a Maister": Sir Walter Ralegh's "The History of the World" as a Public Text'. *Studies in Philology* 91, no. 4 (1994): 432–63.

Beilin, Elaine V. '"Some Freely Spake Their Minde": Resistance in Anne Dowriche's The French Historie'. In *Women, Writing, and the*

Reproduction of Culture in Tudor and Stuart Britain, edited by Mary Elizabeth Burke, Jane Donawerth, Karen Nelson, and Linda L. Dove, 119–40. Syracuse: Syracuse University Press, 2000.

'"The World Reproov'd": Writing Faith and History in England'. In *Culture and Change: Attending to Early Modern Women*, edited by Margaret Mikesell and Adele F. Seeff, 266–80. Newark; London: University of Delaware Press, 2003.

Bennett, R. E. 'Sir William Cornwallis's Use of Montaigne'. *PMLA* 48, no. 4 (1933): 1080–9.

Beverley, Tessa. 'Blundeville, Thomas (1522?–1606?)'. Oxford Dictionary of National Biography, October 2009. www.oxforddnb.com/view/article/2718.

Bireley, Robert. *The Counter-Reformation Prince: Anti-Machiavellianism or Catholic Statecraft in Early Modern Europe*. Chapel Hill: University of North Carolina Press, 1990.

Blau, Adrian. 'Hobbes on Corruption'. *History of Political Thought* 30, no. 4 (2009): 596–616.

Blau, Adrian, A. P. Martinich, and Kinch Hoekstra. 'Reason, Deliberation and the Passions'. In *The Oxford Handbook of Hobbes*, online. Oxford: Oxford University Press, 2013.

Blythe, James M. '"Civic Humanism" and Medieval Political Thought'. In *Renaissance Civic Humanism: Reappraisals and Reflections*, edited by James Hankins, 30–74. Cambridge: Cambridge University Press, 2000.

Bom, Erik De. *(Un)Masking the Realities of Power: Justus Lipsius and the Dynamics of Political Writing in Early Modern Europe*. Leiden: Brill, 2011.

Bonadeo, Alfredo. 'The Function and Purpose of the Courtier in "The Book of the Courtier" by Castiglione'. *Philological Quarterly* 50, no. 1 (1971): 36–46.

Born, Lester Kruger. 'The Perfect Prince: A Study in Thirteenth- and Fourteenth-Century Ideals'. *Speculum* 3, no. 4 (1928): 470–504.

Boschung, Dietrich. *Kairos as a Figuration of Time: A Case Study*. Munich: Wilhelm Fink, 2013.

Bowers, R. H. 'Introduction'. In *Discourses Upon Seneca the Tragedian (1601)*. Gainesville: Scholar's Facsimiles, 1952.

Bradshaw, Leah. 'Political Rule, Prudence and the "Woman Question" in Aristotle'. *Canadian Journal of Political Science* 24, no. 3 (1991): 557–73.

Braun, Harald E. 'Knowledge and Counsel in Giovanni Botero's *Ragion Di Stato*'. *Journal of Jesuit Studies* 4, no. 2 (2017): 270–89.

Brooke, Christopher. *Philosophic Pride: Stoicism and Political Thought from Lipsius to Rousseau*. Princeton: Princeton University Press, 2012.

Brunner, Jose. 'Modern Times: Law, Temporality and Happiness in Hobbes, Locke and Bentham Critical Modernities: Politics and Law beyond the Liberal Imagination'. *Theoretical Inquiries in Law* 8 (2007): 277–310.

Bulman, William J. 'The Practice of Politics: The English Civil War and the "Resolution" of Henrietta Maria and Charles I'. *Past & Present* 206, no.1 (2010): 43–79.

Burgess, Glenn. *Absolute Monarchy and the Stuart Constitution*. New Haven: Yale University Press, 1996.

'The Impact on Political Thought: Rhetorics for Troubled Times'. In *The Impact of the English Civil War*, edited by John Stephen Morrill and Glenn Burgess, 67–83. London: Collins & Brown, 1991.

Burke, Peter. 'Tacitism, Scepticism, and Reason of State'. In *The Cambridge History of Political Thought 1450–1700*, edited by J. H. Burns, 477–98. Cambridge: Cambridge University Press, 1991.

Butler, Sophie. 'Sir William Cornwallis the Younger (c1579–1614) and the Emergence of the Essay in England'. PhD Thesis, University of Oxford, 2013.

Carter, Michael. 'Stasis and Kairos: Principles of Social Construction in Classical Rhetoric'. *Rhetoric Review* 7, no. 1 (1988): 97–112.

Cavallo, JoAnn. 'Joking Matters: Politics and Dissimulation in Castiglione's *Book of the Courtier*'. *Renaissance Quarterly* 53, no.2 (2000): 402–24.

Coates, Hannah. 'The Moor's Counsel: Sir Francis Walsingham's Advice to Elizabeth I'. In *Queenship and Counsel in Early Modern Europe*, edited by Helen Matheson-Pollock, Joanne Paul and Catherine Fletcher, 187–214. Cham: Springer International Publishing, 2018.

Colclough, David. *Freedom of Speech in Early Stuart England*. Cambridge: Cambridge University Press, 2005.

Coleman, Janet. 'A Culture of Political Counsel: The Case of Fourteenth-Century England's "Virtuous" Monarchy vs Royal Absolutism and Seventeenth-Century Reinterpretations'. In *Monarchism and Absolutism in Early Modern Europe*, edited by Cesare Cuttica and Glenn Burgess, 19–31. London: Routledge, 2012.

Collins, Robert J. 'Montaigne's Rejection of Reason of State in "De l'Utile et de l'honneste"'. *The Sixteenth Century Journal* 23, no. 1 (1992): 71–94.

Collinson, Patrick. *Elizabethan Essays*. London: Bloomsbury, 1994.

'John Foxe as Historian'. The Acts and Monuments Online. www.johnfoxe.org/index.php?realm=more&gototype=&type=essay&book=essay3.

Condren, Conal. 'Reason of State and Sovereignty in Early Modern England: A Question of Ideology?' *Parergon* 28, no. 2 (2012): 5–27.

Conrad, F.W. 'A Preservative Against Tyranny: Sir Thomas Elyot and the Rhetoric of Counsel'. In *Reformation, Humanism, and 'Revolution': Papers Presented at the Folger Institute Seminar 'Political Thought in the Henrician Age, 1500–1550'*, edited by Gordon J. Schochet, 191–206. Washington, DC: The Folger Institute, 1990.

'The Problem of Counsel Reconsidered: The Case of Sir Thomas Elyot'. In *Political Thought and the Tudor Commonwealth: Deep Structure, Discourse and Disguise*, edited by Paul Fideler and Thomas Mayer, 77–110. London: Routledge, 2003.

Considine, John. 'Golding, Arthur (1535/6–1606)'. Oxford Dictionary of National Biography, 2004. www.oxforddnb.com/view/article/10908.

Cox, Virginia. 'Introduction'. In *The Book of the Courtier*. London: J. M. Dent & Sons Ltd/Everyman's Library, 1994.

'Machiavelli and the *Rhetorica ad Herennium*: Deliberative Rhetoric in The Prince'. *The Sixteenth Century Journal* 28, no. 4 (1997): 1109–41.

Crane, Mary Thomas. '"Video et Taceo": Elizabeth I and the Rhetoric of Counsel'. *Studies in English Literature, 1500–1900* 28, no. 1 (1988): 1–15.

Croft, Pauline. 'Howard, Henry, Earl of Northampton (1540–1614)'. Oxford Dictionary of National Biography, 2004. www.oxforddnb.com/view/article/13906.

Cromartie, Alan. 'Parliamentary Sovereignty, Popular Sovereignty, and Henry Parker's Adjudicative Standpoint'. In *Popular Sovereignty in Historical Perspective*, edited by Richard Bourke and Quentin Skinner, 142–63. Cambridge: Cambridge University Press, 2016.

Curtright, Travis. 'Thomas More on Humor'. *Logos: A Journal of Catholic Thought and Culture* 17, no.1 (2014): 13–35.

Dahl, Norman O. 'Aristotle on Action, Practical Reason, and Weakness of the Will'. In *A Companion to Aristotle*, edited by Georgios Anagnostopoulos, 498–510. Blackwell Companions to Philosophy. Chichester: Wiley-Blackwell, 2009.

D'Andrea, Antonio. 'The Political and Ideological Context of Innocent Gentillet's *Anti-Machiavel*'. *Renaissance Quarterly* 23, no. 4 (1970): 397–411.

De Bom, Erik. 'Realism vs Utopianism'. In *Utopia 1516–2016: More's Eccentric Essay and Its Activist Aftermath*, edited by Han van Ruler and Giulia Sissa, 109–42. Amsterdam: Amsterdam University Press, 2017.

Deist, Rosemarie. *Gender and Power: Counsellors and Their Masters in Antiquity and Medieval Courtly Romance*. Heidelberg: Winter, 2003.

Dodds, Gregory D. *Exploiting Erasmus: The Erasmian Legacy and Religious Change in Early Modern England*. Toronto: University of Toronto Press, 2009.

Doig, J. C. *Aquinas's Philosophical Commentary on the Ethics: A Historical Perspective*. Dordrecht; Boston: Springer, 2001.

Donaldson, Peter S., ed. *A Machiavellian Treatise*. Cambridge: Cambridge University Press, 2009.

Doran, Susan. 'Elizabeth I and Counsel'. In *The Politics of Counsel in England and Scotland, 1286–1707*, edited by Jacqueline Rose, 151–61. Oxford: Oxford University Press, 2017.

Ferente, Serena. 'Popolo and Law: Late Medieval Sovereignty in Marsilius and the Jurists'. In *Popular Sovereignty in Historical Perspective*, edited by Richard Bourke and Quentin Skinner, 73–95. Cambridge: Cambridge University Press, 2016.

Ferguson, Arthur B. *The Articulate Citizen and the English Renaissance*. Durham, NC: Duke University Press, 1965.

Fernández-Santamaria, J. A. *The State, War and Peace: Spanish Political Thought in the Renaissance 1516–1559*. Cambridge: Cambridge University Press, 1977.

Ferster, Judith. *Fictions of Advice: The Literature and Politics of Counsel in Late Medieval England*. Philadelphia: University of Pennsylvania Press, 1996.

Fiaschi, Giovanni. 'Hobbes on Time and Politics'. *Hobbes Studies* 18, no.1 (2005): 3–26.

Fitzmaurice, Andrew. 'The Commercial Ideology of Colonization in Jacobean England: Robert Johnson, Giovanni Botero, and the Pursuit of Greatness'. *The William and Mary Quarterly* 64, no. 4 (2007): 791–820.

Fontana, Biancamaria. *Montaigne's Politics: Authority and Governance in the* Essais. Princeton: Princeton University Press, 2008.

Fox, Alistair. 'English Humanism and the Body Politic'. In *Reassessing the Henrician Age: Humanism, Politics and Reform, 1500–1550*, edited by Alistair Fox and John Guy, 34–51. Oxford: B. Blackwell, 1986.

Fox, Matthew. *Cicero's Philosophy of History*. Oxford: Oxford University Press, 2007.

Garver, Eugene. *Machiavelli and the History of Prudence*. Madison: University of Wisconsin Press, 1987.

Gaukroger, Stephen. *Francis Bacon and the Transformation of Early-Modern Philosophy*. Cambridge: Cambridge University Press, 2001.

Geiger, Joseph. '*Lives* and *Moralia*: How Were Put Asunder What Plutarch Hath Joined Together'. In *The Unity of Plutarch's Work*, edited by Anastasios Nikolaidis, 5–12. Walter de Gruyter, 2008.

Giancarlo, Matthew. '"Al Nys but Conseil": The Medieval Idea of Counsel and the Poetry of Geoffrey Chaucer'. PhD Thesis, Yale University, 1997.

Gnoza, Jonathan. 'Isocrates in Italy: The Reception of Isocrates among the Romans and the Renaissance Humanists'. Phd Thesis, Yale University, 2012.

Grafton, Anthony. 'Humanism and Political Theory'. In *The Cambridge History of Political Thought 1450–1700*, edited by J. H. Burns, 7–29. Cambridge: Cambridge University Press, 1991.

'Prelude'. In *The Praise of Folly*, vii–xxii. Princeton: Princeton University Press, 2015.

Grendler, Paul F. 'Francesco Sansovino and Italian Popular History 1560-1600'. *Studies in the Renaissance* 16 (1969): 139–80.

Griffiths, Ralph Alan. *The Reign of King Henry VI: The Exercise of Royal Authority, 1422–1461*. Berkeley: University of California Press, 1981.

Gunn, Steven. *Henry VII's New Men and the Making of Tudor England*. Oxford: Oxford University Press, 2016.

Guy, John. 'The Henrician Age'. In *The Varieties of British Political Thought, 1500–1800*, edited by Gordon J. Schochet, J. G. A. Pocock, and Lois Schwoerer, 13–46. Cambridge: Cambridge University Press, 1994.

'The King's Council and Political Participation'. In *Reassessing the Henrician Age: Humanism, Politics and Reform, 1500–1550*, edited by Alistair Fox and John Guy, 121–47. Oxford; New York: Blackwell Pub, 1986.

ed. *The Reign of Elizabeth I: Court and Culture in the Last Decade*. Cambridge: Cambridge University Press, 1995.

'The Rhetoric of Counsel in Early Modern England'. In *Tudor Political Culture*, edited by Dale Hoak, 292–310. Cambridge: Cambridge University Press, 1995.

Tudor Monarchy. London: Hodder Education Publishers, 1997.

Hadfield, Andrew. 'Literature and the Culture of Lying Before the Enlightenment'. *Studia Neophilologica* 85, no. 2 (2013): 133–47.

Literature, Travel, and Colonial Writing in the English Renaissance, 1545–1625. Oxford: Clarendon Press, 1998.

Hankins, James. 'Machiavelli, Civic Humanism, and the Humanist Politics of Virtue'. *Italian Culture* 32, no. 2 (2014): 98–109.

Harbage, Alfred. 'Essayes by Sir William Cornwallis the Younger (Review)'. *Modern Language Quarterly* 9, no. 1 (1948): 107–8.

Hardin, Richard F. 'The Literary Conventions of Erasmus' *Education of a Christian Prince*: Advice and Aphorism'. *Renaissance Quarterly* 35, no. 2 (1982): 151–63.

Hardy, Robert B. 'A Study of Erasmus's Editions of the Works of Lucius Annaeus Seneca'. Honours Dissertation, Oberlin College, 1986.

Haskins, Ekaterina V. *Logos and Power in Isocrates and Aristotle*. Columbia: University of South Carolina Press, 2004.

Heil, Andreas, and Gregor Damschen. *Brill's Companion to Seneca: Philosopher and Dramatist*. Leiden: Brill, 2013.

Hexter, J. H. 'Thomas More and the Problem of Counsel'. In *Quincentennial Essays on St. Thomas More: Selected Papers from the Thomas More College Conference*, 55–66. Boone: Albion, 1978.

Hicks, Michael. 'A Story of Failure: The Minority of Edward V'. In *The Royal Minorities of Medieval and Early Modern England*, edited by Charles Beem, 197–210. New York: Palgrave Macmillan, 2008.

Hill, Christopher. *Intellectual Origins of the English Revolution – Revisited*. Oxford: Clarendon Press, 1997.

Hoak, Dale. 'A Tudor Deborah?: The Coronation of Elizabeth I, Parliament, and the Problem of Female Rule'. In *John Foxe and His World*, edited by Christopher Highley and John N. King, 73–89. Aldershot: Ashgate, 2002.

Hoekstra, Kinch. 'Athenian Democracy and Popular Tyranny'. In *Popular Sovereignty in Historical Perspective*, edited by Richard Bourke and Quentin Skinner, 15–51. Cambridge: Cambridge University Press, 2016.

Hogrefe, Pearl. 'Sir Thomas Elyot's Intention in the Opening Chapters of the "Governour"'. *Studies in Philology* 60, no. 2 (1963): 133–40.

The Life and Times of Sir Thomas Elyot, Englishman. Ames: Iowa State University Press, 1967.

Höpfl, Harro. 'History and Exemplarity in the Work of Lipsius'. In *(Un)Masking the Realities of Power: Justus Lipsius and the Dynamics of Political Writing in Early Modern Europe*, edited by Erik Bom, Marijke Janssens, and Toon van Houdt, 43–72. Leiden: Brill, 2010.

Jesuit Political Thought: The Society of Jesus and the State, c.1540–1630. Cambridge: Cambridge University Press, 2004.

'Orthodoxy and Reason of State'. *History of Political Thought* 23, no. 2 (2002): 211–37.

'Thomas Fitzherbert's Reason of State'. *History of European Ideas* 37, no. 2 (2011): 94–101.

Houston, Chloë. *The Renaissance Utopia: Dialogue, Travel and the Ideal Society*. Burlington, VT: Routledge, 2014.

Houten, A. V. 'Prudence in Hobbes's Political Philosophy'. *History of Political Thought* 23, no. 2 (2002): 266–70.

Howard, Edwin. 'Sir Thomas Elyot on the Turning of the Earth'. *Philological Quarterly* 21 (1942): 441–3.

Howard, Keith David. 'Fadrique Furió Ceriol's Machiavellian Vocabulary of Contingency'. *Renaissance Studies* 26, no. 5 (2012): 641–57.

The Reception of Machiavelli in Early Modern Spain. Woodbridge: Boydell & Brewer, 2014.

Hoyle, R. W. *The Pilgrimage of Grace and the Politics of the 1530s*. Oxford: Oxford University Press, 2001.

Hudson, Hoyt Hopewell. 'The Folly of Erasmus'. In *The Praise of Folly*, xxv–lv. Princeton: Princeton University Press, 2015.

Hughes, Ann. *The Causes of the English Civil War*. Basingstoke: Palgrave Macmillan, 1998.

Hunt, Alice. 'The Monarchical Republic of Mary I'. *The Historical Journal* 52, no. 3 (2009): 557–72.

'Imminent, Adj.' In *OED Online*. Oxford University Press. www.oed.com/view/Entry/91904.

Ives, E. W. 'Henry VIII's Will – a Forensic Conundrum'. *The Historical Journal* 35, no.4 (1992): 779–804.

Jacobs, Susan. 'Plutarch's Deterrent Lives: Lessons in Statesmanship'. DPhil Thesis, Columbia University, 2011.

Javitch, Daniel. '*Il Cortegiano* and the Constraints of Despotism'. In *Castiglione: The Ideal and the Real in Renaissance Culture*, edited by Robert W. Hanning and David Rosand, 17–28. New Haven: Yale University Press, 1983.

Jones, David Martin. 'Aphorism and the Counsel of Prudence in Early Modern Statecraft: The Curious Case of Justus Lipsius'. *Parergon* 28, no. 2 (2012): 55–85.

Jones, Howard. 'Thorius, John (b. 1568)'. Oxford Dictionary of National Biography, 2004. www.oxforddnb.com/view/article/27335.

Kahn, Victoria. 'Reading Machiavelli: Innocent Gentillet's Discourse on Method'. *Political Theory* 22, no. 4 (1994): 539–60.

Keller, Vera. 'Mining Tacitus: Secrets of Empire, Nature and Art in the Reason of State'. *BJHS* 45, no. 2 (2012): 189–212.

Kidd, I. G. 'Moral Actions and Rules in Stoic Ethics'. In *The Stoics*, edited by John M. Rist, 247–58. Berkeley: University of California Press, 1978.

Kincaid, Arthur. 'Cornwallis, Sir William, the Younger (c.1579–1614)'. Oxford Dictionary of National Biography, 2004. www.oxforddnb.com/view/article/6345.

Kinneavy, James. 'Kairos: A Neglected Concept in Classical Rhetoric'. In *Rhetoric and Praxis: The Contribution of Classical Rhetoric to Practical Reasoning*, edited by Jean Dietz Moss, 79–105. Washington, DC: Catholic University of America Press, 1986.

Kintgen, E. R. *Reading in Tudor England*. Pittsburgh: University of Pittsburgh Press, 1996.

Knoppers, Laura Lunger. *Politicizing Domesticity from Henrietta Maria to Milton's Eve*. Cambridge: Cambridge University Press, 2011.

Lake, Peter. *Bad Queen Bess?: Libels, Secret Histories, and the Politics of Publicity in the Reign of Queen Elizabeth I*. Oxford, New York: Oxford University Press, 2016.

Lane, Melissa. *Method and Politics in Plato's Statesman*. Cambridge: Cambridge University Press, 1998.

Langer, Ullrich. *The Cambridge Companion to Montaigne*. Cambridge: Cambridge University Press, 2009.

Lawrence, Gavin. 'Human Excellence in Character and Intellect'. In *A Companion to Aristotle*, edited by Georgios Anagnostopoulos, 419–41. Blackwell Companions to Philosophy. Chichester: Wiley-Blackwell, 2009.

Lee, Daniel. *Popular Sovereignty in Early Modern Constitutional Thought*. Oxford: Oxford University Press, 2016.

Lefort, Claude. *Machiavelli in the Making*. Northwestern University Press, 2012.

Lehmberg, Stanford E. 'Elyot, Sir Thomas (c. 1490–1546), Humanist and Diplomat'. Oxford Dictionary of National Biography, 2008. https://doi.org/10.1093/ref:odnb/8782.

Sir Thomas Elyot, Tudor Humanist. Austin: University of Texas Press, 1960.

'English Humanists, the Reformation, and the Problem of Counsel'. *Archiv Für Reformationsgeschichte – Archive for Reformation History* 52 (1961): 74–91.

Levy Peck, Linda. 'Kingship, Counsel and Law in Early Stuart Britain'. In *The Varieties of British Political Thought, 1500–1800*, edited by Gordon J. Schochet, J. G. A. Pocock and Lois Schwoerer, 80–116. Cambridge: Cambridge University Press, 1994.

Lipscomb, Suzannah. *The King Is Dead: The Last Will and Testament of Henry VIII*. London: Head of Zeus, 2015.

López, Modesto Santos. 'El pensamiento realista y liberal de Bartolomé Felippe, el fiel discípulo de Fadrique Furió'. *Cuadernos constitucionales de la Cátedra Fadrique Furió Ceriol*, no. 56 (2006): 5–24.

Luciani, Vincent. 'Sansovino's *Concetti Politici* and Their Debt to Machiavelli'. *PMLA* 67, no. 5 (1952): 823–44.

Macdonald, Alan R. 'Consultation, Counsel and the "Early Stuart Period" in Scotland'. In *The Politics of Counsel in England and Scotland, 1286–1707*, edited by Jacqueline Rose, 193 210. Oxford: Oxford University Press, 2017.

Malcolm, Noel. 'An Unknown Policy Proposal by Thomas Hobbes'. *The Historical Journal* 55, no. 1 (2012): 145–60.

Aspects of Hobbes. Oxford: Oxford University Press, 2002.

Reason of State, Propaganda, and the Thirty Years' War: An Unknown Translation by Thomas Hobbes. Oxford: Oxford University Press, 2010.

ed. *Thomas Hobbes: Leviathan: Editorial Introduction*. Oxford: Oxford University Press, 2012.

Martin, Randall. 'Anne Dowriche's *The French History* and Innocent Gentillet's *Contre-Machiavel*'. *Notes and Queries* 44, no. 1 (1997): 40–2.

'Anne Dowriche's "The French History", Christopher Marlowe, and Machiavellian Agency'. *Studies in English Literature, 1500–1900* 39, no. 1 (1999): 69–87.

Martinich, A. P. *A Hobbes Dictionary*. Cambridge: Blackwell, 1995.

The Two Gods of Leviathan: Thomas Hobbes on Religion and Politics. Cambridge: Cambridge University Press, 1992.

Mayer, Thomas F. 'Faction and Ideology: Thomas Starkey's Dialogue'. *The Historical Journal* 28, no. 1 (1985): 1–25.

'Introduction'. In *A Dialogue Between Pole and Lupset*. London: Royal Historical Society, 1989.

'Thomas Starkey, an Unknown Conciliarist at the Court of Henry VIII'. *Journal of the History of Ideas* 49, no. 2 (1988): 207–27.

Thomas Starkey and the Commonwealth: Humanist Politics and Religion in the Reign of Henry VIII. Cambridge: Cambridge University Press, 2002.

McCabe, Richard A. '"Ut Publica Est Opinio": An Utopian Irony'. *Neophilologus; Groningen, Netherlands* 72, no. 4 (1988): 633–9.

McClure, Christopher Scott. *Hobbes and the Artifice of Eternity*. New York: Cambridge University Press, 2016.

McCrea, Adriana. *Constant Minds: Political Virtue and the Lipsian Paradigm in England, 1584–1650*. Toronto: University of Toronto Press, 1997.

McKenzie, Lionel A. 'Natural Right and the Emergence of the Idea of Interest in Early Modern Political Thought: Francesco Guicciardina and Jean de Silhon'. *History of European Ideas* 2, no.4 (1981): 277–98.

McLaren, A. N. 'Delineating the Elizabethan Body Politic: Knox, Aylmer and the Definition of Counsel 1558-88'. *History of Political Thought* 17, no. 2 (1996): 224–52.

Political Culture in the Reign Elizabeth of I: Queen and Commonwealth 1558–1585. Cambridge: Cambridge University Press, 2004.

Mears, Natalie. 'Counsel, Public Debate, and Queenship: John Stubbs's "The Discoverie of a Gaping Gulf", 1579'. *The Historical Journal* 44, no.3 (2001): 629–50.

Mendle, Michael. *Henry Parker and the English Civil War: The Political Thought of the Public's 'Privado'*. Cambridge: Cambridge University Press, 2003.

'Parker, Henry [Called the Observator] (1604–1652), Political Writer'. Oxford Dictionary of National Biography, 2004. https://doi.org/10.1093/ref:odnb/21307.

Michaelis, Loralea. 'Hobbes's Modern Prometheus: A Political Philosophy for an Uncertain Future'. *Canadian Journal of Political Science/Revue Canadienne de Science Politique* 40, no. 1 (March 2007): 101–27.

Millstone, Noah. 'Evil Counsel: The Propositions to Bridle the Impertinency of Parliament and the Critique of Caroline Government in the Late 1620s'. *Journal of British Studies* 50, no. 4 (2011): 813–39.

Manuscript Circulation and the Invention of Politics in Early Stuart England. Cambridge: Cambridge University Press, 2016.

'Seeing like a Statesman in Early Stuart England'. *Past and Present* 223, no.1 (2014): 77–127.

Moran, Jo Ann Hoeppner. *The Growth of English Schooling, 1340–1548: Learning, Literacy, and Laicization in Pre-Reformation York Diocese*. Princeton: Princeton University Press, 2014.

Nederman, Cary J. *Community and Consent: The Secular Political Theory of Marsiglio of Padua's Defensor Pacis*. London: Rowman & Littlefield, 1995.

'Nature, Sin and the Origins of Society: The Ciceronian Tradition in Medieval Political Thought'. *Journal of the History of Ideas* 49, no. 1 (1988): 3–26.

'Rhetoric, Reason, and Republic: Republicanisms – Ancient, Medieval, and Modern'. In *Renaissance Civic Humanism: Reappraisals and Reflections*, edited by James Hankins, 247–69. Cambridge: Cambridge University Press, 2000.

Nelson, Eric. 'The Problem of the Prince'. In *The Cambridge Companion to Renaissance Philosophy*, edited by James Hankins, 319–37. Cambridge: Cambridge University Press, 2007.

Newman, Jonathan M. 'Satire of Counsel, Counsel of Satire: Representing Advisory Relations in Later Medieval Literature'. PhD Thesis, University of Toronto, 2009.

Norton, Glyn P. 'Improvisation, Time, and Opportunity in the Rhetorical Tradition'. In *The Oxford Handbook of Critical Improvisation Studies*, edited by George E. Lewis and Benjamin Piekut, 262–88. Oxford: Oxford University Press, 2016.

O'Callaghan, Michelle. '*Coryats Crudities* (1611) and Travel Writing as the "Eyes" of the Prince'. In *Prince Henry Revived: Image and Exemplarity in Early Modern England*, edited by Timothy Wilks, 85–103. Seattle: University of Washington Press, 2007.

O'Connor, Desmond. 'Florio, John (1553–1625)'. Oxford Dictionary of National Biography, 2004. www.oxforddnb.com/view/article/9758.

Onians, Richard Broxton. *The Origins of European Thought: About the Body, the Mind, the Soul, the World, Time, and Fate*. Cambridge: Cambridge University Press, 2011.

Pade, Marianne. *The Reception of Plutarch's Lives in Fifteenth-Century Italy*. Copenhagen: Museum Tusculanum Press, University of Copenhagen, 2007.

Parrish, John Michael. 'A New Source for More's "Utopia"'. *The Historical Journal* 40, no.2 (1997): 493–8.

Patterson, Annabel. *Reading Holinshed's Chronicles*. Chicago: University of Chicago Press, 1994.

Paul, Joanne. 'Counsel and Command in Anglophone Political Thought, 1485–1651'. PhD Thesis, Queen Mary, University of London, 2013.

'Counsel, Command and Crisis'. *Hobbes Studies* 28, no. 2 (2015): 103–131.

'Sovereign Council or Counselled Sovereign: The Marian Conciliar Compromise'. In *The Birth of a Queen: Essays on the Quincentenary of Mary I*, edited by Sarah Duncan and Valerie Schutte, 135–53. New York: Palgrave Macmillan, 2016.

'The Use of Kairos in Renaissance Political Philosophy'. *Renaissance Quarterly* 67, no. 1 (2014): 43–78.

Thomas More. Cambridge: Polity, 2016.

Paul, Joanne, and Kurosh Meshkat. 'Johnson's *Relations*: Visions of Global Order, 1601–1630'. *Journal of Intellectual History and Political Thought* 2 no.1 (2013): 108–40.

Paul, Joanne, with Valerie Schutte. 'Royal Counsel in Early Modern Europe'. In *The Routledge History of Monarchy*, edited by Elena Woodacre, Lucinda H. S. Dean, Chris Jones, Zita Rohr, and Russell Martin. London: Routledge, 2019.

Peck, D. C. 'Introduction'. In *Leicester's Commonwealth: The Copy of a Letter Written by a Master of Art of Cambridge (1584) and Related Documents*. Athens, OH: Ohio University Press, 1985.

Peltonen, Markku. *Classical Humanism and Republicanism in English Political Thought, 1570–1640*. Cambridge: Cambridge University Press, 2004.

Rhetoric, Politics and Popularity in Pre-Revolutionary England. Cambridge: Cambridge University Press, 2013.

Petrina, Alessandra. *Machiavelli in the British Isles: Two Early Modern Translations of The Prince*. Farnham: Ashgate Publishing, Ltd., 2009.

'Reginald Pole and the Reception of the Principe in Henrician England'. In *Machiavellian Encounters in Tudor and Stuart England: Literary and Political Influences from the Reformation to the Restoration*, edited by Alessandro Arienzo and Alessandra Petrina, 12–28. New York: Routledge, 2016.

Pocock, J. G. A. 'A Discourse of Sovereignty: Observations on the Work in Progress'. In *Political Discourse in Early Modern Britain*, edited by Nicholas Phillipson and Quentin Skinner, 377–428. Cambridge: Cambridge University Press, 1993.

Politics, Language, and Time: Essays on Political Thought and History. Chicago: University of Chicago Press, 1989.

The Machiavellian Moment: Florentine Political Thought and the Atlantic Republican Tradition. New Haven: Princeton University Press, 2009.

Poole, Thomas M. *Reason of State: Law, Prerogative and Empire*. Cambridge: Cambridge University Press, 2015.

Popper, Nicholas. *Walter Ralegh's 'History of the World' and the Historical Culture of the Late Renaissance*. Chicago: University of Chicago Press, 2012.

Quillet, Jeannine. 'Community, Counsel and Representation'. In *The Cambridge History of Medieval Political Thought c.350–c.1450*, edited by J. H. Burns, 520–72. Cambridge: Cambridge University Press, 1988.

Raab, Felix. *The English Face of Machiavelli: A Changing Interpretation, 1500–1700*. London: Routledge & K. Paul, 1964.

Raalte, M van. '*More Philosophico*: Political Virtue and Philosophy in Plutarch's *Lives*'. In *The Statesman in Plutarch's Works: Proceedings of the Sixth International Conference of the International Plutarch Society Nijmegen/Castle Hernen, May 1–5, 2002*, edited by Lukas De Blois, Jereon Bons, Ton Kessels, and Dirk M. Schenkeveld, 75–112. Leiden: Brill, 2004.

Rathé, C. Edward. 'Innocent Gentillet and the First "Anti-Machiavel"'. *Bibliothèque d'Humanisme et Renaissance* 27, no. 1 (1965): 186–225.

Rebecchini, Guido. 'The Book Collection and Other Possessions of Baldassarre Castiglione'. *Journal of the Warburg and Courtauld Institutes* 61 (1998): 17–52.

Recio, Leticia Álvarez. 'Opposing the Spanish Match: Thomas Scott's *Vox Populi*'. *Sederi* 19 (2009): 5–22.

Redmond, James. 'A Critical Edition of Sir Thomas Elyot's "Pasquil the Playne"'. PhD Thesis, Purdue University, 1971.

Redworth, Glyn. '"Matters Impertinent to Women": Male and Female Monarchy under Philip and Mary'. *The English Historical Review* 112, no. 447 (1997): 597–613.

Remer, G. 'Justus Lipsius, Morally Acceptable Deceit and Prudence in the Ciceronian Tradition'. *History of Political Thought* 37, no.2 (2016): 238–70.

Roisman, Hanna M. 'Nestor the Good Counsellor'. *The Classical Quarterly* 55, no.1 (2005): 17–38.

Rose, Jacqueline. 'Councils, Counsel and the Seventeenth-Century Composite State'. In *The Politics of Counsel in England and Scotland, 1286–1707*, edited by Jacqueline Rose, 271–94. Oxford: Oxford University Press, 2017.

'Kingship and Counsel in Early Modern England'. *The Historical Journal* 54, no. 1 (2011): 47–71.

'Sir Edward Hyde and the Problem of Counsel in Mid-Seventeenth-Century Royalist Thought'. In *The Politics of Counsel in England and Scotland, 1286–1707*, edited by Jacqueline Rose, 249–69. Oxford: Oxford University Press, 2017.

ed. *The Politics of Counsel in England and Scotland, 1286–1707*. Proceedings of the British Academy. Oxford: Oxford University Press, 2016.

Ruler, Han van. 'Bodies, Morals, and Religion'. In *Utopia 1516–2016: More's Eccentric Essay and Its Activist Aftermath*, edited by Han van Ruler and Giulia Sissa, 71–106. Amsterdam University Press, 2017.

Rummel, Erika. *Desiderius Erasmus*. London: Continuum, 2004.

The Humanist-Scholastic Debate in the Renaissance & Reformation. Boston: Harvard University Press, 1998.

Rundle, David. '"Not so Much Praise as Precept": Erasmus, Panegyric, and the Renaissance Art of Teaching Princes'. In *Pedagogy and Power: Rhetorics of Classical Learning*, edited by Niall Livingstone and Yun Lee Too, 148–69. Cambridge: Cambridge University Press, 1998.

Russell, Conrad. *Parliaments and English Politics 1621–1629*. Oxford: Oxford University Press, 1979.

The Causes of the English Civil War: The Ford Lectures Delivered in the University of Oxford, 1987–1988. Oxford: Clarendon Press, 1990.

Ryan, Lawrence V. 'Book Four of Castiglione's *Courtier*: Climax or Afterthought?' *Studies in the Renaissance* 19 (1972): 156–79.

Schafer, John. *Ars Didactica: Seneca's 94th and 95th Letters*. Göttingen: Vandenhoeck & Ruprecht, 2009.

Schieberle, M. *Feminized Counsel and the Literature of Advice in England, 1380–1500*. Turnhout: Brepols Publishers, 2014.

Schofield, Malcolm. *Saving the City: Philosopher-Kings and Other Classical Paradigms*. London: Routledge, 1999.

Shackleton, Robert. 'Botero, Bodin and Robert Johnson'. *The Modern Language Review* 43, no. 3 (1948): 405–9.

Sharpe, Kevin. *Faction and Parliament: Essays on Early Stuart History*. Clarendon Press, 1978.

Sims, Liam. 'Charles I and the *Eikon Basilike* – Cambridge University Library Special Collections'. https://specialcollections.blog.lib.cam.ac.uk/?p=6793.

Sipiora, Phillip. 'The Ancient Concept of Kairos'. In *Rhetoric and Kairos: Essays in History, Theory and Praxis*, edited by Phillip Sipiora and James S Baumlin, 1–22. New York: State University of New York Press, 2002.

Sissa, Giulia. '*Familiaris Reprehensio Quasi Errantis*. Raphael Hythloday, between Plato and Epicurus'. *Moreana* 49 (Number 187–188), no. 1–2 (2012): 121–50.

Skinner, Quentin. 'Hobbes on Representation'. *European Journal of Philosophy* 13, no. 2 (2005): 155–84.

Machiavelli: A Very Short Introduction. Oxford; New York: Oxford University Press, 2000.

'Paradiastole: Redescribing the Vices as Virtues'. In *Renaissance Figures of Speech*, edited by Sylvia Adamson, Gavin Alexander and Katrin Ettenhuber, 149–65. Cambridge: Cambridge University Press, 2007.

Reason and Rhetoric in the Philosophy of Hobbes. Cambridge: Cambridge University Press, 1996.

The Foundations of Modern Political Thought: Volume 1: The Renaissance. Cambridge: Cambridge University Press, 1978.

'Thomas More's *Utopia* and the Virtue of True Nobility'. In *Visions of Politics: Volume 2: Renaissance Virtues*, 213–44. Cambridge: Cambridge University Press, 2002.

Visions of Politics: Volume 3. Cambridge: Cambridge University Press, 2002.

'Why States Need Time'. Presented at Political Thought, Time and History: An International Conference, Cambridge, 10 May 2018.

Slomp, Gabriella. 'The Inconvenience of the Legislator's Two Persons and the Role of Good Counsellors'. *Hobbes Studies* 19, no. 1 (2016): 68–85.

Smith, Victoria. '"For Ye, Young Men, Show a Womanish Soul, Yon Maiden a Man's": Perspectives on Female Monarchy in Elizabeth's First Decade'. In *Gender and Political Culture in Early Modern Europe, 1400–1800*, edited by James Daybell and Svante Norrhem, 143–57. London; New York: Routledge, 2016.

Soll, Jacob. 'The Reception of *The Prince* 1513–1700, or Why We Understand Machiavelli the Way We Do'. *Social Research* 81, no. 1 (2014): 31–60.

Sommerville, Johann P. 'Introduction'. In *King James VI and I: Political Writings*, xv–xxviii. Cambridge: Cambridge University Press, 1995.

'The Authorship and Dating of Some Works Attributed to Filmer'. In *Filmer: 'Patriarcha' and Other Writings*, xxxii–xxxvii. Cambridge: Cambridge University Press, 1991.

Sorabji, Richard. 'Aristotle On the Role of Intellect in Virtue'. *Proceedings of the Aristotelian Society* 74, no.1 (1974): 107–29.

Stacey, Peter. *Roman Monarchy and the Renaissance Prince*. Cambridge: Cambridge University Press, 2007.

Stanciu, Diana. 'Prudence in Lipsius's *Monita et Exampla Politica*: Stoic Virtue, Aristotelian Virtue or Not a Virtue at All?' In *(Un)Masking the Realities of Power: Justus Lipsius and the Dynamics of Political Writing in Early Modern Europe*, edited by Erik Bom, Marijke Janssens and Toon van Houdt, 233–62. Leiden: Brill, 2010.

Starnes, DeWitt T. 'Introduction'. In *The Gouernaunce of Kynges and Prynces, the Pynson Edition of 1511; a Translation in Verse*, v–xviii. Gainesville: Scholars' Facsimiles & Reprints, 1957.

Stone, Lawrence. *The Causes of the English Revolution 1529–1642*. London: Routledge, 2017.

Sukič, Christine. '"A True Sign of a Readie Wit": Anger as an Art of Excess in Early Modern Dramatic and Moral Literature'. *XVII–XVIII. Revue de La Société d'études Anglo-Américaines Des XVIIe et XVIIIe Siècles*, no. 71 (2014): 85–98.

Sullivan, Robert, and Arthur E. Walzer, eds. *Thomas Elyot: Critical Editions of Four Works on Counsel*. Leiden; Boston: Brill, 2018.

Suzuki, Mihoko. 'Warning Elizabeth with Catherine de' Medici's Example: Anne Dowriche's *French Historie* and the Politics of Counsel'. In *The Rule of Women in Early Modern Europe*, edited by Anne J. Cruz and Mihoko Suzuki, 174–93. Urbana: University of Illinois Press, 2009.

Swartz, N. P. 'Thomas Aquinas: On Law, Tyranny and Resistance'. *Acta Theologica* 30, no.1 (June 2010): 145–57.

Tessitore, Aristide. *Reading Aristotle's Ethics: Virtue, Rhetoric, and Political Philosophy*. New York: SUNY Press, 1996.

Tuck, Richard. 'Democratic Sovereignty and Democratic Government'. In *Popular Sovereignty in Historical Perspective*, edited by Richard Bourke and Quentin Skinner, 115–41. Cambridge: Cambridge University Press, 2016.

'Humanism and Political Thought'. In *The Impact of Humanism on Western Europe During the Renaissance*, edited by A. Goodman and Angus Mackay, 43–65. London; New York: Routledge, 1990.

Philosophy and Government 1572–1651. Cambridge: Cambridge University Press, 1993.

The Sleeping Sovereign: The Invention of Modern Democracy. The Seeley Lectures. Cambridge: Cambridge University Press, 2016.

Tudor, H. '*L'Institution Des Princes Chrestiens*: A Note on Boaistuau and Clichtove'. *Bibliothèque d'Humanisme et Renaissance* 45, no.1 (1983): 103–6.

Tyler, Colin. 'Drafting the Nineteen Propositions, January–July 1642'. *Parliamentary History* 31, no. 3 (1 October 2012): 263–312.

Tytler, Patrick Fraser. *England Under the Reigns of Edward VI. and Mary: With the Contemporary History of Europe*. London R. Bentley, 1839.

Untersteiner, Mario. *The Sophists*. Translated by Kathleen Freeman. New York: Blackwell, 1954.

Viroli, Maurizio. *From Politics to Reason of State: The Acquisition and Transformation of the Language of Politics 1250–1600*. Cambridge: Cambridge University Press, 1992.

'Machiavelli and the Republican Idea of Politics'. In *Machiavelli and Republicanism*, edited by Gisela Bock, Maurizio Viroli and Quentin Skinner, 143–72. Cambridge: Cambridge University Press, 1991.

Waldron, Jeremy. 'The Wisdom of the Multitude: Some Reflections on Book 3, Chapter 11 of Aristotle's *Politics*'. *Political Theory* 23, no.4 (1995): 563–84.

Waley, P. J, and D. P Waley. 'Introduction'. In *The Reason of State and The Greatness of Cities*, vii–xi. London: Routledge & Kegan Paul, 1956.

Walker, Greg. *Writing Under Tyranny: English Literature and the Henrician Reformation*. Oxford: Oxford University Press, 2007.

Walzer, Arthur E. 'Parrēsia, Foucault, and the Classical Rhetorical Tradition'. *Renaissance Society Quarterly* 43, no.1 (2013): 1–21.

'Rhetoric of Counsel in Thomas Elyot's Pasquil the Playne'. *Rhetorica: A Journal of the History of Rhetoric* 30, no. 1 (2012): 1–21.

'The Rhetoric of Counsel and Thomas Elyot's Of the Knowledge Which Maketh a Wise Man'. *Philosophy and Rhetoric* 45, no. 1 (2012): 24–45.

Ward, Allyna E. *Women and Tudor Tragedy: Feminizing Counsel and Representing Gender*. London: Rowman & Littlefield, 2013.

Wareh, Tarik. *The Theory and Practice of Life: Isocrates and the Philosophers*. Hellenic Studies Series 54. Washington, DC: Center for Hellenic Studies, 2013.

Watter, Pierre. 'Jean Louis Guez de Balzac's *Le Prince*: A Revaluation'. *Journal of the Warburg and Courtauld Institutes* 20, no. 3/4 (1957): 215–47.

Watts, John. 'Counsel and the King's Council in England, c.1340-c.1540'. In *The Politics of Counsel in England and Scotland, 1286–1707*, edited by Jacqueline Rose, 63–85. Oxford: Oxford University Press, 2017.

Weiss, Roberto. *Humanism in England During the Fifteenth Century*. Oxford: Basil Blackwell, 1957.

White, Micheline Monica. '"Cunning in Controversies": English Protestant Women Writers and Religious and Literary Debates, 1580–1615'. Ph.D Thesis, Loyola University Chicago, 1998.

Whitt, P. B. 'New Light on Sir William Cornwallis, the Essayist'. *The Review of English Studies* 8, no. 30 (1932): 155–69.

Williams, Steven J. *The Secret of Secrets: The Scholarly Career of a Pseudo-Aristotelian Text in the Latin Middle Ages*. Ann Arbor: University of Michigan Press, 2003.

Williamson, Elizabeth. 'A Letter of Travel Advice? Literary Rhetoric, Scholarly Counsel and Practical Instruction in the *Ars Apodemica*'. *Lives and Letters* 3, no.1 (2011): 1–22.

Woodman, A. J. *Rhetoric in Classical Historiography*. Portland: Taylor & Francis, 2003.

Woodruff, Paul. 'Euboulia as the Skill Protagoras Taught'. In *Protagoras of Abdera: The Man, His Measure*, edited by J.M. van Ophuijsen, M. van Raalte and P. Stork, 179–93. Leiden: Brill, 2013.

Younger, Neil. 'Securing the Monarchical Republic: The Remaking of the Lord Lieutenancies in 1585'. *Historical Research* 84, no. 224 (2011): 249–65.

Zatta, Claudia. 'Democritus and Folly: The Two Wise Fools'. *Bibliothèque d'Humanisme et Renaissance* 63, no.3 (2001): 533–49.

Zeitlin, Samuel Garrett. 'Political and Moral Vision in the Thought of Francis Bacon'. *Journal of Intellectual History and Political Thought* 1, no. 1 (2012): 32–55.

Index

IDEAS IN CONTEXT

Edited by David Armitage, Richard Bourke, Jennifer Pitts and John Robertson

1. RICHARD RORTY, J. B. SCHNEEWIND AND QUENTIN SKINNER (eds.)
   Philosophy in History
   Essays in the Historiography of Philosophy
   PB 9780521273305

2. J. G. A. POCOCK
   Virtue, Commerce and History
   Essays on Political Thought and History, Chiefly in the Eighteenth Century
   PB 9780521276603

3. M. M. GOLDSMITH
   Private Vices, Public Benefits
   Bernard Mandeville's Social and Political Thought
   HB 9780521300360

4. ANTHONY PAGDEN (ed.)
   The Languages of Political Theory in Early Modern Europe
   PB 9780521386661

5. DAVID SUMMERS
   The Judgment of Sense
   Renaissance Naturalism and the Rise of Aesthetics
   PB 9780521386319

6. LAURENCE DICKEY
   Hegel Religion, Economics and the Politics of Spirit, 1770–1807
   PB 9780521389129

7. MARGO TODD
   Christian Humanism and the Puritan Social Order
   PB 9780521892285

8. LYNN SUMIDA JOY
   Gassendi the Atomist
   Advocate of History in An Age of Science
   PB 9780521522397

9. EDMUND LEITES (ed.)
   Conscience and Casuistry in Early Modern Europe
   PB9780521520201

10. WOLF LEPENIES
    Between Literature and Science
    The Rise of Sociology
    PB 9780521338103

11. TERENCE BALL, JAMES FARR AND RUSSELL L. HANSON (eds.)
Political Innovation and Conceptual Change
PB 9780521359788

12. GERD GIGERENZER et al.
The Empire of Chance
How Probability Changed Science and Everyday Life
PB 9780521398381

13. PETER NOVICK
That Noble Dream
The 'Objectivity Question' and the American Historical Profession
HB 9780521343282
PB 9780521357456

14. DAVID LIEBERMAN
The Province of Legislation Determined
Legal Theory in Eighteenth-Century Britain
PB 9780521528542

15. DANIEL PICK
Faces of Degeneration
A European Disorder, c.1848–c.1918
PB 9780521457538

16. KEITH BAKER
Inventing the French Revolution
Essays on French Political Culture in the Eighteenth Century
PB 9780521385787

17. IAN HACKING
The Taming of Chance
HB 9780521380140
PB 9780521388849

17. GISELA BOCK, QUENTIN SKINNER AND MAURIZIO VIROLI (eds.)
Machiavelli and Republicanism
PB 9780521435895

18. DOROTHY ROSS
The Origins of American Social Science
PB 9780521428361

19. KLAUS CHRISTIAN KOHNKE
The Rise of Neo-Kantianism
German Academic Philosophy between Idealism and Positivism
HB 9780521373364

20. IAN MACLEAN
Interpretation and Meaning in the Renaissance

The Case of Law
HB 9780521415460
PB 9780521020275

21. MAURIZIO VIROLI
From Politics to Reason of State
The Acquisition and Transformation of the Language of Politics 1250–1600
HB 9780521414937
PB 9780521673433

22. MARTIN VAN GELDEREN
The Political Thought of the Dutch Revolt 1555–1590
HB 9780521392044
PB 9780521891639

23. NICHOLAS PHILLIPSON AND QUENTIN SKINNER (eds.)
Political Discourse in Early Modern Britain
HB 9780521392426

24. JAMES TULLY
An Approach to Political Philosophy: Locke in Contexts
HB 9780521430609
PB 9780521436380

25. RICHARD TUCK
Philosophy and Government 1572–1651
PB 9780521438858

26. RICHARD YEO
Defining Science
William Whewell, Natural Knowledge and Public Debate in Early Victorian Britain
HB 9780521431828
PB 9780521541169

27. MARTIN WARNKE
The Court Artist
On the Ancestry of the Modern Artist
HB 9780521363754

28. PETER N. MILLER
Defining the Common Good
Empire, Religion and Philosophy in Eighteenth-Century Britain
HB 9780521442596
PB 9780521617123

29. CHRISTOPHER J. BERRY
The Idea of Luxury
A Conceptual and Historical Investigation
PB 9780521466912

30. E. J. HUNDERT
The Enlightenment's 'Fable'
Bernard Mandeville and the Discovery of Society
HB 9780521460828
PB 9780521619424

31. JULIA STAPLETON
Englishness and the Study of Politics
The Social and Political Thought of Ernest Barker
HB 9780521461252
PB9780521024440

32. KEITH TRIBE
Strategies of Economic Order
German Economic Discourse, 1750–1950
HB 9780521462914
PB 9780521619431

33. SACHIKO KUSUKAWA
The Transformation of Natural Philosophy
The Case of Philip Melanchthon
HB 9780521473477
PB 9780521030465

34. DAVID ARMITAGE, ARMAND HIMY AND QUENTIN SKINNER (eds.)
Milton and Republicanism
HB 978521551786
PB 9780521646482

35. MARKKU PELTONEN
Classical Humanism and Republicanism in English Political Thought 1570–1640
HB 9780521496957
PB 9780521617161

36. PHILIP IRONSIDE
The Social and Political Thought of Bertrand Russell
The Development of an Aristocratic Liberalism
HB 9780521473835
PB 9780521024761

37. NANCY CARTWRIGHT, JORDI CAT, LOLA FLECK AND THOMAS E. UEBEL
Otto Neurath
Philosophy between Science and Politics
HB 9780521451741

38. DONALD WINCH
Riches and Poverty
An Intellectual History of Political Economy in Britain, 1750–1834
PB 9780521559201

39. JENNIFER PLATT
A History of Sociological Research Methods in America
HB 9780521441735
PB 9780521646499

40. KNUD HAAKONSSEN (ed.)
Enlightenment and Religion
Rational Dissent in Eighteenth-Century Britain
HB 9780521560603
PB 9780521029872

41. G. E. R. LLOYD
Adversaries and Authorities
Investigations into Ancient Greek and Chinese Science
HB 9780521553315
PB 9780521556958

42. ROLF LINDNER
The Reportage of Urban Culture
Robert Park and the Chicago School
HB 9780521440523
PB 9780521026536

43. ANNABEL BRETT
Liberty, Right and Nature
Individual Rights in Later Scholastic Thought
HB 9780521562393
PB 9780521543408

44. STEWART J. BROWN (ed.)
William Robertson and the Expansion of Empire
HB 9780521570831

45. HELENA ROSENBLATT
Rousseau and Geneva
From the First Discourse to the Social Contract, 1749–1762
HB 9780521570046
PB 9780521033954

46. DAVID RUNCIMAN
Pluralism and the Personality of the State
HB 9780521551915
PB 9780521022637

47. ANNABEL PATTERSON
Early Modern Liberalism
HB 9780521592604
PB 9780521026314

48. DAVID WEINSTEIN
Equal Freedom and Utility
Herbert Spencer's Liberal Utilitarianism
HB 9780521622646
PB 9780521026864

49. YUN LEE TOO AND NIALL LIVINGSTONE (eds.)
Pedagogy and Power
Rhetorics of Classical Learning
HB 9780521594356
PB 9780521038010

50. REVIEL NETZ
The Shaping of Deduction in Greek Mathematics
A Study in Cognitive History
HB 9780521622790
PB 9780521541206

51. MARY S. MORGAN AND MARGARET MORRISON (eds.)
Models as Mediators
Perspectives in Natural and Social Science
HB 9780521650977
PB 9780521655712

52. JOEL MICHELL
Measurement in Psychology
A Critical History of a Methodological Concept
HB 9780521621205
PB 9780521021517

53. RICHARD A. PRIMUS
The American Language of Rights
HB 9780521652506
PB 9780521616218

54. ROBERT ALUN JONES
The Development of Durkheim's Social Realism
HB 9780521650458
PB 9780521022101

55. ANNE MCLAREN
Political Culture in the Reign of Elizabeth I
Queen and Commonwealth 1558–1585
HB 9780521651448
PB 9780521024839

56. JAMES HANKINS (ed.)
Renaissance Civic Humanism
Reappraisals and Reflections

HB 9780521780902
PB 9780521548076

57. T.J. HOCHSTRASSER
Natural Law Theories in the Early Enlightenment
HB 9780521661935
PB 9780521027878

58. DAVID ARMITAGE
The Ideological Origins of the British Empire
HB 9780521590815
PB 9780521789783

59. IAN HUNTER
Rival Enlightenments
Civil and Metaphysical Philosophy in Early Modern Germany
HB 9780521792653
PB 9780521025492

60. DARIO CASTIGLIONE AND IAIN HAMPSHER-MONK (eds.)
The History of Political Thought in National Context
HB 9780521782340

61. IAN MACLEAN
Logic, Signs and Nature in the Renaissance
The Case of Learned Medicine
HB 9780521806480

62. PETER MACK
Elizabethan Rhetoric Theory and Practice
HB 9780521812924
PB 9780521020992

63. GEOFFREY LLOYD
The Ambitions of Curiosity
Understanding the World in Ancient Greece and China
HB 9780521815420
PB 9780521894616

64. MARKKU PELTONEN
The Duel in Early Modern England
Civility, Politeness and Honour
HB 9780521820622
PB 9780521025201

65. ADAM SUTCLIFFE
Judaism and Enlightenment
HB 9780521820158
PB 9780521672320

66. ANDREW FITZMAURICE
Humanism and America
An Intellectual History of English Colonisation, 1500–1625
HB 9780521822251

67. PIERRE FORCE
Self-Interest before Adam Smith
A Genealogy of Economic Science
HB 9780521830607
PB 9780521036191

68. ERIC NELSON
The Greek Tradition in Republican Thought
HB 9780521835459
PB 9780521024280

69. HARRO HÖPFL
Jesuit Political Thought
The Society of Jesus and the State, c.1540–1640
HB 9780521837798

70. MIKAEL HORNQVIST
Machiavelli and Empire
HB 9780521839457

71. DAVID COLCLOUGH
Freedom of Speech in Early Stuart England
HB 9780521847483

72. JOHN ROBERTSON
The Case for the Enlightenment
Scotland and Naples 1680–1760
HB 9780521847872
PB 9780521035729

73. DANIEL CAREY
Locke, Shaftesbury, and Hutcheson
Contesting Diversity in the Enlightenment and Beyond
HB 9780521845021

74. ALAN CROMARTIE
The Constitutionalist Revolution
An Essay on the History of England, 1450–1642
HB 9780521782692

75. HANNAH DAWSON
Locke, Language and Early-Modern Philosophy
HB 9780521852715

76. CONAL CONDREN, STEPHEN GAUKROGER AND IAN HUNTER (eds.)
The Philosopher in Early Modern Europe
The Nature of a Contested Identity
HB 9780521866460

77. ANGUS GOWLAND
The Worlds of Renaissance Melancholy
Robert Burton in Context
HB 9780521867689

78. PETER STACEY
Roman Monarchy and the Renaissance Prince
HB 9780521869898

79. RHODRI LEWIS
Language, Mind and Nature
Artificial Languages in England from Bacon to Locke
HB 9780521874750

80. DAVID LEOPOLD
The Young Karl Marx
German Philosophy, Modern Politics, and Human Flourishing
HB 9780521874779

81. JON PARKIN
Taming the Leviathan
The Reception of the Political and Religious Ideas of Thomas Hobbes in England 1640–1700
HB 9780521877350

82. D WEINSTEIN
Utilitarianism and the New Liberalism
HB 9780521875288

83. LUCY DELAP
The Feminist Avant-Garde
Transatlantic Encounters of the Early Twentieth Century
HB 9780521876513

84. BORIS WISEMAN
Lévi-Strauss, Anthropology and Aesthetics
HB 9780521875295

85. DUNCAN BELL (ed.)
Victorian Visions of Global Order
Empire and International Relations in Nineteenth-Century Political Thought
HB 9780521882927

86. IAN HUNTER
The Secularisation of the Confessional State

The Political Thought of Christian Thomasius
HB 9780521880558

87. CHRISTIAN J. EMDEN
Friedrich Nietzsche and the Politics of History
HB 9780521880565

88. ANNELIEN DE DIJN
French Political thought from Montesquieu to Tocqueville
Liberty in a Levelled Society?
HB 9780521877886

89. PETER GARNSEY
Thinking About Property
From Antiquity to the Age of Revolution
HB 9780521876773
PB 9780521700238

90. PENELOPE DEUTSCHER
The Philosophy of Simone de Beauvoir
Ambiguity, Conversion, Resistance
HB 9780521885201

91. HELENA ROSENBLATT
Liberal Values
Benjamin Constant and the Politics of Religion
HB 9780521898256

92. JAMES TULLY
Public Philosophy in a New Key
Volume 1: Democracy and Civic Freedom
HB 9780521449618
PB 9780521728799

93. JAMES TULLY
Public Philosophy in a New Key
Volume 2: Imperialism and Civic Freedom
HB 9780521449663
PB 9780521728805

94. DONALD WINCH
Wealth and Life
Essays on the Intellectual History of Political Economy in Britain, 1848–1914
HB 9780521887533
PB 9780521715393

95. FONNA FORMAN-BARZILAI
Adam Smith and the Circles of Sympathy

Cosmopolitanism and Moral Theory
HB 9780521761123

96. GREGORY CLAEYS
Imperial Sceptics British
Critics of Empire 1850–1920
HB 9780521199544

97. EDWARD BARING
The Young Derrida and French Philosophy, 1945–1968
HB 9781107009677

98. CAROL PAL
Republic of Women
Rethinking the Republic of Letters in the Seventeenth Century
HB 9781107018211

99. C. A. BAYLY
Recovering Liberties
Indian Thought in the Age of Liberalism and Empire
HB 9781107013834
PB 9781107601475

100. FELICITY GREEN
Montaigne and the Life of Freedom
HB 9781107024397

101. JOSHUA DERMAN
Max Weber in Politics and Social Thought
From Charisma to Canonizaion
HB 9781107025882

102. RAINER FORST
(translated by Ciaran Cronin)
Toleration in Conflict Past and
Present HB 9780521885775

103. SOPHIE READ
Eucharist and the Poetic Imagination in Early Modern England
HB 9781107032736

104. MARTIN RUEHL
The Italian Renaissance in the German Historical Imagination 1860–1930
HB 9781107036994

105. GEORGIOS VAROUXAKIS
Liberty Abroad J. S. Mill on International Relations
HB 9781107039148

106. ANDREW FITZMAURICE
Sovereignty, Property and Empire, 1500–2000
HB 9781107076495

107. BENJAMIN STRAUMANN
Roman Law in the State of Nature
The Classical Foundations of Hugo Grotius' Natural Law
HB 9781107092907

108. LIISI KEEDUS
The Crisis of German Historicism
The Early Political Thought of Hannah Arendt and Leo Strauss
HB 9781107093034

109. EMMANUELLE DE CHAMPS
Enlightenment and Utility
Bentham in French, Bentham in France
HB 9781107098671

110. ANNA PLASSART
The Scottish Enlightenment and the French Revolution
HB 9781107091764

111. DAVID TODD
Free Trade and its Enemies in France, 1814–1851
HB 9781107036932

112. DMITRI LEVITIN
Ancient Wisdom in the Age of the New Science
HB 9781107105881

113. PATRICK BAKER
Italian Renaissance Humanism in the Mirror
HB 9781107111868

114. COLIN KIDD
The World of Mr Casaubon Britain's Wars of Mythography, 1700–1870
HB 9781107027718

115. PETER SCHRÖDER
Trust in Early Modern International Political Thought, 1598–1713
HB 9781107175464

116. SIMON GROTE
The Emergence of Modern Aesthetic Theory
Religion and Morality in Enlightenment Germany and Scotland
HB 9781107110922

117. NIALL O'FLAHERTY
Utilitarianism in the Age of Enlightenment

The Moral and Political Thought of William Paley
Hb 9781108474474

118. GREGORY CONTI
Parliament the Mirror of the Nation
Representation, Deliberation, and Democracy in Victorian Britain
HB 9781108428736

119. MARK MCCLISH
The History of the Arthaśāstra
Sovereignty and Sacred Law in Ancient India
HB 9781108476904

120. WILLIAM SELINGER
Parliamentarism From Burke to Weber
HB 9781108475747

121. JULIA NICHOLLS
Revolutionary Thought after the Paris Commune, 1871–1885
HB 9781108499262

122. ANNA K. BECKER
Gendering the Renaissance Commonwealth
HB 9781108487054

123. IAIN STEWART
Raymond Aron and Liberal Thought in the Age of Extremes
HB 9781108484442

Printed in Great Britain
by Amazon